RSA Security's Official Guide to Cryptography

Keller Graduate School of Management of DeVry University Edition

Steve Burnett and Stephen Paine

McGraw-Hill/Osborne

New York   Chicago   San Francisco
Lisbon   London   Madrid   Mexico City
Milan   New Delhi   San Juan
Seoul   Singapore   Sydney   Toronto

McGraw-Hill/Osborne
2100 Powell Street, 10th floor
Emeryville, California 94608
U.S.A.

To arrange bulk purchase discounts for sales promotions, premiums, or
fund-raisers, please contact **McGraw-Hill**/Osborne at the above address.
For information on translations or book distributors outside the U.S.A.,
please see the International Contact Information page immediately
following the index of this book.

**RSA Security's Official Guide to Cryptography Keller Graduate School
of Management of DeVry University Edition**

1234567890 FGR FGR 01987654

Book p/n 0-07-225495-5 and CD p/n 0-07-225496-3
parts of
ISBN 0-07-225494-7

Publisher
Brandon A. Nordin

**Vice President &
Associate Publisher**
Scott Rogers

Executive Editor
Steven Elliot

Senior Project Editor
LeeAnn Pickrell

Acquisitions Coordinator
Alexander Corona

Technical Editors
Blake Dournaee
Jessica Nelson

Copy Editor
Betsy Hardinger

Composition and Indexer
MacAllister Publishing Services, LLC

Illustrators
Michael Mueller
Beth Young
Lyssa Sieben-Wald

To Pao-Chi, Gwen, Ray, Satomi, Michelle, Alexander, Warren, Maria, Daniel, and Julia

—Steve Burnett

To Danielle, thanks for understanding while I worked on this book

To Alexis and Elizabeth, a father could not ask for better children

—Stephen Paine

Contents

Credits	xiii
Foreword	xv
Acknowledgments	xvii
Preface	xix
About the Authors	xxii

Chapter 1 Why Cryptography? 1

Security Provided by Computer Operating Systems	2
How Operating Systems Work	2
Default OS Security: Permissions	3
Attacks on Passwords	4
Attacks That Bypass Operating Systems	6
Data Recovery Attack	6
Memory Reconstruction Attack	9
Added Protection Through Cryptography	11
The Role of Cryptography in Data Security	12

Chapter 2 Symmetric-Key Cryptography 15

Some Crypto Jargon	18
What Is a Key?	20
Why Is a Key Necessary?	22
Generating a Key	22
A Random Number Generator	27
A Pseudo-Random Number Generator	28
Attacks on Encrypted Data	30
Attacking the Key	30
Breaking the Algorithm	36
Measuring the Time It Takes to Break Your Message	37
Symmetric Algorithms: The Key Table	37
Symmetric Algorithms: Block Versus Stream Ciphers	38
Block Ciphers	38
Stream Ciphers	41
Block Versus Stream: Which Is Better?	45
Digital Encryption Standard	46
Triple DES	47
Commercial DES Replacements	49
Advanced Encryption Standard	50

Summary   51
Real-World Example: Oracle Databases   51

Chapter 3   Symmetric-Key Management   53

Password-Based Encryption   54
  Programming Convenience   59
  Breaking PBE   63
  Slowing Down an Attack on a Password   64
  Good Passwords   65
  Password Generators   67
Hardware-Based Key Storage   69
  Tokens   69
  Crypto Accelerators   73
  Hardware Devices and Random Numbers   75
Biometrics   75
Summary   76
Real-World Examples   76
  Keon Desktop   77
  Other Products   79

Chapter 4   The Key Distribution Problem and Public-Key Cryptography   81

Sharing Keys in Advance   83
  Problems With This Scheme   84
Using a Trusted Third Party   85
  Problems With This Scheme   86
Public-Key Cryptography and the Digital Envelope   88
Security Issues   91
  Breaking a Public-Key Algorithm   92
Some History of Public-Key Cryptography   93
How Public-Key Cryptography Works   94
  The RSA Algorithm   98
  The DH Algorithm   105
  The ECDH Algorithm   111
Comparing the Algorithms   117
  Security   117
  Key Sizes   119
  Performance   120
  Transmission Size   122
  Interoperability   122

Protecting Private Keys   122
Using the Digital Envelope for Key Recovery   123
  Key Recovery via a Trusted Third Party   124
  Key Recovery via a Group of Trustees   126
  Key Recovery via Threshold Schemes   127
  How a Threshold Scheme Works   130
Summary   132
Real-World Example   133

Chapter 5   The Digital Signature   137

The Uniqueness of a Digital Signature   138
Message Digests   141
  Collisions   145
  The Three Important Digest Algorithms   148
  A Representative of Larger Data   149
  Data Integrity   153
Back to Digital Signatures   154
Trying to Cheat   156
Implementing Authentication, Data Integrity, and Nonrepudiation   159
Understanding the Algorithms   159
  RSA   160
  DSA   161
  ECDSA   163
Comparing the Algorithms   163
  Security   163
  Performance   164
  Transmission Size   165
  Interoperability   165
Protecting Private Keys   166
Introduction to Certificates   166
Key Recovery   169
Summary   169
Real-World Example   170

Chapter 6   Public-Key Infrastructures and the X.509 Standard   171

Public-Key Certificates   172
  Unique Identifiers   174
  Standard Version 3 Certificate Extensions   175
  Entity Names   177

ASN.1 Notation and Encoding   179
The Components of a PKI   179
  Certification Authority   180
  Registration Authority   180
  Certificate Directory   181
  Key Recovery Server   182
  Management Protocols   182
  Operational Protocols   184
Registering and Issuing Certificates   184
Revoking a Certificate   185
  Certificate Revocation Lists   186
  Suspending a Certificate   190
  Authority Revocation Lists   190
Trust Models   191
  Certificate Hierarchies   192
  Cross-Certification   193
  X.509 Certificate Chain   194
  The Push Model Versus the Pull Model   195
Managing Key Pairs   196
  Generating Key Pairs   197
  Protecting Private Keys   197
  Managing Multiple Key Pairs   198
  Updating Key Pairs   199
  Keeping a History of Key Pairs   200
Deploying a PKI   201
The Future of PKI   201
  Roaming Certificates   201
  Attribute Certificates   203
Certificate Policies and Certification Practice Statements   204
Summary   206
Real-World Examples   206
  Keon Certificate Server   207
  Keon Web PassPort   207

Chapter 7   Network and Transport Security Protocols   209

Internet Protocol Security   209
  IP Security Architecture   210
  IPSec Services   211
The Authentication Header Protocol   211
  Integrity Check Value Calculation   212

Transport and Tunnel Modes   213
The Encapsulating Security Payload Protocol   215
    Encryption Algorithms   216
    ESP in Transport and Tunnel Modes   217
Security Associations   218
    Combining Security Associations   219
Security Databases   220
    Security Policy Database   222
    Security Association Database   222
Key Management   223
    Internet Key Exchange   224
Secure Sockets Layer   227
    The History of SSL   227
Session and Connection States   228
The Record Layer Protocol   230
The Change Cipher Spec Protocol   231
The Alert Protocol   232
The Handshake Protocol   233
    The Client Hello Message   234
    The Server Hello Message   235
    The Server Certificate Message   236
    The Server Key Exchange Message   236
    The Certificate Request Message   237
    The Server Hello Done Message   237
    The Client Certificate Message   237
    The Client Key Exchange Message   238
    The Certificate Verify Message   238
    The Finished Message   239
    Ending a Session and Connection   239
    Resuming Sessions   240
    Cryptographic Computations   240
    Encryption and Authentication Algorithms   240
Summary   241
Real-World Examples   242

Chapter 8   Application-Layer Security Protocols   243

S/MIME   243
    Overview   244
    S/MIME Functionality   245
    Cryptographic Algorithms   245

S/MIME Messages 247
Enhanced Security Services 252
Interoperability 253
Secure Electronic Transaction (SET) 253
Business Requirements 254
SET Features 255
SET Participants 256
Dual Signatures 257
SET Certificates 258
Payment Processing 260
Summary 264
Real-World Examples 265

Chapter 9 Hardware Solutions: Overcoming Software Limitations 267

Cryptographic Accelerators 267
Authentication Tokens 269
Token Form Factors 270
Noncontact Tokens 270
Contact Tokens 275
Smart Cards 275
Smart Card Standards 276
Types of Smart Cards 276
Readers and Terminals 278
JavaCards 279
History and Standards 279
JavaCard Operations 280
Other Java Tokens 281
Biometrics 282
Biometric Systems Overview 282
Recognition Methods 285
Biometric Accuracy 288
Combining Authentication Methods 289
Summary 291
Vendors 291

Chapter 10 Digital Signatures: Beyond Security 293

Legislative Approaches 295
Legal Guidelines from the American Bar Association 295
Legal Concepts Related to Digital Signatures 296

Nonrepudiation 296
Authentication 298
Written Versus Digital Signatures 299
Requirements for the Use of Digital Signatures 299
Public Key Infrastructures 300
Control of Key Revocation 300
Time-Stamping 300
Current and Pending Legislation 302
The E-SIGN Act 303
Dealing with Legal Uncertainties 306
Summary 307
Real-World Examples 307

Chapter 11   Doing It Wrong: The Break-Ins 309

Measuring Losses 309
Types of Security Threats 310
Unauthorized Disclosure of Data 311
Unauthorized Modification of Data 311
Unauthorized Access 312
Disclosure of Network Traffic 313
Spoofing of Network Traffic 314
Identifying Intruders 314
Insiders 315
Hackers 315
Terrorists 315
Foreign Intelligence Services 316
Hactivists 316
Intruder Knowledge 317
Case Studies 317
Data in Transit 317
Data at Rest 318
Authentication 319
Implementation 320
Information Security: Law Enforcement 321
Summary 322

Chapter 12   Doing It Right: Following Standards 323

Security Services and Mechanisms 324
Authentication 324

Confidentiality   326
Integrity   326
Nonrepudiation   327
Standards, Guidelines, and Regulations   327
The Internet Engineering Task Force   327
ANSI X9   328
National Institute of Standards and Technology   328
Common Criteria   330
The Health Insurance Portability Act   330
Developer Assistance   331
Insurance   332
Security Research   332
Case Studies   333
Implementation   333
Authentication   334
Data at Rest   335
Data in Transit   336
Summary   336

Appendix A Bits, Bytes, Hex, and ASCII   339

Appendix B A Layman's Guide to a Subset of ASN.1, BER, and DER   347

Appendix C Further Technical Details   387

Appendix D Chapter Review   407

Index   489

Credits

Foreword

Welcome to the second book from RSA Press, RSA Security's Official Guide to Cryptography!

As the Internet becomes a more pervasive part of daily life, the need for e-security becomes even more critical. Any organization engaged in online activity must assess and manage the e-security risks associated with this activity. Effective use of cryptographic techniques is at the core of many of these risk-management strategies. This book provides a practical guide for the use of cryptographic e-security technologies to provide for privacy, security, and integrity of an organization's most precious asset: data.

It is an exciting time for cryptography, with important technical, business, and legal events occurring in quick succession. This book can help the reader better understand the technology behind these events.

In January 2000, the United States Government announced a significant relaxation in restrictions on the export of strong cryptography. This decision has permitted U.S. companies to now compete for cryptographic business on a worldwide basis. Previously, many of the algorithms discussed in this book were treated as munitions and were subject to severe restrictions on their export from the U.S.

In September 2000, the patent on the RSA algorithm, arguably the most important patent in cryptography, expired. Now any firm or individual can create implementations of this algorithm, further increasing the pervasiveness of one of the most widespread technologies in the history of computing.

In October 2000, the United States National Institute of Standards and Technology announced its selection of the winner of the *Advanced Encryption Standard* (AES) selection process, an algorithm called Rijndael developed by two Belgian researchers. The AES algorithm is intended to replace the venerable, and increasingly vulnerable *Data Encryption Standard* (DES) algorithm. AES is expected to become the most widely used algorithm of its type in a short time.

The security technology industry has undergone explosive growth in a short period of time, with many new options emerging for the deployment of e-security techniques based on cryptography. Ranging from new developments in cryptographic hardware to the use of personal smart cards in public key infrastructures, the industry continues to increase the range of choices available to address e-security risks. This book provides the reader with a solid foundation in the core cryptographic techniques of e-security—including RSA, AES, and DES mentioned previously, and many others—and then builds on this foundation to discuss the use of these techniques in practical applications and cutting-edge technologies.

While this book does discuss the underlying mathematics of cryptography, its primary focus is on the use of these technologies in familiar, real-world settings. It takes a systems approach to the problems of using cryptographic techniques for e-security, reflecting the fact that the degree of protection provided by an e-security deployment is only as strong as the weakest link in the chain of protection.

We hope that you will enjoy this book and the other titles from RSA Press. We welcome your comments as well as your suggestions for future RSA Press books. For more information on RSA Security, please visit our web site at www.rsasecurity.com; more information on RSA Press can be found at www.rsapress.com.

Burt Kaliski
Director and Chief Scientist
RSA Laboratories
bkaliski@rsasecurity.com

Acknowledgments

The first person I'd like to thank is Stephen Paine. He did the work of putting together the original proposal and outline. Later on, he reorganized the structure to make the book better. He planned; I just wrote.

Betsy Hardinger and LeeAnn Pickrell at McGraw Hill/Osborne are the two editors who made many suggestions (most of which we accepted) to improve the language, readability, and flow of the content. Stephen Paine and I have our names on the book, but I think they deserve plenty of credit for their contributions.

Blake Dournaee of RSA did a great job of reviewing. If it hadn't been for Blake, I would be suffering from great embarrassment for a couple of mistakes he caught. Of course, any errors still residing in this book belong entirely to Stephen and me.

We received help from many people for the examples. Mark Tessin of Reynolds Data Recovery and Dennis Vanatta of 4Sites Internet Services gave me the information and screen shot for the data recovery discussion in Chapter 1. Mary Ann Davidson and Kristy Browder of Oracle helped me put together the example in Chapter 2. For the Keon example, Peter Rostin and Nino Marino of RSA were my sources.

The people at McGraw Hill/Osborne said we had complete control over the acknowledgments, so I'd like to thank some people who didn't contribute to the book so much as contributed to my career. If it hadn't been for Dave Neff at Intergraph, I don't think I would have been much of a programmer and hence never could have been successful enough at RSA to be chosen to write this book. It was Victor Chang, then the VP of engineering at RSA, who hired me, let me do all kinds of wonderful things in the field and industry of cryptography, and made RSA engineering a great place to work. The geniuses of RSA Labs, especially Burt Kaliski and Matt Robshaw, taught me most of the crypto I know today, and the engineers at RSA, especially Dung Huynh and Pao-Chi Hwang, taught me all about the crypto code.

—*Steve Burnett*

The first person I'd like to thank is Steve Burnett. I am positive that if he had not agreed to co-author this book with me, I might have given up before I began.

RSA Press definitely must be thanked for giving Steve Burnett and me a chance to write this book. Also, I'd like to thank Steve Elliot, Alex Corona, Betsy Hardinger, LeeAnn Pickrell, and all of the other employees of McGraw Hill/Osborne who worked to make this book possible.

Both Jessica Nelson and Blake Dournaee did an excellent job providing technical review—thank you. I'd like to offer a special thanks to Mohan Atreya and Scott Maxwell of RSA Security; both were a source of excellent ideas and technical input.

Thanks to my friends at RSA Security for being patient and understanding while I worked long hours on the book.

I especially want to thank Jerry Mansfield, a great friend who taught me to take life as it comes. Finally, I would like to thank my family for their support.

—*Stephen Paine*

Preface

Application developers never used to add security to their products because the buying public didn't care. To add security meant spending money to include features that did not help sales. Today, customers demand security for many applications. The Federal Bureau of Investigation published the following Congressional Statement on February 16, 2000:

> "There were over 100 million Internet users in the United States in 1999. That number is projected to reach 177 million in United States and 502 million worldwide by the end of 2003. Electronic commerce has emerged as a new sector of the American economy, accounting for over $100 billion in sales during 1999; by 2003 electronic commerce is projected to exceed $1 trillion."

At the same time, the *Computer Security Institute* (CSI) reported an increase in cybercrime, "55% of the respondents to our survey reported malicious activity by insiders." Knowing this, you can be sure growing corporations need security products.

The most important security tool is cryptography. Developers and engineers need to understand crypto in order to effectively build it into their products. Sales and marketing people need to understand crypto in order to prove the products they are selling are secure. The customers buying those products, whether end users or corporate purchasing agents, need to understand crypto in order to make well-informed choices and then to use those products correctly. IT professionals need to understand crypto in order to deploy it properly in their systems. Even lawyers need to understand crypto because governments at the local, state, and national level are enacting new laws defining the responsibilities of entities holding the public's private information.

This book is an introduction to crypto. It is not about the history of crypto (although you will find some historical stories). It is not a guide to writing code, nor a math book listing all the theorems and proofs of the underpinnings of crypto. It does not describe everything there is to know about crypto; rather, it describes the basic concepts of the most widely used crypto in the world today. After reading this book, you will know what computer cryptography does and how it's used today. For example, you will

- Understand the difference between a block cipher and a stream cipher and know when to use each (if someone tries to sell you an application that reuses a stream cipher's key, you will know why you shouldn't buy it).

- Know why you should not implement key recovery on a signing-only key.

- Understand what SSL does and why it is not the security magic bullet solving all problems, which some e-commerce sites seem to imply.

- Learn how some companies have effectively implemented crypto in their products.

- Learn how some companies have used crypto poorly (smart people learn from their own mistakes; brilliant people learn from other people's mistakes).

There are, of course, many more things you will learn in this book.

Chapter 1 delves into why cryptography is needed today; Chapters 2 through 5 describe the basic building blocks of crypto, such as symmetric keys and public keys, password-based encryption, and digital signatures. In Chapters 6 through 8, you will see how these building blocks are used to create an infrastructure through certificates and protocols. In Chapter 9, you will learn how specialized hardware devices can enhance your security. Chapter 10 explores the legal issues around digital signatures. Finally, Chapters 11 and 12 show you some real-world examples of companies doing it wrong and doing it right.

Throughout this book we use some standard computer hexadecimal notation. For instance, we might show a cryptographic key such as the following:

```
0x14C608B9 62AF9086
```

Many of you probably know what that means, but if you don't, read Appendix A. It's all about how the computer industry displays bits and bytes in hexadecimal. It also describes ASCII, the standard way letters, numerals, and symbols are expressed in computers.

In Chapter 6, you'll find a brief description of ASN.1 and BER/DER encoding. If you want to drill down further into this topic, read Appendix B.

In Appendix C, you will find further detailed information about many of the topics discussed in the book. These details are not crucial to understanding the concepts presented in the main body of the book; but for those who wish to learn more about the way crypto is used today, this appendix will offer interesting reading.

Appendix D contains a handy summary for each chapter. You'll also find a list of key terms, a key terms quiz, a multiple-choice quiz, and an essay quiz to test your knowledge of each chapter's content, as well as one or two lab projects per chapter.

At the end of the book there is a list of addtional online resources and a page devoted to the contents of the CD.

About the Authors

Steve Burnett With degrees in math from Grinnell College in Iowa and The Claremont Graduate School in California, Steve Burnett has spent most of his career converting math into computer programs, first at Intergraph Corporation and now with RSA Security. He is currently the lead crypto engineer for RSA's BSAFE Crypto-C and Crypto-J products, which are general purpose crypto software development kits in C and Java. Burnett is also a frequent speaker at industry events and college campuses.

Stephen Paine Stephen Paine has worked in the security field throughout most of his career—formerly for the United States Marine Corps and SUN Microsystems. He is currently a systems engineer for RSA Security, where he explains security concepts to corporations and developers worldwide and provides training to customers and RSA employees.

About the Reviewers

Blake Dournaee Blake Dournaee joined RSA Security's developer support team in 1999, specializing in support and training for the BSAFE cryptography toolkits. Prior to joining RSA Security, he worked at NASA-Ames Research Center in their security development group. He has a B.S. in Computer Science from California Polytechnic State University in San Luis Obispo and is currently a graduate student at the University of Massachusetts.

Jessica Nelson Jessica Nelson comes from a strong background in computer security. As an officer in the United States Air Force, she spearheaded the 12 Air Force/Southern Command Defensive Information Warfare division. She built programs that integrated computer and communications security into the DoD's Information Warfare. She graduated from UCSD with a degree in physics and has worked with such astrophysicists as Dr. Kim Griest and Dr. Sally Ride. She currently acts as technical sales lead in the western division of a European security company.

CHAPTER 1

Why Cryptography?

"According to the affidavit in support of the criminal complaint, the Secret Service began investigating this matter when it learned that there had been unauthorized access to [online brokerage] accounts of several [anonymous company] employees. One [anonymous company] employee told authorities that approximately $285,000 had been drained from his [online brokerage] account when an unknown person was able to access his account by calling the online broker and providing a name and social security number. It was later determined that at least eight [anonymous company] employees had been victimized this past spring, and that these eight had lost a total of $700,000 from their stock accounts . . . [anonymous company] officials revealed that while working in the financial department, [the accomplice] had access to confidential employee information such as social security numbers and home addresses."*

If someone tells you, "I don't need security. I have no secrets, nothing to hide," respond by saying, "OK, let me see your medical files. How about your paycheck, bank statements, investment portfolio, and credit card bills? Will you let me write down your Social Security number,

---

*Source: U.S. Department of Justice, July 20, 2000

credit card numbers, and bank account numbers? What's the PIN for your ATM, credit card, or phone card? What's your password to log on to the network at work? Where do you keep your spare house key?"

The point is that we all have information we want kept private. Sometimes the reason is simply our natural desire for privacy; we would feel uncomfortable if the whole world knew our medical history or financial details. Another good reason is self-protection—thieves could use some kinds of information to rob us. In other words, the motives for keeping a secret are not automatically nefarious.

Corporations also have secrets—strategy reports, sales forecasts, technical product details, research results, personnel files, and so on. Although dishonest companies might try to hide villainous activities from the public, most firms simply want to hide valuable information from dishonest people. These people may be working for competitors, they might be larcenous employees, or they could be *hackers* and *crackers*: people who break into computer networks to steal information, commit vandalism, disrupt service, or simply to show what they can do.

Security Provided by Computer Operating Systems

In the past, security was simply a matter of locking the door or storing files in a locked filing cabinet or safe. Today, paper is no longer the only medium of choice for housing information. Files are stored in computer databases as well as file cabinets. Hard drives and floppy disks hold many of our secrets. How do you lock a hard drive?

How Operating Systems Work

Before we talk about how computer data is protected, let's take a brief look at how computers get and store information. The usual way to access data on a computer or network is to go through the *operating system* (OS), such as DOS, Windows, Windows 95, Windows NT, MacOS, UNIX, Linux, Solaris, or HP/UX. The OS works like an application, taking input, performing operations based on the input, and returning output. Whereas, for example, a spreadsheet application takes the numbers you type into it, inserts them into cells, and possibly performs calculations such as adding columns, an OS takes your commands in the form of mouse clicks, joysticks, touch screens, or keyboard input-commands such as "show a listing of the files in this directory"—and performs the request, such as printing to the screen a list of files. You can also ask the OS to launch a particular application—say, a text editor. You then tell the text editor to open a file. Behind the scenes, the editor actually asks the OS to find the file and make its contents available to the editor.

Virtually all computers built today include some form of protection courtesy of the OS. Let's take a look at how such protection works.

Default OS Security: Permissions

Virtually all operating systems have some built-in *permissions*, which allow only certain people access to the computer (its hard drive, memory, disk space, and network connection). Such access is implemented via a *login* procedure. If the user does not present the appropriate credentials (perhaps a user name and password), the OS will not allow that individual to use the computer. But even after a user is logged in, certain files may still be off-limits. If someone asks to see a file, the OS checks to see whether that requester is on the list of approved users; if not, the OS does not disclose the contents (see Figure 1-1).

Access to most business computers and networks is controlled by someone known as a *superuser* or *system administrator* (often shortened to *sys admin*). This system administrator is the person charged with creating and closing user accounts and maintaining the systems and network. A typical task of this superuser account is to override protections. Someone forgot a password? A file is read-protected (meaning that it cannot be opened and read)? The superuser has permission to circumvent the OS permissions to respond to these problems. (This is where the name "superuser" comes from; this individual can do anything.)

How does the OS know that the person requesting such system overrides is the superuser? The OS grants this access by user name and password. The superuser user name is usually "su" or "root" or "administrator." Unfortunately, techniques for circumventing these default defenses are widely known.

Figure 1-1

(a) In Windows
NT, a file's
permission is
given in its
Properties screen.
(b) In UNIX, you
type **ls -l** to see a
file's permission

```
camry% ls -l
total 216
-rw-r--r--    1 burnetts eng        93392 Feb 13 10:48 rc6.txt
-rw-r--r--    1 burnetts eng         2500 Feb 13 10:47 rc6opt.txt
-rw-r--r--    1 burnetts eng        12721 Feb 13 10:47 rc6perf.txt
camry% chmod 664 rc6.txt
camry% ls -l
total 216
-rw-rw-r--    1 burnetts eng        93392 Feb 13 10:48 rc6.txt
-rw-r--r--    1 burnetts eng         2500 Feb 13 10:47 rc6opt.txt
-rw-r--r--    1 burnetts eng        12721 Feb 13 10:47 rc6perf.txt
camry% █
```

Attacks on Passwords

Many computers or operating systems come with a preset superuser
account and password. In many cases, several passwords are used for various
superuser functions. The superuser may have a password to create
accounts, a different password to control network functionality, another to
conduct or access nightly backups, and so on.

For a cracker, logging on to a system as the superuser is possibly the best way to collect data or do damage. If the superuser has not changed an operating system's preprogrammed passwords, the network is vulnerable to attack. Most crackers know these passwords, and their first attempt to break into a network is simply to try them.

If an attacker cannot log on as the superuser, the next best thing might be to figure out the user name and password of a regular user. It used to be standard practice in most colleges and universities, and in some commercial companies, to assign every student or employee an account with a user name and an initial password—the password being the user name. Everyone was instructed to log on and change the password, but often, hackers and crackers logged on before legitimate users had a chance. In other cases, some people never actually used their accounts. Either way, intruders were able to gain access. This "user name as password" system is still used on many campuses and corporate settings to this day.

If the password of a particular user name is not the user name itself, crackers may try to guess the correct password. Guessing a password might be easy for an insider (such as a fellow employee), who probably knows everyone's user name. It's common for people to use a spouse's name or a birthday as a password. Others write down their passwords, and a quick search of a desk might yield the valuable information. Some systems have guest accounts, with a user name of "guest" and a password of "guest."

But even if the intruder is not very good at guessing passwords, applications are available that automate exhaustive password searches. These applications, called *password cracking* software, are made by a variety of people for various reasons—some legitimate and others not so legitimate. To use one of these tools, the intruder needs access to your computer (network access may be sufficient). Once connected, the hacker simply runs the password cracking application. If the password is weak, within minutes the hacker will have privileged access.

Figure 1-2 shows a popular application known as l0phtCrack. This application is designed to allow systems administrators to test the passwords in use by their users. The idea is that if a sys admin can crack a password, so can crackers.

Figure 1-2

l0phtCrack is
used to test
passwords for
vulnerability

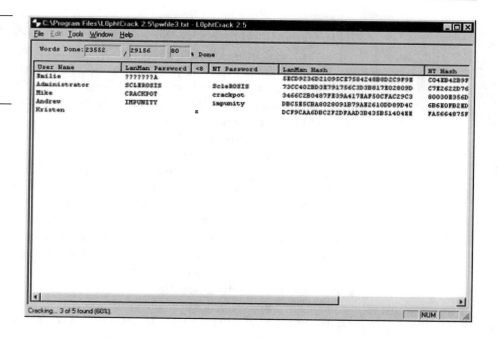

Figure 1-2

l0phtCrack is
used to test
passwords for
vulnerability

Attacks That Bypass Operating Systems

An operating system tags certain files and prevents unapproved people
from seeing the contents. Although a cracker or thief might be able to gain
access to such files by posing as the superuser or a regular user, another
possibility is to ignore the OS altogether and get the contents in some
other way.

Data Recovery Attack

One function of a computer's operating system is to help users find and
use the specific data or application they want. In this way, an OS works
like the index of a book. Just as an index directs you to the specific page
where you'll find the piece of information you want out of all the pages in
a book, the OS organizes data under a directory file structure and uses file
extensions to direct you to the data you want on the hard disk. But as far
as the computer is concerned, the data is simply so many electronic bits.

If you don't care what order they're in, it's possible to read those bits as bits and not as files of text or numbers. Human beings can't read bits in this way, but software and hardware devices are available that can scan storage media and read the bits. These tools bypass the OS and grab the raw bits of data, which can then be reconstructed into the original files.

In fact, an entire industry has been built on the concept of reading bits as bits, a process called *data recovery*. When you have a system crash or some kind of physical damage to a hard drive, you can take your computer to a data recovery expert, who often can reconstruct the files on the disk. These companies provide a valuable service, helping to prevent total losses in the event of a natural disaster or computer failure.

Reynolds Data Recovery of Longmont, Colorado, performs data recovery and also sells software that allows you to perform your own recovery (see Figure 1-3). According to the company's advertising, one of its products, Inspector Copier, "does not reference the OS installed on the devices, [and] this allows copies of different systems such as NT, Novell, UNIX, Linux or Windows 2000!"

Figure 1-3

Inspector Copier from Reynolds Data Recovery (courtesy of Mark Tessin of Reynolds Data Recovery)

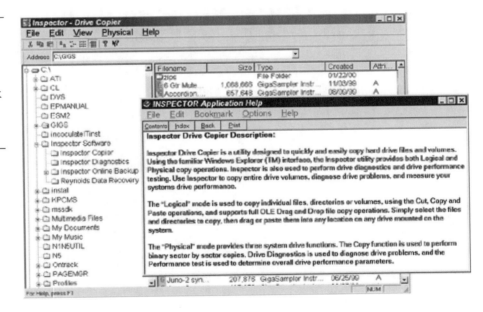

But the techniques of data recovery can also be used by attackers to circumvent OS protections. To extend Inspector Copier, Reynolds sells a network backup service that remotely backs up data on hard drives. It uses Inspector Copier to extract the bits so that even if a hard drive is damaged, a clean backup can be made. Although this service can be valuable to many companies, it also means that the data recovery program can be run remotely. Mark Tessin of Reynolds points out that the service can even circumvent Windows NT security. Suppose your PC is connected to a network but you don't want the outside world to see your C: drive. You can set the permissions on your drive so that only you have read or write permission to it (see Figure 1-4). The Reynolds network backup service can circumvent that permission and read the files anyway. This is not to imply that Reynolds Data Recovery will steal your data, only to illustrate that it is possible.

Figure 1-4

Setting network permissions on a local drive using Windows NT

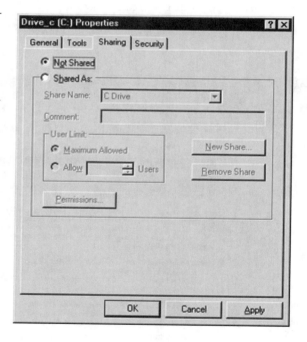

For serious disk drive failures (such as fire damage), data recovery might be possible only through specialized hardware devices. But an attacker is not trying to steal your data from a damaged drive. Data recovery software is so sophisticated and effective that it's all anyone needs to extract bits from a healthy storage medium.

To ensure the security of your data, you must assume that even though some protections may be sufficient against some opponents, there will likely be someone out there with the resources to mount a successful attack. Only if such an individual never comes after your data are you safe.

Memory Reconstruction Attack

Often, sensitive material is not stored on hard drives but does appear in a computer's memory. For example, when the program you're running allocates some of the computer's memory, the OS tags that area of memory as unavailable, and no one else can use it or see it. When you're finished with that area of memory, though, many operating systems and programs simply "free" it—marking it as available—without overwriting it. This means that anything you put into that memory area, even if you later "deleted" it, is still there. A memory reconstruction attack involves trying to examine all possible areas of memory. The attacker simply allocates the memory you just freed and sees what's left there.

A similar problem is related to what is called "virtual memory." The memory managers in many operating systems use the hard drive as virtual memory, temporarily copying to the hard drive any data from memory that has been allocated but is momentarily not being used. When that information is needed again, the memory manager *swaps* the current virtual memory for the real memory. In August 1997, *The New York Times* published a report about an individual using simple tools to scan his hard drive. In the swap space, he found the password he used for a popular security application.

On UNIX systems, the OS "dumps core" in response to certain system errors. Core dump has become almost synonymous with a program exiting ungracefully. But on UNIX, the core file that results from a core dump is actually a snapshot of memory at the time the error occurred. An attacker who wants to read memory may be able to induce a core dump and peruse the core file.

Figure 1-5 illustrates how memory reconstruction attacks work.

Figure 1-5

Your sensitive material, such a password, is not stored on a hard drive but does appear in memory. An attacker may read the data in memory in the swap space, in a core file, or simply after you free it

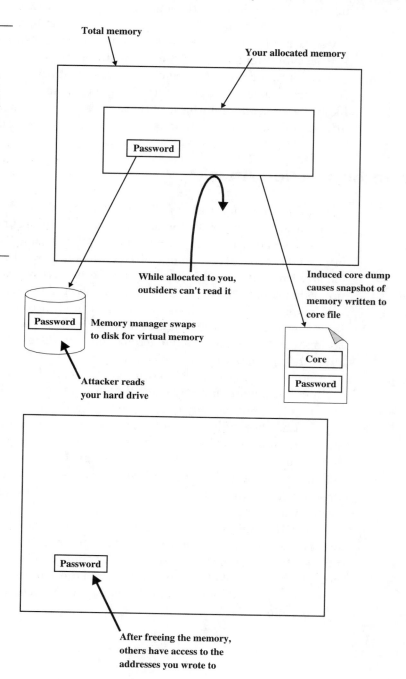

Added Protection Through Cryptography

For your secrets to be secure, it may be necessary to add protections not provided by your computer system's OS. The built-in protections may be adequate in some cases. If no one ever tries to break into or steal data from a particular computer, its data will be safe. Or if the intruder has not learned how to get around the simple default mechanisms, they're sufficient. But many attackers do have the skills and resources to break various security systems. If you decide to do nothing and hope that no skilled cracker targets your information, you may get lucky, and nothing bad will happen. But most people aren't willing to take that risk.

As you'll learn in the chapters to come, one of the most important tools for protecting data is *cryptography,* any of various methods that are used to turn readable files into gibberish. For example, suppose your sensitive material looks like this:

```
do not believe that the competition can match the new feature set,
yet their support, services, and consulting offerings pose        a
serious threat to our salability. We must invest more money in our
```

Here is what the data looks like when it's encrypted:

```
ú?Sdï:1/41Yïõ´]Y çmúcA‡[< _b:vH˜_ô UGØ>e´œ_%` ,<_lo¡`üùØ_"G
ri§õêìqY_Ë•ùK_æ7ÁFT1≅Ó_ . . . À ªR8'» ÿÄh . . . o-
2ñ?í•çÕ(tm)ÇvéR]'Î_¬'(r)<Ñ_UéR`q3/4¥Ü_Ã‡ÁuÉ•¶ _>FômÈÕ6_cêàB1/28#ùh&(G
[gh_!>¶≅Oædtn*´bô1/4jWM1/4B-Â_≅_¬1/4<"-ÏEÿåb{=.AÛH__
```

Even if an attacker obtains the contents of the file, it is gibberish. It does not matter whether or not the OS protections worked. The secret is still secret.

In addition to keeping secrets, cryptography can add security to the process of authenticating people's identity. Because the password method used in almost all commercial operating systems is probably not very strong against a sophisticated (or even an unsophisticated) attacker, it's important to add protection. The cryptographic techniques for providing data secrecy can be adapted to create strong digital identities. If attackers want to pose as someone else, it's not a matter simply of guessing a password. Attackers must also solve an intractable mathematical problem (see Figure 1-6).

Figure 1-6

To pose as Steve Burnett of RSA Security, you'd have to factor this number (see also Chapter 4)

111,103,906,294,152,860,689,339,031,055,865,718,
797,834,178,049,634,993,529,562,676,343,628,611,
324,998,912,180,711,483,651,242,218,389,147,835,
598,353,467,199,134,664,870,577,824,583,579,439,
533,042,724,963,790,890,892,988,756,173,576,982,
820,529,088,558,175,928,394,148,986,383,304,407,
218,632,861,415,573,872,050,375,072,884,180,285,
838,244,342,451,974,820,729,610,630,901,524,541,
854,611,490,009,870,503,127

The Role of Cryptography in Data Security

In the physical world, security is a fairly simple concept. If the locks on your house's doors and windows are so strong that a thief cannot break in to steal your belongings, the house is secure. For further protection against intruders breaking through the locks, you might have security alarms. Similarly, if someone tries to fraudulently withdraw money from your bank account but the teller asks for identification and does not trust the thief's story, your money is secure. When you sign a contract with another person, the signatures are the legal driving force that impels both parties to honor their word.

In the digital world, security works in a similar way. One concept is *privacy*, meaning that no one can break into files to read your sensitive data (such as medical records) or steal money (by, for example, obtaining credit card numbers or online brokerage account information). Privacy is the lock on the door. Another concept, *data integrity*, refers to a mechanism that tells us when something has been altered. That's the alarm. By applying the practice of *authentication*, we can verify identities. That's comparable to the ID required to withdraw money from a bank account (or conduct a transaction with an online broker). And finally, *nonrepudiation* is a legal driving force that impels people to honor their word.

Cryptography is by no means the only tool needed to ensure data security, nor will it solve all security problems. It is one instrument among many. Moreover, cryptography is not foolproof. All crypto can be broken, and, more importantly, if it's implemented incorrectly, it adds no real security. This book provides an introduction to cryptography with a focus on the proper use of this tool. It is not intended as a complete survey of all there is to know about cryptography. Rather, this book describes the most widely used crypto techniques in the world today.

CHAPTER 2

Symmetric-Key Cryptography

Cryptography converts readable data into gibberish, with the ability to recover the original data from that gibberish. The first flavor of crypto is called symmetric-key. In this approach, an algorithm uses a key to convert information into what looks like random bits. Then the same algorithm uses the same key to recover the original data.

Pao-Chi is a sales rep for a company that makes printing machinery. He sells to newspapers, magazines, independent printing houses large and small, and even universities. His product line includes presses, tools, replacement parts, repair services, and training. The end of the quarter is coming up in a couple of weeks, and he's just received a memo from Gwen, the vice president of sales. The company is having difficulty "making its numbers," the memo says. Then it outlines a new, complex pricing policy.

This new policy lists the asking prices for all their products and also indicates the lowest prices sales reps are allowed to negotiate. In the past, they've based the amount of the discounts they give on the size of the order, expectations of future sales with a given client, and other factors. But now, the memo states, sales reps have the authority to give even bigger discounts.

Pao-Chi wants to closely limit who has access to this information. If potential customers knew how far he was willing to go in discounting, they would have the edge in negotiations. Existing customers might demand rebates, and competitors would gain knowledge that could aid them in winning contracts. In addition, stock analysts or business reporters could report the company's slow sales this quarter, affecting its reputation.

How can Pao-Chi and Gwen keep this memo secret? They could choose not to let it leave the office, or maybe Pao-Chi could simply memorize it. But it's more than 20 pages long and too complex to memorize, and he'll need to consult it while trying to make a sale.

So Pao-Chi keeps an electronic copy of the memo on his laptop, and takes steps to protect the file. In Chapter 1, we saw that typical protection techniques are not sufficient. Pao-Chi can lose his laptop, or someone might steal it or simply look through the files while he's at lunch. To protect the file, he decides to encrypt it.

Let's say Pao-Chi buys a computer program to encrypt sensitive files. When running the program, he simply flips the switch to "Encrypt" and feeds the file to the program (see Figure 2-1). When the file comes out of the program, it looks like gibberish. If intruders get their hands on it, they will have no idea what it means.

Figure 2-1

If you feed your sensitive files to an encryption program, you get what looks like gibberish

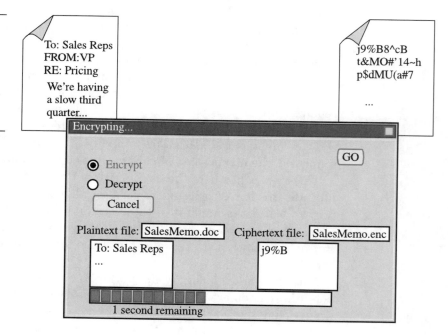

The problem is that as long as the file is gibberish Pao-Chi won't be able to read it either. To read it, he must somehow convert it back to its original form. The program has just such a feature: he flips the switch to "Decrypt," feeds in the gibberish, and out comes the file in its former condition.

But there's one problem with this scenario. If intruders are able to obtain the encrypted file, surely they can obtain the program that converts it back. Even if they can't, where can Pao-Chi safely store the program? If he can keep the program out of the hands of attackers, why not store his file there as well?

No, he doesn't have a place where he can keep the encrypting and decrypting program safe. And if Pao-Chi has access to it, he must assume that attackers can gain access. That's why he uses encryption in the first place. By itself, an encryption machine cannot protect secrets. Pao-Chi needs additional protection.

That additional protection is a secret number. If he feeds the file *and* a secret number to the program, the program will encrypt the file. Until the program has a secret number, it will not run. To decrypt the file, Pao-Chi must present the gibberish and the same secret number (see Figure 2-2).

Figure 2-2

To get encrypted gibberish, you feed sensitive data and a secret number to the encryption machine. To recover the file, you flip the switch to "Decrypt" and then feed it the gibberish and the secret number

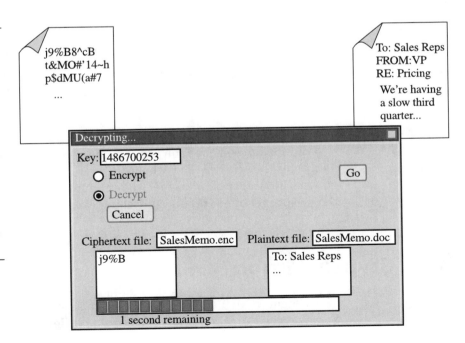

If an attacker somehow obtains a copy of the gibberish and feeds it to the program for recovery, it won't work. The program asks for the number, which the attacker does not know. It's possible to try numbers at random (or to try all possible numbers systematically), but every time a wrong number is inserted, the application simply spits out different gibberish (see Figure 2-3).

Figure 2-3

If attackers try numbers other than the secret value, they get only more gibberish

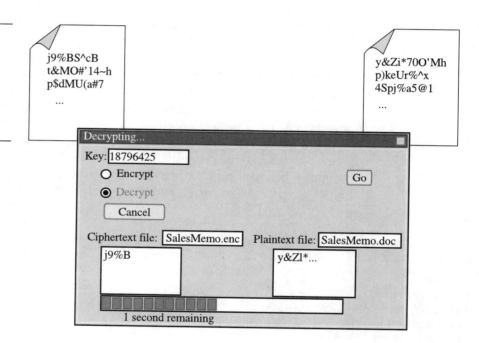

Even though someone can use the same program Pao-Chi used, it never re-creates the original file without the secret number. Even if the attacker guesses a number close to the original number, even if it is off by only 1, the program will not produce anything close to the correct encrypted file.

Some Crypto Jargon

The system we've just described is known as *symmetric-key cryptography*. Some people call it *secret-key cryptography*. Here are some official terms.

When you want to convert sensitive information to gibberish, you *encrypt* the data. To convert it back, you *decrypt* it.

To do this, you use an *algorithm*. The word "algorithm" is a scientific term for a recipe or step-by-step procedure. It is a list of instructions or things to do in a particular order. An algorithm might have a rigid list of commands to follow, or it might contain a series of questions and depending on the answers, describe the appropriate steps to follow. A mathematical algorithm might list the operations to perform in a particular order to "find x." For example, an automobile diagnostic algorithm may ask questions about oil pressure, torque, fluid levels, temperature, and so on, to determine what's wrong. A computer program can also implement an algorithm, meaning the program converts the algorithm's list of commands, questions, and operations into the computer's language, enabling it to perform the steps in the appropriate order. In computer cryptography, algorithms are sometimes complex mathematical operations or simply bit manipulations. Many encryption algorithms exist, and each one has its own particular list of commands or steps. Just as you can have a program that plays Solitaire or one that computes the trajectory of satellites, you can have a program that implements an encryption algorithm that takes your data and converts it to gibberish.

The data that you want to keep secret is called *plaintext* (some call it *cleartext*). Your plaintext could be a human-readable text file, such as the memo. Or it could be a binary file, which looks like nonsense to human eyes but makes perfect sense to a computer program. For example, if you open a PowerPoint file using Windows' Edit text editor, the file looks like gibberish because the program can't convert the PowerPoint formatting information; but if you open the same file in PowerPoint, it appears as intended. Whether or not your information is readable by a human or a given program, it's called plaintext.

After the data is encrypted, it's known as *ciphertext*.

The algorithm encrypts your plaintext into ciphertext, but it needs one more thing—a *key*. In our sales rep example, the secret number used to encrypt the pricing memo was its key. In computer crypto, the key is always a number or a set of numbers.

We've also met the *attacker*, someone trying to steal information. Actually, an attacker may try to do more than simply uncover someone else's secrets. Some attackers try to pose as people they are not, disable Web sites, delete someone else's information, prevent customers from buying at a particular online merchant, slow down systems, and on and on and on. The term "attacker" is simply a catchall for the individual from whom you must protect your digital assets.

The study of breaking cryptographic systems is known as of *cryptanalysis*. Similar to the attacker, the *cryptanalyst* looks for weaknesses in algorithms. All algorithms can be "broken;" the good ones are simply the algorithms strong enough to withstand an attack for so long the break comes "too late." So a cryptanalyst's job is to find weaknesses that may help someone break the algorithm faster. Attackers may use cryptanalytic techniques to do damage, but they may also use other tools.

The *cryptographer* develops crypto systems; the cryptanalyst looks for weaknesses. It's important for the crypto community to know about the weaknesses because attackers are looking for them as well. Attackers are almost certainly not going to announce their discoveries to the world, so cryptanalysts perform a service, letting us all know what attackers probably know but won't tell us.

What Is a Key?

The term "key" comes from the fact that the secret number you choose works in the same way that a conventional key works. To protect the contents of your house, you install a lock on the door. To operate the lock, you insert the key and turn it. The lock's tumblers and mechanisms work with the key in a prescribed way to activate a barrier that prevents the door from being opened. To unlock the door, you insert the key and turn it in the opposite direction. The tumblers and mechanisms work with the key to reverse the process and allow the door to be opened.

In cryptography, to protect the contents of your files, you install a lock (an encryption algorithm) on your door (the computer). To operate the lock (encrypt the data), you insert the key (the secret number) and execute it (instead of turning this key, you operate the program by double-clicking, clicking OK, or pressing ENTER). The algorithm performs its steps using the key to alter the plaintext and convert it to ciphertext. To unlock the encrypted file, you insert the same key and execute. The algorithm reverses the steps and converts the ciphertext back to the original plaintext.

Just as only the correct house key can open your front door, only the correct encryption key can decrypt data. In symmetric-key cryptography, the key that is used to encrypt data is the same key that is used to decrypt it. "Symmetric" essentially means "the same on two sides," and that's what we have here: the same key on two sides of the encryption process. Figure 2-4, a picture you'll see quite a bit in this book, is the image we use to visualize cryptography.

Figure 2-4

This encryption algorithm uses the key to convert plaintext to ciphertext. In symmetric-key cryptography, the key used for encryption is also necessary for decryption

In this book we talk about some of the many different encryption algorithms you have to choose from, but remember that keys are not interchangeable among algorithms. For example, suppose that you encrypt data using the Triple *Digital Encryption Standard* (DES) algorithm (discussed later in the section titled "Triple DES"). If you try to decrypt the data using the *Advanced Encryption Standard* (AES) cipher (discussed later in the section titled "Advanced Encryption Standard"), even if you use the same key, you will not get the correct result.

Why Is a Key Necessary?

All computer crypto operates with keys. Why is a key necessary? Why not create an algorithm that doesn't need a key?

As you saw in the memo example, if attackers can understand the algorithm, they can recover secret data simply by executing the algorithm. That's like installing a deadbolt on your front door with the lock on the outside. It's true that when the deadbolt is in place, the door cannot be opened. But anyone can open the door simply by turning the lock.

It might seem that the solution is to keep the algorithm secret, but that approach has several problems. First, attackers always crack the algorithm (see "Historical Note: They Always Figure Out The Algorithm," later in this chapter). What's more, suppose you do manage to keep the algorithm secret. Unless you are a cryptography expert and develop your own algorithms, you also must trust the company that wrote your algorithm never to reveal it deliberately or accidentally. Does anyone have that much trust in a corporate entity?

Here's the real question: Which would you trust more to keep secrets— an algorithm that must be kept secret, or an algorithm that can do its job even if everyone in the world knows exactly how it works? That's where keys come in.

Keys relieve you of the need to worry about the algorithm used in your encryption scheme. If you protect your data with a key, you need protect only the key, something that's easier to do than protecting an algorithm. In this book you'll learn a lot about key protection. Also, if you use keys to protect your secrets, you can use different keys to protect different secrets. This means that if someone breaks one of your keys, your other secrets are still safe. If you're depending on a secret algorithm, an attacker who breaks that one secret gets access to all your secrets.

Generating a Key

In a symmetric-key cryptographic system, the key is only a number. It can be any number as long as it's the right size, so you simply pick a number at random. Then, the next time you need a key, you pick another number at random. The question is, how do you pick a number at random?

Historical Note: They Always Figure Out the Algorithm

Cryptographers are often asked a key question: "Can't I just encrypt my data and simply not tell the attackers what algorithm I used and how big the key is? How can they break my message then?" There are three answers.

Answer 1: They Always Figure It Out Anyway

Attackers can deduce your algorithm without any help from you. Eventually, they always figure it out. Always. Without exception. Never in the history of cryptography has someone been able to keep an algorithm secret.

In war, spies have always found ways of discovering the algorithm, whether it originates in a mathematical operation or a machine. They steal it or get someone to reveal it, maybe through blackmail, extortion, or the time-tested cryptanalytic technique known as "the rubber-hose attack." Agents have always uncovered the algorithm or gotten a copy of the machine. For example, in World War II, Polish soldiers captured the German Enigma machine early in the war. Enigma was the crypto machine the German military used. The allies (namely the British) were able to crack the code more easily because they had the machine in their possession.

Alternatively, the cryptanalysts simply figure out the algorithm. In World War II, U.S. codebreakers were able to determine the inner workings of the Japanese code machines without having one of the machines in their possession.

In modern times, a company called Gemstar Development created a code that converted date, time, and channel indicators into a single code number. These code numbers were published in TV listings as "VCR+." People who bought a GemStar control box could program their VCRs simply by punching in the numbers, simplifying the process and thus benefiting people who owned the product. Only the Gemstar box knew how to decrypt the code numbers. But Ken Shirriff, Curt Welch, and Andrew Kinsman broke the Gemstar algorithm, and they published it in the July 1992 issue of *Cryptologia,* a trade journal. Now, anyone who wants to decode those numbers

continues

(such as VCR manufacturers) can do it without buying a Gemstar control box.

Another example is RC4, an algorithm invented in 1987 but never published. Cryptanalysts and other experts studied it and determined that RC4 was a good way to keep data secret. But the company that created it, RSA Data Security, never made the inner workings of the RC4 algorithm public. This secrecy was for monetary and not security reasons; the company hoped that by keeping it secret no one else would implement and sell it. In 1994, anonymous hackers posted the algorithm on the Internet. How did they figure it out? It was probably by stepping through a copy of the object code with an assembly language debugger. Incidentally, RC4 is now used as part of *Secure Socket Layer* (SSL), the World Wide Web's secure communication protocol (see Chapter 7). RC4 is arguably the most commonly used symmetric cipher, even more so than DES, discussed later in this chapter in the section "Digital Encryption Standard."

If a cryptographic system is hardware-based, engineers open it and look at the internals. In 1998, David Wagner and Ian Goldberg, at the time graduate students at the University of California at Berkeley, opened a supposedly secure digital cell phone and cracked its code.

Sometimes it is possible to keep an algorithm secret long enough to be effective, but eventually the enemy figures it out. For example, in World War II, the U.S. Army used Navajo soldiers to communicate. They simply spoke in Navajo. The Japanese military did not have anyone in its employ who spoke Navajo, nor did it have dictionaries or other reference material. The encryption worked because the algorithm (the Navajo language itself) was kept secret.

Now, of course, any large military has linguists on staff who either know or can easily learn any language used to encrypt secrets.

Answer 2: You Can't Make Money Developing Secret Algorithms

Gemstar did make money for a while using a secret algorithm, but only until someone cracked it. The ultimate problem, though, goes deeper. Think about it this way: How can you sell something without letting buyers see what they're buying?

continues

Suppose, for example, that you sell a software cryptographic system to an e-mail vendor, enabling it to encrypt messages. How could you prevent this client, or anyone else, from looking at your code? There are plenty of ways to reverse-engineer software, as shown in the RC4 story.

"Fine," you may counter, "I won't sell my algorithm to just anyone. I'll make sure that only people I trust can use it." Is it possible to trust enough people to make money that way? And how are your trusted clients going to use your algorithm? About the only thing they could do so is store their data and talk to each other. But people want to communicate with others who do not purchase their algorithm from the same vendor. As a result, the algorithms must be standardized, and that means they must be public.

The other problem with trying to sell algorithms arises on the buyer's side of the arrangement. If you want to use cryptography, you must employ a hardware device or a software program. The problem is this: Just as you have access to the product, so do attackers. Where did you get your hardware or software—a retail software store, a business-to-business vendor? Attackers can go to the same source and get their own copies.

In short, if you use your own algorithm and want to keep it secret, you can't sell it. As a result, you can't make any money.

Answer 3: Publicly Known Algorithms Are More Secure

Let's say you're the purchasing agent for your company and it's up to you to decide which cryptographic algorithm to buy. Your company will use this algorithm to store data and communicate securely. Two sales reps offer their products. One warns, "This algorithm is secure as long as the attacker does not know its inner workings." The other proclaims, "You can tell attackers what the algorithm is and how long the key is, but they can never retrieve your sensitive data without the key."

Which one would you buy?

If it is possible to build a cryptographic system in which the algorithm is completely known, and if attackers still can't break it without the key, isn't that system more secure than one that can be broken if the algorithm is uncovered? Well, it is possible to build such cryptographic systems.

continues

When algorithms are made public, cryptanalysts and computer engineers get a chance to examine them for weaknesses. If an algorithm is vulnerable, you can choose not to use it. Otherwise, you can be confident that your data is safe. If an algorithm is kept secret, on the other hand, analysts will not be able to find any weaknesses it may have. Does that mean it has no weaknesses? Not necessarily; it simply means that you don't know whether or not it is vulnerable. Maybe a cracker, lurking somewhere in a basement, has obtained a copy of the algorithm (remember, they always do) and has already found a successful attack. But this cracker has decided not to share the information. If you use the secret algorithm, all your data is compromised but you don't know it.

When an algorithm is made public, however, that's no guarantee that it is secure. Maybe analysts have not yet found the weakness, and the basement-dwelling cracker has found it. But great minds thrive on finding flaws in public cryptographic systems. There's prestige (and sometimes a little money) in finding chinks in the armor. If the cryptographic community cannot find something wrong with an algorithm, there's a good chance that no one else will.

Sources: See David Kahn's *The CodeBreakers* for the histories of the Enigma, Purple, and Navajo codetalkers. See Cecil Adams' *Return of the Straight Dope* for the Gem-Star story.

To answer that question, let's consider what the word "random" means. You probably have an intuitive idea of randomness, and most likely it's correct. To be more formal than intuition, we could put it this way: "If someone knows what the *current* numbers are, is it possible to predict the *next* numbers?" To put it the way cryptographers prefer, random values are simply sets of numbers that pass statistical tests of randomness and are unrepeatable.

Suppose that you choose a few thousand numbers and ask a mathematician, "Are these numbers random?" To simplify things and to conform to computer conventions, you make the numbers *binary*, meaning that they are sequences of 1's and 0's. The mathlete will draw on a set of tests

Figure 2-5

Testing numbers
for randomness.
Here, the pattern
110 appears too
often, so it fails

that examine the numbers. Among these tests (see Figure 2-5) are questions such as these: Are there roughly the same count of 1's and 0's? Do some patterns of 1's and 0's appear "too often"? Do some patterns of 1's and 0's appear "not often enough"? If the numbers pass the tests, we say that the numbers are probably random. "Probably" random? Can't we say "definitely" random? No, we can't, and in a few paragraphs you'll see why.

A Random Number Generator

If you have a few thousand numbers, you can test them for randomness. But where do you get those few thousand numbers in the first place? One source is a *random number generator* (RNG). These devices work by gathering numbers from various kinds of unpredictable inputs, such as by measuring radioactive decay, examining atmospheric conditions in the vicinity, or calculating minute variances in electrical current. These numbers pass the tests of randomness.

If you ask the machine for a second group of numbers, you will virtually never receive the same sequence again. That's because the output is based on input that's always changing. The numbers are unrepeatable.

So to return to our original definition, we can ask, "Can anyone predict what the next numbers will be?" To do that, someone would have to predict the minor variations in the radioactive decay, atmospheric conditions, or electricity of the current. These are things we assume that no one can do.

Intel produces an RNG that uses system thermal noise as its variable and unpredictable input. Currently, this device does not ship automatically with every Pentium-based PC, although maybe in the future it will. Other companies (such as nCipher, Chrysalis, and Rainbow) sell devices known as cryptographic accelerators (discussed in Chapters 3 and 9). These devices come with RNGs.

A Pseudo-Random Number Generator

Where can you get random numbers if you don't have an RNG? It turns out there are algorithms called *pseudo-random number generators* (PRNGs). Just as there are algorithms that convert plaintext into ciphertext, there are algorithms that produce what are called "pseudo-random" numbers.

If you use one of these algorithms to generate a few thousand numbers and apply the statistical tests, the numbers pass. What makes these numbers pseudo-random and not random is that they are repeatable. If you install the same PRNG on another computer, you get the same results. If you run the program two weeks later, you get the same results.

This is one reason we say that numbers that pass statistical tests of randomness are "probably" random. Even if they pass, do we know whether they are repeatable? The math tests give us only part of the answer.

If the numbers are repeatable, what good is a PRNG? The answer is that you can change the output by using what is known as a *seed*. Just as RNGs take input (radioactive decay, atmospheric conditions, electrical variances), a PRNG takes input (the seed). If you change the input, you change the output. With RNGs, the input is constantly changing on its own, unpredictably. With a PRNG, it's up to you to make sure the input changes each time you want to generate new numbers.

What is this seed? In the real world, a seed can be lots of things: the time of day down to the millisecond, various constantly changing computer state measurements, user input, and other values. Maybe you've seen a user-input seed collector. An application may ask you to move the mouse around. At selected intervals, the program looks at where, on the screen, the arrow is located. This value is a pair of numbers: how many pixels up from the bottom of the screen and how many pixels over from the left. Any one input is not sufficient, but if you put them all together you have unpredictability (see Figure 2-6).

You may be thinking, "Why use a PRNG to generate the numbers? Why not just use the seed?" There are two main reasons. The first reason is the need for speed. Seed collection is often time-consuming. Suppose you need

Figure 2-6

A random number generator (left) collects unpredictable information and converts it into random numbers. A pseudo-random number generator (right) collects seed information and converts it into numbers that pass statistical tests of randomness but can be repeated

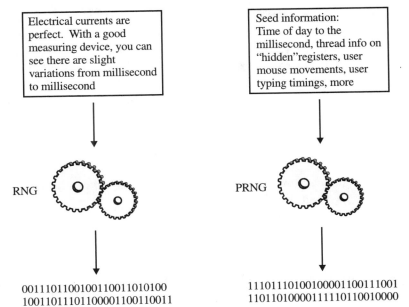

Electrical currents are perfect. With a good measuring device, you can see there are slight variations from millisecond to millisecond

Seed information: Time of day to the millisecond, thread info on "hidden" registers, user mouse movements, user typing timings, more

RNG

PRNG

0011101100100110011010100
1001101110110000110011001

1110111010010000110011001
1101101000011110110010000

only a few thousand bits of random data. A seed collector may take several minutes to gather the necessary numbers. When was the last time you waited several minutes for a program to do something without getting frustrated? To save time, you can gather 160 or so bits of seed (which may take little time), feed it to the PRNG, and get the required thousands of bits in a few milliseconds.

The second reason to use a PRNG is *entropy*, a term that describes chaos. The greater the entropy, the greater the chaos. To put it another way, the more entropy, the more random the output. Suppose you want 128 bits of entropy. A seed may have that, but it is spread over 2,400 bits. For example, the time of day down to the millisecond is represented in 64 bits. But the year, the month, the date, and maybe even the hour and minute might be easy to guess. The millisecond—two or three bits of the time of day—is where the entropy is. This means that out of 64 bits of seed, you have 2 bits of entropy. Similarly, your other seed data may suffer the same condition. A PRNG will take that 2,400 bits of seed and compress it to 128 bits.

Well, then, why not take the seed and throw away the low-entropy bits? In a sense, that's what a PRNG does. You can do it, or you can have a PRNG do it, and the latter means less work for you.

By the way, most PRNGs use *message digests* to do the bulk of the work. We talk about the details of digests in Chapter 5, but for now, let's just say that they are the "blenders" of cryptography. Just as a blender takes recognizable food and purees it into a random, unrecognizable blob, a message digest takes recognizable bits and bytes and mixes them up into a random, unrecognizable blob. That sounds like what we look for in a PRNG.

A good PRNG always produces pseudo-random numbers, regardless of the seed. Do you have a "good" seed (one with lots of entropy)? The PRNG will produce numbers that pass tests of randomness. Do you have a "bad" seed (or no seed at all)? The PRNG will still produce good numbers that pass the tests.

Then why do you need a good seed? The answer is given in the next section.

Attacks on Encrypted Data

Someone wants to read the data you've encrypted. This person, known as the *attacker*, must first decrypt the data. To do that, the attacker must either identify the key or break the algorithm.

Attacking the Key

If attackers can figure out what your key is, they can decrypt your data. One approach, the *brute-force attack,* is to try every possible key until the right one is identified. It works this way. Let's say your key is a number between 0 and 100,000,000,000 (one hundred billion). The attacker takes your ciphertext (perhaps only 8 or 16 bytes' worth) and feeds it to the decryption algorithm along with the "alleged key" of 0. The algorithm does its job and produces a result. If the resulting data appears reasonable, 0 is probably the correct key. If it's gibberish, 0 is not the true key. In that case, you try 1, and then 2, 3, 4, and so on (see Figure 2-7).

Remember, an algorithm simply performs its steps, regardless of the input. It has no way of knowing whether the result it produces is the correct one. Even if the value is close to the key, maybe off by only 1, the result is gibberish. So it's necessary to look at the result to tell whether it might be the key. Smart attackers write programs to examine the result. Is it a series of letters of the alphabet? Yes? Pass this key to the attacker. No? Try the next key.

Figure 2-7

The brute force attack. If you know that the key is a number between 1 and 100,000,000,000, you try each number in turn until a number produces something that's not gibberish

It usually takes very little time to try a key. The attacker can probably write a program that tries many keys per second. Eventually, the attacker could try every possible number between 0 and 100 billion, but that may not be necessary. Once the correct key is found, there's no need to search any more. On average, the attacker will try half of all possible keys—in our example, 50 billion keys—before finding the correct one. Sometimes it takes more time, sometimes less, but, on average, about half the possible keys must be tried.

How long would it take an attacker to try 50 billion keys? Three years? Three days? Three minutes? Suppose you want to keep your secret safe for at least three years, but it takes an attacker only three minutes to try 50 billion values. Then what do you do? You choose a bigger range. Instead of finding a number between 0 and 100 billion, you find a number between 0 and 100 billion billion billion billion. Now the attacker will have to try, on average, many more keys before finding the right one.

This concept of the range of possible keys is known as *key size*. Gold is measured in troy ounces, atoms are measured in moles, and cryptographic keys are measured in bits. If someone asks, "How big is that key?" the answer might be 40 bits, 56 bits, 128 bits, and so on. A 40-bit key means that the range of possible values is from 0 to about 1 trillion. A 56-bit key is 0 to about 72 quadrillion. The range of a 128-bit key is so large that it's easier just to say it's a 128-bit key (see Figure 2-8).

Figure 2-8

The larger the key size, the greater the range of possible values a key can be. Each bit in each position, whether 0 or 1, is important

40-bit keys (in hex)
```
00 00 00 00 00
00 00 00 00 01
00 00 00 00 02
     ...
6F 55 81 D2 0C
     ...
FF FF FF FF FF
```

64-bit keys (in hex)
```
00 00 00 00 00 00 00 00
00 00 00 00 00 00 00 01
00 00 00 00 00 00 00 02
          ...
59 C6 71 DD 54 E4 40 92
          ...
FF FF FF FF FF FF FF FF
```

128-bit keys (in hex)
```
00 00 00 00 00 00 00 00 00 00 00 00 00 00 00 00
00 00 00 00 00 00 00 00 00 00 00 00 00 00 00 01
00 00 00 00 00 00 00 00 00 00 00 00 00 00 00 02
                      ...
20 14 86 AE 18 84 5A CF E9 80 98 B2 44 3C 11 D2
                      ...
FF FF FF FF FF FF FF FF FF FF FF FF FF FF FF FF
```

Each bit of key size you add doubles the time required for a brute-force attack. If a 40-bit key takes 3 hours to break, a 41-bit key would take 6 hours, a 42-bit key, 12 hours, and so on. Why? Each additional bit doubles the number of possible keys. For example, there are eight possible numbers of size 3 bits:

```
000   001   010   011   100   101   110   111
```

These are the numbers from zero to seven. Now add one more bit:

```
0000  0001  0010  0011  0100  0101  0110  0111  1000  1001  1010  1011  1100  1101  1110  1111
```

Every number possible with 3 bits is possible with 4 bits, but each of those numbers is possible "twice": once with the first bit not set, and again with it set. So if you add a bit, you double the number of possible keys. If you double the number of possible keys, you double the average time it takes for brute-force attack to find the right key.

In short, if you want to make the attacker's job tougher, you choose a bigger key. Longer keys mean greater security. How big should a key be? Over the years, RSA Laboratories has offered challenges. The first person or organization to crack a particular message wins a money prize. Some of the challenges have been tests of brute-force time. In 1997, a 40-bit key fell in 3 hours, and a 48-bit key lasted 280 hours. In 1999, the Electronic Frontier Foundation found a 56-bit key in 24 hours. In each case, a little more than 50 percent of the key space was searched before the key was found. In January 1997, a 64-bit challenge was issued. As of December 2000, it has still not been solved.

In all these situations, hundreds or even thousands of computers were operating cooperatively to break the keys. In fact, with the 56-bit DES challenge that the Electronic Frontier Foundation broke in 24 hours, one of those computers was a custom-built DES cracker. This kind of computer does only one thing: check DES keys. An attacker working secretly would probably not be able to harness the power of hundreds of computers and might not possess a machine built specifically to crack a particular algorithm. That's why, for most attackers, the time it takes to break the key would almost certainly be dramatically higher. On the other hand, if the attacker were a government intelligence agency with enormous resources, the situation would be different.

We can devise worst-case scenarios. Let's use as our baseline an exaggerated worst-case scenario: examining 1 percent of the key space of a 56-bit key takes 1 second, and examining 50 percent takes 1 minute (see Table 2-1). Each time that we add a bit to the key size, we double the search time.

Currently, 128 bits is the most commonly used symmetric-key size. If technology advances and brute-force attackers can improve on these numbers (maybe they can reduce the 128-bit times to a few years), then we would need to use a 256-bit key.

You may be thinking, "Technology is always advancing, so I'll have to keep increasing key sizes again and again. Won't there come a time when I'll need a key so big it becomes too unwieldy to handle?" The answer is

Table 2-1

A Worse Than Worst-Case Scenario: How Long a Brute-Force Attack Will Take for Various Key Sizes

Bits	1 percent of Key Space	50 percent of Key Space
56	1 second	1 minute
57	2 seconds	2 minutes
58	4 seconds	4 minutes
64	4.2 minutes	4.2 hours
72	17.9 hours	44.8 days
80	190.9 days	31.4 years
90	535 years	321 centuries
108	140,000 millennia	8 million millennia
128	146 billion millennia	8 trillion millennia

that you'll almost certainly never need a key longer than 512 bits (64 bytes). Suppose that every atom in the known universe (there are about 2^{300} of them) were a computer and that each of these computers could check 2^{300} keys per second. It would take about 2^{162} millennia to search 1 percent of the key space of a 512-bit key. According to the Big Bang theory, the amount of time that has passed since the universe came into existence is less than 2^{24} millennia. In other words, it is highly unlikely that technology will ever advance far enough to force you to use a key that's "too big."

That may not matter, though, because there's another attack on the key. Instead of trying to reproduce the key, attackers can try to reproduce the PRNG and seed that were used to produce the key. It works like this. Attackers know the particular PRNG and seed-collection method you used. (Remember, as discussed earlier in this chapter in "Historical Note: They Always Figure Out the Algorithm," the attacker will always know your algorithms and methods.) If attackers can guess your seed, they can seed the PRNG and produce the same key. If you used a small seed, attackers will try every possible value until they find the correct one. This happened to Netscape, as described in "Historical Note: Netscape's Seed."

Your defense against this kind of attack is to use a good seed. A PRNG will always produce good pseudo-random numbers regardless of seed. But the seed must also be strong enough to withstand a brute-force attack.

Historical Note: Netscape's Seed

Symmetric-key cryptography is one component of SSL (see Chapter 7), which was invented by researchers at Netscape. Not surprisingly, Netscape offered an implementation of SSL that is part of all Netscape browsers (after version 1.0).

At some point in an SSL session, the code must generate a key. To do so, Netscape's implementation uses a PRNG. In version 1.1 (released in 1995), the code collected the time of day, the process ID, and the parent process ID as the seed for the PRNG.

Ian Goldberg and David Wagner (remember them from the earlier historical note?) decided to test how good a seed these three sources would produce. They discovered that the process IDs were easy to capture if one had access to the computer. If one did not have access to the computer, all it took was a little brute-force testing because each ID was only 15 bits. The time of day? Well, the year, the month, the date, and even the hour and minute were known; an attacker simply had to look at when the SSL session occurred. The second? There were only 60 possible values (Netscape used time of day only down to the second and not the millisecond).

On September 17, 1995, Goldberg and Wagner reported to the Cypherpunks newsgroup that they could find the seed, and hence the key, in less than a minute. Whether the key was 40 bits or 128 bits, it took only one minute.

Netscape fixed the problem in version 2.0 by adding more seed. Each platform (Windows, Mac, and UNIX) has different seed sources, but among the many platform-dependent seeds Netscape now uses are cursor or mouse position, memory status, last key pressed, audio volume, and many others.

Sources: Gary McGraw and John Viega, "Make Your Software Behave: Playing The Numbers," *Reliable Software Technologies,* April 4, 2000.
Keith Dawson, "Tasty Bits from the Technology Front," http://www.tbtf.com, Sept. 20, 1995.
Taher El Gamal, letter to the Internet community posted on many Web sites, Sept. 25, 1995. El Gamal was, at the time, director of security for Netscape.

Breaking the Algorithm

Suppose that someone figured out that with a given algorithm, every 14th bit of a given ciphertext is the same as every 12th bit of its plaintext. In other words, if the 14th bit of ciphertext is 1, the 12th bit of plaintext is 1, the 28th bit of ciphertext is 0, the 24th of plaintext is 0, and so on, no matter what the key. Furthermore, the attacker sees that if certain combinations of bits appear in certain locations in the ciphertext, a corresponding portion of the plaintext must be another pattern.

If an algorithm had such weaknesses, an attacker could look at the ciphertext and decipher parts of the plaintext even without knowing the key. This knowledge might be enough to enable the attacker to recover enough of the original message to do damage (see Figure 2-9).

Figure 2-9

If an algorithm has a weakness, an attacker might figure out portions of plaintext without the key, reconstructing most or all of the message

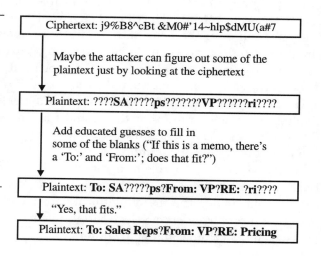

Ciphertext: j9%B8^cBt &M0#'14~hlp$dMU(a#7

Maybe the attacker can figure out some of the plaintext just by looking at the ciphertext

Plaintext: ????**SA**?????**ps**???????**VP**??????**ri**????

Add educated guesses to fill in some of the blanks ("If this is a memo, there's a 'To:' and 'From:'; does that fit?")

Plaintext: **To: SA**?????**ps**?**From: VP**?**RE:** ?**ri**????

"Yes, that fits."

Plaintext: **To: Sales Reps**?**From: VP**?**RE: Pricing**

Here's another possible weakness. Suppose the attacker knows what some of the plaintext and its corresponding ciphertext is. And suppose this attacker is able to therefore deduce the key. But if the attacker knows what the plaintext is, why bother figuring out the key? The answer is that the attacker might know, or be able to guess, only a portion of the plaintext. Recall the memo at the beginning of the chapter. An attacker might see the ciphertext, realize it's a Word for Windows document, and guess some of the control characters at the beginning.

Furthermore, the attacker guesses the document is a memo from the conventional "TO:", "FROM:", and, "RE:" In short, if someone can compute the key from a chunk of ciphertext and its corresponding plaintext, the rest of the message will follow. This is known as a *known-plaintext* attack. Obviously, you don't want to use an algorithm that might be susceptible to such an attack.

Measuring the Time It Takes to Break Your Message

How long will your secret remain secret? The answer is, as long as it takes the attacker to break it. The attacker has two kinds of tools: the brute-force attack and attacks that exploit weaknesses in your algorithm.

In analyzing the security of your message, a key question is how long would a successful brute-force attack take. There's no rigid, specified time, since the attacker may get lucky and find it early or may get unlucky and find it later, but as shown in Table 2-1, you can estimate the variables based on worst-case scenarios. In general, the bigger the key, the longer a brute-force attack will take. But if the algorithm is weak, it doesn't matter how long the key is. The statement "Longer keys mean more security" doesn't apply to a weak algorithm. The point is this: If you pick a weak algorithm, you have no control over how strongly your secret is protected.

So the best strategy is to pick an algorithm that is not weak and further deter an attacker by using a longer key.

That statement may seem so obvious that it's not worthwhile even to mention it. If you're curious about what happens when people overlook these obvious protections, however, read "Crypto Blunders" in the accompanying CD for a couple of stories on using weak algorithms and small keys.

Symmetric Algorithms: The Key Table

Virtually all symmetric ciphers use the key to build a *key table*, which is usually a pseudo-random array of a particular size in a particular format. This process is known as *key setup*, or initialization. It's the key table that does the encryption.

Why have a key table? One reason is that you might want to use keys of varying lengths depending on the application. The algorithm needs a *key value* that is the same size from one use to the next, but your key might vary from 64 bits to 128 to 192 or even 256 bits. For that reason, you build a key table (which is bigger than the biggest possible key size) from the key. It's easier to create a constant-sized key table at the beginning of your encryption session than to do it repeatedly while encrypting data.

Another reason to use a key table is to prevent attacks on the algorithm. Recall that there are two ways to break security: a brute-force attack and attacks on an algorithm's weaknesses. If you use a big, pseudo-random key table, it's easier to do serious scrambling. With good scrambling, the ciphertext looks nothing like the plaintext. If the algorithm cannot do a good job of creating gibberish unless it has a good key, that is be an algorithmic weakness. A good algorithm will simply expand the key into a bigger value and make sure that no matter what key it's given, the key table is random. An attacker could try a brute-force attack on the key table, but that would be more time-consuming than an attack on the key.

The user should give the algorithm a good key. But even with a bad key, it is possible to create a good key table. Just as a PRNG produces good numbers no matter what the seed is, a good encryption algorithm produces a good key table no matter what the key is. With a good key table, the algorithm produces a good scramble, the resulting ciphertext is not at all close to the plaintext, and the attacker cannot exploit an algorithm's weakness.

Symmetric Algorithms: Block Versus Stream Ciphers

If you're using symmetric-key cryptography, how do you choose a good algorithm? There are two types of symmetric-key algorithms: block and stream ciphers. What are they, and which is better?

Block Ciphers

A *block cipher* operates on blocks of data. When you give the algorithm a chunk of data to encrypt or decrypt, it breaks the plaintext into blocks and operates on each block independently (see Figure 2-10). Usually, blocks are 8 or 16 bytes long.

Figure 2-10

A block cipher grabs each block of the input data (usually 8 or 16 bytes) and uses the key table to produce a unique block of output, continuing until all the blocks are encrypted

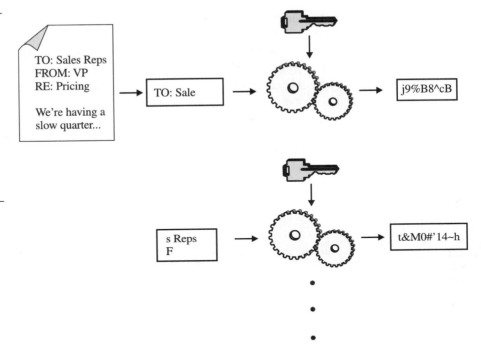

Suppose that your plaintext is 227 bytes long and the cipher you're using operates on 16-byte blocks. The algorithm grabs the first 16 bytes of data, encrypts them using the key table, and produces 16 bytes of ciphertext. Then it starts over, encrypting the next 16 bytes of plaintext. No matter which block it is working with, the cipher encrypts it by starting over from scratch. The key table does not change from block to block.

After encrypting 14 blocks (224 bytes), the algorithm is left with 3 more bytes. But your block cipher cannot operate on 3 bytes; it needs 16 bytes. To encrypt the last 3 bytes, you must *pad* the data: add extra bytes to an incomplete block to make it complete. Whoever decrypts the ciphertext must be able to recognize (and ignore) the padding.

The most popular padding scheme determines the number of bytes to be padded and repeats that value in the final bytes in the data. In our example, the padding scheme must add 13 bytes to the plaintext so that it has a full block. So it repeats the byte "13" in each of the final 13 otherwise empty spaces. During decryption, you look at the last byte of decrypted data; this byte, a number from 1 to 16, indicates how many pad bytes have been added. In this example, after decrypting, we would know that the last 13 bytes of data should be discarded (see Figure 2-11). (Each of the last 13 bytes should be the number 13, so as an extra check, we make sure that each of them is 13.) If the length of the plaintext had been a multiple of 16, there would have been no need to pad. Nevertheless, it makes sense to always pad your data. Then, when decrypting, you know that the last byte decrypted is indeed a pad byte. To do that, you tack on 16 bytes, each of them the number 16.

Figure 2-11

When the last block of plaintext ends in blank bytes, use padding to bring it up to size

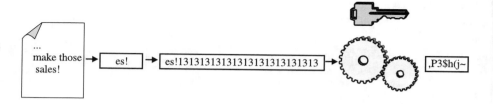

Remember the known-plaintext attack? If an algorithm is susceptible, that doesn't mean an attacker will automatically be able to break a message; it's necessary to find a plaintext/ciphertext pair first. The last block of data might be that known plaintext, because it contains padding. Of course, it's easy to simply use an algorithm that is not susceptible to the known-plaintext attack.

One problem with block ciphers is that if the same block of plaintext appears in two places, it encrypts to the same ciphertext. In our printing machinery company memo, for example, the phrase "slow third quarter" may show up a number of times. Each time the first 16 bytes of that phrase is encrypted, it will produce the same ciphertext, and an attacker might identify this repeated pattern. To avoid having these kinds of copies in the ciphertext, you can use *feedback modes*. A number of these modes are discussed in the FAQ contained in the accompanying CD.

The most common feedback mode is *cipher block chaining* (CBC), shown in Figure 2-12. In this scheme, you XOR the current block of plaintext with the preceding block of ciphertext (see "Technical Note: XOR" later in this chapter). For the first block of plaintext, there is no preceding block of ciphertext, so you XOR with an *initialization vector* (IV). When you decrypt the data, you copy a block of ciphertext, decrypt it, and XOR

Figure 2-12

Cipher block chaining. The first block of plaintext is XOR'd with the IV and then encrypted. Each successive block is XOR'd with the preceding block of ciphertext

the result with the preceding block of ciphertext (which you saved right before you decrypted it). This technique ensures that any duplicate block in the plaintext does not encrypt to the same ciphertext. That's all it does. It adds no other security. The encryption algorithm provides the security.

Stream Ciphers

To understand stream ciphers, the second type of symmetric-key algorithm, you need to first understand the cryptographic technique called a *one-time pad,* which is popular with spies. In one variation of this technique, you generate a bunch of random numbers, each from 0 to 25. Then you print two copies of the series. That's the "pad." One copy stays at your headquarters, and the spy takes the other copy out into the field.

To send a message back home, the spy encrypts each letter of the message with a number on the pad. The first letter of the message is encrypted with the first number on the pad, the second letter with the second number, and so on. Encryption is simply a matter of adding a numeric value assigned to the letter plus the number. Here's how the numeric value is assigned. If the plaintext letter is G and the number on the pad is 11, the ciphertext letter is R (R is the eleventh letter after G, or $G + 11 = R$). If the plaintext letter is Y and the number is 4, the ciphertext letter is C, or $Y + 4$ (Y, Z, A, B, C; when you reach the end of the alphabet, you start over at A).

Technical Note: XOR

The term *XOR* stands for "exclusive OR," a type of bit manipulation. The first concept to understand is an OR. An OR is a bit manipulation that says, "Look at two bits. If one OR the other is set, set the result."

```
0 OR 0 = 0 (zero OR zero equals 0)
0 OR 1 = 1 (zero OR  one equals 1)
1 OR 0 = 1 ( one OR zero equals 1)
1 OR 1 = 1 ( one OR  one equals 1)
```

An exclusive OR says, "Look at two bits. If one is exclusively set, OR if the other is exclusively set, set the result." If both bits are set, then there's no exclusivity, so the result bit is not set.

```
0 XOR 0 = 0 (zero XOR zero equals 0)
0 XOR 1 = 1 (zero XOR  one equals 1)
1 XOR 0 = 1 ( one XOR zero equals 1)
1 XOR 1 = 0 ( one XOR  one equals 0)
```

XOR is a useful bit manipulation in cryptography because half of the time the result is 1, and the other half of the time it's 0. If one bit is plaintext, and one bit is key stream, then the key stream sometimes changes the bit and sometimes doesn't change the bit.

In grade school, we learned how to add, subtract, and multiply using columns:

```
1,482        77        204
+ 319       - 5       *   8
1,801        72       1632
```

Similarly, we can perform XOR operations on longer numbers. Computers, of course, see all numbers as binary values.

```
values as binary text                                    values as hex text
    0111 0100 0110 0101 0111 1000 0111 0100              0x74 65 78 74
XOR 1001 1011 0010 1100 0110 0011 1000 0100              0x9B 2C 63 84
    1110 1111 0100 1001 0001 1011 1111 0000              0xEF 49 1B F0
```

continues

The first row (the row that begins 0111 0100) in the preceding table is the ASCII bit formation of the word "text." ASCII gives us a standard way to map characters to numbers. For example, lowercase *t* is represented as the number 0x74 (binary 0111 0100), which is decimal 116. Punctuation marks are also included; a comma, for example, is 0x2C, which is decimal 44. You see 0111 0100 and so on, but the computer sees the word "text." Suppose that word "text" is our plaintext. To encrypt it, we perform the steps the algorithm prescribes, namely XOR it with the key stream. If the second row (the row with the binary values beginning 1001 1011) is the key stream and we perform the XOR operation, what do we get? We get the bottom row (the row beginning 1110 1111)—that would be the ciphertext.

What does this ciphertext say? It says "?9??" As it happens, the first, third, and fourth characters are not standard characters (they are numbers outside the ASCII range). The second is the character 9. So the algorithm converted the "e" in "text" to a "9", but what about the other characters? Because the numbers are not standard character numbers, each computer or software package gets to decide what they mean. One computer or software package might print the ciphertext as "µ9←≡". Another computer or software package might print it as "☐9☐☐". Whichever you use, it looks like gibberish; it's nothing like the plaintext.

If you start with the ciphertext and XOR it with the key stream, what do you get? You get the plaintext.

```
values as binary text                                  values as hex text
     1110 1111 0100 1001 0001 1011 1111 0000            0xEF 49 1B F0
XOR  1001 1011 0010 1100 0110 0011 1000 0100            0x9B 2C 63 84
     0111 0100 0110 0101 0111 1000 0111 0100            0x74 65 78 74
```

That's another reason that the XOR operation is popular in cryptography: It's symmetric.

When the home office gets the encrypted message, the translator simply reverses the algorithm. If the ciphertext is R and the associated number in the pad is 11, compute $R-11 = G$. As long as the spy and the home office use the same pad, the communication will be successful. Figure 2-13 shows an example of the one-time pad. Where does the pad come from? Probably an RNG.

Figure 2-13

A one-time pad

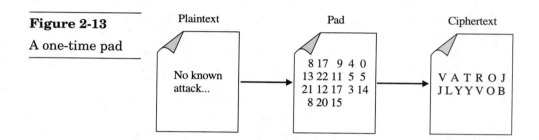

A *stream cipher* is similar to a one-time pad. To encrypt data, the algorithm generates a pad based on the key. The pad can be as big as it needs to be. The algorithm will XOR the plaintext with the pad (see Figure 2-14 and the technical note on the XOR function). With the one-time pad, the spy and the home office generate a pad (actually, probably many pads) in advance. The stream cipher generates its pad on-the-fly, only when needed. In cryptography circles, the "pad" is called a *key stream*. A true pad would be random; a stream cipher produces pseudo-random values and technically can't be called a pad.

Figure 2-14

A stream cipher

Most stream ciphers work this way. First, you use the key to build a key table. Then to encrypt the data, you take one byte of plaintext, go to the key table, somehow get a byte of key stream, and XOR it with the plaintext byte. Next, you throw away the key stream byte and remix the key table. Then you get the next byte of data and continue. The key table, and hence the key stream, does not depend on the input data.

In the example of the one-time pad, the spy added numbers to letters to encrypt the data and the home office subtracted them to decrypt. A stream cipher uses the XOR operation because encrypting and decrypting are the same operation. Only one program and not two exist.

Block Versus Stream: Which Is Better?

Stream ciphers are almost always faster and generally use far less code than do block ciphers. The most common stream cipher, RC4, is probably at least twice as fast as the fastest block cipher. RC4 can be written in perhaps 30 lines of code. Most block ciphers need hundreds of lines of code.

On the other hand, with a block cipher, you can reuse keys. Remember that the stream cipher is rather like a one-time pad. "One-time" implies that you should use a pad only once (see "Crypto Blunders" on the accompanying CD for a story of multiple uses of one-time pads). Similarly, you should use a stream cipher key only once. Generally, that's not a problem, but sometimes it will be necessary to encrypt many things using the same key. For example, an e-commerce company may have a database of customer information, including credit card numbers. Rather than encrypt each entry with a different key (and hence manage hundreds or even thousands of keys), the company can encrypt all of them with one key. When one entry is needed, decrypt it with the one key. Key management is much easier when there's only one key to manage.

Another factor is standardization. Everyone has two algorithms—DES and AES-both of which are block ciphers. For reasons of interoperability, you may want an algorithm that is widely used. The entity on the other end of your data link may or may not have RC4, but it's almost a guarantee that it has DES and AES. You choose a block cipher because it's a standard.

In other words, neither type is "better." If you need to reuse keys, use a block cipher. If you must guarantee interoperability, it's best to use AES. Otherwise, use a stream cipher. Table 2-2 lists some applications and the type of cipher you might want to use with each one.

	Application	Cipher to Use	Comments
Table 2-2 Choosing an Algorithm by Application	Database	Block	Interoperability with other software is not an issue, but you will need to reuse keys.
	E-mail	AES	Although each e-mail message has its own key and you could use a stream cipher, you gain interoperability with all e-mail packages by using the standard AES.
	SSL (secure connections on the Web)	RC4 (stream cipher)	Speed is extremely important, each connection can have a new key, and virtually all Web browsers and servers possess RC4.
	File encryption (storing your files securely)	Block	Interoperability is not an issue, but you can encrypt each file with the same key and then protect that key (see Chapter 3).

Digital Encryption Standard

A computer can be programmed to perform any encryption algorithm. By the 1970s, though, it was known that the old algorithms were not very strong. They had weaknesses and were difficult to implement.

The advent of computers made it possible to throw out the old rules of cryptography and create a new paradigm. Researchers at IBM decided to develop a new algorithm for the computer age, and built on a scheme called Lucifer, an algorithm invented by cryptographer Horst Feistel. They also enlisted the help of the *National Security Agency* (NSA), the agency charged with protecting the U.S. government's secret data, a duty that includes cryptography. The fruit of the group's labor was DES.

DES is a block cipher that uses a 56-bit key—no more, no less—to build a key table. Using the key table, DES performs bit manipulations on plaintext. To decrypt ciphertext, it simply does everything in reverse.

After its introduction, DES became freely available and widely studied. Throughout the 1980s, the consensus among cryptographers was that it had no weaknesses. This meant that the fastest way to break a message encrypted with DES was to use the brute-force attack. Because a 56-bit key is a number between 0 and about 72 quadrillion, even the fastest computers took years to break a single message.

By the 1990s, though, cryptographers knew that DES couldn't last. Computers were becoming faster and eventually would be fast enough to mount a brute-force attack on a 56-bit key in a reasonable amount of time. In addition, researchers discovered potential weaknesses that led them to conclude that someday it might be possible to break the algorithm. The brute-force attack was still the fastest attack, but those potential weaknesses were troubling.

In 1999, at the RSA Conference, the Electronic Frontier Foundation broke a DES key in less than 24 hours. The world needed a replacement.

Triple DES

One widely used replacement for DES is Triple DES. The name says it all: Triple DES performs the DES algorithm three times. That's it. You run your block of data through DES using a key, and then you encrypt that result with another DES key. Then you do it a third time (see Figure 2-15).

You use three keys, each 56 bits. That's essentially the same as using one 168-bit key. You may be thinking, "If it takes 24 hours to break one key, then shouldn't it take 72 hours to break three keys?" Here's the answer. It takes 24 hours to break one key if you know you've broken it. But with Triple DES, you don't know you've stumbled onto the first key until you combine it with the other two correct keys.

Think of it this way. Suppose that the three keys are called A, B, and C, and each possible key value is numbered from 0 to 72 quadrillion. Suppose also that the correct key combination is A = 1, B = 33,717, and C = 1,419,222. An attacker could try value 0 with key A, value 0 with key B, and value 0 with key C. That doesn't produce the correct answer, so try A = 1, B = 0, C = 0. As shown in Figure 2-16, the first key is correct. But the value the attacker got from trying the three-key combination is not the right value. The correct plaintext appears only when all three keys are correct. So how can the attacker know that the first key is correct?

Figure 2-15

Triple DES is
simply DES run
on the data three
times

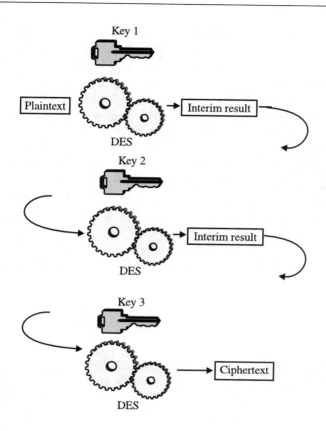

Figure 2-15

Triple DES is
simply DES run
on the data three
times

Triple DES, however, presents two problems. First, cryptanalysts have figured out a way to streamline the brute-force attack. You'd think it would require a "168-bit" brute-force attack, but there are clever ways to reduce it to the equivalent of a 108-bit brute-force attack. A key that is equivalent to 108 bits is still secure (see Table 2-1 for worst-case estimates of a 108-bit brute-force attack), but this "weakness" is troubling. Will more research expose more cryptanalytic weaknesses? Will the security of Triple DES be compromised even further?

The second problem is speed. DES takes a long time to encrypt or decrypt data, and Triple DES is three times as slow. Some applications need high-speed throughput of many megabytes worth of information. Triple DES reduces the performance so much that some applications cannot function.

For these two reasons, people needed a new algorithm.

Figure 2-16

To break Triple DES, you must know all three keys

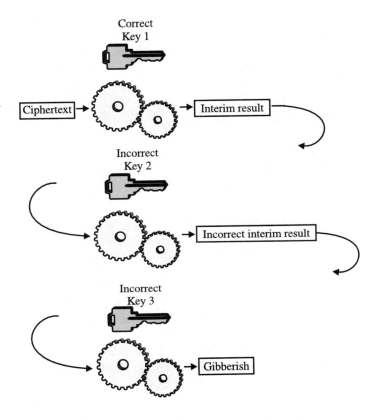

Commercial DES Replacements

In response to the key size and performance problems of Triple DES, many cryptographers and commercial companies developed new block ciphers. The most popular offerings were RC2 and RC5 from RSA Data Security, IDEA from Ascom, Cast from Entrust, Safer from Cylink, and Blowfish from Counterpane Systems.

All these algorithms were faster than Triple DES, and they were able to operate with variable-sized and bigger keys. Whereas DES and Triple DES keys require fixed-length keys, the new algorithms could be made stronger. Recall that you can choose a key size that is big enough to make your cryptographic system immune to the brute-force attack or at least to make the brute-force attack unfeasible. At one time, a 56-bit key was big enough. But when that was no longer secure enough, 64 bits was a popular key size. Even though DES cannot increase its key size, the commercial replacements can.

The various commercial DES replacements caught on to some degree, and companies built products using the algorithms. But none became a worldwide standard comparable to DES and Triple DES.

In response, the U.S. government, through the *National Institute of Standards and Technology* (NIST), set about creating a new standard. The idea was to name a particular algorithm as the U.S. government standard. Once the U.S. government adopted a standard, the thinking went, the rest of the world would almost certainly follow.

Advanced Encryption Standard

The NIST plan was formally announced on January 2, 1997, when the agency invited anyone to submit an algorithm as the new standard, to be known as AES. As a condition for entry into the AES process, developers promised to give up any intellectual property rights to the selected algorithm. Many individuals and companies responded, and on August 20, 1998, NIST named 15 candidates.

The next step was for the world to analyze the algorithms. The criteria were security (no algorithmic weaknesses), performance (it had to be fast on many platforms), and size (it couldn't take up much space or use much memory). Many of the original 15 algorithms did not last long. Weaknesses were discovered, and some were shown to be simply too big or too slow.

In August 1999, NIST trimmed the list to five candidates. For the next year, researchers, cryptanalysts, and vendors of computer hardware and software tested the algorithms to decide which they liked best. Many papers were published, and volumes of statistics were released comparing the finalists. Each had its strengths and weaknesses.

Finally, on October 2, 2000, NIST announced the winner: an algorithm called Rijndael (commonly pronounced "Rhine-doll") invented by two Belgian researchers: Vincent Rijmen and Joan Daemen.

From now on, the AES algorithm is free for anyone to develop, use, or sell. As with DES, it is expected that AES will become a worldwide standard. You can expect that within a short time, if someone has cryptography, he or she has AES.

Summary

If you want to encrypt something, follow these steps.

1. Select a symmetric algorithm and a PRNG. You should choose an encryption scheme that is not susceptible to attacks on the algorithm. It should also allow key sizes big enough to thwart a brute-force attack. If you need to reuse your cryptographic keys, choose a block cipher. If you need to guarantee interoperability with other cryptographic programs or products, choose AES. Otherwise, you might want to choose a stream cipher for performance reasons.

2. Collect your seed value and feed it to the PRNG. Make sure that your seed contains enough entropy to thwart a brute-force attack. It's best to combine several seeds, including user input.

3. Using the PRNG, generate a key. Choose a key size that requires a brute-force attack that is so time-consuming that it is unfeasible. Currently, the most popular key size is 128 bits.

4. Apply the symmetric algorithm, which will work with the key to encrypt your plaintext.

5. Save and protect your key. The next chapter talks about how to protect keys.

To recover the data you encrypted, follow these steps.

1. Retrieve your key.

2. Apply the symmetric algorithm, which will work with the key to decrypt your plaintext.

Real-World Example: Oracle Databases

How do people and companies use symmetric-key cryptography today? Here is one example.

Most companies store volumes of sensitive information in databases. A database is a software package that stores data in a systematic way and enables users to easily and quickly find what they're looking for. For example, a company may have personnel files containing names, addresses, salaries, and Social Security numbers of all employees.

A hospital may keep medical records of hundreds of patients. An e-commerce company might store credit card numbers and customers' purchasing histories.

The owners of the databases may want to make sure that only the appropriate people have access to the information. One way to protect the data is to encrypt it. If attackers break into the database, they still can't read the sensitive material.

Oracle sells a database product, Oracle 8*i*, release 8.1.6, that comes with an encryption package. If you are a developer using the database, and you want to encrypt the elements before storing them, you generate some random or pseudo-random bytes to be used as the key and then call on the package to perform the encryption. The calls to the encryption function are PL/SQL, which are standard database language conventions. For instance, to encrypt the data, you would add a line of code that looks something like this.

```
dbms_obfuscation_toolkit.DESEncrypt(input_string => plaintext,
            key => keyData, encrypted_string => ciphertext);
```

And that's it. Well, you also need to save the key somewhere (not in the same location). The next chapter talks about how to do that. If your application was using SQL, it would now have the opportunity to store the data in the clear (plaintext) or encrypted (ciphertext). This line shows that you are using DES, but Triple DES is also available. When your program needs to retrieve data, you recall it from the database, recover your key, and make something like the following call:

```
dbms_obfuscation_toolkit.DESDecrypt(input_string => ciphertext,
            key => keyData, decrypted_string => plaintext);
```

Thanks to Mary Ann Davidson and Kristy Browder of Oracle for providing this example.

CHAPTER 3

Symmetric-Key Management

Symmetric-key encryption can keep your secrets safe, but because you need your keys to recover encrypted data, you must also keep them safe. The process of keeping all your keys safe and available for use is known as key management. This chapter is about managing symmetric keys.

In Chapter 2, "Symmetric-Key Cryptography," Pao-Chi generated a random or pseudo-random key, and used it to encrypt data. If he wants to decrypt the data, he must use the same key. This means he has to either memorize the key or store it somewhere. Memorizing it isn't practical, so he must store it so that *he* can recall it when he wants to, but no one else can. Right now you're probably asking, "If there's some place Pao-Chi can keep his key safe, why doesn't he just put his sensitive information there as well?" The answer is that it's easier to protect a small key than many megabytes worth of information. In fact, some of the key storage solutions you'll see in this chapter are small devices designed in part to protect keys. So the idea is to use symmetric-key crypto to protect the megabytes of information and some other technique to protect the 16 bytes (or so) of keys.

Password-Based Encryption

The key used to encrypt the megabytes of information, or bulk data, is generally known as the *session key*. A session is simply an instance of encryption, possibly during an email exchange, a World Wide Web connection, or a database storage. In Pao-Chi's case, a session involves encrypting a file before storing it on his hard drive. Some systems generate a new key for each session; others use the same key from session to session. One way to store the session key securely is to encrypt it using a symmetric-key algorithm. Someone who finds the session key has really found the encrypted key. The attacker would have to break the encryption to get the key that protects the megabytes of information. Of course, the process of encrypting the session key itself needs a key. That is, the key needs a key. There's the session key and then the *key encryption key*, as shown in Figure 3-1. In the crypto literature, not surprisingly, the latter is often known as the KEK.

You may be thinking that if Pao-Chi uses a KEK, he now has to store and protect it as well. Actually, he does not store the KEK, and therefore does not need to protect it. When he needs a KEK to encrypt, Pao-Chi will generate it, use it, and then throw it away. When he needs to decrypt the data, he generates the KEK again, uses it, and throws it away. He is able to generate the KEK a second time and produce the same value as before because it is based on a password. Pao-Chi uses an RNG or PRNG to gen-

Figure 3-1

A session key protects data, and a *key encryption key* (KEK) protects the session key

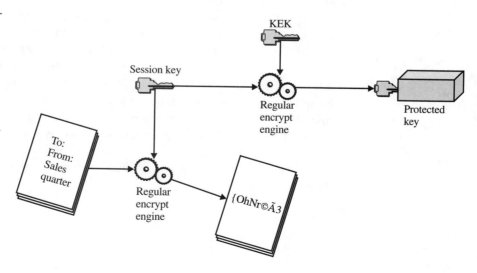

erate a session key, he uses *password-based encryption* (PBE) to build the KEK. It usually works like this (see Figure 3-2).

1. Enter the password.
2. Use an RNG or PRNG to generate a *salt*.

NOTE:

What's a salt? We describe the salt and its purpose in a few paragraphs.

---

3. Using a mixing algorithm, blend the salt and password together. In most cases, the mixing algorithm is a message digest. And that's the second time we've mentioned this tool—the message digest. The first time was in discussing PRNGs. Remember, a digest is a blender, taking recognizable data and mixing it up into an unrecognizable blob. We'll talk more about message digests in Chapter 5.
4. The result of step 3 is a bunch of bits that look random. Take as many of those bits as needed for the KEK and use it with a symmetric-key algorithm to encrypt the session key. When the session key has been encrypted, throw away the KEK and the password. Save the salt.
5. When storing the now encrypted session key, be sure to store the salt along with it. It is necessary to decrypt.

When it comes time to decrypt the data, here's the process.

1. Enter the password.
2. Collect the salt. The same salt used to encrypt is required (that's why you saved it with the encrypted session key).
3. Using the same mixing algorithm used to encrypt, blend the salt and password together. If one or more of the salt, password, or mixing algorithm is different, the result will be a KEK; however, it will be the wrong KEK. If all three elements are the same, the result is the correct KEK.
4. Use this KEK from step 3 along with the appropriate symmetric-key algorithm to decrypt the session key.

You probably have four questions.

Figure 3-2

In *password-based encryption* (PBE), (1) blend the password and the salt to form a KEK and then (2) use it to encrypt the session key. To decrypt the data, use the same password and salt

Mixing Algorithms and KEK

Why use a mixing algorithm? Why not just use the password as the KEK?

A password does not have much entropy. Recall from Chapter 2 that entropy is the measure of randomness. But a password is made up entirely of keystrokes (characters associated with the keys on a keyboard), which are not sufficiently chaotic. Using a mixing algorithm on the password (and salt) ensures that the KEK looks random.

The Necessity of Salt

Why is a salt needed in the first place?

The salt is there to prevent precomputations. If the password were the only thing used to generate the KEK, an attacker could create a dictionary of common passwords and their associated keys. Then a brute force attack would not be necessary; the attacker would try only the precomputed keys (logically enough, this is called a *dictionary attack*). With a salt, the attacker must wait until seeing the salt before finding the KEK any particular password produces (see Figure 3-3).

Figure 3-3

Using a salt foils a dictionary attack

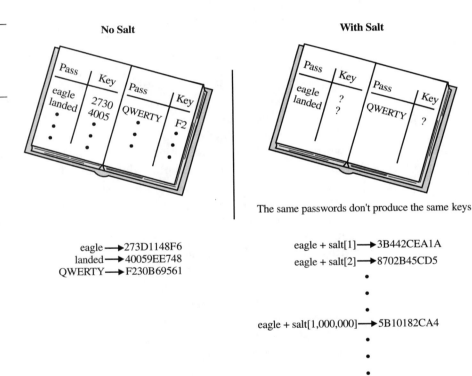

Storing Salt with Ciphertext

If the salt is stored with the ciphertext, then won't the attacker be able to see it? Wouldn't it be safer to keep the salt secret?

As just explained, a salt's only purpose is to prevent precomputations. That's worth repeating: the salt does not add security; it only prevents a dictionary attack. Even though the salt is not secret, it achieves that goal. Besides, if the salt is secret, how is it recovered when needed?

Reasons for Using Two Keys, a Session Key, and KEK

Wouldn't it be easier to simply use PBE to encrypt the bulk data? Why is it necessary to have two keys (the session key and the KEK)?

There are a couple of reasons to use a session key and a KEK. First, suppose you need to share the data with other people and you want to keep it stored encrypted. In that case, you generate one session key, and everyone gets a copy of it. Then everyone protects his or her copy of the session key using PBE. So rather than share a password (something everyone would need for decrypting if you had used PBE to encrypt the bulk data), you share the key (see Figure 3-4).

The second reason for using both keys is that it's easier to break a password than to break a key (more on this soon), and attackers might have easier access to the encrypted data than to the encrypted key. For instance, suppose Pao-Chi's data is on the network and the encrypted session key (the value encrypted by PBE using the KEK) is on his own personal computer (or other storage facility). Suppose Ray, an attacker, breaks into the network and steals the encrypted bulk data. To decrypt, Ray would have to break the session key or else perform a second break in (possibly into a more secure location) to find the encrypted session key and then break the password. Alternatively, if Pao-Chi used PBE to protect the data, Ray can recover the information by breaking the password (see Figure 3-5).

Of course, it is possible to use PBE to do the bulk encryption. In this book we don't discuss that option. From a programming point of view, it's not much more difficult to use a session key and then PBE to encrypt the session key, so you might as well because of the reasons given.

Figure 3-4

Using a session key for bulk data and protecting it with PBE means that users don't have to share passwords

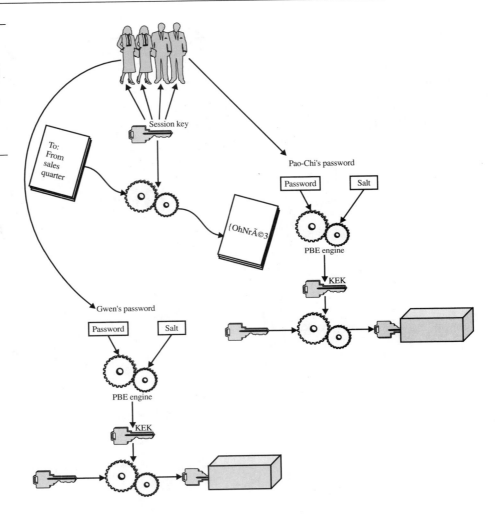

Programming Convenience

A PBE program will do its work, even with the wrong password. Suppose the wrong password were entered, the program would have no way of knowing it was an incorrect password. It would simply mix the "bad" value with the salt and produce a KEK. It wouldn't be the correct KEK, but the

Figure 3-5

If Pao-Chi uses PBE to protect bulk data, Ray can recover it by breaking the password. If Pao-Chi uses PBE to protect the session key, Ray must find the encrypted key

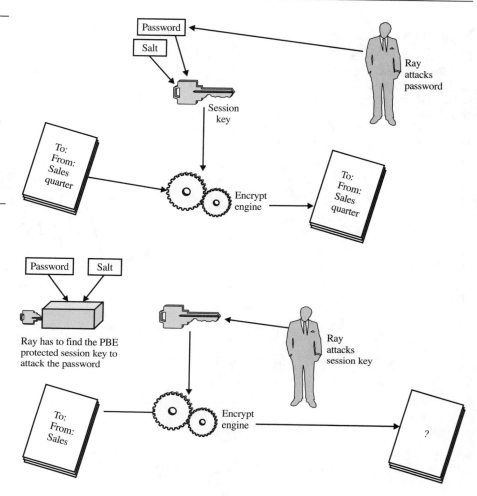

program wouldn't know that; it just blindly follows instructions. It would then use that KEK to decrypt the session key. That would work; some value would come out as a result. It would be the wrong value, but there would be something there. Then the program would use this supposed session key to decrypt the ciphertext. The resulting data would be gibberish, but only then would it be possible to see that something went wrong.

For this reason, it would have been more convenient if, when entering the password, there were some way to know immediately whether it's the correct password or not. That would be better than decrypting the entire bulk data before finding that out.

One solution is to use the KEK to encrypt the session key along with something else, the "something else" being some recognizable value, such as the salt. Then when decrypting, the program checks this recognizable value first. If it's correct, continue using the session key to decrypt the bulk data. If not, the password was wrong and the process should start over.

The overall process looks like this. To encrypt bulk data:

1. Generate a random or pseudo-random session key. Use this key to encrypt the data.

2. Enter the password, generate a salt, and mix the two together to produce the KEK.

3. Encrypt the salt and session key using the KEK. Store the encrypted data with the salt.

4. Store the encrypted session key, which is actually the session key and the salt (see Figure 3-6).

To decrypt the data, follow these steps.

1. Collect the salt and password and mix the two together to produce what is presumably the KEK.

2. Using this KEK, decrypt the session key. The result is really the session key and the salt.

3. Check the decrypted salt. Is it correct?

   a. If it is not correct, don't bother using the generated session key to decrypt the data; it's not the correct value. The user probably entered the wrong password. Go back to step 1.

   b. If it is correct, use the session key to decrypt the data.

Instead of the salt, you can use a number of things as a check. For example, it could be an eight-byte number, the first four bytes being a random value and the second four, that random value plus 1. When decrypting, check the first eight bytes; if the second four bytes is the first four plus 1, it's the correct password. This may be more palatable than the salt, since if the salt is the check, there is now some known plaintext. Presumably, the cipher is immune to a known-plaintext attack, but nonetheless,

Figure 3-6

Use a KEK to encrypt the session key along with a recognizable value such as the salt. Entering the wrong password produces the wrong KEK/salt combination

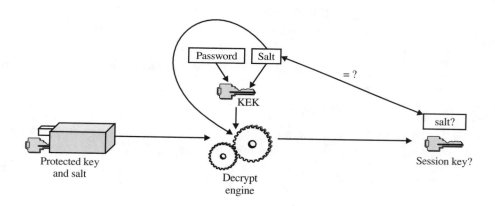

some people might feel it is more secure without any known plaintext. Of course, it is possible to use the wrong password and get a KEK that decrypts the check into a different eight-byte value that by sheer coincidence passes the test. The chances of this happening are so small, it will probably never happen in a million years.

Another check could be an algorithm identifier. This would be some sequence of bytes that represents the algorithm being used. Or it could be a combination of some of these values. In the real world, you'll probably find that engineers come up with complex procedures that include multiple checks. In these schemes, maybe one check accidentally passes, but not all of them.

Breaking PBE

Our attacker (who we're calling Ray) has two ways to break PBE. First, he could break it like any symmetric-key encryption and use brute-force on the KEK. Second, he could figure out what the password is.

Although the KEK is the result of mixing together the password and salt, Ray doesn't have to bother with those things; he could simply perform a brute-force attack on the KEK, use it to decrypt the session key, and then decrypt the data. This might be plausible if the session key is larger than the KEK. In Chapter 2, though, we saw that if a key is large enough, that's not going to happen. Hence, Ray will probably try the second way, which is to figure out what the password is. Once he has the password, he can reconstruct the key-generating process and have the KEK.

How can Ray figure out what the password is? One way would be to try every possible keystroke combination. This would be another flavor of the brute-force attack. If Pao-Chi entered the password from the keyboard, Ray could try every possible one-character password. Then he would try every two-character combination (AA, AB, AC, AD, . . .), then three-character values, and so on. In this way, eight-character or less passwords (on a keyboard with 96 possible values) would be approximately equivalent to a 52-bit key. Ten-character passwords are equivalent to about 65-bit keys.

Another attack is for Ray to build up a dictionary of likely passwords, such as every word in the English, German, French, and Spanish languages, along with common names, easy-to-type letter combinations, such as "qwertyuiop." He could add to that dictionary lists of common passwords that are available from hacker sites and bulletin boards (if you've thought of a password, someone else probably thought of it also). When confronted with PBE, he runs through the dictionary. For each entry, he mixes it with the salt and generates an alleged KEK. He tries that KEK on the chunk of PB-encrypted data. Did it produce the session key? Because the original PBE probably has a check in it (such as the salt encrypted along with the session key), it's probably easy to determine. If the check passes, that was the correct password and it produced the correct KEK, which in turn will properly decrypt the session key, which will then decrypt the bulk data.

This dictionary attack tries fewer passwords than does the brute force attack. Any password the dictionary attack tries, the brute force attack also tries, but the brute-force attack tries many additional passwords that the dictionary attack does not. As a result, the dictionary attack is faster than the brute force attack.

Of course, if Pao-Chi comes up with a password not in Ray's dictionary, it will never succeed. If Ray is smart, he'll probably start with a dictionary attack and if that fails, move on to a modified brute-force attack.

Slowing Down an Attack on a Password

To check a password, Ray has to mix the salt and password the same way Pao-Chi did. Pao-Chi can slow Ray down by making that a lengthy task. His goal will be to make the process quick enough that it doesn't make his own encryption or decryption process too expensive, but slow enough to be a drain on Ray. He can do this by repeating the mixing over and over.

First, mix the salt and password together. Then take the result of that and run it through the blender again. Then take the result of that and run it through the blender. And on and on, say 1,000 times.

The blender is probably pretty fast, the mixing is almost certainly done with a message digest, and these algorithms are generally very fast, so for Pao-Chi to do 1,000 iterations of the mixing process won't be too time-consuming. In fact entering a password is going to be far more time-consuming than 1,000 mixings. So relatively speaking, for Pao-Chi, the mixing takes up a very small portion of the total time. But Ray is going to have to do 1,000 mixings for every password he tries. That can add up.

Let's say Pao-Chi has an eight-character password. In an earlier section we said that an eight-character password is equivalent to a 52-bit key. But actually, Ray cannot try one password as quickly as one key. If he tries the brute-force attack on a key, here's the process (BFK stands for "brute-force on the key"):

BFK1   Get a candidate key.

BFK2   Do key setup (recall the key table from Chapter 2).

BFK3   Decrypt some ciphertext, yielding some purported plaintext.

BFK4   Check the plaintext.

But for each password Ray checks, on the other hand, here's the process (BFP stands for "brute-force on the password"):

BFP1   Get a candidate password.

BFP2   Perform the mixing to build the candidate key.

BFP3   Do key setup.

BFB4   Decrypt the ciphertext, yielding the purported check and session key.

BFB5   Perform the check.

How long it takes to do one BFK depends on four things. How long it takes to do one BFP depends on those same four things, plus one more. If step BFP2 is as long as the other four steps combined, that's going to double the amount of time to check one password. That's like adding one bit to your password. The eight-character password which was equivalent to a 52-bit key is now more like a 53-bit key.

In our experiments, performing 1,000 iterations (doing step BFP2 1,000 times) is about 136 times slower than the other steps combined (more or less, depending on the encryption algorithm; we used RC4, a very fast algorithm). On one Pentium-based PC, step BFP2 took 4.36 milliseconds, whereas checking one key took 0.032 milliseconds (a millisecond is "one one-thousandth" of a second; Pao-Chi is going to pay this 4 millisecond penalty when he encrypts or decrypts). Although Ray could check 31,000 keys per second, he could check only 230 passwords per second. The eight-character password is now equivalent to a 59-bit key. The 10-character password is more like a 72-bit key.

Incidentally, you may be thinking, "In a lot of places I've used passwords, there's a limit to how many times I can enter the wrong password before the program won't work. So if I try too many wrong passwords even if I later on do enter the correct password, the application won't run. Can't I just make PBE work the same?"

It's possible to write such a program, but the attacker will simply use a different PBE program that mimics the original. That is, Pao-Chi used his program to encrypt. Ray would simply obtain a copy of the ciphertext and run it through another program that looks like Pao-Chi's, except Ray's program puts no limits on the number of passwords allowed.

Good Passwords

In choosing a password, your goal is to choose one that doesn't appear in a dictionary and would thwart a brute-force attack. For example, the following password probably does not appear in a password dictionary:

14G:c*%3<wM*-l6g]_Bnp?~ d86

Editorial: The "Three-Try" Password Limit, A Pain in the Neck

by Steve Burnett

Many programs, especially login programs, place a limit on the number of wrong password tries they will accept before locking up. Usually, the limit is three. Enforcing a limit is a good security measure, but it's very annoying that the limit is so low. Furthermore, a low limit does not add any significant security compared to a larger limit.

Suppose you enter a password and the program denies access. You check and see that you accidentally have the CAPS LOCK on. You fix that and type in a password again. But this one didn't work either. What happened? Did you forget the password? Or did you simply misspell (for instance, how many times have I typed in "teh" for "the" or even "Bunrett" and that's my own name!)? Did you accidentally press a stray key? There's no way to know since you can't see what you typed. You've made two tries and gotten it wrong both times; are you going to try a third time? Probably not, because if you get it wrong, you'll be locked out. So it really isn't it a "three-try" password but a "two-try."

Now what about attackers? If the password is so weak that you need to limit intruders to no more than three tries, it's too weak. The security department should be talking to the employees about using better passwords. What's more, attackers may not even be trying the password through the user interface. Instead, they're probably grabbing information and trying the attack offline.

Given this, why not set the limit of password tries to, say, 10? That would make things easier for the user and most likely wouldn't give attackers any significant assistance. "Three tries and you're out" is just a pain in the neck.

It's a possible password, but attackers probably won't get around to trying it for a very long time. The problem with this password, of course, is that it's not easy to remember, and even if you could remember it (maybe you have a photographic memory), it's easy to mistype.

If you're using PBE, you need a good password. What makes a good password? The following list comes from an RSA Security manual. Other sources might offer other guidelines, but this is a good start.

1. Use at least 10 characters.

2. Mix in uppercase and lowercase letters, numbers, spaces, punctuation, and other symbols.

3. Avoid using a character more than twice.

4. Avoid using actual words.

5. Avoid using personal information, such as the name of a spouse, child, parent, or friend, or your phone number, Social Security number, license plate number, or birthday.

6. Do not write it down. Instead, memorize it.

Number 6 is the hardest if you follow recommendations 1 through 5. In addition, if you have several applications, security experts recommend that you use a different password for each one. What's more, some applications enforce a policy that requires you to change your password periodically.

Given all that, what's the average user to do? So far, there are no easy answers to the password dilemma. Later sections describe some alternatives to passwords, along with ways to use passwords more effectively. Unfortunately, these techniques require new hardware, and for some of them the technology is years away from perfection or public acceptance.

Password Generators

Programs are available that will generate passwords for you. These programs work like PRNGs but produce keystrokes instead of numbers. For example, the program may collect some seed bytes, including your mouse movement and keystrokes. Then it spits out a password that probably looks random. Most programs allow you to specify how long the password will be, whether the password combines uppercase and lowercase letters, or whether it should contain punctuation or other marks. You might get results like this:

tiFXFCZcZ6

K6($xV]!h1

M?a84z9W,g

Technical Note: You Never Know Where Attackers Will Look Next

Do you think that you can choose a key or password that will force a brute force attack to run to completion? For example, if the brute force attack on the password begins with *A,* then *B,* and then so on through the alphabet to *AA, AB,* and so on, you might think it would be clever to choose ZZZZZZZZZZZZ as your password. After all, that's a long way away from the beginning of the list.

Unfortunately, brute force attacks usually don't work that way. First, most brute force attacks use more than one computer, and each computer works with some of the possible key or password space.

Here's how it works. A computer that wants to be part of the cracking process applies to a central "bureaucrat" computer. This central computer keeps track of the keys or passwords that have been searched. It generates a range of keys or passwords for the "worker" computer to check, which then searches all the values in that range. If the worker computer finds the key or password, it reports the good news to the bureaucrat. But if the worker searches its entire allotted range with no success, it goes back to the bureaucrat to get another range.

How is a range determined? Probably not systematically. In other words, the first range is not going to be *A* to *ZZZ,* the second range from *AAAA* to *ZZZZ,* and so on. Instead, the ranges are probably parceled out randomly. The first applicant gets something like EV9A3LGP to FBMA111G, the second applicant gets W6MWC0O to ARH7ZD2F, and so on.

Even if only one computer is involved in the brute force attack, it operates as both a bureaucrat and a worker. As a result, you never know which part of the space will be searched next.

These passwords were generated using the JavaScript Source password generator (see http://javascript.internet.com/).

They are good passwords, but they're harder to memorize. Still, if you want a "random" password, one that will withstand a dictionary attack, a program such as this one might be a good choice.

Make sure that you trust the program you choose. Imagine a malicious password generator programmer. Suppose our attacker Ray creates a program that produces what looks like random passwords. But actually the program is limited to how many it can really create, say 10 million. Now Ray simply looks at who buys the product, and then has a leg up on cracking that customer's passwords.

Hardware-Based Key Storage

We've just examined PBE as a possible way to store cryptographic keys. Another storage place is on a hardware device. Some devices are tiny computers called *tokens*. Others are larger, tamperproof boxes, generally called *crypto accelerators*.

Tokens

A token is not a cell phone or a *personal digital assistant* (PDA) such as Palm, iPaq, and so on, but rather is something even smaller that fits inside your wallet or shirt pocket: a plastic "smart" card, a plastic "key," a small USB port attachment, or even a ring you wear on your finger. (Smart cards and USB port attachments, the most common types of tokens, are discussed in the following two sections.) A token contains a small chip with a processor, an operating system of sorts, and limited input/output, memory, and hard drive storage space. Some tokens are very small or thin, are slow, have very little storage space, and do very little. Others may have more power and can store as much information as a 1970s era PC. Figure 3-7 shows some tokens.

Figure 3-7

Some tokens

Java ring

iKey 2000

Datakey

Smarty smart card and reader

RSA SecurID 3100 smart card

The advantage of using tokens is that the attacker does not have access to them. If our attacker Ray is in Elbonia, he can probably use the internet to access Pao-Chi's computers' hard drives and does not need to be in his office to break in. (As you may know, Elbonia is a fictional country featured in the *Dilbert* comic strip by Scott Adams.) But Pao-Chi's token is not connected to the network (it's in his wallet or on his key chain or finger), so it's not visible. This arrangement thwarts a remote attack. When Pao-Chi *uses* his token, it's connected to his computer, which is ultimately connected to the world, so for a brief while, his secrets are vulnerable. But a few seconds of vulnerability is not as dangerous as the 24 hours a day the network is vulnerable.

Even if Ray obtains Pao-Chi's token, further protections are built-in. Generally, a token performs functions (such as retrieving stored keys) only when a correct password or *personal identification number* (PIN) activates it. Often, a token locks itself if too many incorrect passwords are entered. If someone tries to physically get at the storage space (as in Chapter 1 with data recovery techniques), the token will erase itself—sort of a "scorched earth" policy. This scorched earth thwarts an offline attack on the password.

The problem with tokens is that they need a way to communicate with the computer; once they can communicate with the computer, they can communicate with users through the computer. For example, you communicate with the computer by using the keyboard and mouse. Sound systems communicate using a sound card. A token might use the serial or USB port, or even the floppy drive. Some tokens use a *reader* to one of the ports. It's the reader that communicates with the computer. To use the token, you insert it into the reader, something that's generally easier than inserting it into a port. Of course, this means that you must buy the reader as well as the token and then install it.

Smart Cards

A *smart card* is simply a plastic card, similar to a credit card, that contains a microprocessor. One of the goals of smart card vendors is to replace the current version of the credit card. Just as credit cards with magnetic strips replaced simpler embossed cards, the hope is that smart cards will replace credit cards. But because smart cards contain small computers, they will be able to do more than serve as credit cards.

We'll talk more about smart cards throughout this book, but for now, one of the things you can do with them is to store keys. When you need to use a symmetric key, for example, you transfer it to the computer, which uses it to encrypt or decrypt data. To transfer the key between card and computer, though, you need a smart card reader. Several PC manufacturers have announced that future laptops and keyboards will come with built-in smart card readers.

The *International Organization for Standardization* (ISO) has published several standards outlining the physical characteristics of smart cards, including the dimensions and locations of the contacts, signals and transmission, and more. Virtually all smart cards look alike because they are built to standard. The idea is that all smart cards will be usable with a wide variety of readers. So far, however, many smart cards and readers simply don't work together. Often, to use a particular manufacturer's smart card, you must use that firm's reader. As more PC manufacturers release products with readers built in, this situation should change.

USB Tokens

The Universal Serial Bus port is an industry standard for attaching plug and play devices. Other ports have such functionality (such as PCMCIA), but the USB port is probably the most popular. Since 1998 or 1999, most new PCs and laptops have come with USB ports as standard equipment. If you have a device that connects to your computer through the USB port (such as a camera downloading pictures or a printer), there's no need to attach and reboot. So long as the software to run the device is installed, you simply insert the device and run it. When you're done with one USB device, take it out and insert a new one, or most likely, you can have several attached to the same port.

Several companies have introduced cryptographic tokens that attach to the USB port. Other companies with tokens that are not USB-ready have made adapters to USB ports. These tokens are approximately $2\frac{1}{2}$ by $\frac{1}{2}$ inches in size (about the size of a house key but a little thicker). They have quite a bit more computing power and storage space than smart cards. Hence, they will almost always be much faster, do more work, and store more keys than a smart card.

Tokens as Password Storage Devices

In addition to your keys, tokens can hold passwords. Suppose you have several places to log in: your network account, e-mail, various computer accounts, electronic commerce accounts (such as an account with an online travel agent or bookstore), and so on. For each account, you'd like a different password. In that way, if someone figures out one password (for example, the online travel agent might know your password for that account), he or she won't have them all.

The solution is to use a token to generate big random passwords and store those passwords. When you need to log in to an account, you hook up the token and have it send the password. You don't have to remember the password, so it can be random and very long, perhaps 20 or 30 characters.

You probably have access to the token through a password, so if attackers obtain your token and figure out that password, they've got all your passwords. That is a danger, but using a token does help thwart a remote attack. For example, suppose Ray, the attacker, goes to your online bank account and logs in as you. Although he need not be at your computer to do this—he can be in Elbonia—he does need to enter your password. A long, random password is much more difficult to crack than passwords you might otherwise use for your various accounts because they're easier to remember.

Crypto Accelerators

The larger hardware crypto devices are generally called *crypto accelerators* (see Figure 3-8) because they usually have specialized chips that perform cryptographic operations faster than general-purpose microprocessors. Crypto accelerators can also store data more securely than can a regular computer. The problem with, for example, your desktop PC is that the hard drive is visible to the outside world. As you saw in Chapter 1, attackers can probably read your computer's hard drive, and even if you have firewalls around your sensitive information, attackers can use tools, such as data recovery software, to read that data as well. But a crypto accelerator is built so that its storage space is not visible. There is very limited access to it using normal channels, and if attackers try to pry open the cover to physically access the hard drive, the device erases itself. If you store your key on such a box, it's extremely unlikely that someone will be able to extract it.

Many crypto accelerators do not let the key leave the device. With a token, if you want to encrypt 10 megabytes (MB) of data, you must get the key from the token and let your PC do the encrypting. While the key is in memory—and afterward, as you saw in Chapter 1 with memory reconstruction attacks—it is vulnerable. With a crypto accelerator, you send the

Figure 3-8

Some crypto
accelerators

nShield key management and
acceleration

Cryptoswift PCI E-Commerce Accelerator

Luna CA^3

AXL 300

plaintext to the device, and it encrypts and returns the ciphertext. This arrangement further limits the key's vulnerability.

One problem with crypto accelerators is that they are connected to your computer 24 hours a day. This is in contrast to tokens, which are connected only for a few seconds at a time, limiting their vulnerability. Presumably, the crypto accelerator I/O is secure so that if attackers have remote access to your computer, they still cannot get access to the accelerator. "Presumably," however, may not be adequate security in some situations. That's why most crypto accelerators work in conjunction with tokens—that is, they don't operate without a token inserted.

If you store your keys on the box, you can recover them by presenting the correct token and entering the correct password. For attackers to access your keys, they must somehow obtain your token (another token by the same manufacturer won't work, just as two credit cards don't refer to the same account) and the ability to use that token (usually a password). And, of course, they must have physical contact with the accelerator (to insert the token), again thwarting a remote attack.

Hardware Devices and Random Numbers

Tokens and crypto accelerators usually come with an RNG (see Chapter 2 for details about RNGs and PRNGs). You must be careful, though, because some tokens don't have true RNGs. Rather, they have PRNGs seeded at the factory. Even if your device constantly collects seed material each time it is used—a better approach than a PRNG seeded at the factory—it's still a PRNG.

Biometrics

A hardware device stores your keys securely, but it usually relinquishes them when someone enters a password. Good passwords can be strong, but in real life, not everyone uses good passwords.

Another way to authorize a device to unleash the key is through *biometrics,* which uses your unique physical characteristic to verify your identity. The most well-known biometric is the fingerprint. It's common knowledge that everyone, even an identical twin, has unique fingerprints. If a machine could read fingerprints, it could determine whether the appropriate person is requesting an operation. Such machines exist. (It's macabre, but some of these machines can even tell whether the finger being used is actually attached to the body and whether the body is alive.)

Other biometrics include retina scans, voiceprints, and even DNA. Biometrics companies are attempting to build hardware that can be programmed to identify you by scanning your eye, voice, or DNA and then appropriately release secure information or perform a cryptographic function.

Biometric devices are not currently in widespread use for a couple of reasons. One is the cost of the devices, and the other is their reliability. A number of concerns have been raised. Will the device return an erroneous "positive ID" on someone who isn't the identified subject? Will it always return a positive ID on the subject? What if the subject has cut his or her right thumb—will the fingerprint reader still function? Can it instead use the left thumb? Another finger? For a voiceprint reader, what if the person has a cold—will it still work? And so on. A password works virtually 100 percent of the time. If you enter the wrong password, access is denied. With the correct password, you always get access. With biometrics, there may be some errors.

The technology is advancing, and companies are building better and cheaper readers. Someday, maybe a smart card will contain not only a chip but also a fingerprint reader. Maybe your cell phone will have built-in voice recognition.

Summary

After you've generated a symmetric key and used it to encrypt data, how do you protect the key? One of the most common techniques is password-based encryption. In PBE, you use a password and a salt to build the key encryption key. You then use the KEK to encrypt the session key. Another method of protecting your session key is to store it on a hardware device, such as a token or crypto accelerator.

Real-World Examples

How do companies protect keys in the real world? One class of products for protecting session keys is file encryption applications. These products encrypt the files on your hard drive using symmetric-key cryptography. Protecting bulk data keys can be done in several ways.

Keon Desktop

RSA Security makes a family of products called Keon. One component is Keon Desktop. Among the features of this product is file encryption. You register directories with Keon, and it will encrypt all files in those directories (see Figures 3-9 and 3-10). When you open one of those files, Keon will decrypt it. When you close it, Keon will encrypt it again. That means if the file is on your hard drive, it is encrypted. It is decrypted only when you want to see it.

Figure 3-9

Registering a directory with Keon. Once registered, all files in this directory will be automatically encrypted when not in use, and decrypted when accessed

Figure 3-10

After creating a protected directory, choose the algorithm you want to use to encrypt the files. The key menu is for choosing where to store the session key, on a smart card or a virtual smart card

Keon uses RC5 at 128 bits or DES at 56 bits to encrypt. It uses a PRNG to generate the key. The seed is various machine states and user input. Once the key has been used to encrypt the files, it's necessary to store that key. Keon stores it in the user's Credential Store. If the user has a smart card, Keon will use it as the Credential Store. If not, Keon will create a virtual smart card on the user's hard drive or on a floppy disk or both. The keys on this virtual smart card are protected using PBE.

If you keep your Credential Store on a mobile medium (the smart card or floppy), you can use Keon to encrypt or decrypt files from any computer you work on (as long as it has Keon Desktop installed), whether it is your office computer, home computer (for telecommuting), or a laptop on a business trip.

To read your encrypted file, an attacker will have to either break the encryption algorithm, create a substitute Credential Store (which would entail finding the session key through a brute-force attack) or break your Credential Store to obtain the bulk data key. The first two are highly unlikely, so an attack, if it occurs, will probably be mounted against your Credential Store. If you keep it on a smart card or floppy, the attacker will have to steal it. And then it will still be necessary to either break the smart card or break your password.

Other Products

If you search the Web, you will find dozens or even hundreds of applications out there that offer file encryption. Some are freeware, others are shareware, and some are regular products.

One of the most commonly used file encryption programs is PGP. The letters stand for *Pretty Good Privacy*. PGP was originally a freeware program written by Phil Zimmerman using RSAREF, the cryptographic reference library produced by RSA Data Security. According to the documentation, it has file encryption through PBE (it does not generate a key and protect the key with PBE; it encrypts the file using PBE). It also offers an advanced "enveloping" file encryption that uses a key on your "key ring." Once again, your key ring can be a number of devices, including a PBE-protected file.

CHAPTER 4

The Key Distribution Problem and Public-Key Cryptography

Symmetric-key encryption can keep your secrets safe, but if you need to share secret information with other people, you must also share the keys. How can you securely send keys to other individuals? This chapter describes some solutions, including the revolutionary concept of public-key cryptography.

Chapters 2 and 3 describe how Pao-Chi (the sales rep on the road) can keep secrets by encrypting his data and then safely storing the encrypting key. But suppose he wants to share some of his secrets with other people? For example, let's say Pao-Chi has just met with Satomi, a potential customer, and wants to discuss strategy with Gwen, the VP of sales and Pao-Chi's boss. Normally, Pao-Chi and Gwen could handle the conversation by phone, but they need to send complex documents back and forth, and they figure the best way to do that is through e-mail. Being a little paranoid, they want to ensure the security of this exchange of sensitive data. After all, Pao-Chi will likely be hooking up his laptop to Satomi's phone lines or Internet connection, and who knows what sort of sniffers are attached to her company's wires?

The simple solution is for Pao-Chi to encrypt any files he sends to Gwen. In that way, if Satomi intercepts the message, all she sees is gibberish. The problem is that when the message gets to Gwen, she also sees only gibberish. To decrypt the message, Gwen needs the key. Pao-Chi has the key, but how can he send it to Gwen? He can't send it in another message; if Satomi can intercept the data message, she can also intercept the key message. And if Pao-Chi could find a channel to send the key securely, he could simply send the secret via that route.

The problem facing Pao-Chi and Gwen is known as the *key distribution problem*—namely, how can two or more people securely send keys over unsecure lines? In more general terms, how can people securely send any sensitive information over unsecure lines? Because we can encrypt the data, though, we can reduce the general problem to the smaller problem of securely sending the key. If you have 10MB of sensitive material, you could try to figure out a way to send that bulk data securely, or you could encrypt it using a 128-bit symmetric key and then try to come up with a way to securely send the key. If you solve the key distribution problem, you also solve the bulk data distribution problem (Figure 4-1).

Figure 4-1

The key distribution problem: How can Pao-Chi send Gwen sensitive information, when Satomi might be eavesdropping?

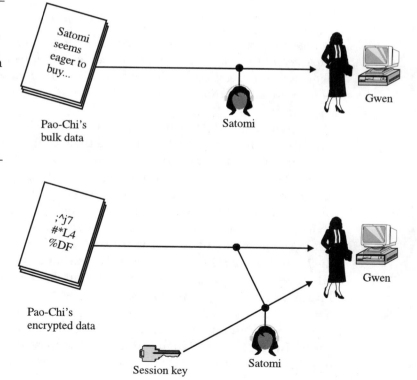

Sharing Keys in Advance

In Chapter 3, you saw how Pao-Chi can encrypt bulk data with a session key and then store that key securely. He can store that key using, for example, PBE or a token. To solve the key distribution problem, Pao-Chi and Gwen can get together in advance to generate a key, and then each of them can store the key. To send secure messages to each other, they use the key to encrypt the data.

So before Pao-Chi leaves on his trip, he stops by Gwen's office with his laptop. He generates a 128-bit key and stores it somehow—maybe using PBE, maybe on a token. He then puts a copy of the key onto a floppy disk and hands Gwen the disk. She inserts the disk into her computer, copies the key, and stores it securely. Now the two parties share a key that they can use whenever they want to send sensitive material. This key, by the way, likely will not be the same key Pao-Chi uses to encrypt the files on his hard drive. If it were, Gwen could read all his sensitive data. If that's not OK with Pao-Chi, he has the option of encrypting his data using a key only he can access.

If the two of them had chosen to exchange the key online, Pao-Chi would not have had to go to Gwen's office in person. But their goal is to send no sensitive data in the clear over unsecure lines, and that includes the company network. Even if the network is secure from outsiders, that doesn't eliminate the possibility of an inside job. Another employee—maybe the system administrator or simply someone who is adept at hacking—might be able to intercept such a key exchange. So the safest way to exchange the encrypting key in advance is to do so in person.

Another possibility is for Pao-Chi to generate the key, encrypt it using PBE, and send the encrypted key to Gwen. Anyone intercepting the message would not be able to decrypt it without the password. Of course, Gwen needs the password, so Pao-Chi can give it to her by phone. In this way, the sensitive data (the password) is never sent over the network lines. But is the phone line secure? Maybe, maybe not. Still, whoever wants to steal the key will have to break into both the network and the phone system. Although this makes the attacker's job more difficult, it still means sending sensitive data over unsecure lines.

Problems With This Scheme

Pao-Chi and Gwen now share a key. This scheme will work; if attackers try to intercept their messages encrypted using that key, the attackers will not be able to recover the information. But this solution does have its problems.

Suppose the parties want to share keys with more than one person. Pao-Chi is not the company's only sales rep, and he may want to securely send information to his sales colleagues as well as people in the engineering, accounting, and shipping departments. To communicate securely with all these people, Pao-Chi will have to visit their offices and perform the key exchange. What's more, Gwen will have to make similar visits (or her colleagues will have to visit her—after all, she is the VP). Everyone will have to exchange keys in person with everyone with whom they share confidential information.

The logistics quickly become burdensome. Some colleagues may have offices in other parts of the country or even in other countries. The company can't send everyone on all the trips required to exchange keys. Maybe the solution would be to gather all the employees at one location and have a giant key exchange party. But what happens when the company hires someone new? Does it have yet another key exchange party? Send the new employee on a worldwide trip to exchange keys?

Furthermore, as more people need to share keys, the number of required meetings grows dramatically. When two people share a key, there's one meeting. When three people share keys, there are two meetings; with four people, six meetings, and so on. In general, n people, must make $1/2(n^2 - n)$ key exchanges. If your company has 10 employees involved in secure data sharing, that's $1/2(100 - 10)$ key exchanges, or $1/2(90) = 45$. For 20 employees, it's 190 meetings. A company with 1,000 employees would need to perform 499,500 key exchanges.

One solution is for everyone in the company to share the same key. You could have a "key master" who gives the key to all employees. The drawback is what happens when someone leaves the company. If the company does not change the key, an unauthorized individual can now decrypt sensitive materials. If, on the other hand, the company changes keys, the key master will have to revisit everyone in the company.

A second problem with the shared secret key is that if attackers crack one message, they crack them all. Because all messages between two people are encrypted with the same key, finding the key for one message means finding the key for all messages. It's not likely that attackers will find the key if the correspondents use a 128-bit key and an algorithm with no weaknesses. On the other hand, if it is possible to easily use a separate key for each message, why not take that extra measure of precaution? Although this is a drawback of the shared key approach, it's trivial compared with the pitfalls of trying to exchange keys in person.

Using a Trusted Third Party

If sharing keys in advance is not an option, Pao-Chi and Gwen can try using a *trusted third party* (TTP). This is a variation on the key master solution. In this scheme, the trusted third party—let's call her Michelle—shares a key with each individual in the company. Actually, the keys are *key-encrypting keys*, or KEKs. Pao-Chi visits Michelle and asks for a KEK. She generates one, stores it securely, and gives a copy to Pao-Chi. The two of them now share a KEK. Gwen also visits Michelle, and the two of them share a different KEK (see Figure 4-2).

When Pao-Chi wants to communicate with Gwen, he sends a message to Michelle, requesting a session key he can use in his messages with Gwen. To fulfill the request, Michelle generates a new session key and sends it to Pao-Chi. She encrypts the new session key using the KEK she shares with him, so anyone intercepting that message cannot identify this new key. Michelle also sends this same new session key to Gwen, encrypting it using the KEK those two share (see Figure 4-2).

Pao-Chi and Gwen now share a key, and neither had to make a trip to the other's office. Anyone else wanting to share a key with any other employee simply establishes a KEK with Michelle, who distributes the key. In a trusted third party scheme, the correspondents are the first two parties. In our example, Michelle is the third party. Just as important, Michelle must be trusted because she has everyone's keys. When Pao-Chi and Gwen exchange encrypted messages, normally they are the only people who can decrypt them. But now Michelle also has their session key, so she can decrypt their messages. Pao-Chi and Gwen must trust Michelle not to read their sensitive material or release their key to anyone else.

The trusted third party still has to exchange keys with all the employees in person. As you saw in the preceding section, that's a daunting task. To make things easier, you can create a hierarchy of trusted third parties. Everyone goes to a local TTP, each of whom has established a key with every other TTP. For all the TTPs to exchange keys is still a formidable

Figure 4-2

Michelle acts as a trusted third party, distributing keys between Pao-Chi and Gwen

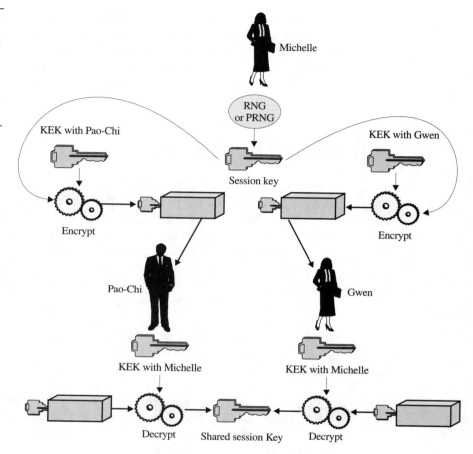

project, but it is more manageable than having a single companywide TTP. If two correspondents are in the same office, they can use the services of a shared TTP. If they are in separate offices, each one communicates with his or her own TTP. Then the two TTPs communicate with each other to bridge the gap (see Figure 4-3).

Problems With This Scheme

The first problem is that the TTP can read all the messages. The whole idea of encrypting messages is to limit their exposure to only the corre-

Figure 4-3

TTP Michelle
(San Francisco)
shares keys with
TTP Alexander
(New York),
creating a
hierarchy that
serves Pao-Chi
and Daniel in the
two cities

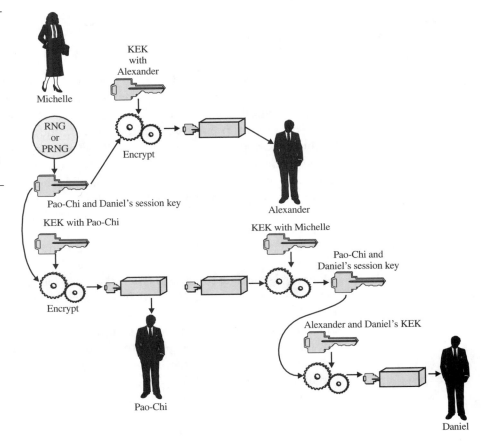

spondents. Now a third person has access. If the correspondents can live with that, this scheme will work. Otherwise, they'd better look for another solution.

The second problem is that when the TTP leaves the company it must hire a new TTP and start the process over from the ground up. Otherwise, the outgoing TTP can gain access to all sensitive materials.

An alternative is to contract the job of TTP to an outside company. In this arrangement, the TTP is not an individual but a corporate entity. In this case, you must trust that the company has checks in place that prevent its employees from gaining access to the keys.

Public-Key Cryptography and the Digital Envelope

In the 1970s, researchers invented *asymmetric-key cryptography,* a new way to securely send keys. This scheme uses two different keys. Although they are related to each other—they are partners—they are significantly different. The relationship is mathematical, and what one key encrypts the other key decrypts. In symmetric crypto, the same key is used to encrypt and decrypt (hence the word "symmetric"—the same on both sides); if you use any other key to decrypt, the result is gibberish. But with asymmetric crypto (see Figure 4-4), the key that's used to encrypt the data does not decrypt it; only its partner does (hence the word "asymmetric,"— each side different).

An analogy is the asymmetric lockers often found in airports, train stations, skating rinks, and many other public places. To securely store your belongings, you put them into the locker and lock it by inserting money. Just as your house key locks your front door, the money locks the locker—in a sense, your money is the key. After you lock the door, you receive another key—perhaps an actual key that looks like your house key or car key, or perhaps a piece of paper that contains a number. To reopen the locker, you use the key or enter the number on a key pad (sort of like using a temporary *personal identification number* or PIN).

Suppose thieves want to steal your belongings. To open the locker, they need a key. The key you used to lock it was money. But if the thieves insert more money into the locker, it won't open. They can stuff money into it all day long, and it still won't open. The key that was used to lock the locker will not unlock it. Only the second, different key will unlock the door.

Similarly, it's possible to create a cryptographic algorithm in which one key encrypts data and the other key decrypts it. Another term for this model (the term we use in this book) is *public-key cryptography*. Because both keys are needed to lock and unlock the data, one of them can be made public without jeopardizing security. This key is known as the *public key*. Its partner is called the *private key*. You encrypt data with the public key and decrypt it with the private key. Just as thieves can know what key was used to lock the asymmetric locker—can even have access to that key—and still not be able to open the door, an attacker can have access to a cryptographic public key and still not be able to decrypt the data. Only the private key can be used to decrypt it, and if the owner of

Figure 4-4

In asymmetric crypto, the encrypting key cannot be used to decrypt; you must use its partner

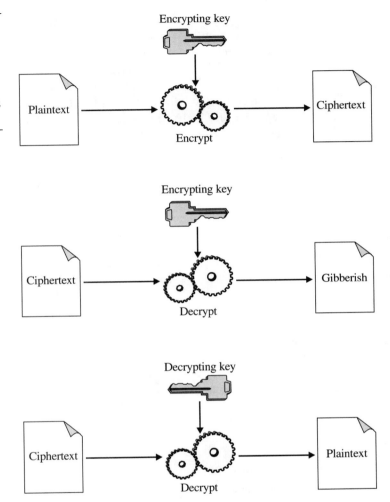

that key keeps it private (as the name implies), plaintext encrypted with the public key will remain secure.

Let's return to our sales rep example. If Gwen has a public and private key pair, she makes the public key publicly available (what else are you going to do with a key called "public"). She is the only one who has access to the private key. Pao-Chi uses a symmetric algorithm with a session key to encrypt his e-mail, and then he uses Gwen's public key to encrypt the session key. Then he sends both the encrypted message and the encrypted session key (see Figure 4-5). This arrangement is similar to password-based encryption, in which the session key is used to encrypt the bulk data, and the KEK (based on the password) is used to encrypt the session key. In PBE, only the owner of the password can recover the session key and consequently decrypt the bulk data. In public-key cryptography, only the owner of the private key can recover the session key and decrypt the bulk data.

Figure 4-5

You use a session key with a symmetric algorithm to encrypt the bulk data and then encrypt the session key with the recipient's public key

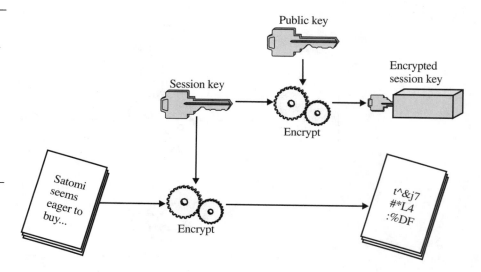

Now you're probably asking, "Why does Pao-Chi use a session key with a symmetric algorithm to encrypt the bulk data and then encrypt the session key with the public key? Why doesn't he simply encrypt the bulk data with the public key?" The answer has to do with performance: Public-key algorithms are slow, whereas symmetric-key crypto can encrypt bulk data very quickly. Depending on the platform, some symmetric algorithms can operate at speeds of 10MB, 20MB, 50MB (or even more) per second. In contrast, a public-key algorithm operates at probably 20KB to 200KB per second, depending on the algorithm, platform, and other factors. That's too slow for processing bulk data, but encrypting 128 bits (the probable size of a symmetric key) would not take much time. So if Pao-Chi's e-mail (the plaintext) is a few megabytes, it's more efficient to use this combination of symmetric-key and public-key crypto.

You may ask, "Why not simply develop a public-key algorithm that can encrypt as fast as the symmetric algorithms?" You're welcome to try.

This process of encrypting bulk data using symmetric-key crypto, and encrypting the symmetric key with a public-key algorithm, is called a *digital envelope*. The idea is that the symmetric key is wrapping the data in an envelope of encryption, and the public key is wrapping the symmetric key in an envelope (see Figure 4-6).

Figure 4-6

A digital envelope. The session key wraps the bulk data in an envelope of encryption, and the public key wraps the session key in another envelope

Notice the huge advantage of this method compared with a shared secret (discussed in the section "Sharing Keys in Advance"). With a shared secret scheme, Pao-Chi and Gwen have a key they use each time they communicate. Each of them must have separate session keys to use when communicating with anyone else. And they must keep all these keys secure. Using a digital envelope, Pao-Chi and Gwen still have to keep a separate key for each individual, but this time it's a public key, which doesn't need to be protected. Furthermore, they probably don't need to store the public keys themselves; directories of public keys are readily available. We talk about these directories in Chapter 6. For now, it's sufficient to know that you can leave the task of managing all those public keys to someone else.

Security Issues

Suppose Pao-Chi sends an e-mail to Gwen using a digital envelope, and Satomi indeed intercepts the message. Will Satomi be able to read it? The bulk data was encrypted using a symmetric algorithm, so she needs the session key. To decrypt the data she could try a brute force attack, but if the key is 128 bits, that would take billions or even trillions of millennia (as you saw in Chapter 2). But because the session key is right there, part of the message itself, it seems she doesn't need to try this attack—except the session key is also encrypted. To decrypt the session key, she needs the partner to the public key that was used to encrypt it because that's the only key that will decrypt it. That's the private key, but only Gwen has that.

Maybe Satomi can break the public-key algorithm or perform a brute force attack to find the private key. Recall that there were two ways to recover messages encrypted using a symmetric-key crypto: break the algorithm or find the key using brute force. The same is true for public-key crypto. If Satomi can figure out what the private key is by breaking the algorithm or using brute force, she can decrypt the session key and use it to decrypt the bulk data.

To determine the private key, Satomi must finds a 160-bit to 510-bit (or possibly higher) number. If a brute force attack on a 128-bit value (the symmetric key) is outside the realm of feasibility, then so is such an attack on a 160-bit number. So a brute force attack on the 160-bit or 510-bit number is not a realistic option.

What about the algorithm? Can a public-key algorithm be broken? It turns out that all public-key algorithms can be broken by determining what the private key is, based on the public key. Remember that the public and private keys are partners, that they're related, and that this relationship is mathematical. Math computations can be used to derive the private key from the public key.

Luckily, these math computations are time-consuming. As with symmetric-key crypto, the longer the public key, the longer it will take to derive the private key from it. If the keys are long enough, solving the math problem would take as much time as a brute force attack on a 96-bit to 128-bit key. In the section titled "Key Sizes," we talk about key sizes for public-key algorithms.

Breaking a Public-Key Algorithm

In Chapter 2, we say that you should use only symmetric algorithms with no weaknesses that the fastest way to break them should be a brute force attack. Why, then, are we now telling you to use public-key algorithms that can be broken? For these algorithms, the brute force attack is not the fastest attack. Why the change of heart?

The answer is simple: No one has been able to develop a public-key algorithm that has no weaknesses. For all public-key algorithms, there are techniques that will break them faster than brute force. Think of these techniques as shortcuts. But most users are willing to live with the shortcuts for two reasons. First, cryptographers have performed a tremendous amount of research quantifying the time required by the shortcuts. Even though an algorithm is susceptible to an attack faster than brute force, the research shows it still takes a long time. For most people, that amount of time is sufficient security. Second, people are willing to use algorithms that suffer from shortcuts because these algorithms are the best way to solve the key distribution problem.

For people who don't trust public-key cryptography, the only recourse is to use a shared secret scheme for key distribution. Otherwise, until someone comes up with a public-key algorithm with no shortcuts, we'll have to live with them.

Actually, though, having the shortcuts is not too bad. Using brute force, an attacker might get lucky and find the key in one of the first few tries, theoretically reducing the time of a successful attack to almost zero. In contrast, cryptographers know how long they can expect it will take to break a public-key algorithm using a shortcut. These attacks usually must run their entire course before coming up with the answer, almost never hitting on a lucky early answer, so researchers have established a more concrete minimum attack time.

Some History of Public-Key Cryptography

In the mid-1970s, Stanford University graduate student Whitfield Diffie and professor Martin Hellman investigated cryptography in general and the key distribution problem in particular. The two came up with a scheme whereby two people could create a shared secret key by exchanging public information. They could communicate over public lines, sending information back and forth in a form readable by eavesdroppers, at the same time generating a secret value not made public. The two correspondents would then be able to use that secret value as a symmetric session key (discussed in more detail soon). The name given to this scheme is Diffie-Hellman, or DH.

DH solves a problem-sharing a key—but it's not encryption. That does not make it unusable; in fact, DH is in use to this day. But it was not the "ultimate" algorithm, one that could be used for encryption. Diffie and Hellman published their result in 1976. That paper outlined the idea of public-key cryptography (one key encrypts, the other decrypts), pointed out that the authors did not yet have such an algorithm, and described what they had so far.

Ron Rivest, a professor at MIT, was intrigued by Diffie and Hellman's idea of public-key cryptography and decided to create the ultimate algorithm. He recruited two colleagues—Adi Shamir and Len Adleman—to work on the problem. In 1977, the trio developed an algorithm that could indeed encrypt data. They published the algorithm in 1978, and it became known as RSA, the initials of its inventors.

In 1985, working independently, two men—Neal Koblitz of the University of Washington and Victor Miller of IBM's Watson Research Center—proposed that an obscure branch of math called elliptic curves could be used to perform public-key cryptography. By the late 1990s, this class of algorithms had begun to gain momentum.

Since 1977 (and 1985), many researchers have invented many public-key algorithms. To this day, however, the most commonly used public-key algorithm for solving the key distribution problem is RSA. In second place is DH, followed by elliptic curves. We talk about these algorithms in the following sections.

How Public-Key Cryptography Works

It's easy to imagine symmetric-key crypto. Using the key, you follow a step-by-step procedure to scramble the outgoing data. To decrypt it, you perform the steps in reverse. If the last thing the encryptor did was to rotate a word, the first thing the decryptor does is to rotate the ciphertext word in the other direction by the same amount (see Figure 4-7). If the key used to encrypt the data is the key used to decrypt it, the rotation number will be the same. (If the key is wrong, there is a chance that particular rotation may still be correct, but almost all the rest of the operations down the line, maybe an XOR here or an AND there, will be wrong.)

But with public-key cryptography, such a procedure won't work. You can't simply reverse the steps. Why not? The quick answer has to do with math. Whereas symmetric-key crypto simply operates on the data as bits

Who Invented Public-Key Cryptography?

Because they published the first papers on the subject, Whitfield Diffie and Martin Hellman, along with Ron Rivest, Adi Shamir, and Len Adleman, are generally credited with inventing public-key cryptography in the mid 1970s. Another researcher, Ralph Merkle, also deserves credit for his pioneering work.

Yet British and U.S. information security organizations claim that they developed these techniques in the 1960s and 1970s. Did they?

The Code Book, Simon Singh's history of crypto, gives ample evidence that James Ellis of the *British Communications Electronic Security Group* (CESG) proposed the idea of asymmetric encryption in the 1960s. Apparently, he was inspired after reading an anonymous paper written at Bell Labs during World War II. Ellis had difficulty finding an algorithm that would work. In 1973, mathematician Clifford Cocks joined the CESG. Ellis described the concept to him, and within a few minutes Cocks had devised a solution that was essentially the algorithm known today as RSA. In 1974, Malcolm Williamson, another Ellis colleague, described yet another algorithm, this one similar to the one we call Diffie-Hellman. Because this work was secret (the CESG is a secret organization, called by some people a spy group), it was never published, and the authors did not receive credit until years later.

The U.S. *National Security Agency* (NSA) also claims to have invented public-key crypto in the 1960s. Whitfield Diffie has remarked that part of his inspiration for public-key crypto was hearing about the secure phone system at the NSA. Although Diffie did not know how the NSA had solved the key distribution problem, he explains that because he knew it was possible, he figured he could come up with the solution. The NSA system—which, it was later learned, used public-key crypto—was up and running by the mid-1970s, perhaps indicating that years of study preceded deployment. In addition to the NSA phone system, a document with the exciting title "National Security Action Memorandum 160" outlines a proposal for installing "permissive links" onto nuclear weapons. Apparently, this memo was submitted to President John F. Kennedy; it

continued

bears his signature. Along with NSAM 160 is the "Weisner Memorandum," which includes more details about permissive links. It can be inferred that the authors proposed equipping nuclear arms with cryptographic switches. Bombs could be activated only with the correct codes, with a form of public-key crypto guaranteeing correct codes (two principles referred to as authentication and nonrepudiation; see Chapter 5).

What about the former Soviet Union or the People's Republic of China? Did these nations have public-key algorithms before 1976? Or how about Hungary or Japan—or any other government? If they did, they're not saying.

Figure 4-7

In symmetric-key crypto, generally the last thing done in encrypting is the first thing done (in reverse) in decrypting

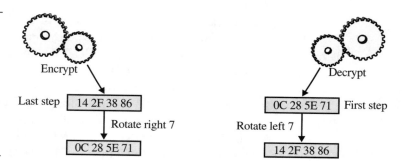

and manipulates them using computer operations, public-key crypto operates on the data as numbers and plays with the numbers (see Figure 4-8). And the math is one-way: It's easy in one direction but not in the other direction. In fact, the foundation of any good public-key algorithm is a *one-way function,* the class of math problems on which public-key crypto is built. Actually, public-key one-way functions are more accurately described as one-way with a trap door. To the rest of the world the functions are one-way, but the private key operates as a trap door that allows the owner to recover the original data (see Figure 4-9). There are true one-way functions, and we talk about some of them in Chapter 5.

Figure 4-8

Public-key crypto treats all data as numbers and performs mathematical operations on them

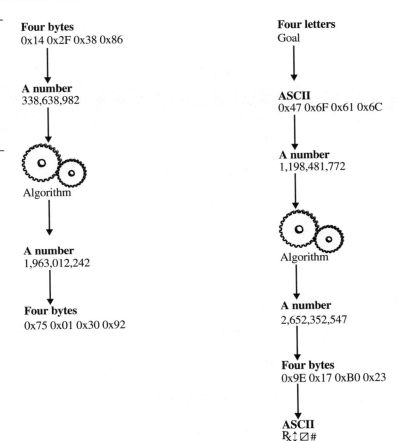

Four bytes
0x14 0x2F 0x38 0x86

A number
338,638,982

Algorithm

A number
1,963,012,242

Four bytes
0x75 0x01 0x30 0x92

Four letters
Goal

ASCII
0x47 0x6F 0x61 0x6C

A number
1,198,481,772

Algorithm

A number
2,652,352,547

Four bytes
0x9E 0x17 0xB0 0x23

ASCII
R↕☒#

In this book, we don't describe the full details of the math behind the various algorithms; you can find that in the RSA Labs FAQ on the accompanying CD. But in the following sections we talk about the three most widely used algorithms for solving the key distribution problem: RSA, DH, and ECDH (Elliptic Curve Diffie-Hellman). We tell you the names of the one-way functions and outline the problems.

Figure 4-9

A one-way function with a trap door. Performing operations in one direction is easy, but reversing the steps is difficult unless you know the secret trap door

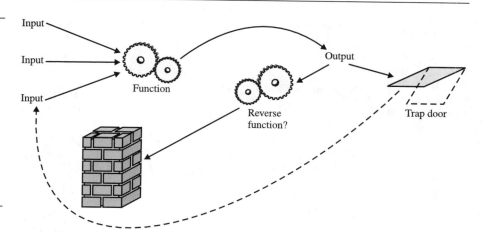

The RSA Algorithm

The RSA algorithm encrypts data. If you feed your plaintext to the algorithm along with the public key, you get ciphertext as a result. With the digital envelope, the plaintext is the session key. It's certainly possible to use RSA to encrypt data other than a session key, but RSA is not as fast as the symmetric algorithms. For example, RC4 (probably the fastest symmetric algorithm in wide use today) will encrypt data at a rate 700 times faster than 1,024-bit RSA (1,024 bits is the most commonly used RSA key size). RC5 (one of the fastest block ciphers) is about 500 times faster.

NOTE:

Incidentally, the R in RC4 and RC5 is the same R as in RSA.

So the best way to use RSA is to create a digital envelope. For example, Pao-Chi can generate a random or pseudo-random 128-bit RC4 key, use it to encrypt his e-mail message to Gwen, and then use Gwen's RSA public key to encrypt the RC4 key. Encrypting the RC4 key (16 bytes) will take only a few milliseconds on most platforms. Pao-Chi's message to Gwen consists of two parts: the encrypted session key and the encrypted bulk data (see Figure 4-10). Gwen separates the two components, uses her RSA private key to decrypt the session key, and then uses that decrypted RC4 key to decrypt the bulk data.

Figure 4-10

In Pao-Chi's message, the encrypted session key comes first and the encrypted bulk data follows

```
fõøý®2S7"F•!$å§Õy=n
```

Encrypted key

```
Ê9öYÆz@ÑvO\•{7r
‰¬Øj²ÖQ+á+"˜~j°_(Œ:
rÑ©öæêå"Æœ4ç±>øÍé
ÖÔšv•pŠæâ+ˆî-
‡¨¤Š†§-¾0ÍíRà¼Ñä"
x'®kÝêÍØsu)¦ÐV•³]
\îàµ[ðüª|˜
¹ÉÝ"³9iãaÛ¾ï'‡É5Å
âQ§f't>[ZCõ{»¡P•Ã
PV˜®îÙî²©0"_Ày}™5"4
í±XC•%ÝçC¾àâ'xÿˆFÝ
kÍöe,û]fc¿£<t4)¨½/,rF
•t•F^ì,²¦uG"†Má•û•
Õ{°*8Xƒˆïu»M8øU!ÁÒ
«mßÖãõ¯DÂq§`4az§
ÀD™XF\³\Mÿ½'š•ýjh
•@(háüå¿z7ð'•ƒ•f,•à
z|•aƒ;¿Ñ¬"r•§2Q¡Ês
Zë¨°@5à5-`m%ú°H
Ä!s_£u>¼*JM\üý>S~£
```

Encrypted bulk data

An RSA public key consists of two numbers: a modulus and a public exponent. The private key is made up of the same modulus and a private exponent (see Figure 4-11). The modulus, incidentally, is the product of two very large prime numbers. (A prime number, or prime, cannot be evenly divided; for example, 3, 5, 7, 13, and 17 are primes.) In the cryptographic literature, these numbers are usually given the romantic names $n, e,$ and $d,$ where n is the modulus, e is the public exponent, and d is the private exponent. Equally poetic are the names for the two primes that make up the modulus: p and q.

When you generate an RSA key pair (or rather, when the program you're running generates an RSA key pair), you decide on a public exponent $e,$ find two large primes p and q that work with the e you've chosen, multiply p and q to get the modulus $n,$ and finally compute your private

Figure 4-11

A 1,024-bit RSA key pair. The number n is the modulus, e is the public exponent, and d is the private exponent

Public Key:

$n =$

```
c6 2c 3f 8c fe c2 95 d1 d9 11 55 ae 94 62 1d b4
f3 0d f2 22 ea a1 62 01 13 22 95 89 3c 0f 89 9f
5e f3 01 2c e8 45 3f d9 2f 99 90 37 4e fa 35 89
0b cf e4 83 cf 9e f7 28 92 a8 89 2b 0b 0b e8 f1
ec 00 f1 e9 30 6f ae 32 16 29 0c 64 71 48 b9 f6
d7 e5 73 db b0 4b be ab d8 a3 83 3f 34 1e 0d 03
d0 70 51 f1 40 df 11 f3 6c 29 6e 7d 5a a6 dc b1
c8 d8 13 1f 57 14 a0 ff 4e d7 de a9 ef 4a 9c b7
```

$e =$ `03`

Public Key:

(Use the same n as the public key)

$d =$

```
84 1d 7f b3 54 81 b9 36 90 b6 39 1f 0d 96 be 78
a2 09 4c 17 47 16 41 56 0c c1 b9 06 28 0a 5b bf
94 a2 00 c8 9a d8 d5 3b 75 11 0a cf 89 fc 23 b0
b2 8a 98 57 df bf 4f 70 61 c5 b0 c7 5c b2 9b 4a
c5 56 70 ff 91 e0 c9 e2 67 25 4e f7 d0 a5 f8 73
f5 ec 07 83 73 24 06 76 ed d8 1e e7 d2 f3 6c 3b
af 1c 0b 3e ba 33 e3 34 08 24 f3 b9 51 20 68 0d
ee a4 e3 e7 42 71 90 a6 20 5e 2e dc 2b 4c c0 db
```

exponent d based on e, p, and q. Then you throw away p and q (see Figure 4-12). Incidentally, finding large primes is easy using the Fermat test (in the 1600s, Pierre de Fermat discovered interesting things about numbers, one of which led to a test of primality). Furthermore, researchers have shown in the Prime Number Theorem that there are more primes of 512 bits or fewer than there are atoms in the known universe. This means that we'll never "run out" of primes, and the probability that two people will pick the same prime are so small that we can safely assume it will never happen.

Suppose that Satomi, our attacker, wants to determine Gwen's private key. If Satomi knows the key, she can open Pao-Chi's digital envelope. She must figure out n and d. Because the public key is, well, public, she knows

Figure 4-12

Generating an RSA public and private key pair

(1) Choose a public exponent

3   17   65,537

(2) Find p, q

Not all primes work with the public exponent you choose; you may have to reject some primes before finding two compatible numbers

p, q

(3) Multiply to get n $n = p \times q$

(4) Find d $e, p, q \longrightarrow$ Extended Euclid

d

(5) Destroy p, q p, q

n because it's part of the public key. So really, all she has to do is figure out d. It turns out that d is simply the inverse of e modulo $\phi(n)$. Satomi knows what e is, so all she has to do is find $\phi(n)$ and perform a modular inverse function. That's very easy to do using the Extended Euclidean Algorithm.

NOTE:

Here's an interesting bit of history. Euclid published his algorithm in about 400 BCE, but researchers have concluded that he didn't invent it. It's believed that the algorithm had been around for about 200 years before Euclid presented it. Who was the true inventor? No one knows, but there is a lesson to be learned from this anonymous mathematician: If you get a good idea, publish!

By the way, $\phi(n)$ is known as Euler's phi-function (ϕ is the Greek letter *phi*, pronounced "fee"). Leonhard Euler (pronounced "Oiler") was an 18th-century mathematician who noticed some interesting things about numbers. For example, if n is the product of those two primes p and q, then $\phi(n)$ is $(p - 1)(q - 1)$. That's "the quantity p minus 1 times the quantity q minus 1" (see the FAQ on the accompanying CD for more details).

So Satomi's problem, which began as "find d" and was reduced to "find $\phi(n)$," has now been further reduced to "find p and q." She knows n and knows that $p \times q = n$, so all she has to do is factor n, which is the hard problem at the foundation of the RSA algorithm.

In other words, in RSA, the one-way function is multiplication. That's right, multiplication. You're probably thinking, "That's not one-way. To reverse multiplication, all you have to do is divide." That's true—if you know what to divide by. But if someone multiplies two numbers and tells you the result, can you determine the original two numbers? That's known as *factoring*, and it happens to be difficult.

Suppose n is 35. What are p and q? That's easy—they're 5 and 7 because $5 \times 7 = 35$. The numbers 5 and 7 are the prime factors of 35. When you break 35 into its prime factors, you're factoring.

Now suppose n is 893. Factor that. (The answer is given in the next paragraph.) If you factored 893, you probably discovered that it was a little more time-consuming than factoring 35. The longer the number, the more time it takes to factor it. Researchers have written computer programs to factor numbers. For those programs, factoring 893 would be trivial. But just as with humans, it takes these programs longer to factor bigger numbers. You can pick a number so big that the amount of time it would take to factor, even for the fastest computers, would be prohibitive.

Remember Satomi's problem? If she finds p and q, she can compute $\phi(n)$. With $\phi(n)$ and e, she can determine d. When she has d, she can open Pao-Chi's digital envelope. Because $p \times q = n$ and because she knows what n is (remember, that's part of the public key), all she has to do is factor n—and that's how factoring can break RSA. (The answer from the preceding paragraph is 19 and 47.) Because the modulus (that's n) is the number Satomi needs to factor, we'll say that the size of the modulus is the size of the RSA key. Hence, an RSA key that uses a modulus of 1,024 bits is a 1,024-bit key.

No one has been able to factor big numbers in a reasonable amount of time. How big is big? Currently, the most commonly used RSA key size is 1,024 bits. The record for factoring (as of December 2000) is 512 bits. In that case, p and q were each 256 bits long. It took a team using 292 off-the-shelf computers a little more than five months to do the job. With a brute force attack, each time you add a bit to the key size, you double the time it takes to break. But with the technique used by the current factoring champions, each time you add a bit to the number, you don't quite double the time to factor. Each added bit makes the program run about 1.035 to 1.036 times longer. So if a 512-bit key is broken in five months, a 1,024-bit key can be broken in about 3 to 30 million years (see Figure 4-13).

Figure 4-13

In a popular 1,024-bit RSA key, the modulus is 1,024 bits, built by multiplying two 512-bit primes

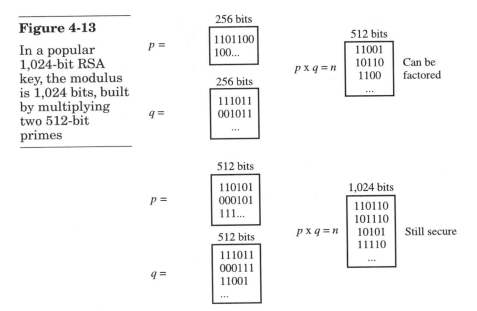

You may wonder why the modulus has to be the product of two primes. Why can't the modulus itself be a prime number? The reason is that for a prime number p, $\phi(p)$ is $(p - 1)$. Because your modulus is public, if the modulus were p, a prime number, any attacker would be able to find $\phi(p)$; it's simple subtraction. Armed with $\phi(p)$, an attacker can easily find d.

Incidentally, Satomi has a couple of brute force opportunities. First, she could try to find d by trying every value it could possibly be. Fortunately, d is a number as big as the modulus. For a 1,024-bit RSA private key, d is 1,024 bits long (maybe a bit or two smaller). No, brute force on d is not an option. A second possibility is to find p or q. Satomi could get a number b (call it b for brute force candidate) and then compute $n \div b$ (n divided by b). If that doesn't work (b does not divide n evenly; there is a remainder), she tries another b. She keeps trying until she finds a b that works (one that divides n evenly). That b will be one of the factors of n. And the answer to $n \div b$ is the other factor. Satomi would then have p and q. But the factors of n are half the size of the modulus (see "Technical Note: MultiPrime RSA"). For a 1,024-bit RSA key, p and q are 512 bits each. So Satomi would be trying a brute force attack on a 512-bit number, and

Technical Note: MultiPrime RSA

Faster performance is always a goal of programmers, so anything that would speed up the RSA algorithm would be welcome. The first speed improvement came in 1982 from Belgian researchers Jean-Jacques Quisquater and C. Couvreur. They showed that it's possible to make private key operations (opening a digital envelope) faster if you keep the p and q around, by using what is known as the *Chinese Remainder Theorem* (CRT). This theorem dates to the fourth century and originated in, as the name implies, China. It's a result of research into how to count columns and columns of soldiers more quickly.

Remember that an RSA private key is made up of the two numbers n and d, where n is built by multiplying two primes, p and q. When you have your d, you throw away p and q. According to the theorem, if you don't throw away your p and q, and if, while generating your key pair, you make a few other calculations and save a few more values, the private key operations you perform can run almost three times faster. The fundamental reason is that p and q are smaller than n (there's more to it than that, but at its foundation, that is the reason). Because p and q must be kept private, this technique will not help public key operations. But, as you'll see in the section "Performance," RSA public key operations are already rather fast. Recently, people have been looking into using three or more primes to make up n. Here's why.

When you multiply two numbers, if you add the sizes of those two numbers you get the size of the result. For example, if you multiply a 512-bit number by a 512-bit number, you get a 1,024-bit number because $512 + 512 = 1{,}024$ (it could end up being 1,023 bits, but let's not quibble). Actually, you could multiply a 612-bit number by a 412-bit number to get a 1,024-bit result, but for security reasons, it's better to have the numbers the same size or very close. Virtually all programs that generate RSA key pairs find two 512-bit primes and multiply them to make n.

If you want a 1,024-bit number as a result of multiplying three smaller numbers, how big should they be? One possibility is 341, 341, and 342 bits. If p and q are each 512 bits, and if private key operations are faster because they are smaller than n (which is

continued

1,024 bits), will operations improve even more if p, q, and r (let's call our third prime r) are smaller still?

The answer is yes. The more primes that make up the modulus, the faster the private key operations run. It's all because of the Chinese Remainder Theorem.

The problem is that the more primes that make up the modulus, the easier it is to factor. More precisely, if "too many" primes make up the modulus, it's easier. How many is too many? That depends on the size of the modulus. The bigger the modulus, the safer it is to use more primes. Using three primes to build a 1,024-bit modulus will not help an attacker; it will take just as long to factor as does a two-prime number. But should you use four primes to generate a 1,024-bit modulus? That may be too dangerous. If your modulus is 2,048 bits, four primes is safe, but five might not be.

Actually, that issue is still under contention. How many primes is it safe to use at various sizes of moduli? Although there is disagreement in some areas, it is widely believed that using three primes is safe for a 1,024-bit modulus. Research continues on the topic.

So if you hear about MultiPrime RSA, you'll know that it has to do with making private key operations faster by using more than two primes to build a modulus.

that's out of the question. Actually, because p and q are primes, they are odd, so the least significant bit is set; and because they are 512 bits long, the most significant bit is also set, so Satomi would know at least 2 of the 512 bits. So it's not brute force on 512 bits but rather on 510—but that's not much better.

The DH Algorithm

The Diffie-Hellman algorithm is not used for encryption, so how can it solve the key distribution problem? After all, don't you have to encrypt the session key to create a digital envelope?

With DH, you don't generate a symmetric session key and distribute it using public-key technology; instead, you use public-key technology to generate the symmetric session key. Each corresponding party possesses a secret value and a public value. If you combine a private value with the other public value, each individual will generate the same secret value (see Figure 4-14).

Figure 4-14

With Diffie-Hellman, you combine your private value with the other party's public value to create a secret. The other party combines his or her private value with your public value and creates the same secret

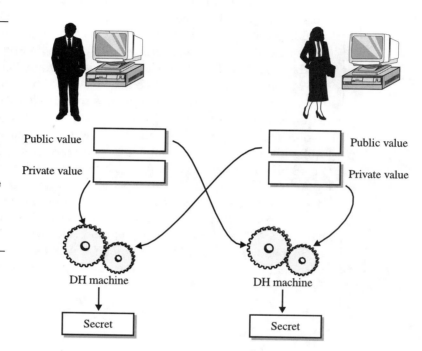

Public value

Private value

Public value

Private value

DH machine

DH machine

Secret

Secret

Here's how Pao-Chi and Gwen would make it work. Gwen has a DH key pair; the public key is (obviously) publicly available, and she keeps her private key someplace where only she has access. Inside Gwen's public key is enough information for Pao-Chi to generate his own temporary DH key pair. Now both of them have a DH key pair (see Figure 4-15). For each of the key pairs, the public and private keys are related. But Pao-Chi's and Gwen's key pairs themselves are also related. Pao-Chi uses his private key and Gwen's public key together to generate a number, called a *secret value*.

To encrypt the bulk data, Pao-Chi needs a session key. Instead of using an RNG or PRNG to generate the key, he uses the secret value result from the DH computations. For Gwen to read the message, though, she needs

Figure 4-15

Pao-Chi generates a temporary DH key pair using the information from Gwen's public key. Now both parties have related key pairs, and each can create the same secret

Pao-Chi

Gwen's public DH key

PRNG

DH machine

Pao-Chi's temporary DH keypair

the session key. Since Pao-Chi used the DH secret value as his session key, that means Gwen needs the secret value. She can generate the secret value using her private key and Pao-Chi's temporary public key, which he sends along with the message (see Figure 4-16).

Figure 4-16

Pao-Chi's message has his public value first followed by the encrypted bulk data

```
VÚvãõœBÕNñÝm_LÂ£

ØCª…K‾BÖ•ˎZÖ=¤
C•°=Mþiðªq¢A
'É‰ọ'RÄ!ä'˜øáS×íXPÚj¡ý
ò~5OÔÐ¦/)zyÆN˙Ù•4
"•£ÙÂôÜlçlWÛÁRéŸC
^ᴺᴺë-Á'‡!_Ôÿ½i%˳÷$÷,ù
^aZww"#Èb¥h}WãÜZà¾
‡Ê†À¨éåÅ94Ç' Ãj—X
û9•3÷ÎO"‡¹Yì•3Æcµ8Y
ýÍ,@³þµ"W<ñëk.bî0Ù
d[0ynG‾k'@ Æÿ,!±Ø¥þu
•$?½VTØ\)•À¼zo"¿œ/
Ý½H›ô×øþs?ÿÆå<óõÉ
"l¶î#†n7©tza›
%° *ðÍflüëcDEhø -äÐ¥#
ë®L—7ûXÄÊ ‡9,ê¢«í
```

Pao-Chi's temporary DH public key

Encrypted bulk data

The Diffie-Hellman algorithm does not encrypt data; instead, it generates a secret. Two parties can generate the same secret and then use it to build a session key for use in a symmetric algorithm. This procedure is called *key agreement*. Two parties are agreeing on a key to use. Another name found in the literature is *key exchange*. That description is not as accurate, but some people use it. It means that two parties perform an exchange, the result of which is a shared key.

But if Pao-Chi and Gwen can generate the secret, why can't Satomi? Satomi knows Gwen's public key and, if she's eavesdropping, Pao-Chi's temporary public key. If she puts those two keys together, what does she have? Nothing useful. The secret appears only when combining a public and a private value (each from a different person). Satomi needs one of the private keys—not both, just one.

A DH public key consists of a generator, a modulus, and public value. The private key is the same modulus along with a private value. As with RSA, cryptographers exercise their creativity to give these numbers more melodious names: g, p, y, and x. The generator is g, the modulus is p, the public value is y, and the private value is x (see Figure 4-17). Here, p is a prime number; note that it's not the product of two or more prime numbers but rather is itself a prime. You generate a key pair by finding the prime p first, then a generator g that works well with your p, and then a random or pseudo-random x. If you combine those numbers using modular exponentiation (see Figure 4-18), you get y.

$$y = g^x \bmod p$$

We have said that there is a way to break all public-key algorithms. That includes DH. Satomi can break DH by deriving one of the private keys from its public partner. Because Satomi needs only one of the private keys, she'll probably go after Gwen's, which has been out there longer (remember, Pao-Chi generates his temporary private key only when he sends the message). Gwen's public key consists of y, g, and p. All Satomi has to do is find x. In the preceding equation, Satomi knows all the values except one. High school algebra describes this as "one equation in one unknown." That's solvable, right?

Yes, it's solvable. It's known as the *discrete log* problem (finally, a more interesting name), and computer programs will solve it. But the longer the p, the more time the computer programs will take—in fact, the same time as it would take to factor. As it happens, the factoring problem and the discrete log problem are related. It's commonly believed that if you solve one you solve them both. So in use, p should be 1,024 bits long.

Figure 4-17

A 1,024-bit DH key pair. The number p is the modulus, g is the generator, y is the public value, and x is the private value

Public Key:

$p =$

```
ab  db  22  1a  70  1f  14  7d  84  7d  18  4d  fe  f2  3e  2a
b1  24  00  05  0e  71  a0  38  d9  cc  3b  fa  6d  07  ac  8b
a4  fd  96  75  70  a0  a9  36  a5  0c  03  04  74  4d  48  df
9f  8f  80  3c  69  68  35  ee  d0  da  14  9c  a5  78  f8  72
0d  f6  79  a7  03  24  10  32  65  36  69  e5  0c  21  72  d5
c3  af  bd  ba  4f  3b  b4  c5  67  ff  e2  db  0f  4f  80  80
a5  a1  2b  1f  69  4a  3e  87  c1  2d  51  cb  5a  80  13  b2
b1  f0  bd  3a  7f  0b  cd  87  9c  62  75  c5  e6  45  2d  75
```

$g =$

```
8e  af  41  2d  ae  f4  89  e7  77  4d  af  f9  cd  d8  8d  32
46  c1  3f  ca  b8  a6  16  04  c8  84  51  19  a8  f9  67  87
f1  13  5c  5c  3c  38  9e  20  e0  93  dd  01  ea  7a  1e  16
e8  96  b5  6c  f1  60  a8  eb  76  c2  c2  42  f5  d8  66  99
ef  cd  0a  a9  dd  42  33  2f  a5  bb  f3  73  e1  9c  62  61
e7  47  fc  14  da  8f  d2  42  4e  d7  e1  57  48  70  d0  c5
6c  dd  4e  e4  2f  5b  92  d4  96  d3  2e  e3  ed  1d  d2  3a
b0  54  b6  3c  a1  f1  e0  7f  ea  ad  68  b2  dd  02  f8  b8
```

$y =$

```
29  0e  a7  68  b8  72  d6  a3  2b  19  9c  46  62  a8  ab  06
9a  11  08  d5  17  08  ef  06  c7  15  2c  09  82  37  01  e6
62  76  30  0e  60  ea  00  5f  69  31  2d  c1  36  f0  0d  16
13  1b  fa  b6  55  26  6d  93  bd  16  73  77  18  4b  7a  b3
d4  37  44  c3  0d  9f  a4  33  0c  f6  ef  d8  89  8d  6d  62
fa  f8  db  7e  d4  0b  b2  e4  a4  03  2c  e2  d7  34  cf  c3
df  fd  62  73  f4  e1  6d  6a  60  8f  01  03  a7  51  21  26
ef  ad  e1  19  e1  2a  d5  6a  74  eb  42  99  f6  0c  50  46
```

Private Key:
(Use the same p as the public key)

$x =$

```
b7  f0  a0  92  0d  87  27  6b  02  47  d7  cb  98  a2  09  02
13  15  aa  39
```

Figure 4-18

Generating a DH
public and
private key pair

(1) Generate a prime

p

(2) Generate a generator
that works well with p

(3) Generate a private
exponent

(4) Compute the public
value y $y = g^x \bmod p$

With RSA, you find two 512-bit primes and multiply them to get a 1,024-bit modulus. With DH, you find one 1,024-bit prime and use it as the modulus.

NOTE:

"Discrete log" doesn't refer to a felled tree that's good at keeping secrets (that would be a "discreet log"). The word "discrete" means that we're working with the math of integers only—no fractions or decimal points— and the word "log" is short for "logarithm."

With RSA, you can't use a single prime as the modulus; you must multiply two primes. But with DH, you use a single prime as the modulus. Why is it that single-prime RSA can be broken but single-prime DH cannot? The answer is that the two algorithms do different things. RSA encrypts data, whereas DH performs key agreement. With RSA, you use a value called d that is dependent on $\phi(n)$. With DH, you don't use d, and you don't mess around with $\phi(n)$.

So Satomi will need a few million years to break Gwen's private key by going the discrete log route. What about brute force—would that work? The private key is really just x, a random or pseudo-random number that can be as long as Gwen wants it to be. If she wants it to be 160 bits, she can make it 160 bits. Then Satomi won't be able to mount a brute force attack on it. Gwen could make x even longer, but the longer it is, the longer it will take her to perform her calculations. So for performance reasons, she wants it as short as possible, and for security reasons, she wants it as long as possible. Today, 160 bits is probably the most common size of x.

The ECDH Algorithm

The first thing to know about Elliptic Curve Diffie-Hellman is what an *elliptic curve* (EC) is, and that's shown in Figure 4-19. This curve is not the only form an EC can take, but it's a common one. Actually, it's not even a cryptographic EC, but when cryptographers talk about EC, they generally show a picture similar to Figure 4-19.

Figure 4-19

An elliptic curve. This also shows EC addition

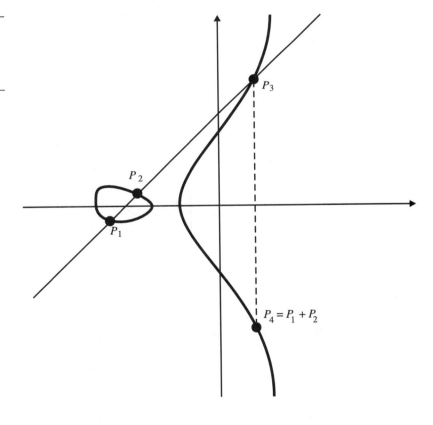

Elliptic curves date to the 1800s. They are actually a form of the Weierstrass equation (a "smooth" Weierstrass equation, to be a little more precise). Karl Weierstrass was a 19th-century mathematician who did pioneering work on number theory. Elliptic curves played a role in the proof of Fermat's Last Theorem and are also involved in factoring.

Cryptographers use only a few of the many flavors of ECs. The curves used by cryptographers fall into two main categories, generally called "odd" and "even." Another way to categorize the types of curves used in crypto is Fp, F2 Polynomial, and F2 Optimal Normal (see Figure 4-20). These latter categories can be broken down to even more classes of curves.

Figure 4-20

Classes of elliptic curves used by cryptographers

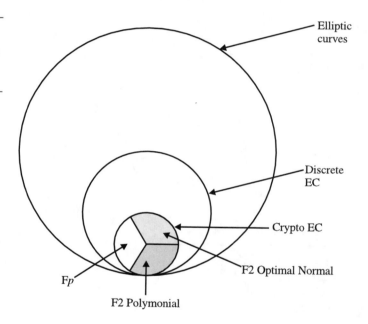

A cryptographic EC is discrete (only integers; no fractions or decimal points). All numbers fall within a certain range. The bigger the range, the more secure the curve; the smaller the range, the faster the computations.

An elliptic curve has *points*; a point is an *x,y*-coordinate. For example, in Figure 4-19, the point labeled $P3$ could also be described as (3,8). The *x*-coordinate is 3, so you start at the origin and go to the right 3 units (the unit—inches, millimeters, or something else—depends on the scale). Then you use the y-coordinate to go up 8 units. The point $P2$ could be $(-6, 1)$: left 6 units (the negative in -6 means left) and up 1 unit. As the figure shows, you can add points on an EC. Notice that it's not an intuitive sense of "adding." You find two points you want to add, draw a line through them, and see where that line intersects the EC. That point is not the solution; the negative of that point is the solution. Why isn't $P3$ the sum of $P1$ and $P2$? Here's why. If you added $P1$ and $P2$ and got $P3$, then what would $P3 - P2$ be? It would be $P1$. But what would $P3 + P2$ be? It would also be $P1$. You can't have $P3 + P2 = P3 - P2$ (unless $P2$ were zero, and it's not). So there's a different set of rules for addition.

The graphical form of elliptic curves (the curve itself, the points, the addition rules, and more) can be described with mathematical equations. You don't deal with pictures; instead you deal only with numbers and equations. And if you're dealing with only numbers and equations, you can write computer programs to do the work. If you have programs that manipulate numbers, maybe you can get crypto. All you need now is a one-way function (with a trap door).

The one-way function is called *scalar multiplication*: You add a point to itself some number of times. We have a point, generally called $P0$ (that's a capital P and a zero; the point is "P − zero"). Add it to itself: $P0 + P0$. Figure 4-19 shows the addition of two distinct points, but there is a way, via another strange rule, to add a point to itself. The special thing about elliptic curves is that if you add a point on the curve to another (or the same) point on the curve, the result is also a point on the curve. If you have an elliptic curve and a point or two on that curve, when you add a point following the special rules you will get another point on that curve—guaranteed. If you have a curve and one or two points on that curve, and the result of adding is not on the curve, it is not an elliptic curve.

So the answer to $P0 + P0$ is another point; let's call it $P1$. Now add $P0$ to that result; let's call it $P2$. $P1 + P0 = P2$. What you've actually done is to find $P0 + P0 + P0$. Another way of saying that is $3 \times P0$. You're multiplying 3, a *scalar* (the mathematical term for a single number), by $P0$, a point (a point cannot be described using a single number; you need two numbers: the x-coordinate and the y-coordinate). You could compute any such scalar multiplication. What's $120 \times P0$? Why, that's $P0$ added to itself 120 times. What's $d \times P0$? That's $P0$ added to itself d times. The result of any scalar multiplication is another point on the curve.

There are shortcuts. If you want to find $120 \times P0$, you don't actually have to do 120 additions; instead, you can use a multiplication program. We just wanted to show you how scalar multiplication is defined.

We said that scalar multiplication is a one-way function. Here's how it works. Suppose you find an elliptic curve (that's not hard to do) and a point on that curve. Cryptographers have again demonstrated their lyrical side by calling the curve E and the point P. You now generate a random or pseudo-random scalar called d. Now you multiply, finding $d \times P$. The answer is some point on the curve; let's call it Q. Now you show the world your curve and those two points; E, P, and Q are publicly available, so the challenge is to find d. That is, if $dP = Q$ inside E, and if you know E, P, and Q, your task is to find d. As with Diffie-Hellman, you have one equation in one unknown.

This is known as the elliptic curve discrete log problem, and, as long as the curve is big enough, no one has found a way to solve it in a reasonable amount of time. Recall that in cryptography, elliptic curves are defined over a specific range. The technical term for this range is *field*. In the three kinds of curves we've mentioned—Fp, F2 polynomial, and F2 optimal normal—the F stands for "field." The p in Fp stands for "prime number." That's a lowercase p, not to be confused with the uppercase P used as the point in the description of the EC discrete log problem (cryptographers sure know how to choose names, don't they?). The 2 in F2 is indeed 2. Actually, it would be more accurate to say F2^m.

If you want to work with an Fp curve, you find a big prime p, and all your calculations will use integers from 0 to $p - 1$. If you want to work in F2^m, choose a size m and all your calculations will use integers from 0 to $2^m - 1$. For more security, you should use a bigger range. But the bigger the range, the slower your computations will be. The most common size is 160 bits to 170 bits.

Here's how Pao-Chi and Gwen would use elliptic curve cryptography (ECC). Gwen generates an EC called E. She finds a point, P, on that curve. Then she generates a random or pseudo-random scalar d and finds $Q = d \times P$. Her public key is E, P, and Q (see Figure 4-21). Her private key is the same curve E coupled with the random or pseudo-random d, which is most likely the same size as the range of the curve.

To send Gwen a message, Pao-Chi gets her public key. It contains enough information for Pao-Chi to generate his own temporary ECDH key pair. Now both correspondents have an ECDH key pair. For each of the key pairs, the public and private keys are related. But Pao-Chi's and Gwen's key pairs themselves are related as well. Pao-Chi uses his private key and Gwen's public key together to generate a secret point on the curve. He uses that secret value somehow as a session key. Because a point is a pair of numbers x and y, the two correspondents will have to decide in advance which bits from those numbers to use as the key. The most common ECDH applications use x), so they just throw away the y (see Figure 4-22).

Figure 4-21

A 160-bit F2 EC key pair. The numbers under E describe an elliptic curve (composed of 2^m field, a, b, order, and cofactor), and P and Q are two points on the curve related by d, a scalar

Public key

$E =$

2^m field =

```
01 00 00 00 00 00 20 00 00 00 00 00 00 00 00 00
00 00 00 00 07
```

$a =$
```
00
```

$b =$
```
0d a9 e3 58 04 7f 39 7a 9d 7a 01 e4 60 67 80 37
e2 38 44 de
```

order =
```
0d a9 e3 58 04 7f 39 7a 9d 7a 01 e4 60 67 80 37
e2 38 44 de
```

cofactor =
```
04
```

$P =$
```
x-coordinate:
52 2f 38 09 b9 4e dc 39 23 f5 23 60 0e 3b 0b 59
7e cd c8 35
y-coordinate:
3c b3 ff 5d 20 40 c5 38 11 4b 73 fa 82 74 f3 b7
92 26 6a e5
```

$Q =$
```
x-coordinate:
ea f6 59 3c 0d 9d e1 de 4b 91 f9 95 e5 26 09 a6
93 23 92 8d
y-coordinate:
df 84 76 34 5a b5 69 3b ba 91 d2 f8 f5 38 6e 07
68 39 f4 49
```

Private key:
(use the same E as the public key)

$d =$
```
32 83 65 87 cc e7 f6 1c 50 1a 72 7d 75 e8 16 d3
bc b2 cb 4e
```

Figure 4-22

Pao-Chi combines
his temporary
private key with
Gwen's public
key to get a
secret point

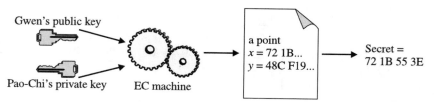

To read the message, Gwen needs the session key. She gets it by combining her private key with Pao-Chi's temporary public key (he sends his temporary public key along with the encrypted message).

This sounds just like Diffie-Hellman. In that scheme, two people combine public and private keys in a special way to generate a shared secret. In this scheme, the same thing is happening. The difference is the underlying math, and that explains the name Elliptic Curve Diffie-Hellman.

To read Pao-Chi's intercepted message, Satomi needs one of the private keys, knowing both of the public keys will not do the trick. To break Gwen's private key (probably Satomi's first choice), Satomi must figure out d. That would require her to solve the EC discrete log problem, something that would take a few million years, so Satomi might try a brute force attack. The problem is that d is the same size as the underlying field. Gwen probably chose a 160-bit or 170-bit EC, meaning that d is also 160 bits to 170 bits, so brute force won't work either.

Remember that RSA and DH were based on related problems, and that's why the key sizes are the same. But with ECC, you use a different key size because the underlying problems are different. And solving the EC discrete log problem is harder than solving the factoring or discrete log problem.

By the way, it's possible to use ECC to do encryption. However, in the real world, it's not used very much for security and performance reasons. Recall that as you increase the key size, you slow down the computations. And for ECES (elliptic curve encryption scheme) or ECRSA to achieve the level of security of regular RSA, you must use bigger keys. The keys need to be so big that you take too big a hit in performance.

Comparing the Algorithms

The three algorithms we've discussed can be used to solve the key distribution problem. Which one is the best? There's probably no answer to that question because each has its advantages and disadvantages. A more appropriate question might be, "Which algorithm works best in which situation?" When you're evaluating each approach, it's a good idea to look at five areas: security, key size, performance, transmission size, and interoperability.

Security

Is one of the algorithms more secure than the others? There's no truly objective answer. It depends on what you think is important.

ECC is based on the EC discrete log problem, which is "harder"; does this mean it's more secure than RSA, which is based on factoring, or DH, which is based on the discrete log problem? Not necessarily.

Thousands of mathematicians have been studying the factoring problem for many years (most intently since 1978). Some of them think that if a solution could have been found, it would have been found by now. On the other hand, it took about 300 years to come up with a proof of Fermat's Last Theorem, so maybe the ultimate factoring solution simply has not yet been found. Considering the enormous bank of research available to build on, finding a solution may become easier over time.

ECC is newer and less well understood. Far fewer researchers have been attacking it, and for a shorter time. Some people think that more time and effort are needed to develop a better sense of security. Furthermore, despite the "lag" in research, some classes of curves have been found to be susceptible to cryptanalysis. Of the many flavors of elliptic curves, not all of them are used in crypto. For some flavors, it was known early that they contained more weaknesses than others and that there were ways to break them faster than security requirements allowed. Such curves have never been proposed for use in crypto. Other flavors that were proposed for such use were later shown to possess weaknesses. All the weaknesses found so far lie in the F2 area. At this point, it's believed that no application has ever been deployed in the real world with a weak EC. But because some curves have fallen, some cryptographers are not confident in F2 ECC, and others do not trust any curve at all—Fp or F2.

Some people prefer RSA because DH and ECDH are susceptible to the man-in-the-middle attack. In our sales rep example, the potential attacker is a woman in the middle, Satomi. She could intercept all messages between Pao-Chi and Gwen, establishing DH or ECDH keys with each of them. Pao-Chi would think he's computing a shared secret key with Gwen but would really be computing one with Satomi. Similarly, Gwen would compute a shared secret key with Satomi, thinking she was talking with Pao-Chi. Then if Pao-Chi sent a message to Gwen, only Satomi would be able to decrypt it. She would decrypt it, store the message, reencrypt it with the key she established with Gwen, and send it on (see Figure 4-23). The man-in-the-middle attack is easily thwarted by using authentication along with the key exchange (Chapter 5 discusses authentication), and most protocols include authentication anyway. So for some people, this attack is no real disadvantage.

Another issue is each correspondent's ability to contribute to the key. With RSA, only the initiator of the contact has any say in what the session key will be. With DH or ECDH, both parties contribute to generating the session key. Each correspondent performs some operations and sends the result to the other; the final secret depends on each individual's contribution. For some people, this arrangement sounds better than trusting someone else entirely to generate a good key. For others, it's not a great feature. After all, they argue, another party who would do a bad job of generating a session key probably wouldn't do any better with the key exchange.

So, the choice of algorithm is a matter of your own feeling of security. At this time, no honest cryptographer can make a definitive statement about which algorithm is more secure.

Figure 4-23

The man-in-the-middle attack

Key Sizes

The bigger the key, the greater the level of security and the slower any public-key algorithm will run. You want the algorithm to run as fast as possible but maintain a particular level of security. The question is, how low can you go before you jeopardize security? The conventional wisdom is that a 1,024-bit RSA or DH key is equivalent in security to a 160-bit ECC key. There is a little contention on that issue, but research continues. In this book, when making comparisons, we look at 1,024-bit RSA or DH, and 160-bit ECC. With RSA, the modulus is made up of three primes; with DH, the private value is 160 bits.

In April 2000, RSA Labs published a paper that analyzed how long it would take to break the RSA algorithm at various key sizes if an attacker had $10 million to throw at the problem. Table 4-1 summarizes the research; the symmetric key and ECC key columns are there for comparison. With ECC, you could probably get the same results with smaller key

Table 4-1	Symmetric Key (Size in Bits)	ECC Key (Size in Bits)	RSA Key (Size in Bits)	Time to Break	Number of Machines	Amount of Memory
Time to Break Keys of Various Sizes with $10 Million to Spend	56	112	430	Less than 5 minutes	105	Trivial
	80	160	760	600 months	4,300	4GB
	96	192	1,020	3 million years	114	170GB
	128	256	1,620	10^{16} years	0.16	120TB

sizes. However, the assumption in the report is that the public key algorithm should use a key size at least twice as long as the symmetric key (regardless of performance) for security reasons.

The table says that with $10 million, an attacker could buy 105 specially made computers to crack a 56-bit symmetric key, a 112-bit ECC key, or a 430-bit RSA key in a few minutes. Actually, that $10 million would probably buy more than 105 machines, but 105 is all it would take. With the same amount of money, at the next key level the attacker could buy 4,300 machines specially built to solve the problem; at the next key level, 114, and at the next level, 0.16.

Why does the money buy fewer machines as the key size increases? The reason is that the amount of required memory increases. The base computer is the same, but to break bigger keys, the attacker needs more memory (120 terabytes, or about 120 trillion bytes, in the case of a 1,620-bit RSA key), and buying memory would eat up the budget. In fact, the attacker will probably need more than $10 million to break a 1,620-bit RSA key because that amount of money would only buy 0.16, or about 1/6, of a machine.

Performance

If no algorithm wins on security, you might think that you should choose the fastest one. But there is no simple answer there. Comparing the performance of the public key operations (initiating the contact, or creating the digital envelope) shows that RSA is significantly faster than ECC, which in turn is faster than DH. For the private key operations (receiving the contact or opening the digital envelope), ECC is somewhat faster than DH, and both are faster than RSA.

For many machines, though, the difference in performance is negligible. The two times might be 0.5 milliseconds and 9 milliseconds. Even though one algorithm may be 18 times faster, there's no discernible difference between times that are that fast. But if the processor performing the action is a slow device, such as a smart card, a Palm device, or other hand-held device, the difference might be 0.5 seconds versus 9 seconds. Or maybe one of the correspondents is a server that must make many connections, maybe several per second. Then the comparison might be 111 per second versus 2,000 per second.

Another factor with ECC is whether you use acceleration tables to speed the private key operations. If you do, you must store extra values in addition to your key. Those extra values amount to about 20,000 bytes. If the device is a server, that's no problem—but will a smart card or hand-held device have that kind of storage space?

So the most suitable algorithm depends on which is more important—public-key or private-key operations—in your application. Table 4-2 lists estimates from RSA Security Engineering on the relative performance of the two algorithms. The baseline is an RSA public-key operation, which is 1 unit. As shown in the table, if a particular computer can create an RSA digital envelope in 1 millisecond, it would take that same computer 13 milliseconds to open it. Or it would take that same computer 18 milliseconds to initiate an ECDH exchange and 2 milliseconds to receive one using acceleration tables.

Table 4-2 Estimated Relative Performance of the Public-Key Algorithms		RSA	DH	ECC	ECC with Acceleration
	Public key (initiate contact)	1	32	18	
	Private key (receive message)	13	16	6	2
	Combined	14	48	24	20

Transmission Size

What if the amount of money it costs or the time it takes to transmit bits across the wire (or in the air) is significant? It turns out that the algorithms differ in the size of the transmission. With RSA and DH, transmission size is the same as the key size. With ECC, you send twice the key size. So using a 1,024-bit RSA or DH key pair means that each time you send a digital envelope, you're adding 1,024 bits to the message. With a 160-bit ECC key, you're adding 320 bits.

Interoperability

With symmetric-key crypto, if you want to make sure that someone else can decrypt your ciphertext, you should use DES, Triple DES, or AES. Any correspondents who have crypto will have those algorithms. You may want to use RC4 or RC5 because they're faster, but to ensure interoperability, you might choose the algorithm you know everyone has.

Can the same be said in the public-key world? For the most part, yes. RSA is almost ubiquitous and has become the de facto standard. If you send an RSA digital envelope, the recipient will almost certainly be able to read it, whether or not your correspondent uses the same application you do. With DH, there's a good chance that the other party will have the necessary code, but it's not as widespread. ECC is even less prevalent than DH. Most applications using ECC today are closed, meaning that they talk only to themselves. The vast majority of those are in the United States. You will find very little ECC used in Europe.

Another problem with ECC and interoperability is that the flavors of curves (Fp and F2) are not interoperable. If you have code that does Fp and your correspondent has code that does F2, you can't talk to each other. In the future, the interoperability issue may go away for ECC if more people adopt it and the world settles on a single class. But until that time, your best bet is to use RSA.

Protecting Private Keys

Throughout this chapter, we emphasize the importance of keeping a private key private. How do you do that? The quick answer is that most of the techniques mentioned in Chapter 3 for protecting session keys apply to private keys.

For example, suppose you want a key pair. You'll most likely run a program that generates it for you. You make the public key available to the world, and you store the private key on your computer. Of course, simply storing data on your computer is not safe, so you'll probably store it encrypted, using password-based encryption. When you run the program that uses the private key (for example, when you receive some encrypted e-mail), it loads the data. You enter your password, the program uses it to decrypt the key, and now you can open the envelope.

You can also store the private key on a smart card or other token. The card will generate the key pair and return the public key for you to distribute, but it probably won't allow the private key to leave the device. To open an envelope, you give the token the encrypted session key (if you're using RSA) or the sender's temporary public key (if you're using DH or ECDH). The token performs the private key operation and returns the session key to you. For servers, crypto accelerators might be used. They behave the same way as tokens except that they're much faster.

Using the Digital Envelope for Key Recovery

If you lose your car key, you can often call a dealer in the area who can make a new one. If you lose your house key, you can call a locksmith who can create a new one. If you lose a cryptographic key, there's no one to call. It's gone. That's why many companies implement a key recovery plan.

When Pao-Chi generates a symmetric key to encrypt his files or generates a public/private key pair to be used for key distribution, he stores the symmetric and private keys in such a way that only he can recover them. If he has a key recovery plan, though, he also creates copies of the keys and stores them in such a way that someone else can recover them. In addition, it is possible to store them so that it takes more than one person to recover the keys. In that way, no one single individual can surreptitiously recover the keys and examine Pao-Chi's secret information.

The most common form of key recovery is the RSA digital envelope. Pao-Chi has a software program that encrypts his files. It generates a symmetric session key and uses that key to encrypt each file. He then stores that key securely, possibly using PBE or a token. At the time the session key is generated, he also encrypts it using the key recovery RSA public key (see Figure 4-24). This arrangement is essentially a digital envelope. If Pao-Chi loses his key, the owner of the key recovery private key can open the digital envelope and retrieve Pao-Chi's encrypting session key.

There are three basic entities that can act as a *key recovery agent*:

- A trusted third party
- A group of trustees, each holding a portion of the key
- A group of trustees using a threshold scheme

Figure 4-24

Pao-Chi encrypts his session key with the key recovery public key, storing that digital envelope for emergencies

Key Recovery via a Trusted Third Party

Earlier in this chapter in the section titled "Using a Trusted Third Party," you met Michelle, a TTP who creates session keys for Gwen and Pao-Chi. Now Michelle is going to be their key recovery agent. Michelle generates her RSA key pair and distributes the public key to each individual who will participate in the key recovery program. Pao-Chi's software, for example, can have that public key built-in. When he generates his keys (the session key or public/private key pair), he encrypts them with this public key. He could send this digital envelope to Michelle, but he probably prefers to keep it himself. In that way, Michelle cannot open the envelope without his knowledge. Michelle is a trusted third party, but Pao-Chi's trust in her has some limit. Hence, he will probably store the digital envelope on a floppy disk and keep the disk in his locked desk drawer. Then if Pao-Chi forgets a password, loses his smart card, has a hard drive failure, and so on, and needs to recover a key, he takes the digital envelope to Michelle. She opens it using her RSA private key and gives Pao-Chi the output, namely his key. After he uses the key, Pao-Chi again protects the key.

The Difference Between Key Recovery and Key Escrow

Many elements of cryptography go by different names. There's "symmetric-key" crypto, which is also known as "secret-key" crypto. "Asymmetric-key" crypto also goes by the name of "public-key" crypto, and the terms "message digest" and "hash" (see Chapter 5) are often interchangeable. Now we come to an area of crypto-key recovery and key escrow—in which two terms appear to describe the same thing but are actually significantly different.

Key recovery and key escrow are not the same thing. *Key recovery* is a method that's implemented to restore keys that get lost. *Key escrow* is the practice of giving keys to a third party so that the third party can read sensitive material on demand. "Key escrow" is almost always used to describe a way for governments to obtain keys in order to collect evidence for investigations.

Consider the analogy of your house key. With key recovery, if you lose your key, you hire a locksmith to create a new one. With key escrow, the day you buy the house, you surrender a copy of the key to the police so that they can enter your house when they want to, possibly without your knowledge.

This book is not concerned with the political or practical implications of key escrow. It is our intention only to point out the difference between the two terms. The actual techniques used to implement key recovery and proposed key escrow plans are often the same. So for the rest of this chapter, we describe key recovery schemes.

The advantage of this system is that recovering the key is easy. The disadvantage is that Michelle has access to all the keys. It is possible for her to recover keys without anyone's knowledge. Another disadvantage is that Pao-Chi must depend on Michelle. What does he do when she is away on vacation? What does the company do if she leaves for another job? In that case, the company will have to get a new TTP, generate a new key recovery key pair, distribute the new public key, and have everyone create new digital envelopes with all their keys.

Key Recovery via a Group of Trustees

Some companies and individuals do not like the idea of one person having access to all keys. In such situations, a better scheme is to break the key into parts and distribute them among several individuals. Suppose those individuals are the company's TTPs—Michelle and Alexander—and Gwen, the VP of sales. Now Pao-Chi's software comes preloaded with three public keys. Each of his keys is broken into three parts, and three digital envelopes are created. For example, Pao-Chi has a 128-bit symmetric key that he uses to encrypt the files on his hard drive; this key is separated into three blocks of five bytes, five bytes, and six bytes. Michelle's public key protects five of the bytes, Alexander's protects another five, and Gwen's protects the last six. Now if Pao-Chi needs to recover his key, all three trustees must gather to reconstruct the data.

The advantage here is that no one individual can recover keys secretly. For keys to be recovered surreptitiously, all three trustees would have to agree to subvert the system, a scenario less likely to occur than if only one individual possessed the ability to recover keys.

The scheme as described here has a problem. Because each trustee has a portion of the key, it would be possible for an individual to recover the known portion and then perform a brute force attack on the rest. Gwen has the largest portion—six bytes (48 bits)—so her task would be equivalent to breaking an 80-bit key. Such an attack is not likely, but it would be better if that avenue were closed.

One way around this problem is to create a 384-bit value and split that into three 128-bit components. Each trustee knows 128 bits but is missing 256 bits of the total value. The 384-bit value is actually used to derive the key. That is, Pao-Chi generates a 384-bit value and uses it as a seed for a PRNG. The PRNG produces the session key. Each trustee gets a portion of the 384-bit value. To recover the key, you must put all three of the trustees' components together and re-create the PRNG (see Figure 4-25).

This splitting of the secret into multiple digital envelopes has the advantage of preventing one individual from wielding too much power. But it has the disadvantage of being more difficult to implement and also carries all the disadvantages of the TTP approach: If one trustee is on vacation, the key is still lost. Furthermore, if one trustee leaves the company, the key recovery process must start over from scratch, new public/private key pairs have to be generated and public keys distributed, and all employees must create new digital envelopes.

Figure 4-25

Pao-Chi creates a 128-bit session key using a 384-bit seed value and splits the 384-bit value into three portions, encrypting each portion with one trustee's public key. Recovering the session key means recovering the 384-bit value and recreating the PRNG

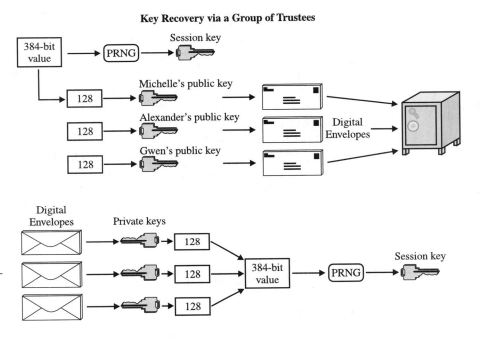

Key Recovery via a Group of Trustees

Key Recovery via Threshold Schemes

Probably the most common key recovery method involves *threshold schemes,* also called *secret sharing* or *secret splitting*. A secret, such as a key, is split into several shares, some number of which must be combined to recover the secret. For example, a secret can be split into 6 shares, any 3 of which can be combined to reproduce the value. Or the secret can be split among 10 shares, any 4 of which can recover the item, or 12 shares with a threshold of 11, or 5 shares with a threshold of 5, or 100 shares with a threshold of 2. Almost any reasonable share and recovery count is possible (as long as the threshold is less than or equal to the share count). For key recovery, the secret is an RSA private key.

If Pao-Chi's company implements a threshold scheme, it might work like this. The company decides how many shares there will be, how many are needed to implement key recovery, and who the trustees will be. Suppose the policy is for six trustees and three shares needed. The trustees are a system or network administrator, the HR director, and representatives from several departments. Say the sys admin is Warren, the HR director is Maria, Gwen represents sales and marketing, the shipping department sends Daniel, Julia comes from engineering, and Michelle is the key recovery administrator.

To start the process, all the trustees gather to generate and collect shares. First, an RSA key pair is generated. Then the threshold program splits the private key into six shares, with each trustee getting one share (see Figure 4-26). The program generating the shares takes as input the private key, the number of shares (six), and the threshold count (three) and produces as output six shares. It's up to the trustees to protect their shares, although the company probably has a policy that defines the procedure. They can simply use PBE on the shares and store them on floppy disks, or they can store them on smart cards or other tokens. After the shares are generated and distributed, the public key is distributed and the private key is destroyed.

Figure 4-26

An RSA key pair is generated, and each trustee gets one share of the private key, which is then destroyed

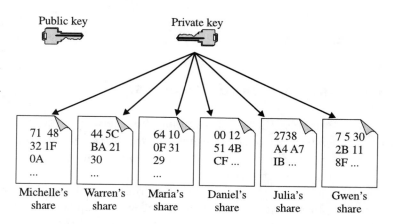

Key Recovery via Threshold Schemes

Now employees can copy their keys (symmetric encryption keys, key exchange or digital enveloping keys) and encrypt them using the key recovery public key.

Suppose Pao-Chi encrypts sensitive files on his hard drive and keeps the key on a token. Furthermore, suppose he participates in the key recovery and has created a digital envelope of his session key using the key recovery public key. He keeps that digital envelope on a floppy in his desk drawer. Now suppose he loses his token. How can he recover his data?

To recover the data, Pao-Chi takes the floppy containing the digital envelope to Michelle, the key recovery administrator. If Michelle is out that day, he could take it to Warren, the system administrator, or Gwen, the VP of sales, or any of the other trustees. The trustee he visits must then find two other trustees. The combination of trustees might be Warren, Daniel and Julia, or Maria, Daniel, and Julia. Maybe it would be Warren, Maria, and Gwen, or if Michelle were there that day it could be Michelle, Gwen and Daniel. It doesn't matter; the scheme needs three trustees.

The three trustees give their shares to the program running the threshold algorithm, and the program combines them to produce the secret, which in this case is an RSA private key. Now that the private key is reconstructed, Pao-Chi's digital envelope can be opened. The result is the session key he needs to decrypt the data on his hard drive (see Figure 4-27).

Figure 4-27

Three trustees combine their shares to reproduce the key recovery private key

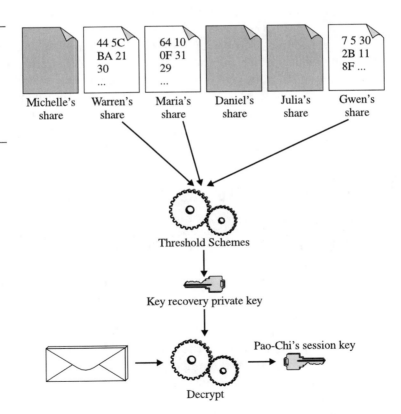

The threshold scheme has many advantages over the key recovery programs described earlier, and it eliminates some of the disadvantages. First, no one person can recover keys; it takes a group acting together. Anyone attempting to be dishonest must find some co-conspirators. Second, if one of the trustees is unavailable, it's still possible to perform the operation. Third, if one of the trustees leaves the company, the secret is still safe, and there's no need to restart the key recovery process from the beginning.

A disadvantage is that if one trustee leaves the company, his or her share is still valid. By itself, this share can't do anything, but if a threshold number of people leave the company, this group of unauthorized people would have the power to recover the company's secrets. For example, suppose that Warren, Maria, and Julia leave the company, either all at once or over a period of time. They might form their own company, start working for another firm, or work for different companies. If the three of them decide to steal their former employer's secrets, they could re-create the key recovery private key.

Of course, that private key won't do them any good without the digital envelopes protecting the session keys of all the employees. So if they want to steal secrets, they still have to find the floppy disks or tokens storing the encrypted session keys. But a company that wants to eliminate such an attack would generate a new key pair and restart the key recovery program from scratch. Fortunately, with a threshold scheme, this step is not necessary every time a trustee leaves but only when several of them leave.

How a Threshold Scheme Works

One of the first threshold algorithms was developed in 1979 by Adi Shamir (the S in RSA). It's probably the easiest to understand.

Consider the case of a key recovery scheme that uses three shares with a threshold of two—that is, three shares are created, any two of which can recover the secret. You can think of the secret as a point on an (x, y) graph. Any point on the graph can be represented by two numbers: the x-coordinate and the y-coordinate. In Figure 4-28, the secret is the point $(0, S)$. For the Shamir algorithm, the secret is always a point on the y-axis. So let's consider the secret a number, call it S, and then use the point $(0, S)$.

Now you generate a random or pseudo-random line that runs through that point. Next, you find three random or pseudo-random points on that line. In Figure 4-28, these points—the shares—are labeled S1, S2, and S3.

Figure 4-28

The Shamir
threshold scheme

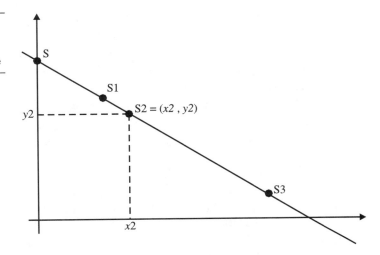

To recover the secret, you take two of the points and find the line that runs through them. You might recall from high school algebra that any two points uniquely define a line. With the line just created, you next determine where it crosses the y-axis. That's the secret. It doesn't matter which points are used: S1 and S2, or S1 and S3, or S2 and S3. Each pair of points generates the same line. If your scheme uses more than three shares, you simply find additional random or pseudo-random points on the line. To create a line, however, you need at least two points. One point is not enough because an infinite number of lines can run through any single point. Which one is the correct line? It's impossible to tell, and that's why one share alone won't recover the secret.

If you use a threshold of three, instead of a line, the algorithm generates a parabola (a curve of degree 2) that intersects the y-axis at the secret. Any three points on a parabola uniquely define it, so any three shares (points on the parabola) can re-create the curve. With the curve, if you find the point where it intersects the y-axis, you find the secret. For any threshold count, then, you simply generate a random curve of the appropriate degree (the degree of the curve will be 1 less than the threshold count) that intersects the y-axis at the secret. Each share will be a random point on that curve. Of course, a program executing the Shamir algorithm will not do this graphically; instead, it will do all the work using math equations.

Summary

To solve the key distribution problem, you can use public-key cryptography. With the RSA algorithm, the data encrypted by the public key can be decrypted only by the private key. To securely transmit the session key, you can use a digital envelope. With Diffie-Hellman or Elliptic Curve Diffie-Hellman, you can use public-key technology to generate a shared secret. Only the correspondents can create this secret value, which can then be used as a session key.

Each of the three algorithms has its advantages and disadvantages, so it's not really possible to say that one or the other is better. But any one algorithm may be better suited for a specific application.

It's possible to lose cryptographic keys by forgetting a PBE password, losing the token where they're stored, and so on. In addition, a company may want to be able to recover material encrypted by an employee who, for example, has left the firm. For these reasons, many organizations implement a key recovery plan. Generally, key recovery involves the use of an RSA digital envelope, encrypting keys with a recovery agent's public key. The key recovery agent might be an individual or a group of trustees. Threshold schemes offer an attractive means of implementing key recovery with checks and balances. With a threshold algorithm (also known as secret sharing or secret splitting), a secret such as an RSA private key is split into a number of shares. To recover the secret, a minimum number of shares must be collected. This method prevents one individual from obtaining keys surreptitiously, while making it possible to reconstruct the keys even if one or more trustees is absent.

Real-World Example

The S/MIME (Secure/Multipurpose Internet Mail Extensions) standard specifies a way to encrypt e-mail. MIME is a widely adopted e-mail standard, and S/MIME is an extension that adds encryption.

S/MIME solves the key distribution problem by using RSA digital envelopes. If your e-mail package is S/MIME-enabled, you can create a digital envelope. All you need to do is get your correspondent's public key and flip the switch to encrypt the message.

If you send e-mail through Netscape Communicator, for example, you can use S/MIME. Here's how. First, launch the Netscape browser. Click the Security button and then click Messenger (along the left-hand column). You'll get a window that looks like the one in Figure 4-29. Click the option Encrypt Mail Messages, When It Is Possible. (The signing options are the topic of Chapter 5.) To encrypt a message, you need to select your correspondent's public key, which you'll find inside a certificate. If you don't already have the certificate, you can search for it in a directory (see Figure 4-30). To get to this menu, click Security Info. Under Certificates (along the left-hand column in the resulting window), click People. Then click Search Directory. After you select the public key, any e-mail you send to that individual will be encrypted using a digital envelope.

If you use Microsoft Outlook 98, click Tools, then Options, and then the Security tab. You'll see a window that looks like the one in Figure 4-31. As with the Communicator program, there is an option to encrypt outgoing messages. Again, you'll need the other party's public key to do that.

Chapter 6 talks about certificates and their directories. For now, you can see that applications today are using public key cryptography to solve the key distribution problem.

Figure 4-29

Netscape
Communicator's
menu for
encrypting e-mail
using S/MIME

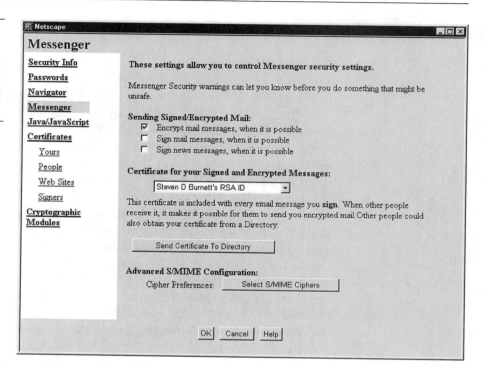

Figure 4-30

A Netscape
Communicator
menu for finding
a public key to
use when
creating the
digital envelope

Figure 4-31

The S/MIME
menu in
Microsoft
Outlook 98

CHAPTER 5

The Digital Signature

Public-key cryptography helps to solve the key distribution problem. It also addresses two other cryptography issues: authentication and nonrepudiation. Authentication allows someone in the electronic world to confirm data and identities, and nonrepudiation prevents people from going back on their electronic word. One way to implement these features is to use a digital signature.

When you use the RSA algorithm, it means that anything encrypted with the public key can be decrypted only with the private key. What would happen if you encrypted plaintext with a private key? Is that possible? And if so, which key would you use to decrypt? It turns out that RSA works from private to public as well as public to private. So you can encrypt data using the private key, and in that case, only the public key can be used to decrypt the data (see Figure 5-1).

You may ask, "What good is that?" After all, if you encrypt data with your private key, anyone can read it because your public key, which is publicly available, can be used to decrypt it. It's true that using RSA in this direction does not let you keep secrets, but it is a way to vouch for the contents of a message. If a public key properly decrypts data, then it must have been encrypted with the private key. In the crypto community, this technique is conventionally called a *digital signature*. If we didn't "all" agree to call it a digital signature, it wouldn't be, it would be just an interesting exercise in math and computer science. But the crypto community

Figure 5-1

If you encrypt
plaintext with an
RSA private key,
you can use the
public key to
decrypt it

called it such, the rest of the computer community (hardware and software vendors) have agreed to this nomenclature, and governments are starting to come on board. At the state and national level, laws are being passed that declare a digital signature as a legally binding way to sign documents. This means that anything you encrypt with your private key is a digital signature. So you shouldn't go around encrypting things with your private key unless you're willing to vouch for them.

The Uniqueness of a Digital Signature

Suppose Pao-Chi sells four printing presses to Satomi and must now communicate the sale to the home office. He sends a message to Daniel in the shipping office:

```
Daniel, I sold 4 presses to Satomi. Ship immediately.
```

Pao-Chi can send this e-mail using a digital envelope (see Chapter 4), and only Daniel can read it. But how can Daniel know that this message really came from Pao-Chi and not someone posing as him? For all Daniel knows, Satomi sent that message, maybe she's trying to get four printing presses shipped to her for free. In the paper world, you can look at the signature on a document. Generally, everyone has a unique way of writing his or her name, a way that is supposed to be hard to forge. If Pao-Chi and Daniel have corresponded by paper in the past, Daniel can probably spot the difference between Pao-Chi's signature and a fake, but with e-mail, there's no such signature.

Pao-Chi could encrypt the plaintext (his e-mail) using his RSA private key, producing ciphertext. Daniel could then use Pao-Chi's public key on the ciphertext. If the result of that decryption were gibberish, Daniel would know it was not encrypted using Pao-Chi's private key and would figure Pao-Chi did not send it (see Figure 5-2). Sure, it's possible that the message came from Pao-Chi and that he actually encrypted it using some key other than his private key. But why would he do that? What would he accomplish? No—he's trying to prove to Daniel that he did indeed send the e-mail and that the contents have not been altered along the way. Daniel can safely conclude that Pao-Chi did not send that message.

Figure 5-2

If Pao-Chi's public key produces gibberish, it means the ciphertext was not encrypted with his private key

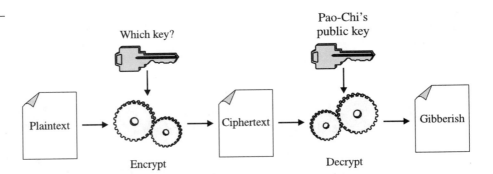

If, on the other hand, using Pao-Chi's public key produces a reasonable message, it must be that his private key was used to encrypt the plaintext. Is it possible that someone other than Pao-Chi produced a chunk of data that looks like ciphertext and, when "decrypted" with Pao-Chi's public key, produces a reasonable message (see Figure 5-3)? As far as we know, no one has yet been able to do that. So we say there is only one way to produce

Figure 5-3

(A) Pao-Chi's digital signature is encrypted using his private key and verified by decrypting with his public key. (B) If the plaintext is encrypted using a different key, can the resulting ciphertext be decrypted with Pao-Chi's public key? (C) Is it possible to perform some operation on the plaintext, possibly using Pao-Chi's public key as a guide, and produce correct ciphertext?

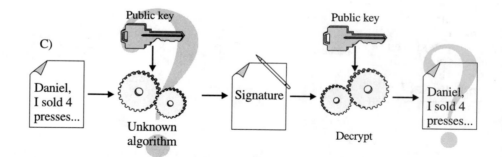

the ciphertext: Start with the plaintext, and encrypt it with the private key. Because the message was encrypted using Pao-Chi's private key and because we're assuming that Pao-Chi is the only person with access to his private key, it must have come from him. Because it must have come from him, we can call the ciphertext a digital signature. A signature is a way of vouching for the contents of a message—of saying, "Yes, I'm the one who wrote it." In addition, a digital signature lets you check that the data has not been altered.

Digital signatures depend on two fundamental assumptions: first, that the private key is safe and only the owner of the key has access to it, and second, that the only way to produce a digital signature is to use the private key. The first assumption has no technical answer except that keys must be protected (for details, see Chapter 3). But the second assumption can be examined from a mathematical point of view. Is it possible to show that a signature is unique?

Figure 5-3a shows the path that data takes to become a digital signature and to be verified. Is it possible to send data on another path that ends up at the same place? An attacker might want to start with the plaintext, encrypt it with a key other than the true private key, and still produce the correct ciphertext (Figure 5-3b). Or maybe the attacker would try to perform some other operation on the plaintext (not regular RSA encryption), possibly using the public key as a guide, and still produce the correct ciphertext (Figure 5-3c). If that were possible, a digital signature would not be unique. If it were not unique, it would not be possible to claim that the owner of the private key is vouching for the plaintext.

The best that cryptographers can say is that no one knows of any such successful attack. The literature contains phrases such as "computationally infeasible," "it is believed to be true," and "for some classes of signatures, it is possible to prove certain security properties." But no one has completely proven signature uniqueness for any signature scheme. Researchers have spent countless hours trying to come up with alternative paths to break uniqueness, and no one has yet come close.

Message Digests

Because public-key crypto is slow (see Chapter 4), it's not a good idea to encrypt the entire plaintext. Imagine creating an e-mail message, encrypting it using the sender's private key, then encrypting the result with a session key (so that eavesdroppers cannot read it), and then encrypting the session key with the recipient's public key. Such a procedure wouldn't be very efficient, and performance would suffer. So instead of encrypting the entire plaintext with the private key, the best method is to encrypt a representative of the data.

The representative of data in cryptography is a *message digest,* a concept we've mentioned in earlier chapters without defining in detail. We said we would talk about it later, and this is finally the time to describe the details. So for the moment, we're going to take a detour from digital signatures to explain message digests.

Probably the best way to begin a description of what a message digest is would be to give two examples. Here are two messages and their associated SHA-1 digests (SHA-1 is generally pronounced "shaw one").

```
message 1:
    Daniel, I sold 4 presses to Satomi. Ship immediately.
SHA-1 digest:
    46 73 a5 85 89 ba 86 58 44 ac 5b e8 48 7a cd 12
    63 f8 c1 5a

message 2:
    Daniel, I sold 5 presses to Satomi. Ship immediately.
SHA-1 digest:
    2c db 78 38 87 7e d3 1e 29 18 49 a0 61 b7 41 81
    3c b6 90 7a
```

The first thing you notice about these digest samples is that even though the messages are 53 bytes long (each character, including spaces and punctuation marks, is 1 byte), the digests are only 20 bytes. The word "digest" means to condense or to reduce and sure enough, we've taken a 53-character message and condensed it to 20 bytes. No matter what you give to SHA-1, the result will be 20 bytes. Is your data 10,000 characters? The result of SHA-1 will be 20 bytes. Do you have a 200MB message? SHA-1 will produce a 20-byte digest. Even if your message is smaller than 20 bytes, the result of SHA-1 will be 20 bytes.

The second thing to notice about the digests is that they "look random." The bytes appear to be gibberish—a bunch of bits thrown together haphazardly. In fact, you could test the results of digests for randomness (recall that discussion in Chapter 2). Tests of randomness need plenty of input, so you could digest lots of different things, string them all together, and see what the tests say. It turns out that the product of message digests passes tests of randomness. Of course, a digest is not truly random. If you digest the same thing twice using the same algorithm, even on two different computers using two different software packages (assuming they've both implemented the algorithm correctly), you'll always get the same result. So the output of a message digest algorithm is pseudo-random. This is why message digests are often the foundation of PRNGs and PBE.

The third thing about the digests is that even though our sample message 2 is almost identical to message 1 (there's really only a 1-bit difference between the two), the digests are dramatically different. That's a quality of a good digest algorithm: If you change the input, you change the output. Two messages that are very similar will produce two digests that are not even close.

So what is a message digest? It's an algorithm that takes any length of input and mixes the input to produce a fixed-length, pseudo-random output. Another word you'll often see used for message digest is *hash*. In fact, the algorithm name SHA-1 stands for *Secure Hash Algorithm*. (The original SHA was shown to be weak, so the designers improved it and called the updated version SHA-1 or SHA1.) The word "hash" can mean a jumble or hodgepodge, which aptly describes the result of a message digest.

Other properties of good digest algorithms aren't as easy to see. First, you can't reconstruct the message from the digest. Here's a suggestion. Have a friend create a message, digest it, and give you the result. Now try to figure out the message. If your friend used a good digest algorithm, that won't be possible. Sure, you could do a brute force attack by trying every possible message, digesting it, and seeing whether it matches. If you did that, you would eventually find it. But your friend's message is one of a virtually infinite number of possible messages. In Chapter 2, you saw how long it would take to find a 128-bit value; imagine how long it would take to find a message that could be of any possible length? For good algorithms, no one has yet been able to figure out the message from only the digest. In other words, it's a one-way function. Remember that Chapter 4 talked about one-way functions with trap doors. A message digest has no trap door.

Another property of a good digest algorithm is that you can't find any message that produces a particular digest. You've seen that you can't find *the* message your friend used to produce the digest, but can you find *any* message that will produce the value? No one has yet come up with a method that can find a message that will produce a given digest.

The last property is that you can't find two messages that produce the same digest. Here, you're not looking for a particular digest but rather two messages that produce the same result, whatever that result may be. Again, with good algorithms, no one has yet been able to do that. The brute force attack would be to digest a message, save the message and result in a table, digest another message, compare it to the first one, and save the result in the table, and then digest another message, compare it to all previously saved values, and so on. Figure 5-4 illustrates these properties with a challenge: Find the message, or any message, and produce the given digest.

Figure 5-4

Can you find the message we used to produce this digest (or any message that will produce it)? If so, you will have found a collision in SHA-1

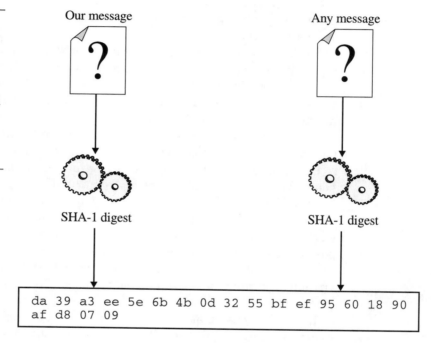

NOTE:

By the way, you probably already know this, but for the sake of completeness, let's say it. A "message" is not necessarily a communication between two people. Any data you give to a digest algorithm is a message, even if it's not in human-readable form. Each byte of input is simply a byte of input, whether or not the byte is an ASCII character.

Collisions

When an algorithm violates one of the last two properties discussed in the preceding section, the result is a *collision*, the technical term to describe a situation in which two messages produce the same digest. A collision occurs when a second message produces the same digest as a previous message, or when two messages—any two messages—produce the same digest whatever that digest is. If two messages collide, they meet at the digest.

Although the number of possible messages is virtually infinite, the number of possible digests is finite. With SHA-1, the number of possible digests is 2^{160}. Clearly, there will be many messages that produce any one digest. To show that, let's use the time-honored mathematical tool known as the *pigeonhole principle*. Suppose you had a cabinet of pigeonholes (see Figure 5-5). Each pigeonhole corresponds to a digest. The zeroth pigeonhole is for the digest 00 00 . . . 00, the first is for 00 00 . . . 01, and so on, until you reach the last pigeonhole, the place for FF FF . . . FF.

Now you start digesting messages. After you digest a message, place the message into the pigeonhole of the digest it produces. For example, the digest of the 1-byte message 00 is

```
5b a9 3c 9d b0 cf f9 3f 52 b5 21 d7 42 0e 43 f6
ed a2 78 4f
```

So you place message 00 into pigeonhole 5B A9 . . . 4F. The digest of message 01 is

```
bf 8b 45 30 d8 d2 46 dd 74 ac 53 a1 34 71 bb a1
79 41 df f7
```

Message 01 goes into pigeonhole BF 8B . . . F7.

Suppose you keep digesting messages, the next message being the preceding message plus 1. The sequence of messages is 00, 01, 02, . . ., FF, 01 00, 01 01, . . ., FF FF, 01 00 00, and so on. Suppose you did this for 2^{160} messages. The last message in the sequence would be

```
FF FF FF FF FF FF FF FF FF FF FF FF FF FF FF FF
FF FF FF FF
```

Message:

00 → Digest → 5B 9A...

01 → Digest → BF 8B...

FF FF FF → Digest → EF F3

All pigeonholes
are now
occupied

Daniel,
I sold all 4
presses to
Satomi . . . → Digest → 46 73

Now suppose that each message produced a different digest. (For all we
know, there were messages that produced the same digest, but for the
sake of argument, let's say each message produced a different digest.) You
had 2^{160} pigeonholes and 2^{160} messages, each message going into a different pigeonhole. This means that all pigeonholes are now occupied. Now
consider Pao-Chi's message to Daniel (ordering four presses for Satomi).
This 424-bit message is not a message you've already examined. So far in
this pigeonhole exercise, if you've operated on a message, it's been 160 or
fewer bits. To place Pao-Chi's message into a pigeonhole, you would place

it into 46 73 . . . 5a. But that pigeonhole, like all the others, is already occupied. Which message it contains doesn't matter; you simply know it's occupied. You have a collision.

Now consider that "all possible messages" includes messages of any size.

Collisions exist, but no one can find a collision on demand (for some digest algorithms, no one has found any collision, even by accident). The worst possible scenario for a digest algorithm would be if someone could take any message and produce a similar message that produces the same digest. Figure 5-6 shows an example of that. One message mentions $1,000,000, and the second message mentions $1,500,000. If someone changes only the 5, the digests will not match. But what if someone could change the 5, change a few other things here and there, maybe add a phrase or two, and get the same digest?

Figure 5-6

If a digest algorithm were predictable enough that an attacker could change a message slightly and produce the same digest, the algorithm would be broken

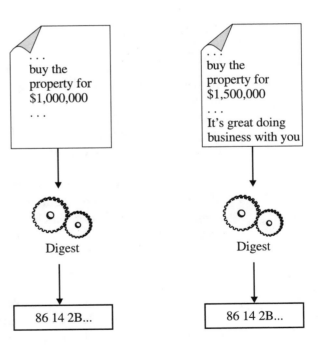

The Three Important Digest Algorithms

There are many digest algorithms, but three have dominated the market: MD2, MD5, and SHA-1.

MD2

Ron Rivest created a digest algorithm and named it MD. Then he thought he could do better and so developed the next generation, MD2. Because MD2 produces a 128-bit (16-byte) digest, it has 2^{128} possible digest values. MD2 has been widely used, but over the years, analysts found flaws with it. Eventually, a few collisions were discovered. Nobody was able to find collisions on demand with any arbitrary message, but certain classes of messages produced collisions. Hence, MD2 isn't used very much anymore except on old certificates created before MD2 lost favor (Chapter 6 describes certificates). Most of those old certificates have probably expired or will expire soon. No good cryptographer would recommend using MD2 in new applications.

MD5

Rivest wanted a faster digest, and when MD2 began to show weaknesses, he also wanted one that was stronger. He started creating new digests. MD3 was a bust, and when he showed MD4 to the world it was quickly shown to be weak. (Despite that weakness, at least one application used it. See "Crypto Blunders" on the accompanying CD for that story.) MD5 was more successful.

MD5, a lot faster and much stronger than MD2, became the dominant algorithm and is still in common use. Like MD2, MD5 is a 16-byte digest. Over the years, research has led to potential weaknesses. MD5 isn't broken, and no one has found collisions; rather, some of the internals of the algorithm are vulnerable. If a component or two were missing from the algorithm, it would be broken. But because those components are there, the algorithm survives.

Some people say that it doesn't matter that the algorithm would be weak if certain pieces were missing; the pieces are there, so it's not weak. Others say that you don't break an algorithm all at once; you break it piece by piece. Now that there are only a few pieces (maybe one or two) preventing a total collapse, they argue, it would be better to move on to another algorithm.

SHA-1

The SHA-1 algorithm looks a lot like MD5 (Ron Rivest played a role in the design of SHA-1). SHA-1 contains stronger internals than MD5, and it produces a longer digest (160 bits compared with 128 bits). Size alone makes it stronger. SHA-1 has survived cryptanalysis and comes highly recommended by the crypto community. In development are SHA-1 variants that produce 192-bit and 256-bit digests.

A Representative of Larger Data

If you're looking for something to produce a representative of a larger amount of data, it's easy to see that a message digest does that job fairly well. First, the output of a digest algorithm is usually smaller than the data itself, and no matter how big the data gets, the digest as a representative will always be the same size. If someone tries to surreptitiously change the original message, the new, fake message will not produce the same digest. If the digest produced by the algorithm does not represent the data, you know that something went wrong (see Figure 5-7). Maybe the data has been altered, maybe the digest is wrong. You might not know what exactly happened, but you do know something happened.

Here's how an application can check a digest. Pao-Chi is sending Daniel some data, such as an e-mail or a contract; for this example, it's the message about selling four units to Satomi. Before Pao-Chi sends the message, he digests it. Now he sends the data and the digest. When Daniel gets the data, he also digests it. If his digest matches Pao-Chi's, he knows the data has not been changed in transit. If Satomi had intercepted and altered the message, the digest that Daniel produced would not have matched the digest Pao-Chi produced. Daniel would know that something happened and would not trust the data.

Your immediate response might be, "If Satomi could alter the data, she could alter the digest." That's true, but there are two ways to prevent that. One is to use a digital signature, a topic we'll return to shortly. For now, let's look at the second way: a keyed digest. The most common keyed digest is called HMAC.

HMAC

MAC stands for message authentication checksum (or message authentication code), and *H* stands for hash or hash-based function, so an HMAC

Figure 5-7

If the data does
not match the
digest, you know
that something
went wrong

Data

> Daniel, I sold
> 4 presses to
> Satomi. Ship
> immediately.

True Representative

46 73 A5...5A

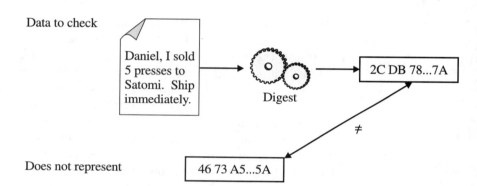

Data to check

> Daniel, I sold
> 5 presses to
> Satomi. Ship
> immediately.

Digest

2C DB 78...7A

≠

Does not represent

46 73 A5...5A

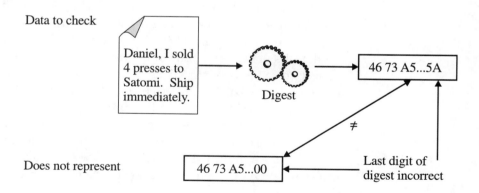

Data to check

> Daniel, I sold
> 4 presses to
> Satomi. Ship
> immediately.

Digest

46 73 A5...5A

≠

Does not represent

46 73 A5...00

Last digit of
digest incorrect

(pronounced "aitch mac") is a hash-based message authentication algorithm. A *checksum* is an algorithm that checks data by summing it. Suppose you had a column of numbers (say, in an accountant's ledger). If the correct numbers are there, the sum of the column is a specific value. Later, to check that the ledger is still correct, you don't compare each number individually; rather, you find the sum of the column. If the second sum matches the first sum, the check passes. Of course, if someone can change one number, it's easy also to change the sum at the bottom of the ledger so that it matches the change in the single number. It would also be easy to change another number in the column to offset the first change. A MAC is a way to detect changes in the data or in the sum. To detect changes in the data, a MAC can be based on a digest, block cipher, or stream cipher (see Chapter 2). To detect changes in the actual checksum, the MAC uses a key.

Most HMACs work this way. Two parties share a secret key (Chapter 4 shows how that's done), and then each digest the key and message. The digest depends on the message and the key, so an attacker would have to know what the key is to alter the message and attach a correct checksum. For example, suppose Pao-Chi sends Daniel message 1 shown earlier (the message instructing him to ship four units to Satomi). Pao-Chi uses an HMAC so that Daniel can verify that the data did not change. Using a key exchange algorithm (RSA, DH, ECDH), the two agree on a 128-bit key. Pao-Chi uses SHA-1 to digest the key and message as one chunk of data. The result is as follows. (The two vertical lines || indicate concatenation; see also Figure 5-8.)

```
Pao-Chi's HMAC result (SHA-1 digest of key || message 1):
    60 c4 65 a8 a4 9d 35 6a 68 36 f8 f0 56 3d d2 7f
    7e 26 35 b2
```

NOTE:

We haven't told you what the key is, so you can't verify that the result we present is the actual result of an HMAC. If you want to know what the key is, you can figure it out. Put together a chunk of data—a key candidate followed by the message—and then digest it. Is it the same result given here? No? Try another key, and another, and so on until you find the correct one. It's a 128-bit key.

Now Pao-Chi sends Daniel the message and the HMAC result together. Suppose that Satomi intercepts the transmission and tries to get Daniel

Figure 5-8

The HMAC
algorithm digests
the key and the
data (in that
order) to produce
a value

to ship five presses instead of four by substituting message 2 for Pao-
Chi's. After replacing the message, she sends it to Daniel. If she failed to
replace the HMAC result, Daniel would digest the key and fake message
and get the following (see Figure 5-9).

```
Daniel's HMAC result (SHA1 digest of key || message 2):
    a8 32 3b 8d f3 6b 3e e1 08 bb 6b 0b f0 cc a5 5b
    26 d4 d1 41
```

Figure 5-9

Daniel digests the
correct key but
the wrong
message, so he
knows that
something is
wrong

The digested message is not the same as Pao-Chi's. (Daniel knows what Pao-Chi got for an HMAC; that's part of the message.) So Daniel knows that what Pao-Chi digested and what he digested are not the same. Something—maybe the key, maybe the actual message, maybe even the HMAC value—was changed. Daniel doesn't know exactly what was changed, but that doesn't matter. He knows something went wrong. He contacts Pao-Chi again, and they start over.

Another possibility is for Satomi to substitute message 2 for message 1 *and* substitute the HMAC. But the problem is that Satomi can't know what the correct HMAC value should be. To demonstrate this, suppose Satomi substitutes six presses for four presses. Here's the SHA-1 digest.

```
    Daniel, I sold 6 presses to Satomi. Ship immediately.
SHA-1 digest:
        66 05 40 8c 24 6e 05 f8 00 20 f4 72 14 08 bc 22
        53 b2 eb d2
```

If Satomi substitutes this digest, Daniel will still know something is wrong because that's not the value he's going to get. He's not digesting the message; rather, he's digesting the key and the message. So what should Satomi use?

Data Integrity

We've described a message digest as the foundation of a pseudo-random number generator or password-based encryption, and now as a representative of a larger message. Another use for a message digest is to check *data integrity,* which is the term used to describe what the HMAC does. If you're concerned that the information may be altered, you send the data along with a check. If the message was altered, the check will also be different. Of course, you must ensure that the check value cannot be altered to match any changes in the message.

If the check value shows no alterations, the data has been shown to have integrity. "Integrity" is a word for honest, sound, and steadfast. When used in relationship to data, it may seem pretentious, but it does describe data that you can count on, at least in terms of its authenticity.

Back to Digital Signatures

In our example, the HMAC seems to serve as a signature. Daniel can know that the data came from Pao-Chi and that no one tampered with it in transit. But HMAC has some shortcomings. The first is the statement, "Daniel can know that the data came from Pao-Chi." Maybe *he* can know it came from Pao-Chi, but can anyone else? After all, to verify that the data came from Pao-Chi, the recipient must know what the key is to create the appropriate HMAC. Daniel knows what the shared secret key is, but no one else does. Daniel could write a bogus message (say, setting the number of presses to eight) and create the correct HMAC. So from anyone else's point of view, the message may have come from Pao-Chi or Daniel; no one else can know for sure who "signed" it. The second drawback is that for someone other than Pao-Chi or Daniel to verify the "signature," the correspondents must reveal the secret key. Now this third party has access to the key and can also create messages that appear genuine.

Usually, HMACs are used only to verify that contents have not been altered in transit. They are meant to be used as an on-the-fly check and not as a permanent record. For that reason, you need another way to create unique, verifiable signatures, and that way is to encrypt the digest with the signer's private RSA key.

It works like this. Pao-Chi digests the message and then encrypts the digest with his private key. He sends Daniel the message along with the encrypted digest, which serves as the signature. Daniel separates the two components and digests the message he received. He has a message in his possession and knows the digest that will produce it (he just computed it). He must determine whether the message he now has is the same message Pao-Chi sent. If Daniel knew what Pao-Chi computed as a digest, he could make that determination. Well, he has Pao-Chi's digest—it's the signature. So Daniel uses Pao-Chi's public key to decrypt the signature. That's the value Pao-Chi signed (see Figure 5-10). Is it the same answer Daniel got? If it is, he knows that the data was not altered in transit and that Pao-Chi is vouching for the contents.

Notice something powerful about the digital signature: Each chunk of data has its own signature. This means that no single digital signature is associated with an individual or key pair. Each signature is unique to the data signed and the keys used. When an individual signs two messages with the same key, the signatures will be different. Moreover, when two people with different keys sign the same data, they will produce different signatures. As a result, someone cannot take a valid signature and append

Figure 5-10

The RSA
signature

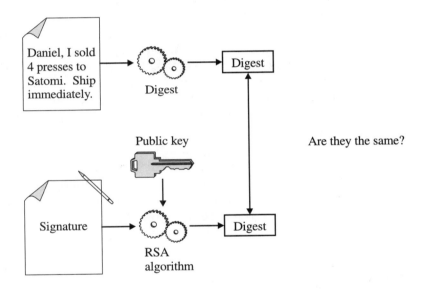

it to the bottom of a different message, something that makes it much more difficult to forge a signature.

Think of it this way. Two people (a sender and a receiver) each have a copy of a message. Are they really copies or was the receiver's copy altered in transit? To find out, they digest the two messages and compare them. If the digests are the same, both parties know that the two versions match. If the digests don't match, something went wrong. How do you know that the sender's digest was not altered? You know that because it was encrypted with the sender's private key. How do you know that it was encrypted with the sender's private key? You know it because the public key decrypts it.

In addition, you can make a couple of other checks. In the real world, there will almost certainly be some digest algorithm identifier bytes (discussed in the next paragraph) and some pad bytes in addition to the digest. A signer will encrypt a block of data that is the padding, the digest algorithm identifier, and the digest. That encrypted value is the signature. Figure 5-11 shows an example. Using the appropriate public key, that signature decrypts to the padded value. The verifier checks not only for the digest but also the pad bytes and the SHA-1 algorithm identifier. (Technically, the program the verifier runs will make these checks.) Having three checks makes it harder to spoof.

The algorithm identifier bytes prevent an attacker from substituting an alternative digest algorithm. Suppose that Satomi looks at Pao-Chi's message and its correct digest. She then finds a second message and digests it using a different algorithm. Further suppose that this second algorithm on the second message produces the same digest as the first algorithm on the first message. If the signature were the encryption of the digest only, that one signature would look as if it also came from the second algorithm. But if you tie a signature to a digest *and* the algorithm, you thwart such an attack. On the one hand, it doesn't seem likely that someone would ever be able to generate the same digest from a different algorithm. On the other hand, might MD2 be broken completely someday? It doesn't cost anything to make the second check, so you might as well use it.

Trying to Cheat

Two people-Satomi and Pao-Chi-might try to cheat. Here's how they can try.

First, suppose that Satomi intercepts the message and replaces "4" with "5." She figures she'll pay Pao-Chi for four units but Daniel will send her five, and she'll get an extra press for free. In this scheme, when Daniel gets the e-mail, he digests it and gets the following value. (Using the same algorithm Pao-Chi used-SHA-1-that information is part of the e-mail although not part of the message digested.)

```
2c db 78 38 87 7e d3 1e 29 18 49 a0 61 b7 41 81
3c b6 90 7a
```

Figure 5-11

A digested
message and the
RSA signature.
The private key
used for this
example is listed
in Chapter 4

Message:

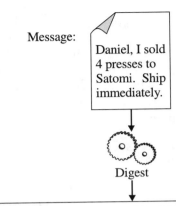

Daniel, I sold
4 presses to
Satomi. Ship
immediately.

Digest

Padded plaintext:

```
00 01 ff ff ff ff ff ff ff ff ff ff ff ff ff ff
ff ff ff ff ff ff ff ff ff ff ff ff ff ff ff ff
ff ff ff ff ff ff ff ff ff ff ff ff ff ff ff ff
ff ff ff ff ff ff ff ff ff ff ff ff ff ff ff ff
ff ff ff ff ff ff ff ff ff ff ff ff ff ff ff ff
ff ff ff ff ff ff ff ff ff ff ff ff 00 30 21 30
09 06 05 2b 0e 03 02 1a 05 00 04 14 46 73 a5 85
89 ba 86 58 44 ac 5b e8 48 7a cd 12 63 f8 c1 5a
```

RSA machine

Signature:

```
4d 86 2e 8e 3e 9e f2 57 6d 03 d2 79 a0 e0 6a b4
d3 a3 86 07 4e c1 53 03 c9 a5 13 5f 59 74 53 37
56 9b d5 9c 38 8e 28 41 64 9b 5b c6 dd 68 94 5c
88 f4 c9 74 a7 cf b7 95 f3 da 63 d4 4e 3f 13 5d
b0 f1 66 d4 7b 4c a0 a7 e5 0e b8 46 31 be 17 86
d1 b8 75 4a 8a 15 e3 5a 50 9c 9d 4e 61 0c a5 ca
5a 5e 03 cc 27 0d ae 08 8f e8 3c 4f a2 8b c1 03
8d 1e e6 4e c8 34 01 7c 23 3f d7 37 e5 37 d5 8d
```

Daniel must find out whether that value is the same one Pao-Chi got when he digested the message he sent. To find out, Daniel uses Pao-Chi's public key to decrypt the signature. After decryption, he gets a chunk of data. Does this data have the correct padding? He sees that the padding is correct, so he just throws that away. The next bytes are the identifying marks indicating that the algorithm is SHA-1; that's correct. Finally, he has the digest.

```
46 73 a5 85 89 ba 86 58 44 ac 5b e8 48 7a cd 12
63 f8 c1 5a
```

Daniel compares the digest value in the decrypted signature to his digest value (the value he just computed from the purported message) and sees that they are different. Something's not right. What went wrong? Daniel doesn't know exactly what caused the discrepancy, but he knows that the message he received is not the same message Pao-Chi sent. Because Daniel doesn't trust the message, he ignores it, asking Pao-Chi to try again. Meanwhile, Daniel doesn't send Satomi anything and she doesn't get her extra unit.

Now let's look at Pao-Chi's attempt at cheating. Suppose he made a mistake and quoted Satomi a price for two units. He got paid for two but told Daniel to ship four. He doesn't want to take the heat for the error, so he claims he wrote "2" instead of "4" in his e-mail. He figures he can shift the blame to Daniel or maybe just technology—some gremlin on the Internet that garbled the message.

Daniel points out that the signature attached to his e-mail matches the message with the number of presses to ship at four. Because that's Pao-Chi's signature and because each signature is unique to a message and private key, Daniel claims that Pao-Chi vouched for the information and can't back out now.

To counter this, Pao-Chi could claim that the signature was forged. To forge a signature would mean that someone was able to create a blob of data, through other means, that was the same as a signature. This would mean that some unknown forger had broken the RSA algorithm. That is highly unlikely (see Chapter 4). No, Pao-Chi signed the message, and he can't claim otherwise.

Or Pao-Chi could try another approach, claiming that someone stole his private key. Maybe it was protected on his hard drive using PBE, and someone cracked his password. Maybe it was stored on a smart card or other token, and someone broke that device or was able to log on as Pao-Chi (possibly by breaking a password). If that really is the case, Pao-Chi did a poor job of protecting his private key, and he will still be in trouble. We return to this subject later in this chapter in the section "Protecting Private Keys."

Implementing Authentication, Data Integrity, and Nonrepudiation

When Daniel checks to make sure that the data has come from Pao-Chi and not someone posing as him, it's called *authentication*. He authenticates Pao-Chi's identity. When Daniel examines the message to make sure it has not been altered in transit, that's called *data integrity checking*. And when Pao-Chi can't go back on his signature, that's called *nonrepudiation*. In addition to privacy, these are the main areas in which cryptography benefits those who use it.

Symmetric-key encryption provides privacy in that the sensitive data looks like gibberish to unauthorized eyes. Public-key technology solves the key distribution problem. A message digest—either a keyed digest such as HMAC or a digital signature—ensures data integrity in that what the sender sends is what the receiver receives. A digital signature also offers authentication in that the other entity in the data exchange is shown to be the entity it claims to be and the data is verified to have come from that entity. A digital signature also provides nonrepudiation in that a signer cannot later disavow any knowledge of the message.

Understanding the Algorithms

You can use the RSA algorithm to sign, but Diffie-Hellman can be used only to perform key exchange and not digital signatures. As discussed in Chapter 4, Diffie and Hellman proposed the idea of the ultimate public key algorithm. It would be one that could be used to encrypt data. The digital signature is the reason that such an algorithm would be the ultimate algorithm. In an interview, Whitfield Diffie explained that when he heard about the NSA's secure phone system, he was less concerned with the key exchange problem than with authentication—that is, verifying that you are talking to the person you think you are talking to.

At Stanford, cryptographer Taher El Gamal came up with a way to extend DH so that it could be used to sign as well as encrypt. But his idea never really caught on, possibly because RSA existed, and possibly because David Kravitz invented a digital signature algorithm for the U.S. government, and with the backing of an entity as powerful as the U.S. government, his algorithm became popular. Kravitz (or someone in the U.S. government) gave the new algorithm the lyrical name "Digital Signature Algorithm," known to this day as DSA. Like DH, DSA is based on the discrete log problem. It became the official U.S. government signature algorithm and probably is second only to RSA in use today. Kravitz was working for the NSA when he developed DSA, and it is based on work by El Gamal and Claus Schnorr, another cryptographer.

Finally, just as elliptic curve math can be adapted to solve the key distribution problem, it can be adapted to create signatures. There are a number of possibilities, but the most common way to use ECC to create signatures is called ECDSA. This approach does essentially the same thing as DSA but with elliptic curves.

NOTE:

Kravitz received a patent for DSA, but the U.S. government owns it because the inventor was working for the NSA at the time. The patent is in the public domain and can be used freely. Claus Schnorr invented a signature algorithm that is very similar to DSA. His patent on that algorithm predates Kravitz's. If you want the whole story, consult a patent attorney.

Many signature algorithms have been proposed over the years, but only RSA, DSA, and ECDSA have shown any long-lasting success in finding adopters. Let's look at these three algorithms in more detail.

RSA

We show RSA in detail in Chapter 4. It's the algorithm that is used to encrypt a digest with a private key to produce a digital signature. To forge an RSA signature, someone must find the private key. Lacking a private key, no one has been able to produce a chunk of data, call it a digital signature, and have it be verified.

DSA

To this point, we've described a digital signature as the private-key encryption of a digest. Now we come to DSA, which does not encrypt data. Although DSA uses the digest of the data, it does not encrypt the digest. Your first thought is likely to be, "If it can't encrypt data, how can it produce a digital signature?" Remember that DH cannot be used to encrypt data but can be used to solve the key distribution problem. Similarly, even though DSA cannot be used to encrypt data, it can be used to create a digital signature. A digital signature is a chunk of data that comes from the message and the private key. Only that particular message coupled with that particular private key will produce that particular signature. If you accomplish that by encrypting the digest, great. If you accomplish that in some other way, that's fine, too.

With DSA, the signer digests the message with SHA-1 and treats that digest as a number (it's a big number: 160 bits long). Another number sent to the algorithm is a random or pseudo-random value, usually called k. The last input is the private key. The algorithm then performs some mathematical operations, one of which is modular exponentiation, the same function at the heart of DH and RSA. The output is two numbers, usually called r and s. These two numbers are the signature.

The verifier computes the SHA-1 digest of the message. Is it the same digest that the signer produced? The verifier does not have that digest available but does have r and s. Using the digest as a number, along with the public key and the s, the verifier performs some mathematical operations. The result of the computations is a number called v. If v is the same as r, the signature is verified (see Figure 5-12).

At its most basic, DSA computes the same number in two different ways. In Diffie-Hellman, two parties can generate the same secret value even though each one is using different input. The same thing is happening here with DSA. Two parties produce the same number using different input. The two sets of input are related. Well, they should be related; if something breaks down, the final answers will differ.

Each side has three inputs. The signer has the digest, k, and the private key. The verifier has the digest, s, and the public key. The digests are related; they should be the same thing. If that relationship breaks down— say, the signed data is not the same as the data being verified and the two parties produce different digests—the final answer from each individual will differ. The k and s are related (they're not the same number, but they're related). If the signature is wrong, the s will be wrong and the two

Figure 5-12

Producing and verifying a DSA signature

players will produce different final answers. The private key and the public key are also related; they are partners related mathematically. If that relationship is not there—if the public key used to verify is not the partner to the private key used to sign—the two agents will produce different final answers.

The security of DSA lies in the discrete log problem, the same problem that gives DH its security. So the size of DSA keys will be the same as that of DH keys. As always, you can find more detailed information in the RSA Labs FAQ on the accompanying CD.

ECDSA

This algorithm looks a lot like DSA. The signer has three inputs: the digest, k, and the private key. The output is r and s. The verifier has the digest, s, and the public key. The output is v. If v and r are the same, the signature is verified; if they're not the same, something went wrong. What went wrong? Was it the wrong digest? The wrong public key? Was the signature mangled in transmission? You probably can't know exactly what happened, but you do know that something went wrong. The math underlying ECDSA is elliptic curves, so key size is the same as with ECDH.

Comparing the Algorithms

Of the three algorithms that produce digital signatures, which one is the best? As we say in Chapter 4 regarding the key distribution problem, there's probably no single answer to that question. Each has its advantages and disadvantages. A more appropriate question might be, "Which algorithm works best in which situation?" Remember that all three of them are in use today because different problems call for different solutions.

Security

Everything we say in Chapter 4 on the security of the three algorithms applies here as well (the security of Diffie-Hellman and DSA are pretty much the same). There's no objective answer to the question of which algorithm is the most secure. It depends on what each individual feels is important.

One other factor with digital signatures, though, may be the concept of *message recovery*. With RSA, a signature verification recovers the message, but with DSA and ECDSA, a signature verification simply compares two numbers. Technically, RSA recovers the digest of the message instead of the message itself; that's really one level of indirection. DSA and ECDSA find a number based on the digest; that's two levels of indirection. Earlier in this chapter in "The Uniqueness of a Digital Signature," we mention that the crypto literature on digital signatures contains statements such as, "For some classes of signatures it is possible to prove certain security properties." Message recovery is one of those security properties. When you perform an RSA verification operation, you get to see what the signer produced; you recover the message digest because you're decrypting it. With DSA and ECDSA, you don't see what the signer produced. Instead, you generate a number, and if that number is equal to another number, you figure you produced the same thing that the signer produced.

Think of it this way. DSA and ECDSA produce surrogate numbers, let's call them the signer's surrogate and the verifier's surrogate. If the two numbers match, the signature is verified. With RSA, there is no surrogate; the verifier actually compares the signer's value.

Because DSA and ECDSA compare surrogates and not originals, it opens an avenue of attack not possible with RSA. An attacker could try to produce the appropriate surrogate number without the correct original key or data. That is, an attacker does not have to find a digest collision to substitute messages, but can try to find a DSA collision. But before you think that makes RSA much stronger than the other two, remember that no one has been able to create such an attack or even to come close. Still, although the probability of such an attack on DSA or ECDSA is extremely low, it's lower still with RSA.

Performance

In Chapter 4, you saw that no algorithm wins the performance race hands-down. Of the several factors, each algorithm compares favorably with the others in one way but unfavorably in another. The same is true with signatures. RSA performance does not change, but DSA and ECDSA are slightly more time-consuming than their DH counterparts.

If you want a faster signature scheme, you should go with ECC. But often, making a connection means that each party has to do two or more verifications; each one must verify a signature and then verify one or more certificates (Chapter 6 talks about certificates). If you have a fast signer (a server, for example) but a slow verifier (a hand-held device or smart card for example), you may get bogged down in verification. Again, each application may have different needs, and even though one algorithm may satisfy one application's needs better than another algorithm, the next application may find a different algorithm more suitable.

Table 5-1 shows some performance comparisons. The numbers are relative; if RSA public-key operations (such as verification) take one unit of time (whatever that unit may be) on a particular machine, the other operations will take the amounts of time shown.

Table 5-1		RSA	DSA	ECC	ECC with Acceleration
Estimated Relative Performance of the Public-Key Algorithms (in Relative Time Units)	Private key (sign)	13	17	7	2
	Public key (verify)	1	33	19	
	Combined	14	50	26	21

Transmission Size

DSA and ECDSA signatures are about 340 bits, regardless of key size. An RSA signature is the same size as the key. So if you use a 1,024-bit RSA key pair, each time you send a digital signature you add 1,024 bits to the message. Again, if transmission size is important, you may want to look at DSA or ECDSA.

Interoperability

The story's the same with signatures as with key distribution. RSA is almost ubiquitous and has become the de facto standard. DSA was promoted by the U.S. government and has become a part of most cryptographic packages. So if you sign using RSA or DSA, other parties will almost certainly be able to verify it, whether or not they use the same application you do. ECC is less prevalent.

Protecting Private Keys

Chapter 3 shows how to protect symmetric keys, and Chapter 4 explains that you protect a private key in a similar way. Tokens such as smart cards add a dimension to protection, but for the most part, the way you protect one key is the way you protect any key. Many protocols (discussed in Chapters 7 and 8) require that you have two keys: a digital envelope (or key exchange key) and a separate signing key. So you'll likely have to protect two private keys.

But if you lose your private key, there are ways to *revoke,* or cancel, the public key affiliated with it. If Pao-Chi claims that someone obtained his private key and is signing under his name, he can have his public key revoked. After the effective date of the revocation, any signatures verified with Pao-Chi's public key are invalid because the public key is invalid. Now Pao-Chi has to generate a new key pair, this time protecting the private key more diligently. Chapter 6 talks about revoking keys.

For now, note that if attackers steal your signing key, they can do a lot more damage than if they steal other types of keys because your signing key lets them pose as you. By stealing your digital envelope or key exchange private key, attackers can get at secrets, but they cannot act on your behalf. If you don't protect your signing key or don't protect it well enough, you're making yourself much more vulnerable.

Introduction to Certificates

Throughout Chapters 4 and 5, we've talked about other individuals using someone else's public key. To send a secure message to Gwen, Pao-Chi found her public key and created a digital envelope. To verify Pao-Chi's message, Daniel acquired Pao-Chi's public key and verified the digital signature. But how can anyone truly know whether a public key belongs to the purported individual?

Pao-Chi has in his possession a public key, which is purportedly Gwen's. The key works; he is able to create a digital envelope. But what if

Satomi somehow substituted her public key for Gwen's? While Pao-Chi was out to lunch, Satomi may have broken into his laptop, found a file called "Gwen's public key" and edited it so that this file contained her public key, not Gwen's. Then when Pao-Chi sends the digital envelope, Satomi will be able to intercept and read it. Gwen won't be able to open it because she does not have access to the private key partner to the public key used.

Suppose the company Pao-Chi and Daniel work for has a centralized directory where everyone's public key is stored. When Daniel wants to verify Pao-Chi's signature, he goes to the directory and find's Pao-Chi's key. But what if Satomi broke into that directory and replaced Pao-Chi's public key with hers? Now she can send a fake message to Daniel with a valid digital signature. Daniel will think it came from Pao-Chi because he verifies the signature against what he thinks is Pao-Chi's public key.

The most common way to know whether or not a public key does belong to the purported entity is through a digital certificate. A *digital certificate* binds a name to a public key. An analogy would be a passport, which binds a photo to a name and number. A passport is supposed to be produced in such a way that it is detectable if someone takes an existing passport and replaces the true photo with an imposter's photo. It may be a valid passport, but not for the person in the photo. Immigration officials will not honor that passport.

A digital certificate is produced in such a way that it is detectable if someone takes an existing certificate and replaces the public key or name with an imposter's. Anyone examining that certificate will know that something is wrong. Maybe the name or public key is wrong , so you don't trust that name/key pair combination.

Here's how it works. Take a name and public key. Consider those two things to be a message, and sign the message. The certificate is the name, public key, and signature (see Figure 5-13). The only thing left to determine is who will sign the certificate. Signing is almost always done by a *certificate authority*, also known as a CA. More on that later.

Gwen originally generated her key pair, protected the private key, and contacted her CA requesting a certificate. Depending on the CA's policy, Gwen may be required to show up in person. The CA verifies Gwen is who she claims to be by examining her passport, driver's license, company ID badge, or whatever method the CA uses to determine identity. Then Gwen uses her private key to sign something (the certificate request, probably). In that way, the CA knows that Gwen does indeed have access to the private key partner to the public key presented, and that the public key has not been replaced. The CA combines Gwen's name and public key into a

Figure 5-13

A certificate is
the name, public
key and signature

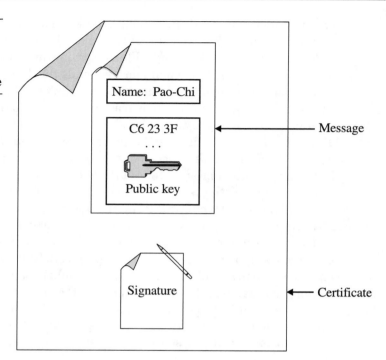

message and signs that message using its private key. Gwen now has a certificate and distributes it. So when Pao-Chi collects Gwen's public key, what he's really collecting is her certificate.

Now suppose Satomi tries to replace Gwen's public key with her own. She finds the file on Pao-Chi's laptop holding Gwen's public key and substitutes the keys. But when Pao-Chi loads the key, he's not loading just the key, he's loading the certificate. He can extract the public key from the certificate if he wants, but before he does that, he verifies that the certificate is valid using the CA's public key. Because the message has been altered, the signature does not verify and Pao-Chi does not trust that public key. Therefore, he will not create a digital envelope using that public key, and Satomi will not be able to read any private communications.

Of course, that scenario assumes that Pao-Chi has the CA's public key and that he can trust no one has replaced it with an imposter's. Because he can extract it from the CA's certificate, Pao-Chi knows he has the true CA public key. Just as Gwen's public key can be wrapped in a certificate, so can the CA's. Who signed the CA's certificate? Probably another CA. This could go on forever.

But it has to stop somewhere and that somewhere is the *root*. A root will sign a CA's certificate, and the root key is distributed outside the certificate hierarchy. Maybe the root is built into software; maybe Pao-Chi will have to enter it himself. Of course, if Satomi is able to substitute the root public key with one of her own, she can subvert the whole system. So Pao-Chi needs to protect the root key as he does his symmetric key and his own private keys.

Key Recovery

As discussed in Chapter 4, it's possible to set up a scheme to restore keys that someone loses by forgetting a password or losing a token. However, it's probably not a good idea to apply a key recovery plan to signing keys. If a signing key can be obtained by someone other than the owner (even if that is a trusted third party or a committee of trustees), that would make it possible to nullify nonrepudiation. Anyway, if someone loses a signing key, it's no great problem; any existing signatures are still valid because only the public key is needed to verify. For new signatures, you simply generate a new key pair and distribute the new public key. For this reason, many protocols specify that participants have separate signing and key exchange keys. As you will see in Chapters 6 and 7, it is possible to define a key as signing only or key encrypting (with the RSA digital envelope) or as key exchange only (with the Diffie-Hellman protocol).

Summary

To verify that a message came from the purported sender, you can use public-key cryptography. A private key is used to sign the data, and the public key is used to verify it. The only known way to produce a valid signature is to use the private key. Also, a signature is unique to a message; each message and private key combination will produce a different signature. So if a public key verifies a message, it must be that the associated private key signed that message. Three main algorithms are used as signature schemes: RSA, DSA, and ECDSA. Each algorithm has its advantages and disadvantages, and it's not really possible to say that one or the other is better. Each algorithm may be better suited for different applications.

For performance reasons, you don't sign the data but rather sign a representative of the data called a message digest. Also known as a hash, a message digest is the foundation of most PRNGs and PBE implementations. A keyed digest, such as HMAC, is also used to check data integrity.

Real-World Example

As discussed in Chapter 4, S/MIME uses public-key cryptography to solve the key distribution problem. As you've probably already surmised, S/MIME uses digital signatures as well. To implement a digital signature, follow these steps. First, launch Netscape Navigator, click the Security button, and then click Messenger (along the left-hand side of the security window). In Chapter 4, you saw the Encrypt choice checked. Notice the two Sign choices as well. If you select these menu items, when you send e-mail or post to newsgroups your message will be signed using your private key.

Before you can sign, you need a key pair. The browser has a module that generates a key pair for you, or, if you have a token (such as a smart card), you can specify that it be used to generate the key pair and store the private key. In the security window, click Yours under Certificates. The resulting window displays a button labeled Get A Certificate. This is the starting point for generating a key pair and getting a certificate. (Chapter 6 discusses certificates.)

With Microsoft Outlook, click Tools and then Options. In the resulting window, click the Security tab. You saw the Encrypt choice in Chapter 4. Here, notice the Sign option. Again, you need a key pair and a certificate. Start the process by clicking the Get A Digital ID button at the bottom of the window.

CHAPTER 6

Public-Key Infrastructures and the X.509 Standard

As you learned in Chapter 4, public-key cryptography gives you not only a powerful mechanism for encryption but also a way to identify and authenticate other individuals and devices. Before you can use this technology effectively, however, you must deal with one drawback. Just as with symmetric-key cryptography, key management and distribution are an issue with public-key crypto. Instead of confidentiality, the paramount issue for public-key crypto is the integrity and ownership of a public key.

For end users and *relying parties* (relying parties are those who verify the authenticity of an end user's certificate) to use this technology, they must provide their public keys to one another. The problem is that, like any other data, a public key is susceptible to manipulation while it is in transit. If an unknown third party can substitute a different public key for the valid one, the attacker could forge digital signatures and allow encrypted messages to be disclosed to unintended parties. That's why it's crucial to assure users that the key is authentic and that it came from (or was received by) the intended party.

Within a small population of trusted users, this task is not very difficult. An end user could distribute the public key by simply hand-delivering it on disk to a recipient, an approach known as manual public-key distribution. For larger groups of individuals, however, this task is much more difficult, especially when the people are geographically dispersed. Manual distribution becomes impractical and leaves room for security holes. For that reason, a better solution has been developed: public-key certificates. Public-key certificates provide a systematic, scalable, uniform, and easily controllable approach to public-key distribution.

A *public-key certificate* (PKC) is a tamperproof set of data that attests to the binding of a public key to an end user. To provide this binding, a set of trusted third parties vouches for the user's identity. The third parties, called *certification authorities* (CAs), issue certificates to the user that contain the user's name, public key, and other identifying information. Digitally signed by the CA, these certificates can now be transferred and stored.

This chapter covers the necessary technology needed to understand and use a *public-key infrastructure* (PKI). First, we describe the X.509 standard and the structure of an X.509 public-key certificate. Then we explain how the PKI components work as a collaborative process to let you create, distribute, manage, and revoke certificates.

Public-Key Certificates

Public-key certificates are a secure means of distributing public keys to relying parties within a network. In many ways, PKCs are analogous to a driver's license. Both a driver's license and a PKC are certified by a trusted third party, which affirms the user's identity and privileges. In its most basic form, a certificate contains a public key, the identity of the individual it belongs to, and the name of the party that is attesting to the validity of these facts.

Various certificates are in use. Some of them, such as *Pretty Good Privacy* (PGP), are proprietary. Other popular certificates are application-specific, such as SET and *Internet Protocol Security* (IPSec) certificates. The most widely accepted certificate format is the International Telecommunication Union's X.509 Version 3. The original X.509 standard was published in 1988 as part of the X.500 directory recommendations. Since then, it has been revised twice—in 1993 and again in 1995. RFC2459, a profile for the X.509 standard, was published in 1999 by the *Internet Engineering Task Force* (IETF). Although RFC2459 is targeted to the Internet community, a number of its useful components can be applied in an enterprise environment. Therefore, we provide references to some of its recommendations where appropriate. Figure 6-1 illustrates the structure of an X.509 certificate.

Figure 6-1

X.509 certificate structure

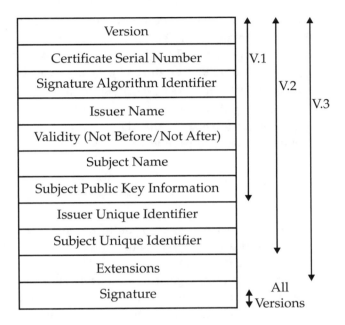

All versions of X.509 certificates contain the following fields:

■ **Version**   This field differentiates among successive versions of the certificate, such as Version 1, Version 2, and Version 3. The Version field also allows for possible future versions.

■ **Certificate Serial Number**   This field contains an integer value unique to each certificate; it is generated by the CA.

■ **Signature Algorithm Identifier**   This field indicates the identifier of the algorithm used to sign the certificate along with any associated parameters.

■ **Issuer Name**   This field identifies the *distinguished name* (DN) of the CA that created and signed this certificate.

- **Validity (Not Before/After)** This field contains two date/time values—Not Valid Before and Not Valid After—which define the period that this certificate can be considered valid unless otherwise revoked. The entry can use the following formats: UTC time (*yymmddhhmmssz*) or generalized time (*yyyymmddhhmmssz*).

- **Subject Name** This field identifies the DN of the *end entity* to whom this certificate refers, that is, the subject who holds the corresponding private key. This field must have an entry unless an alternative name is used in the Version 3 extensions.

- **Subject Public Key Information** This field contains the value of the subject's public key as well as the algorithm identifier and any associated parameters of the algorithm for which this key is used. This field must always have an entry.

Unique Identifiers

Version 2 and 3 certificates may contain unique identifiers that pertain to the subject and issuer. These fields are designed to handle the possibility of reuse of these names over time. RFC2459 recommends that names not be reused for different entities and that Internet certificates not use unique identifiers. This means that CAs conforming to this profile *should not* generate certificates with unique identifiers. Nevertheless, applications conforming to this profile should be capable of parsing unique identifiers and making comparisons.

- **Issuer Unique Identifier** This optional field contains a unique identifier that is used to render unambiguous the X.500 name of the CA in cases when the same name has been reused by different entities over time. This field can be used only in Version 2 and Version 3 certificates, and its use is not recommended according to RFC2459.

- **Subject Unique Identifier** This optional field contains a unique identifier that is used to render unambiguous the X.500 name of the certificate owner when the same name has been reused by different entities over time. This field can be used only in Version 2 and Version 3 certificates, and its use is not recommended according to RFC2459.

Standard Version 3 Certificate Extensions

After the release of Version 2, it was apparent that the certificate profile still contained deficiencies. For this reason, a set of extensions was created to append to the Version 3 format of the certificate. These extensions cover key and policy information, subject and issuer attributes, and certification path constraints.

The information contained in extension fields can be marked as either critical or noncritical. An extension field has three parts: extension type, extension criticality, and extension value. The *extension criticality* tells a certificate-using application whether it can ignore an extension type. If this extension is set to critical and the application does not recognize the extension type, the application should reject the certificate. On the other hand, if the extension criticality is set to noncritical and the application does not recognize the extension type, it is safe for the application to ignore the extension and to use the certificate.

The following standard certificate extension fields are available only in Version 3 certificates:

- **Authority Key Identifier** This extension is used to differentiate between multiple certificate signing keys of the same CA. The CA provides a unique key identifier or provides a pointer to another certificate, which can certify the issuer's key. The RFC2459 mandates the use of this field for any certificate that is not self-signed.

- **Subject Key Identifier** This extension is used to differentiate between multiple certificate signing keys of the same certificate owner. The owner provides a unique key identifier or provides a pointer to another certificate that can certify the issuer's key. RFC2459 mandates the use of this field for any CA signing certificate and also recommends it for end entities.

- **Key Usage** This extension is used to define restrictions on the operations that can be performed by the public key within this certificate. Such operations include digital signature, certificate signing, *certificate revocation list* (CRL) signing, key enciphering, data enciphering, and Diffie-Hellman key agreement. This field can also be flagged as critical or noncritical. If it is flagged critical, it can be used only for its intended use; otherwise, it will be considered in violation of the CA's policy. RFC2459 recommends a flag of critical when this field is used.

- **Extended Key Usage** This extension can be used in addition to or in place of the Key Usage extension to define one or more uses of the public key that is certified within this certificate. This extension enables the certificate to interoperate with various protocols and applications (such as, *Transport Layer Security* [TLS] server authentication, client authentication, time stamping, and others). RFC2459 states that this field may be flagged critical or noncritical.

- **CRL Distribution Point** This extension indicates a *uniform resource identifier* (URI) to locate the CRL structure where revocation information associated with this certificate resides. RFC2459 recommends that this field be flagged noncritical, although it also recommends that CAs and applications support this extension.

- **Private Key Usage Period** Similar to the Validity field of the certificate, this extension indicates the time frame of use for the private key associated with the public key in this certificate. In the absence of this extension, the validity period of use for the private key is that of the associated public key. RFC2459 recommends against the use of this extension.

- **Certificate Policies** This extension identifies the policies and optional qualifier information that the CA associates with the certificate. If this extension is marked critical, the processing application must adhere to at least one of the policies indicated, or the certificate is not to be used. To promote interoperability, RFC2459 recommends against the use of policy identifiers, but it does specify two possible qualifiers: the *certification practice statement* (CPS) qualifier and the user notice qualifier. The CPS qualifier contains a pointer to a CPS that applies to this certificate. The notice reference qualifier can be made up of a notice reference or an explicit notice (or both), which can in turn provide a text message of the policy required for this certificate.

- **Policy Mappings** This extension is used only when the subject of the certificate is also a CA. It indicates one or more policy *object identifiers* (OIDs) within the issuing CA's domain that are considered to be equivalent to another policy within the subject CA's domain.

- **Subject Alternative Name** This extension indicates one or more alternative name forms associated with the owner of this certificate. Use of this field enables support within various applications that employ their own name forms, such as various e-mail products, *electronic data interchange* (EDI), and IPSec. RFC2459 specifies that if no DN is specified in the subject field of a certificate, it must have one or more alternative names and this extension must be flagged critical.

- **Issuer Alternative Name**   This extension indicates one or more alternative name forms associated with the issuer of this certificate. As with the Subject Alternative Name extension, use of this field enables support within various applications.

- **Subject Directory Attributes**   This extension can be used to convey any X.500 directory attribute values for the subject of this certificate. It provides additional identifying information about the subject that is not conveyed in the name fields (that is, the subject's phone number or position within a company). RFC2459 recommends against the use of this extension at this time. However, if it is used, RFC2459 mandates the use of a noncritical flag to maintain interoperability.

- **Basic Constraints**   This extension indicates whether the subject may act as a CA, providing a way to restrict end users from acting as CAs. If this field is present, a certification path length may also be specified. The certification path length limits the certifying powers of the new authority (for example, whether Verisign could allow RSA Inc. to act as a CA but at the same time not allow RSA Inc. to create new CAs). RFC2459 mandates that this extension be present and marked critical for all CA certificates.

- **Name Constraints**   This extension, to be used only within CA certificates, specifies the namespace within which all subject names must be located for any subsequent certificate that is part of this certificate path. RFC2459 mandates that this extension be marked critical.

- **Policy Constraints**   This extension, to be used only within CA certificates, specifies policy path validation by requiring policy identifiers or prohibiting policy mappings (or both). RFC2459 simply states that this extension may be marked critical or noncritical.

Entity Names

In a public-key certificate, entity names for both the issuer and the subject must be unique. Version 1 and 2 certificates use the X.500 DN naming convention.

Distinguished names were originally intended to identify entities within an X.500 directory tree. A *relative distinguished name* (RDN) is the path from one node to a subordinate node. The entire DN traverses a path from the root of the tree to an end node that represents a particular entity. A goal of the directory is to provide an infrastructure to uniquely name every communications entity everywhere (hence the "distinguished" in "distinguished name"). As a result of the directory's goals, names in X.509 certificates are perhaps more complex than one might like (compared with, for example, e-mail addresses). Nevertheless, for business applications, DNs are worth the complexity because they are closely coupled with legal name registration procedures, something not offered by simple names such as e-mail addresses. A distinguished name is composed of one or more RDNs, and each RDN is composed of one or more *attribute-value assertions* (AVAs). Each AVA consists of an attribute identifier and its corresponding value information, for example, "CountryName = US" or "CommonName = Jeff Hamilton".

X.509 Version 3 certificates grant greater flexibility with names, no longer restricting us solely to X.500 name forms. Entities can be identified by one or more names using various name forms. The following name forms are recognized by the X.509 standard:

- Internet e-mail address
- Internet domain name (any official DNS name)
- X.400 e-mail address
- X.500 directory name
- EDI party name
- Web URI, of which a *uniform resource locator* (URL) is a subtype
- Internet IP address (for use in associating public-key pairs with Internet connection endpoints).

Alternative names provide more flexibility to relying parties and applications that may not have any connections to the end user's X.500 directory. For example, a standard e-mail application could use a certificate that provides not only an X.500 name form but also a standard e-mail address.

ASN.1 Notation and Encoding

Most encrypted data ends up being transferred to other entities, so it is crucial that the data follow a standard format, syntax, and encoding so that it makes sense to other users or applications. We've talked about how the X.509 standard provides such a format. In this section we explain the X.509 rules for data syntax and encoding.

The syntax for all certificates that conform to the X.509 standard are expressed using a special notation known as *Abstract Syntax Notation 1* (ASN.1), which was originally created by *Open Systems Interconnection* (OSI) for use with various X.500 protocols. ASN.1 describes the syntax for various data structures, providing well-defined primitive objects as well as a means to define complex combinations of those primitives.

ASN.1 has two sets of rules that govern encoding. *Basic Encoding Rules* (BER, defined in X.690) are a way of representing ASN.1-specified objects as strings of 1's and 0's. *Distinguished Encoding Rules* (DER), a subset of BER, provide a means to uniquely encode each ASN.1 value.

NOTE:
For more information about these rules, see Appendix B, which includes a copy of RSA Laboratories' "A Layman's Guide to a Subset of ASN.1, BER, and DER."

The Components of a PKI

As we've mentioned, CAs serve as trusted third parties to bind an individual's identity to his or her public key. CAs issue certificates that contain the user's name, public key, and other identifying information. Signed by the CA, these certificates are stored in public directories and can be retrieved to verify signatures or encrypt documents. A public-key infrastructure involves a collaborative process between several entities: the CA, a *registration authority* (RA), a certificate repository, a key recovery server, and the end user. In this section we discuss each of these components in detail.

Certification Authority

If we think of a certificate as being similar to a driver's license, the CA operates as a kind of licensing bureau analogous to a state's Department of Motor Vehicles or similar agency. In a PKI, a CA issues, manages, and revokes certificates for a community of end users. The CA takes on the tasks of authenticating its end users and then digitally signing the certificate information before disseminating it. The CA is ultimately responsible for the authenticity of its end users.

In providing these services, the CA must provide its own public key to all the certified end users as well as all relying parties who may use the certified information. Like end users, the CA provides its public key in the form of a *digitally signed* certificate. However, the CA's certificate is slightly different in that the Subject and Issuer fields contain the same information. Thus, CA certificates are considered *self-signed*.

CAs fall into to two categories: public and private. *Public* CAs operate via the Internet, providing certification services to the general public. These CAs certify not only users but also organizations. *Private* CAs, on the other hand, are usually found within a corporation or other closed network. These CAs tend to license only to end users within their own population, providing their network with stronger authentication and access controls.

Registration Authority

Although an RA can be considered an extended component of a PKI, administrators are discovering that it is a necessity. As the number of end entities increases within a given PKI community, so does the workload placed on a CA. An RA can serve as an intermediate entity between the CA and its end users, assisting the CA in its day-to-day certificate-processing functions.

An RA commonly provides these functions:

- Accepting and verifying registration information about new registers
- Generating keys on behalf of end users
- Accepting and authorizing requests for key backup and recovery
- Accepting and authorizing requests for certificate revocation
- Distributing or recovering hardware devices, such as tokens, as needed

RAs are also commonly used for the convenience of end users. As the number of end users increases within a PKI domain, it's likely that they will become more geographically dispersed. CAs can delegate the authority to accept registration information to a local RA. In this way, the CA can be operated as an offline entity, making it less susceptible to attacks by outsiders.

Certificate Directory

After a certificate is generated, it must be stored for later use. To relieve end users of the need to store the certificate on local machines, CAs often use a *certificate directory*, or central storage location. An important component of a PKI, a certificate directory provides a single point for certificate administration and distribution. There is no one required directory standard. Lotus Notes and Microsoft Exchange use proprietary directories, and directories based on the X.500 standard are also gaining popularity.

X.500 directories are becoming more widely accepted because in addition to acting as a certificate repository, they give administrators a central location for entry of personal attribute information. Entries might include network resources such as file servers, printers, and URLs. User information, such as e-mail address, telephone privileges, and certificates, is accessible from numerous clients in a controlled fashion. Directory clients can locate entries and their attributes using a directory access protocol such as *Lightweight Directory Access Protocol* (LDAP).

LDAP, defined by RFCs 1777 and 1778, was designed to give applications a means to access X.500 directories. It has been widely adopted because it is simpler and easier to use than the X.500 standard protocols. Because it is not directory-specific, LDAP has also found its way into various environments, enhancing its interoperability.

NOTE:

Because of the self-verifying nature of certificates, certificate directories themselves do not necessarily have to be trusted. Should a directory be compromised, certificates can still be validated through the standard process of checking the certificate chain through the CA. If the directory server contains personal or corporate data, however, it may be necessary to provide security and access control to it.

Key Recovery Server

In a PKI population of any size, one thing is sure to happen: End users will lose their private keys. Whether the loss results from hardware failure or a forgotten password, it can create a significant burden on all parties in the PKI. With the loss of a private key, for example, the CA must revoke the corresponding PKC; in addition, a new key pair must be generated, and a new corresponding PKC must be created. As a result, all data encrypted before the incident becomes unrecoverable.

One solution is to provide a *key recovery server* (or, more accurately, a key backup and recovery server). As the name implies, the key recovery server gives the CA a simple way of backing up private keys at the time of creation and recovering them later.

Although key recovery servers can save considerable time and money, problems can arise. For example, the key used to decrypt data could be the same key used to sign messages (that is, the user's private key). In this case, an attacker could access the user's private key and forge messages in the user's name. For that reason, some CAs support two key pairs: one for encryption and decryption and another one for signature and verification. We discuss the storage of multiple key pairs later in this chapter in the section titled "Managing Multiple Key Pairs."

NOTE:

The term "escrow" is sometimes used interchangeably with "recovery." There is, however, a clear distinction between the two. A key recovery server is implemented in a given PKI by its administrators to provide recovery functions for end users. In key escrow, on the other hand, a third party (such as a federal or local law enforcement agency) is given keys needed as evidence in an investigation.

Management Protocols

Management protocols assist in the online communication between end users and management within a PKI. For example, a management protocol might be used to communicate between an RA and an end user or between two CAs that cross-certify each other. Examples of PKI management protocols include *Certificate Management Protocol* (CMP) and message formats such as *Certificate Management Message Format* (CMMF) and PKCS #10.

Management protocols should support the following functions:

- **Registration**   This is the process whereby a user first makes herself or himself known to a CA (directly or through an RA).

- **Initialization**   Before an end user system can operate securely, it is necessary to install key materials that have the appropriate relationship with keys stored elsewhere in the infrastructure. For example, the end-user system must be securely initialized with the public key and other assured information of the trusted CA(s), to be used in validating certificate paths. Furthermore, a client typically must be initialized with its own key pair(s).

- **Certification**   This is the process in which a CA issues a certificate for a user's public key and then either returns the certificate to the end user's client system or posts the certificate in a repository (or both).

- **Key recovery**   As an option, end user client key materials (for example, a user's private key used for encryption purposes) can be backed up by a CA or a key backup system. If a user needs to recover these backed-up key materials (for example, as a result of a forgotten password or a lost key chain file), an online protocol exchange may be needed to support such recovery.

- **Key update**   All key pairs must be updated regularly. In this process, key pairs are replaced and new certificates are issued.

- **Revocation**   This process is invoked when an authorized person advises a CA of an abnormal situation requiring certificate revocation.

- **Cross-certification**   Two CAs exchange information used in establishing a cross-certificate. A cross-certificate is a certificate issued by one CA to another CA that contains a CA signature key used for issuing certificates.

NOTE:

Online protocols are not the only way to implement these functions. Offline methods can also be used.

Operational Protocols

Operational protocols are those protocols that enable the transfer of certificates and revocation status information between directories, end users, and relying parties. The X.509 standard does not specify any single protocol for use within a PKI domain. Instead, the standard specifies how the data should be structured for transport. The following protocols are commonly used within an environment: HTTP, FTP, e-mail, and LDAP.

Figure 6-2 illustrates the ways in which the various components of PKI interact.

Figure 6-2

The interaction between the various PKI components

Registering and Issuing Certificates

CAs can register end users in various ways, often depending greatly on the environment. Many end users simply register with the CA or RA via the Internet using a Web browser. A private corporate PKI may use an automated system to register newly hired employees.

In either case, registration is one of the most important processes in a PKI. It is at this point that the end user and the CA establish trust.

Depending on the type of certificate being issued, each party may go to great lengths to validate the other. For its part, the end user may review the CA's published certificate policies and certification practice statements. For the CA to establish trust with the end user, the CA may require financial documentation and proof of identity through in-person communications.

After registration is complete and a relationship of trust has been established between the CA and the end user, a certificate request can be initiated. One of two approaches can be used. The end user generates a key pair and provides the public key in the form of a standard PKCS #10 *certificate-signing request* (CSR), or the CA can generate a key pair on behalf of the end user.

Revoking a Certificate

Certificates are created in the belief that they will be valid and usable throughout the expected lifetime indicated in the Validity field. In some cases, however, an unexpired certificate should no longer be used. For example, the corresponding private key may have been compromised, the CA has discovered that it has made a mistake, or the holder of the key is no longer employed at a company. As a result, CAs need a way to revoke an unexpired certificate and notify relying parties of the revocation.

The most common method is the use of a *certificate revocation list* (CRL). Simply stated, a CRL is a signed data structure containing a time-stamped list of revoked certificates. The signer of the CRL is typically the same entity that originally issued it (the CA). After a CRL is created and digitally signed, it can be freely distributed across a network or stored in a directory in the same way that certificates are handled.

CAs issue CRLs periodically on schedules ranging from every few hours to every few weeks. A new CRL is issued whether or not it contains any new revocations; in this way, relying parties always know that the most recently received CRL is current. A PKI's certificate policy governs its CRL time interval. Latency between CRLs is one of the major drawbacks of their use. For example, a reported revocation may not be received by the relying party until the next CRL issue, perhaps several hours or several weeks later.

NOTE:

Currently, most applications (such as Web browsers and e-mail readers) do not use the various revocation mechanisms that are in place. However, this is beginning to change as PKIs are becoming more widespread.

Certificate Revocation Lists

As stated previously, a CRL is nothing more than a time-stamped, digitally signed list of revoked certificates. The following section describes, in detail, the various fields that make up a CRL. Figure 6-3 illustrates these fields.

Figure 6-3

The standard structure of a CRL

Version
Signature Algorithm Identifier
Issuer Name
This Update (Date/Time)
Next Update (Date/Time)
User Certificate Serial Number / Revocation Date
CRL Entry Extensions
. . .
User Certificate Serial Number / Revocation Date
CRL Entry Extensions
CRL Extensions
Signature

- **Version** This field indicates the version of the CRL. (This field is optional for Version 1 CRLs but must be present for Version 2.)

- **Signature Algorithm Identifier** This field contains the identifier of the algorithm used to sign the CRL. For example, if this field contains the object identifier for SHA-1 with RSA , it means that the digital signature is a SHA-1 hash (see Chapter 5) encrypted using RSA (see Chapter 4).

- **Issuer Name**   This field identifies the DN, in X.500 format, of the entity that issued the CRL.

- **This Update (Date/Time)**   This field contains a date/time value indicating when the CRL was issued.

- **Next Update (Date/Time)**   This optional field contains a date/time value indicating when the next CRL will be issued. (Although this field is optional, RFC2459 mandates its use.)

- **User Certificate Serial Number/Revocation Date**   This field contains the list of certificates that have been revoked or suspended. The list contains the certificate's serial number and the date and time it was revoked.

- **CRL Entry Extensions**   These fields are discussed in the following section.

- **CRL Extensions**   These fields are discussed in the section "CRL Extensions."

- **Signature**   This field contains the CA signature.

CRL Entry Extensions

Just as an X.509 Version 3 certificate can be enhanced through the use of extensions, Version 2 CRLs are provided a set of extensions that enable CAs to convey additional information with each individual revocation. The X.509 standard defines the following four extensions for use with a Version 2 CRL:

- **Reason Code**   This extension specifies the reason for certificate revocation. Valid entries include the following: unspecified, key compromise, CA compromise, superseded, certificate hold, and others. (For valid reasons, RFC2459 recommends the use of this field.)

- **Hold Instruction Code**   This noncritical extension supports the temporary suspension of a certificate. It contains an OID that describes the action to be taken if the extension exists.

- **Certificate Issuers**   This extension identifies the name of the certificate issuer associated with an indirect CRL (discussed later in the section titled "Indirect CRLs"). If this extension is present, RFC2459 mandates that it be marked critical.

- **Invalidity Date**   This noncritical extension contains a date/time value showing when a suspected or known compromise of the private key occurred.

CRL Extensions

The following CRL extensions have been defined on a per-CRL basis:

- **Authority Key Identifier**   This extension can be used to differentiate between multiple CRL signing keys held by this CA. This field contains a unique key identifier (the subject key identifier in the CRL signer's certificate). The use of this field is mandated by RFC2459.

- **Issuer Alternative Name**   This extension associates one or more alternative name forms with the CRL issuer. RFC2459 specifies that if no DN is specified in the subject field of a certificate, it must have one or more alternative names, and this extension must be flagged critical. RFC2459 recommends the use of this extension when alternative name forms are available but mandates that it not be marked critical.

- **CRL Number**   This noncritical extension provides a means of easily recognizing whether a given CRL has been superseded. It contains a unique serial number relative to the issuer of this CRL. Although this extension is noncritical, RFC2459 mandates its use.

- **Delta CRL Indicator**   This critical extension identifies the CRL as a delta CRL and not a base CRL (see later section, "Delta CRLs"). If this extension is present, RFC2459 mandates that it be marked critical.

- **Issuing Distribution Point**   This critical extension identifies the name of the CRL distribution point for a given CRL (see next section). It also indicates whether the CRL covers revocation of end user certificates only or of CA certificates only, and it specifies whether the certificate was revoked for a set reason. This extension can also be used to indicate that the CRL is an indirect CRL. If this extension is present, RFC2459 mandates that it be marked critical.

CRL Distribution Points

What happens when the CRL for a given PKI domain becomes too large? CRL *distribution points* (sometimes referred to as CRL *partitions*) provide a simple solution. The idea is that instead of a single large CRL, several smaller CRLs are created for distribution. Relying servers retrieve and process these smaller CRLs more easily, saving time, money, and bandwidth.

To use CRL distribution points, the CA supplies a pointer to a location within the Issuing Distribution Point extension. Examples of such pointers are a DNS name, an IP address, or the specific filename on a Web server. The pointer enables relying parties to locate the CRL distribution point.

Delta CRLs

A *delta* CRL lists only incremental changes that have occurred since the preceding CRL. In this way, delta CRLs provide a way to significantly improve processing time for applications that store revocation information in a format other than the CRL structure. With this approach, such applications can add new changes to their local database while ignoring unchanged information already stored there. After an initial full CRL (*base* CRL) posting, an accurate list of revoked certificates is maintained through delta CRLs. As a result, delta CRLs can be issued much more often than can base CRLs.

CAs use the Delta CRL Indicator extension to indicate the use of delta CRLs. In addition, a special value, the "Remove from CRL" value, can be used in the Reason Code extension to specify that an entry in the base CRL may now be removed. An entry might be removed because certificate validity has expired or the certificate is no longer suspended.

Indirect CRLs

Indirect CRLs are another alternative for improving the distribution of CRLs. As the name implies, an *indirect* CRL is provided to the relying party by a third party that did not necessarily issue the certificate. In this way, CRLs that otherwise would be supplied by numerous CAs (or other revoking authorities) can be consolidated into a single CRL for distribution. For example, suppose that a private PKI is served by multiple CAs. By using indirect CRLs, the PKI can receive one CRL issued by one CA (or other trusted third party) on behalf of the other CAs.

Two CRL extensions enable the use of indirect CRLs. To indicate that a CRL contains revocation information from multiple CAs, the Indirect CRL attribute is set to True. It's also important to provide the relying party with additional information concerning revocation of each entry. A CRL entry for each certificate is used to identify its CA. If there is no CRL entry, the certificate is assumed to have been issued by the CA listed on the first line of the CRL.

Suspending a Certificate

At times, a CA needs to limit the use of a certificate temporarily but does not require that it be revoked. For example, a corporate end user may be going on vacation. In such cases, the certificate can be *suspended*, disabling the use of PKI-enabled applications that should not be accessed in the employee's absence. When the employee returns, the CA removes the suspension. This approach saves the CA time by not requiring it to revoke and then reissue the certificate. To suspend a certificate, the CA uses the value Certificate Hold in the Reason Code extension of the CRL.

Authority Revocation Lists

Like end users, CAs themselves are identified by certificates. Just as end user certificates may require revocation, so do CA certificates. An *authority revocation list* (ARL) provides a means of disseminating this revocation information for CAs. ARLs are distinguished from CRLs via the Issuing Distribution Point field within the revocation list.

Online Certificate Status Protocol

Depending on the size of the PKI population, CRLs can become unwieldy. Even if you use the CRL techniques we've discussed (CRL distribution points, indirect CRLs, and delta CRLs), the workload associated with CRLs can become burdensome. On the other end, relying parties must spend considerable resources obtaining the most current CRL.

A newer protocol, the *Online Certificate Status Protocol* (OCSP), can be used to check whether a digital certificate is valid at the time of a given transaction. OCSP enables relying parties to conduct these checks in real time, providing a faster, easier, and more dependable way of validating digital certificates than the traditional method of downloading and processing CRLs. Figure 6-4 illustrates the interaction between various OCSP components.

Here's how it works. The CA provides a server, known as an OCSP *responder,* that contains current revocation information. Relying parties can query the OCSP responder to determine the status of a given certificate. The best way to obtain the information is to have the CA feed it directly into the responder. Depending on the relationship between the CA and the OCSP responder, the CA can forward immediate notification of a certificate's revocation, making it instantly available to users.

Figure 6-4

Interaction between a relying part and an OCSP responder

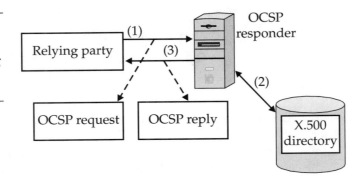

The relying party sends a simple request to the OCSP responder, suspending the use of the certificate in question until a response is received. The OCSP request contains the protocol version, the service requested, and one or more certificate identifiers. The certificate identifier consists of a hash of the issuer's name, a hash of the issuer's public key, and the certificate serial number.

The OCSP responder provides a digitally signed response for each of the certificates in the original request. Replies consist of a certificate identifier, one of three status values (Good, Revoked, or Unknown), and a validity interval (This Update and, optionally, Next Update). The response may also include the time of revocation as well as the reason for revocation.

NOTE:

RFC2560 states that an OCSP request must be protocol-independent, although HTTP is the most common approach in use.

Trust Models

Trust models are used to describe the relationship between end users, relying parties, and the CA. Various models can be found in today's PKIs. The following describes the two most widely used and well known: certificate hierarchies and cross-certification models.

It should be noted, however, that each of these can be used not only alone but in conjunction with one another as well.

Certificate Hierarchies

As a PKI population begins to increase, it becomes difficult for a CA to effectively track the identities of all the parties it has certified. As the number of certificates grows, a single authority may become a bottleneck in the certification process. One solution is to use a *certificate hierarchy,* in which the CA delegates its authority to one or more subsidiary authorities. These authorities, in turn, designate their own subsidiaries, and the process travels down the hierarchy until an authority actually issues a certificate. Figure 6-5 illustrates the concept of certificate hierarchies.

Figure 6-5

This simple certificate hierarchy might occur in a large corporation

Metro Motors Corporate

Metro Motors West

Metro Motors East

Metro Motors Marketing

Metro Motors HR

Metro Motors R&D

Metro Motors Manufacturing

A powerful feature of certificate hierarchies is that not all parties must automatically trust all the certificate authorities. Indeed, the only authority whose trust must be established throughout the enterprise is the highest CA. Because of its position in the hierarchy, this authority is generally known as the *root* authority. Examples of current public root CAs include Verisign, Thawte, and the U.S. Postal Service's root CA.

Cross-Certification

The concept of a single, monolithic PKI serving every user in the world is unlikely to become a reality. Instead, we will continue to see PKIs established between nations, political organizations, and businesses. One reason for this practice is the policy that each CA should operate independently and follow its own rules. Cross-certification enables CAs and end users from different PKI domains to interact. Figure 6-6 illustrates the concept of cross-certification.

Cross-certification certificates are issued by CAs to form a nonhierarchical *trust path*. A mutual trust relationship requires two certificates, which cover the relationship in each direction. These certificates must be supported by a cross-certification agreement between the CAs. This agreement governs the liability of the partners in the event that a certificate turns out to be false or misleading.

After two CAs have established a trust path, relying parties within a PKI domain are able to trust the end users of the other domain. This capability is especially useful in Web-based business-to-business communications. Cross-certification also proves useful for intradomain communications when a single domain has several CAs.

NOTE:

The use of cross-certification instead of or in conjunction with certificate hierarchies can prove to be more secure than a pure hierarchy model. In a hierarchy, for example, if the private key of the root CA is compromised, all subordinates are rendered untrustworthy. In contrast, with cross-certification, the compromising of one CA does not necessarily invalidate the entire PKI.

Figure 6-6

Cross-certification

Metro Motors Corporate

Metro Motors East

USA Steel

Cross-certified

Metro Motors R&D

Metro Motors Manufacturing

USA Steel Order Entry

USA Steel Shipping

X.509 Certificate Chain

A *certificate chain* is the most common method used to verify the binding between an entity and its public key. To gain trust in a certificate, a relying party must verify three things about each certificate until it reaches a trusted root. First, the relying party must check that each certificate in the chain is signed by the public key of the next certificate in the chain. It must also ensure that each certificate is not expired or revoked and that each certificate conforms to a set of criteria defined by certificates higher up in the chain. By verifying the trusted root for the certificate, a certificate-using application that trusts the certificate can develop trust in the entity's public key. Figure 6-7 illustrates certificate chains and how they may be used.

Figure 6-7

A certificate
chain

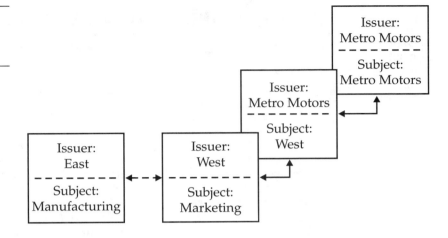

To see this process in action, consider what happens when a client application in the marketing department verifies the identity of the marketing department's Web server. The server presents its certificate, which was issued by authority of the manufacturing department. The marketing client does not trust the manufacturing authority, however, so it asks to see that authority's certificate. When the client receives the manufacturing authority's certificate, it can verify that the manufacturing authority was certified by the corporation's root CA. Because the marketing client trusts the root CA, it knows that it can trust the Web server.

The Push Model Versus the Pull Model

The chaining described here relies on individuals having access to all the certificates in the chain. How does the relying party get these certificates? One way is for the issuer to send an entire chain of certificates when sending one certificate (see Figure 6-8). This is the *push* model, in which the sender pushes the entire chain of certificates to the recipient, and the recipient can immediately verify all the certificates. The *pull* model sends only the sender's certificate and leaves it up to the recipient to pull in the CA's certificate. Because each certificate contains the issuer's name, the recipient knows where to go to verify the certificate. (To make searches easier, Version 3 certificates offer more fields to hold information.) Even with the push model, however, some recipient chaining may be necessary.

Figure 6-8

Internet Explorer
provides a set of
trusted root
certification
authorities

Figure 6-8

Internet Explorer provides a set of trusted root certification authorities

Managing Key Pairs

The management of key pairs—the policies whereby they are generated and protected—is important in any PKI. As described in this section, such policy decisions depend greatly on the intended purpose of the keys. For example, keys that enable nonrepudiation for e-commerce transactions are more likely to be handled with greater care than those used to provide for secure e-mail.

Generating Key Pairs

Keys can be generated in one of two ways. In the first option, key pairs are generated on the end user's system. The second option requires that a trusted third party (such as the CA or its delegated RA) generate the key pair. Which of these options is more appropriate is a matter of debate. Each approach has advantages and disadvantages.

End-user generation of keys can be effective, especially for generating keys for the purpose of nonrepudiation. This option enables the user to build greater confidence in the trust shared with relying parties because the key value is never exposed to another entity. One problem is that the end user must provide software or hardware to generate strong keys. Even though most browsers incorporate this functionality, it tends to be CPU-intensive and slow. In addition, end users face the task of securely transporting the public key to the CA (or corresponding RA) for certification.

The second method, in which a central system such as the CA or one of its RAs generates key pairs, also has its advantages. A central system commonly has greater resources to provide for faster key generation. Furthermore, an end user may require cryptographically strong keys that have been generated by a trusted and independently evaluated cryptographic module. In other cases, an end user may need private key backup, and this service can be easily accommodated without unnecessary transfer of the private key.

Because each approach offers benefits, many CAs support both options. Yet another option is the use of multiple key pairs. Here, end users generate keys used to provide nonrepudiation, and the central system provides the keys for encryption.

Protecting Private Keys

The strength of public-key cryptographic systems and their associated certificates relies greatly on the security of private keys. It is crucial that only the certified owner—the person or organization identified in the certificate—use the corresponding private key. The following mechanisms are used to safeguard and limit access to private keys:

■ **Password protection** This is the most common form of protection employed by PKIs. A password or *personal identification number* (PIN) is used to encrypt the private key, which is stored on the local hard disk. However, if the key can be obtained from the hard disk, the problem of accessing the key is reduced to simple password guessing. As a result, this is considered the least secure method and is generally not thought to be a long-term solution.

- **PCMCIA cards** (Personal Computer Memory Card International Association) To reduce the risk of a key being stolen from the user's hard disk, many vendors have begun to offer the option of storing keys on chip cards. Because the key must still leave the card and enter the system's memory, however, it remains vulnerable to theft. Chip cards are discussed in Chapter 9.

- **Tokens** With *tokens*, the private key is stored in an encrypted format in a hardware device and can be unlocked only through the use of a one-time passcode provided by the token. Although this technique is more secure than those mentioned so far, the token still must be available to the end user whenever the private key is needed, and it can be lost.

- **Biometrics** The key is associated with a unique identifying quality of an individual user (for example, a fingerprint, a retinal scan, or a voice match). The idea is that biometrics can provide the same level of security as tokens while alleviating the need for the user to carry a device that can be lost.

- **Smart cards** In a true smart card (see Chapter 3), the key is stored in a tamperproof card that contains a computer chip, enabling it to perform signature and decryption operations. Thus, the key never leaves the card, and the possibility of compromise is greatly reduced. However, the user must carry a device, and if the card was used for encryption and is lost, the encrypted data may be unrecoverable.

NOTE:

Most users take few or no precautions to protect their private keys from theft. As public-key technology becomes more widely used, organizations will probably devote more time to awareness programs and education.

Managing Multiple Key Pairs

As stated throughout this chapter, it is not uncommon for end users to have more than one certificate for various purposes, and therefore they may have various key-pair types. For example, a key used to digitally sign a document for purposes of nonrepudiation is not necessarily the same one that would be used for the encryption of files. For this reason, it is crucial that end users as well as PKI administrators be aware of the various management techniques used to secure these keys.

A private key that is used to provide digital signatures for the purposes of nonrepudiation requires secure storage for the lifetime of the key. During its lifetime, there is no requirement for backup; if the key is lost, a new key pair should be generated. After the lifetime of the key has expired, the key should not be archived. Instead, it should be securely destroyed. This practice ensures against unauthorized use that may occur years after the key is considered expired. The use of secure time-stamping can also help reduce fraud. To authenticate data signed by these private keys, it is necessary to maintain the corresponding PKC.

NOTE:

For private keys used for nonrepudiation, the ANSI X9.57 standard requires that they be created, used, and destroyed within one secure module.

Conversely, a private key used to support encryption should be backed up during its lifetime to enable recovery of encrypted information. After the private key is considered expired, it should be archived to support later decryption of encrypted legacy data. Whether and how corresponding public keys should be backed up and archived greatly depends on the algorithm in use. With RSA, the public key does not require backup or archiving. If Diffie-Hellman key agreement was used, on the other hand, the public key will be required to recover data at a later time.

Updating Key Pairs

As mentioned earlier in this chapter in the section titled "Management Protocols," good security practices dictate that key pairs should be updated periodically. One reason is that, over time, keys become susceptible to compromise through cryptanalytic attacks. After a certificate has expired, one of two things can occur: The CA can reissue a new certificate based on the original key pair, or a new key pair can be generated and a new certificate issued.

Key pairs can be updated in one of two ways. In a manual update, it is left to the end user to recognize that the certificate is about to expire and request an update. This approach places a considerable burden on users to keep track of a certificate's expiration date. Failing to request a timely update will put the user out of service and unable to communicate securely. As a result, the end user must perform an off-line exchange with the CA.

A better solution is an automated update, in which a system is in place to check the validity of the certificate each time it is used. As the certificate approaches expiration, the automated system initiates a request for key update with the appropriate CA. When the new certificate is created, the system automatically replaces the old certificate. In this way, the end user is free to carry out secure operations uninterrupted.

Keeping a History of Key Pairs

A CA's published policy states the time period during which a given certificate can be considered valid (typically, one year). As a result, it's not uncommon for a user to accumulate three or more key pairs within three years. A key history mechanism provides a way of archiving keys and certificates for later use. The other alternatives, such as decrypting and reencrypting data as new keys are generated, would be impractical in most environments.

Such a history is of great importance to any PKI. For example, suppose that a data file was signed with my private signing key three years ago. How does a relying party get a copy of the corresponding PKC to verify the signature? Similarly, what if the public key from my certificate was used to encrypt some data or another symmetric key to perform a digital enveloping process five years ago? Where can the corresponding private decryption key be found? If a key history has been kept, the necessary keys for both scenarios will be available.

NOTE:

As stated earlier, similar keys can be used for various purposes (for example, private keys can be used not only for decryption but also for signing). Because a key's purpose dictates the method of storage, it may be necessary to have two or more separate key pairs.

Deploying a PKI

As organizations plan for deploying PKIs, they have three basic options: outsourcing, insourcing, or running their own. With *outsourcing,* a third party runs a CA on behalf of the organization. This option requires the organization to have a great deal of trust in the third party and its policies and practices. The advantage of outsourcing is that the organization can leverage outside expertise and resources that it may not have in-house.

With *insourcing,* an organization provides its own resources, but the administrative staff is leveraged from outside. This option enables an organization to maintain control over its own CA policies while taking advantage of outside expertise. Many PKI vendors, including Entrust Technologies and Verisign, include this service in their standard offerings.

Finally, it is possible for an organization to run its own CA. By using PKI-enabling products or building its own, an organization manages every aspect of the PKI. This option greatly benefits organizations that have in-house expertise, affording them the most flexibility and control over the system.

The Future of PKI

PKIs have grown considerably in the past decade as increasing numbers of organizations have become dependent on them. However, many improvements are in the works, not only by noncommercial organizations such as the *International Organization for Standardization* (ISO) and *Internet Engineering Task Force* (IETF) but also by many PKI vendors. Two such improvements are roaming certificates and attribute certificates, discussed in the next two sections.

Roaming Certificates

As you've seen, standard certificates do a great job of binding an individual to a public key, but a new problem has arisen: the need for portability. It is not uncommon for a user to move among several computers within an organization. A certificate can be placed on every possible machine, but in order to be effective, the private key also must be present.

Until recently, only two real solutions have provided the mobility of certificates and their corresponding private keys. The first is smart card technology, in which the public/private key pair is stored on the card. However, this option has drawbacks, such as the inconvenience of carrying an item that can be lost or damaged. In addition, smart cards are usable only on systems that have a smart card reader. The second option, which is not much better, is to copy the certificate and private key onto a floppy for later use. Again, the user is forced to carry an item that can be lost or damaged, and a floppy is not as cryptographically secure as a smart card.

A new solution is the use of *roaming certificates* (perhaps better stated as roaming certificates and private keys), which are provided through third-party software. Properly configured on any system, the software (or plug-in) enables a user access to his or her public/private key pairs. The concept is simple. Users' certificates and private keys are placed in a secure central server. When the user logs into a local system, the public/private key pair is securely retrieved from the server and placed in the local system's memory for use. When the user has completed work and logs off of the local system, the software (or plug-in) scrubs the user's certificate and private key from memory.

To date, this technology has been limited mainly to private PKIs, such as corporations, because of scalability issues. However, as roaming applications and users become more prevalent, it's conceivable that roaming certificate technology will be developed into a cost-effective way of providing virtual PKIs worldwide. Figure 6-9 illustrates the interaction of common roaming certificate systems.

Figure 6-9

Roaming
certificates

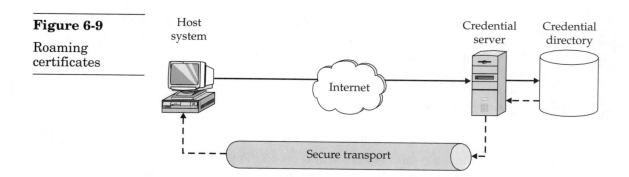

NOTE:

Although the concept of roaming certificates has proven quite useful, some standards do not support this technology. One such standard is ANSI X9.57, which requires that private keys used for the purposes of nonrepudiation be created, used, and destroyed within one secure module.

Attribute Certificates

Another popular emerging standard is the *attribute certificate* (AC). Although ACs are similar in structure to public-key certificates, ACs provide different functionality. ACs do not contain a public key for an individual. Instead, they are used to bind an entity to a set of attributes that specify membership, role, security clearance, or other authorization information. Attribute certificates, like public-key certificates, are digitally signed to prevent changes after the fact.

In conjunction with current authentication services, ACs can provide a means to transport authorization information securely. Applications that can use this technology include those that provide remote access to network resources (such as Web servers and databases) and those that control physical access to buildings and facilities. For example, after a user signs on, his or her identity can be verified through the use of the current public-key certificate. After the user has logged in, his or her public key can be used to create a secure session with an access control server, and the user's attribute certificate can be checked against a list of valid users. Figure 6-10 illustrates a standard attribute certificate.

NOTE:

ISO has defined the basic attribute certificate, and IETF is currently profiling these definitions for use in Internet environments.

Figure 6-10

Controlling
access with
attribute
certificates

Version (V.1 or V.2)
Holder Name (Comparable to Subject's Name)
Issuer Name
Signature
Serial Number
Validity period (Start/End Date/Time)
Attributes
Issuer Unique Identifier
Extensions

Certificate Policies and Certification Practice Statements

Certification authorities act as trusted third parties, vouching for the contents of the certificates they issue. But what exactly does a CA certify? What makes one CA more trusted than another? Two mechanisms are used by CAs to establish trust among end users and relying parties. These are certificate policies and certification practice statements.

The X.509 standard defines a certificate policy as "a named set of rules that indicates the applicability of a certificate to a particular community and/or class of application with common security requirements." One or more certificate policies can be identified in the standard extensions of an X.509 Version 3 certificate. As relying parties obtain a certificate for processing, they can use the policies specified in that certificate to make a decision of trust.

A more detailed description of practices is made available through the use of a certification practice statement, a concept originated by the *American Bar Association* (ABA). According to the ABA's "Digital Signature Guidelines," a CPS is "a statement of the practices which the certification authority employs in issuing certificates." A CPS gives relying parties a basis for making a trust decision concerning a CA.

The relationship between certificate policies and CPSs is not entirely clear. Each kind of document was created for unique reasons by different sources. CPSs tend to provide a detailed statement about a CA's practices, whereas certificate policies tend to provide a broader definition of practices.

RFC2527 outlines the key components of a CPS as follows:

- **Introduction** This part of a CPS provides a general overview of the certificate policy definition, indicating any applicable names or other identifiers (for example, ASN.1 object identifiers) that are used in the statement. It should also provide all contact information (name, phone number, address, and so on) of the responsible authority.

- **General Provisions** This section describes the various obligations, rights, and liabilities of the CA or RA, end users, and relying parties. It also includes information about how and how often certificates and CRLs will be published.

- **Identification and Authentication** This section describes the procedures used by the CA or RA to authenticate an end user applicant. It also describes how end users should request certificate revocations and key updates.

- **Operational Requirements** This section describes the requirements for certificate enrollment, issuance, and acceptance. It also addresses suspension, revocation, and the frequency of CRLs. Various security concerns are also covered, such as audit procedures, compromise and disaster recovery, and procedures for CA termination.

- **Physical, Procedural, and Personnel Security Controls** This section defines the nontechnical controls that are in place to provide for secure key generation, subject authentication, certificate issuance, certificate revocation, audit, and archiving. Such controls, for example, might include off-site record storage and background investigations of employees who fill trusted roles.

- **Technical Security Controls** This section describes the security measures taken by a CA to protect its private keys. Examples include where and how private keys are stored and who can activate and deactivate a private key.

- **Certificate and CRL Profile** This section specifies the format to be used for certificates and CRLs, the current versions supported, and the name forms used by the CA, the RA, and the end user. Also identified here are the supported certificate and CRL extensions and their criticality.
- **Specification Administration** This section specifies how this certificate policy definition or CPS will be maintained. Covered are change procedures for updating this statement, how it will be distributed, and the approval procedures for this and any new statement.

Summary

Although public-key technology solves many of the problems associated with symmetric-key technology, it presents a new set of distribution problems. The most widely accepted standard for public-key technology is the X.509 standard, which describes the format of public-key certificates to assist in the secure distribution of these keys. X.509 Version 3 certificates, for example, contain various fields and extensions that help govern their use.

A public-key infrastructure (PKI) plays an important role in the operation of public-key certificates. A PKI manages the collaboration between end users and relying parties, enabling the secure issuance and operation of these certificates. Certificate revocation and status checking are supported through the use of a CRL or the Online Certificate Status Protocol (OCSP), or both.

Certificate policies and certification practice statements provide end users and relying parties with information on which to base a decision to trust a given CA.

Real-World Examples

Various products are available that provide public-key infrastructure support, including developer toolkits, which assist individuals in creating their own public-key infrastructures, and companies, such as Verisign, that have based their business on providing certificates as a service. The following is a description of two PKI products developed by RSA Security, Inc.

Keon Certificate Server

The Keon certificate server is a fully functional CA\RA with all of the necessary tools to run a full CA. This server provides useful functionality, such as the One Step function. The One Step function actually allows the CA administrator to set up Keon programmatically so that as new employees are added to a human resource database, a certificate is generated and stored for use. This functionality takes a lot of the burden off end users and administrators.

Keon Web PassPort

Another advancement in the PKI arena is the new Keon Web PassPort. The Web PassPort provides roaming-certificate technology, which is similar to certificates discussed in the "Roaming Certificates" section earlier in this chapter. Through the use of a browser plug-in, a user can download the necessary private and public information to make use of PKI-enabled applications. A user may now, through the use of strong authentication and one small plug-in, make use of any computer system anywhere in the world.

CHAPTER 7

Network and Transport Security Protocols

Applications, systems, and networks can be made secure through the use of security protocols, which provide a wide range of encryption and authentication services. Each protocol is placed within several layers of a computing infrastructure (that is, network, transport, and application layers). Figure 7-1 shows the various protocols and their locations within the Transportation Control Protocol/Internet Protocol *(TCP/IP) stack. This chapter and Chapter 8 describe these protocols and explain how they operate within the TCP/IP stack. This chapter first covers the IPSec protocol, which provides security at the network layer. Then we take an in-depth look at the* Secure Sockets Layer *(SSL), which implements security at the transport layer.*

Internet Protocol Security

Internet Protocol Security (IPSec) is a framework of open standards for ensuring secure private communications over IP networks. Based on standards developed by the *Internet Engineering Task Force* (IETF), IPSec ensures confidentiality, integrity, and authenticity of data communications across a public IP network. IPSec is a necessary component of a

Figure 7-1

Protocol locations within TCP/IP: (a) network security and (b) transport security

SMTP	HTTP	NNTP
TCP		
IP/**IPSec**		

(A) Network security

SMTP	HTTP	NNTP
TCP		
SSL		
IP		

(B) Transport security

standards-based, flexible solution for deploying a network-wide security policy.

IPSec implements network layer encryption and authentication, providing an end-to-end security solution in the network architecture. In this way, end systems and applications can enjoy the advantage of strong security without the need to make any changes. Because IPSec encrypted packets look like ordinary IP packets, they can be easily routed through any IP network, such as the Internet, without any changes to the intermediate networking equipment. The only devices that know about the encryption are the endpoints. This feature greatly reduces the cost of implementation and management.

IP Security Architecture

IPSec combines several security technologies to protect the confidentiality, integrity, and authenticity of IP packets. IPSec actually refers to several related protocols as defined in RFCs 2401-2411 and 2451. Two of these standards define IPSec and *Internet Key Exchange* (IKE). IPSec defines the information that is added to an IP packet to enable confidentiality, integrity, and authenticity controls; it also defines how to encrypt the packet data. IKE is used to negotiate the security association between two entities and to exchange keying material. The use of IKE is optional, but it relieves users of the difficult and labor-intensive task of manually configuring security associations. IKE should be used in most real-world applications to enable large-scale, secure communications.

IPSec Services

IPSec provides security services at the IP layer by enabling a system for selecting required security protocols, determining the algorithm(s) to use for the service(s), and implementing any cryptographic keys required to provide the following services:

- Access control
- Connectionless integrity (a detection method of the IP packet itself)
- Data origin authentication
- Rejection of replayed packets (a form of partial sequence integrity)
- Confidentiality (encryption)
- Limited traffic-flow confidentiality

IPSec provides these services through the use of two protocols. The first one, the *authentication header* (AH) protocol, supports access control, data origin authentication, connectionless integrity, and the rejection of *replay* attacks, in which an attacker copies a packet and sends it out of sequence to confuse communicating nodes. The second protocol is the *encapsulating security payload* (ESP) protocol. ESP alone can support confidentiality, access control, limited traffic-flow confidentiality, and the rejection of replay attacks.

NOTE:
ESP and AH can be used in concert to provide all the services.

The Authentication Header Protocol

AH provides data integrity and authentication services for IP packets (see Figure 7-2). These services protect against attacks commonly mounted against open networks. AH uses a keyed-hash function rather than digital signatures because digital signature technology is too slow and would greatly reduce network throughput. Note, however, that AH does not provide confidentiality protection, so data can still be viewed as it travels across a network.

Figure 7-2

The authentication header protocol

Next Header	Payload Length	Reserved
Security Parameters Index (SPI)		
Sequence Number		
Authentication Data (variable length)		

AH contains the following fields:

- **Next Header**   This field identifies the higher-level protocol following AH (for example, TCP, UDP, or ESP).

- **Payload Length**   This field indicates the length of the AH contents.

- **Reserved**   This field is reserved for future use. Currently, this field must always be set to zero.

- **Security Parameters Index**   This field is a fixed-length, arbitrary value. When used in combination with the destination IP address, this value uniquely identifies a security association for this packet (that is, it indicates a set of security parameters for use in this connection).

- **Sequence Number**   The field provides a monotonically increasing number for each packet sent with a given SPI. This value lets the recipient keep track of the order of the packets and ensures that the same set of parameters is not used for too many packets. The sequence number provides protection against replay attacks.

- **Authentication Data**   This variable-length field contains the *integrity check value* (ICV) (see next section) for this packet. It may include padding to bring the length of the header to an integral multiple of 32 bits (in IPv4) or 64 bits (IPv6).

Integrity Check Value Calculation

The ICV, a truncated version of a *message authentication code* (MAC), is calculated by a MAC algorithm. IPSec requires that all implementations support at least HMAC-MD5 and HMAC-SHA1 (the HMAC symmetric authentication scheme supported by MD5 or SHA-1 hashes; see Chapter 6. To guarantee minimal interoperability, an IPSec implementation must support at least these schemes.

The ICV is computed using the following fields:

■ The IP header fields that either do not change in transit or whose values are predictable upon arrival at the endpoint for the AH security association. Other fields are set to zero for the purpose of calculation.

■ The entire contents of the AH header except for the Authentication Data field. The Authentication Data field is set to zero for the purpose of calculation.

■ All upper-level protocol data, which is assumed to be immutable in transit.

NOTE:

The HMAC value is calculated completely, although it is truncated to 96 bytes (the default size for the Authentication Data field).

Transport and Tunnel Modes

AH services can be employed in two ways: in transport mode or in tunnel mode. The actual placement of the AH depends on which mode is used and on whether the AH is being applied to an IPv4 or an IPv6 packet. Figure 7-3 illustrates IPv4 and IPv6 packets before authentication services are applied.

In *transport* mode, the AH applies only to host implementations and provides protection for upper-layer protocols in addition to selected IP header fields. In this mode, AH is inserted after the IP header but before

Figure 7-3

IPv4 and IPv6 before AH is applied

Standard IPv4 packet

Original IP Header (any options)	TCP	Data

Standard IPv6 datagram

Original IP Header (any options)	Extension Headers (if present)	TCP	Data

any upper-layer protocol (such as, TCP, UDP) and before any other IPSec headers that have already been inserted. In IPv4, this calls for placing AH after the original IP header but before the upper-layer protocol. In IPv6, AH is viewed as an end-to-end payload; this means that intermediate routers should not process it. For this reason, the AH should appear after the original IP header, hop-by-hop, routing, and fragmentation extension headers. This mode is provided via the transport *security association* (SA). Figure 7-4 illustrates the AH transport mode positioning in typical IPv4 and IPv6 packets.

Figure 7-4

IPv4 and IPv6 header placement in transport mode

IPv4 AH in transport mode

Original IP Header (any options)	AH	TCP	Data

IPv6 AH in transport mode

Original IP Header	Hop-by-Hop Destination, Routing Fragment	AH	Destination Options	TCP	Data

In *tunnel* mode, the AH can be employed in either host or security gateways. When AH is implemented in a security gateway (to protect transit traffic), tunnel mode must be used. In this mode, the AH is inserted between the original IP header and the new outer IP header. Whereas the inner IP header carries the ultimate source and destination addresses, the new outer IP header may contain distinct IP addresses (such as, addresses of firewalls or other security gateways). In tunnel mode, AH protects the entire inner IP packet, including the entire inner IP header. In tunnel mode, the position of AH relative to the outer IP header is the same as for AH in transport mode. This mode is provided via the tunnel SA. Figure 7-5 illustrates AH tunnel mode positioning for typical IPv4 and IPv6 packets.

NOTE:

ESP and AH headers can be combined in a variety of modes. The IPSec architecture document (RFC2401) describes the combinations of security associations that must be supported.

Figure 7-5

IPv4 and IPv6 header placement in tunnel mode

IPv4 AH in tunnel mode

New IP Header (any options)	AH	Original IP Header (any options)	TCP	Data

IPv6 AH in tunel mode

New IP Header	Extension Headers (if present)	AH	Extension Headers (if present)	TCP	Data

The Encapsulating Security Payload Protocol

The *encapsulating security payload* (ESP) protocol provides confidentiality services for IP data while in transit across untrusted networks. Optionally, ESP also provides authentication services. The format of ESP varies according to the type and mode of the encryption being used. In all cases the key associated with the encryption is selected using the SPI. Figure 7-6 illustrates the components of an ESP header.

Figure 7-6

Components of an ESP header

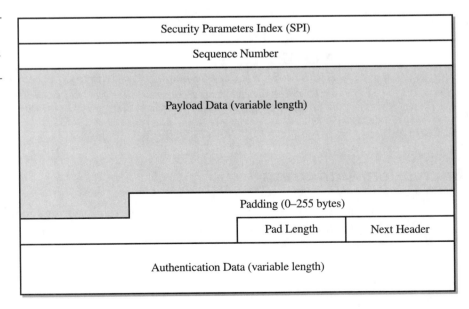

Security Parameters Index (SPI)
Sequence Number
Payload Data (variable length)
Padding (0–255 bytes)
Pad Length / Next Header
Authentication Data (variable length)

The ESP header contains the following fields:

- **Security Parameters Index** This field, as in the AH packet, is used to help uniquely identify a security association to be used.

- **Sequence Number** This field, again as in the AH packet, contains a counter that increases each time a packet is sent to the same address using the same SPI. It lets the recipient keep track of the packet order.

- **Payload Data** This variable-length field contains the actual encrypted data contents being carried by the IP packet.

- **Padding** This field provides space for adding bytes, as required by certain types of encryption algorithms (see Chapter 2). Data padding confuses *sniffers,* who try to access information about encrypted data in transit, in this case by trying to estimate how much data is being transmitted.

- **Pad Length** This field identifies how much of the encrypted payload is padding.

- **Next Header** This field identifies the type of data carried in the Payload Data field.

- **Authentication Data** This variable-length field contains a value that represents the ICV computed over the ESP packet minus the Authentication Data field. This field is optional and is included only if the authentication service is selected within the SA.

NOTE:

All the ESP header components are encrypted except for the Security Parameters Index and Sequence Number fields. Both of these fields, however, are authenticated.

Encryption Algorithms

The IPSec ESP standard currently requires that compliant systems have two cryptographic algorithms. Systems must have the DES algorithm using *cipher block chaining* (CBC) mode (see Chapter 2); compliant systems that require only authentication must have a NULL algorithm. However, other algorithms are defined for use by ESP services. Following are some of the defined algorithms:

- Triple DES
- RC5
- IDEA
- CAST
- BLOWFISH
- 3IDEA

ESP in Transport and Tunnel Modes

Like AH, ESP can be employed in two modes: transport mode and tunnel mode. These modes operate here in a similar way to their operation in AH, with one exception: with ESP, data, called *trailers,* are appended to the end of each packet.

In transport mode, ESP is used only to support host implementations and to provide protection for upper-layer protocols but not for the IP header itself. As with AH, in an IPv4 packet the ESP header is inserted after the original IP header and before any upper-layer protocols (for example, TCP, UDP) and before any other existing IPSec headers. In IPv6, ESP is viewed as an end-to-end payload; that is, intermediate routers should not process it. For this reason, the ESP header should appear after the original IP header, hop-by-hop header, routing header, and fragmentation extension header. In each case, the ESP trailer is also appended to the packet (encompassing the Padding, Pad Length, and Next Header fields). Optionally, the ESP authentication data field is appended if it has been selected. Figure 7-7 illustrates the ESP transport mode positioning in typical IPv4 and IPv6 packets.

Figure 7-7

IPv4 and IPv6 header placement in transport mode

IPv4 ESP in transport mode

Original IP Header (any options)	ESP Header	TCP	Data	ESP Trailer	ESP Authentication

IPv6 AH in transport mode

Original IP Header (any options)	Hop-by-Hop Destination, Routing Fragmentation	ESP Header	Destination Options	TCP	Data	ESP Trailer	ESP Authentication

Tunnel mode ESP can be employed by either hosts or security gateways. When ESP is implemented in a security gateway (to protect subscriber transit traffic), tunnel mode must be used. In this mode, the ESP header is inserted between the original IP header and the new outer IP header. Whereas the inner IP header carries the ultimate source and destination addresses, the new outer IP header may contain distinct IP addresses (such as, addresses of firewalls or other security gateways). In tunnel mode, ESP protects the entire inner IP packet, including the entire inner IP header. The position of ESP in tunnel mode, relative to the outer IP header, is the same as for ESP in transport mode. Figure 7-8 illustrates ESP tunnel mode positioning for typical IPv4 and IPv6 packets.

Figure 7-8

IPv4 and IPv6 header placement in tunnel mode

IPv4 AH in tunnel mode

New IP Header (any options)	ESP Header	Original IP Header (any options)	TCP	Data	ESP Trailer	ESP Authentication

IPv6 AH in tunnel mode

New IP Header	New Extension Headers	ESP Header	Original IP Header	Original Extension Header	TCP	Data	ESP Trailer	ESP Authentication

NOTE:

ESP and AH headers can be combined in a variety of modes. The IPSec architecture document describes the combinations of security associations that must be supported.

Security Associations

To communicate, each pair of hosts using IPSec must establish a *security association* (SA) between them. The SA groups together all the things that you need to know about how to communicate securely with someone else, such as the type of protection used, the keys to be used, and the valid duration of this SA. The SA establishes a one-way relationship between the sender and the receiver. For peer communications, a second SA is needed.

You can think of an SA as a secure channel through the public network to a certain person, group of people, or network resource. It's like a contract with whoever is at the other end. The SA also has the advantage in that it lets you construct classes of security channels. If you need to be a little more careful when talking to one party than another, the rules of your SA with that party can reflect extra caution—for example, specifying stronger encryption.

A security association is uniquely identified by three parameters:

- **Security Parameters Index** This bit string uniquely identifies a security association relative to a security protocol (for example, AH or ESP). The SPI is located within AH and ESP headers so that the receiving system can select the SA under which a received packet will be processed.

- **IP Destination Address** This parameter indicates the destination IP address for this SA. The endpoint may be that of an end user system or a network system such as a gateway or firewall. Although in concept this parameter could be any address type (multicast, broadcast, and so on), currently it can be only a unicast address.

- **Security Protocol Identifier** This parameter indicates whether the association is that of an AH or an ESP security association.

Combining Security Associations

Using a single SA, you can deploy either AH or ESP (but not both) to implement security for IP packets. However, there is no restriction on the use of multiple SAs, usually referred to as an SA *bundle*. The order in which the SAs are bundled is defined by your security policy. IPSec does define two ways of combining SAs: transport adjacency and iterated tunneling.

Transport adjacency refers to the process of applying multiple transport SAs to the same IP packet without using tunneling SAs. This level of combination lets you apply both AH and ESP IP packets but does not enable further nesting. The idea is that strong algorithms are used in both AH and ESP, so further nesting would yield no additional benefits. The IP packet is processed only once: at its final destination. Figure 7-9 illustrates the application of transport adjacency.

In *iterated tunneling,* you apply multiple (layered) security protocols by using IP tunneling. This approach allows multiple levels of nesting. Each

Figure 7-9

Transport
adjacency

tunnel can originate or terminate at a different IPSec site along the path.
Figure 7-10 shows three basic cases of iterated tunneling supported by the
IPSec protocol.

NOTE:

*You can also combine transport adjacency and iterated tunneling. For
example, you could construct an SA bundle from one tunnel SA and one
or two transport SAs applied in sequence.*

Security Databases

IPSec contains two nominal databases: the *Security Policy Database*
(SPD) and the *Security Association Database* (SAD). SPD specifies the
policies that determine the disposition of all IP traffic, inbound or outbound. SAD contains parameters that are associated with each currently
active security association.

Figure 7-10

Three cases of iterated tunneling

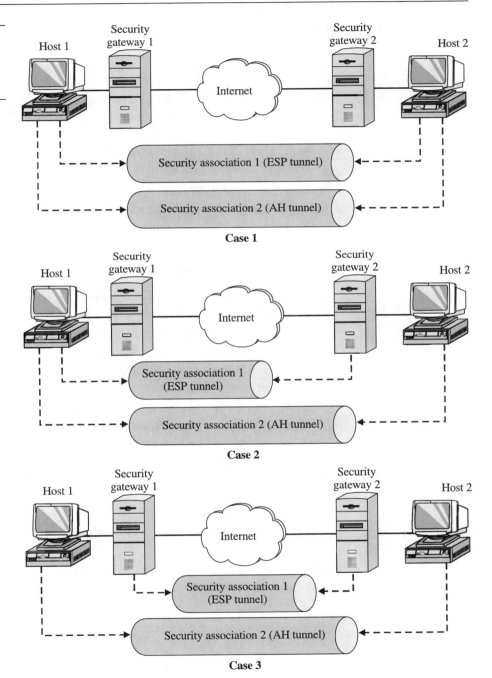

Case 1

Case 2

Case 3

Security Policy Database

An SA is nothing more than a management construct that is used to enforce a security policy. Because SPD is responsible for all IP traffic, it must be consulted during the processing of all traffic (inbound and outbound), including non-IPSec traffic. To support this, SPD requires distinct entries for inbound and outbound traffic; these entries are defined by a set of *selectors,* or IP and upper-layer protocol field values. The following selectors determine an SPD entry:

- **Destination IP Address** This can be a single IP address, a list of addresses, or a wildcard address. Multiple and wildcard addresses are used when you have more than one source system sharing the same SA (for example, behind a gateway).

- **Source IP Address** This can be a single IP address, a range of addresses, or a wildcard address. Multiple and wildcard addresses are used when you have more than one source system sharing the same SA (for example, behind a gateway).

- **Name** This can be either an X.500 distinguished name or a user identifier from the operating system.

- **Data Sensitivity Level** This is used for systems that provide information flow security (for example, unclassified or secret).

- **Transport Layer Protocol** This is obtained from the IPv4 Protocol field or IPv6 Next Header field. It can be an individual protocol number, a list of protocol numbers, or a range of protocol numbers.

- **Source and Destination Ports** These can be individual UDP or TCP port values, or a wildcard port.

Security Association Database

Each implementation of IPSec contains a nominal SAD, which is used to define the parameters associated with each SA. The following parameters are used to define an SA:

- **Sequence Number Counter** A 32-bit value used to generate the Sequence Number field in AH or ESP headers.

- **Sequence Counter Overflow** A flag indicating whether overflow of the sequence number counter should generate an auditable event and prevent transmission of additional packets on the SA.

- **Anti-Replay Window**   A 32-bit counter that is used to determine whether an inbound AH or ESP packet is a replay.
- **AH Information**   Parameters relating to the use of AH (such as authentication algorithms, keys, and key lifetimes).
- **ESP Information**   Parameters relating to the use of ESP (such as encryption algorithms, keys, key lifetimes, and initialization values).
- **Lifetime of This Security Association**   A time interval or byte count that specifies an SA's duration of use. When the duration is complete the SA must be replaced with a new SA (and new SPI) or terminated, and this parameter includes an indication of which of these actions should occur.

NOTE:

If a time interval is employed, and if IKE employs X.509 certificates for SA establishment, the SA lifetime must be constrained by the validity intervals of the certificates and by the "NextIssueDate" of the CRLs used in the IKE exchange for the SA. For more about CRLs, see Chapter 6.

- **IPSec Protocol Mode**   Specifies the mode-tunnel, transport, or wildcard-of AH or ESP that is applied to traffic on this SA.
- **Path MTU**   Any observed path *maximum transferable unit* (MTU) and aging variables. (The MTU is the maximum size of a packet without fragmentation.)

Key Management

As with any security protocol, when you use IPSec you must provide key management, such as supplying a means of negotiating with other people the protocols, encryption algorithms, and keys to be used in data exchange. In addition, IPSec requires that you keep track of all such agreements between the entities. IETF's IPSec working group has specified that compliant systems must support both manual and automated SA and cryptographic key management.

Following are brief descriptions of these techniques:

- **Manual** Manual key and SA management are the simplest forms of key management. A person (usually a systems administrator) manually configures each system, supplying the keying material and SA management data relevant to secure communication with other systems. Manual techniques can work effectively in small, static environments, but this approach is not very practical for larger networks.

- **Automated** By using automated key management protocols, you can create keys as needed for your SAs. Automated management also gives you a great deal of scalability for larger distributed systems that are still evolving. You can use various protocols for automated management, but IKE seems to have prevailed as the current industry standard.

Internet Key Exchange

IKE is not a single protocol; rather, it is a hybrid of two protocols. IKE integrates the *Internet Security Association and Key Management Protocol* (ISAKMP) with the Oakley key exchange protocol.

IKE performs its services in two phases. In the first phase, two IKE peers establish a secure, authenticated channel for communication by using a common IKE security association. IKE provides three modes of exchanging keying information and setting up SAs (see next section); in this first phase, only main or aggressive mode is employed.

In the second phase, SAs are negotiated on behalf of services such as IPSec or any other service that needs keying material or parameter negotiation. The second phase is accomplished via a quick mode exchange.

Main Mode

IKE's *main* mode provides a three-stage mechanism for establishing the first-phase IKE SA, which is used to negotiate future communications. In this mode, the parties agree on enough things (such as authentication and confidentiality algorithms, hashes, and keys) to be able to communicate securely long enough to set up an SA for future communication. In this mode, three two-way messages are exchanged between the SA initiator and the recipient.

As shown in Figure 7-11, in the first exchange, the two parties agree on basic algorithms and hashes. In the second, they exchange public keys for

Figure 7-11

Transactions in
IKE's main mode

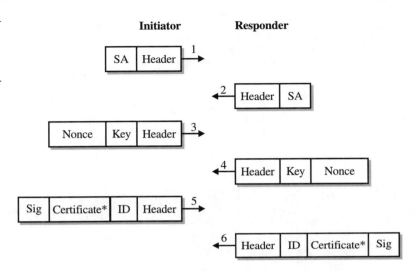

* Indicates inclusion of optional certificate payload

a Diffie-Hellman exchange and pass each other *nonces* (random numbers signed and returned by the other party to prove its identity). In the third exchange, they verify those identities.

Aggressive Mode

Aggressive mode is similar to main mode in that aggressive mode is used to establish an initial IKE SA. However, aggressive mode differs in the way the messages are structured, thereby reducing the number of exchanges from three to two.

In aggressive mode, the proposing party generates a Diffie-Hellman pair at the beginning of the exchange and does as much as is practical with that first packet: proposing an SA, passing the Diffie-Hellman public value, sending a nonce for the other party to sign, and sending an ID packet that the responder can use to check the initiator's identity with a third party (see Figure 7-12). The responder then sends back everything needed to complete the exchange. All that's left for the initiator to do is to confirm the exchange.

The advantage of aggressive mode is its speed, although aggressive mode does not provide identity protection for the communicating parties. This means that the parties exchange identification information before

Figure 7-12

Aggressive mode
transactions

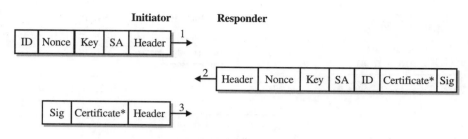

* Indicates inclusion of optional certificate payload

establishing a secure SA in which to encrypt it. As a result, someone monitoring an aggressive mode exchange can identify the entity that has just
formed a new SA.

Quick Mode

After two communicating entities have established an IKE SA using
either main or aggressive mode, they can use *quick* mode. Quick mode,
unlike the other two modes, is used solely to negotiate general IPSec security services and to generate fresh keying material.

Because the data is already inside a secure tunnel (every packet is
encrypted), you can afford to be a little more flexible in quick mode. Quick
mode packets are always encrypted and always start with a *hash payload,*
which is composed using the agreed-upon pseudo-random function and
the derived authentication key for the IKE SA. The hash payload is used
to authenticate the rest of the packet. Quick mode defines which parts of
the packet are included in the hash.

As shown in Figure 7-13, the initiator sends a packet with the quick
mode hash; this packet contains proposals and a nonce. The responder

Figure 7-13

Quick mode
transactions

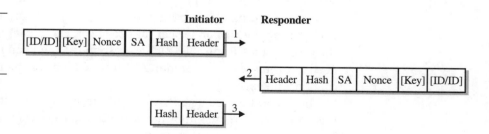

then replies with a similar packet, this time generating its own nonce and including the initiator's nonce in the quick mode hash for confirmation. The initiator then sends back a confirming quick mode hash of both nonces, completing the exchange. Finally, using the derivation key as the key for the hash, both parties perform a hash of a concatenation of the following: the nonces, the SPI, and the protocol values from the ISAKMP header that initiated the exchange. The resulting hash becomes the new password for that SA.

Secure Sockets Layer

Secure Sockets Layer (SSL), the Internet protocol for session-based encryption and authentication, provides a secure pipe between two parties (the *client* and the *server*). SSL provides server authentication and optional client authentication to defeat eavesdropping, tampering, and message forgery in client-server applications. By establishing a shared secret between the two parties, SSL provides privacy.

SSL works at the transport layer (below the application layer) and is independent of the application protocol used. Therefore, application protocols (HTTP, FTP, TELNET, and so on) can transparently layer on top of SSL, as shown in Figure 7-14.

Figure 7-14

SSL in the
TCP/IP stack

SMTP	HTTP	NNTP
TCP		
SSL		
IP		

The History of SSL

Netscape originally developed SSL in 1994. Since then, SSL has become widely accepted and is now deployed and supported in all major Web browsers and servers as well as various other software and hardware products (see Figure 7-15). This protocol currently comes in three versions: SSLv2, SSLv3, and TLSv1 (also known as SSLv3.1). Although all three can be found in use around the world, SSLv3, released in 1995, is the predominant version.

Figure 7-15

The padlock symbol in this browser denotes the use of SSL for Web security

SSLv3 solved many of the deficiencies in the SSLv2 release. SSLv3 enables either party (client or server) to request a new handshake (see next section) at any time to allow the keys and ciphers to be renegotiated. Other features of SSLv3 include data compression, a generalized mechanism for Diffie-Hellman and Fortezza key exchanges and non-RSA certificates, and the ability to send certificate chains.

In 1996, Netscape turned the SSL specification over to the IETF. Currently, the IETF is standardizing SSLv3 in its *Transport Layer Security* (TLS) working group. TLSv1 is very similar to SSLv3, with only minor protocol modifications. The first official version of TLS was released in 1999.

Session and Connection States

Any system of the type discussed in this chapter is composed of two parts: its state and the associated state transitions. The system's *state* describes the system at a particular point in time. The *state transitions* are the processes for changing from one state to another. The combination of all possible states and state transitions for a particular object is called a *state machine*. SSL has two state machines: one for the client side of the protocol and another for the server side. Each endpoint must implement the matching side of the protocol. The interaction between the state machines is called the *handshake*.

It is the responsibility of the SSL handshake protocol to coordinate the states of the client and server, thereby enabling each one's protocol state machine to operate consistently even though the state is not exactly parallel. Logically, the state is represented twice: once as the current operating state and (during the handshake protocol) a second time as the pending state. Additionally, separate read and write states are maintained. An SSL session can include multiple secure connections, and parties can have multiple simultaneous sessions.

The SSL specification defines the elements of a session state as follows:

- **Session Identifier** An arbitrary byte sequence chosen by the server to identify an active or resumable session state.

- **Peer Certificate** X.509v3 certificate of the peer. This element of the state can be null.

- **Compression Method** The algorithm used to compress data before encryption.

- **Cipher Spec** Specifies the bulk data encryption algorithm (null, DES, and so on) and a MAC algorithm (such as MD5 or SHA-1) used for message authentication. It also defines cryptographic attributes such as the hash size.

- **Master Secret** 48-byte secret shared between the client and the server.

- **Is Resumable** A flag indicating whether the session can be used to initiate new connections.

Furthermore, the SSL specification defines the following elements of a connection state:

- **Server and Client Random** Byte sequences that are independently chosen by the server and the client for each connection.

- **Server Write MAC Secret** The secret key that is used in MAC operations on data written by the server.

- **Client Write MAC Secret** The secret key that is used in MAC operations on data written by the client.

- **Server Write Key** The symmetric cipher key for data encrypted by the server and decrypted by the client.

- **Client Write Key** The symmetric cipher key for data encrypted by the client and decrypted by the server.

- **Initialization Vectors** The *initialization vector* (IV) required for each block cipher used in CBC mode. This field is first initialized by the SSL handshake protocol. Thereafter, the final ciphertext block from each record is preserved for use with the following record.

- **Sequence Numbers** Each party maintains separate sequence numbers for transmitted and received messages for each connection. When a party sends or receives a *change cipher spec* message (see later section titled "The Change Cipher Spec Protocol"), the appropriate sequence number is set to zero. Sequence numbers are of type uint64 and may not exceed $2^{64}-1$.

The Record Layer Protocol

As data is transmitted to and received from upper application layers, it is operated on in the SSL record layer (see Figure 7-16). It is here that data is encrypted, decrypted, and authenticated.

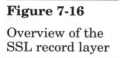

Figure 7-16

Overview of the SSL record layer

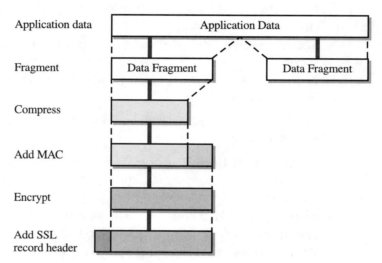

The following five steps take place in the record layer:

1. As the record layer receives an uninterrupted stream of data from the upper application layer, the data is *fragmented*, or broken into manageable plaintext blocks (or *records*). Each record is 16K or smaller.

2. Optionally, the plaintext records are compressed using the compression algorithm defined by the current session state.

3. A MAC is computed for each of the plaintext records. For this purpose, the shared secret key, previously established, is used.

4. The compressed (or plaintext) data and its associated MAC are encrypted using the symmetric cipher that has been previously agreed upon for this session. Encryption may not increase the overall length of the record beyond 1,024 bytes.

5. A header is added to each record as a prefix consisting of the following fields:

> **Content Type** This field indicates the protocol used to process the enclosed record in the next-higher level.
>
> **Major Version** This field indicates the major version of SSL in use. For example, TLS has the value 3.
>
> **Minor Version** This field indicates the minor version of SSL in use. For example, TLS has the value 1.
>
> **Compressed Length** This field indicates the total length in bytes of the plaintext record.

The party receiving this information reverses the process, that is, the decryption and authentication functions are simply performed in reverse.

NOTE:

Sequence numbers are also included with each transmission so that missing, altered, or extra messages are detectable.

The Change Cipher Spec Protocol

The change cipher spec protocol is the simplest of the SSL-specific protocols. It exists to signal a transition in the ciphering strategies. The protocol consists of a single message, which is encrypted and compressed by the record layer as specified by the current cipher specification. Before finishing the handshake protocol, both the client and the server send this message to notify each other that subsequent records will be protected under the just-negotiated cipher specification and associated keys. An unexpected change cipher spec message should generate an unexpected_message alert.

The Alert Protocol

One of the content types supported by the SSL record layer is the *alert* type. The alert protocol conveys alert messages and their severity to parties in an SSL session. Just as application data is processed by the record layer, alert messages are compressed and encrypted as specified by the current connection state.

When either party detects an error, the detecting party sends a message to the other. If the alert message has a fatal result, both parties immediately close the connection. Both parties are required to forget any session identifier, keys, and secrets associated with a failed connection. For all other nonfatal errors, both parties can cache information to resume the connection.

The following error alerts are always fatal:

- **Unexpected_message** This message is returned if an inappropriate message was received.

- **Bad_record_mac** This message is returned if a record is received without a correct message authentication code.

- **Decompression_failure** This message is returned if the decompression function received improper input (for example, the data could not be decompressed or it decompresses to an excessive length).

- **Handshake_failure** The return of this message indicates that the sender was unable to negotiate an acceptable set of security parameters given the available options.

- **Illegal_parameter** A field in the handshake was out of range or inconsistent with other fields.

The remaining alerts are as follows:

- **No_certificate** This message can be sent in response to a certification request if no appropriate certificate is available.

- **Bad_certificate** The return of this message indicates that a certificate was corrupted (that is, it contained a signature that did not verify).

- **Unsupported_certificate** The return of this message indicates that a certificate was of an unsupported type.

- **Certificate_revoked** The return of this message indicates that a certificate was revoked by its signer.

- **Certificate_expired**   The return of this message indicates that a certificate has expired.
- **Certificate_unknown**   The return of this message indicates that some other (unspecified) issue arose in processing the certificate, and it was rendered unacceptable.
- **Close_notify**   This message notifies the recipient that the sender will not send any more messages on this connection. Each party is required to send this message before closing the write side of a connection.

The Handshake Protocol

The SSL handshake protocol is responsible for establishing the parameters of the current session state. As shown in Figure 7-17, both parties agree on a protocol version, select cryptographic algorithms, optionally

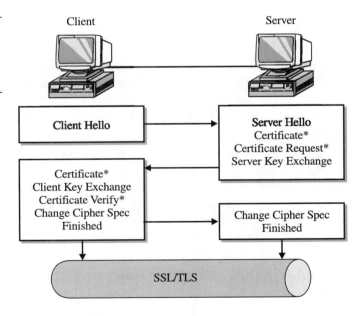

Figure 7-17

Overview of the handshake protocol

* Indicates optional or situation-dependent message

authenticate each other, and use public-key encryption techniques to generate shared secrets (described later under "Cryptographic Computations") through a series of messages exchanged between the client and the server. The following subsections explain in detail the steps of the handshake protocol.

The Client Hello Message

For communications to begin between a client and a server, the client must first initiate a *client hello* message. The contents of this message provide the server with data (such as version, random value, session ID, acceptable ciphers, and acceptable compression methods) about variables that are supported by the client. This message can come as a client response to a hello request (from the server), or on its own initiative the client can use it to renegotiate the security parameters in an existing connection.

A client hello message contains the following fields:

- **Client_version** This field provides the highest SSL version that is understood by the client.

- **Random** This field contains a client-generated random structure that will be used for later cryptographic computations in the SSL protocol. The 32-byte random structure is not entirely random. Rather, it is made up of a 4-byte date/time stamp, with the remaining 28 bytes of data being randomly generated. The date/time stamp assists in the prevention of replay attacks.

- **Session_id** This field contains a variable-length session identifier. This field should be empty if no session identifier is available or if the client wishes to generate new security parameters. If the session identifier does, however, contain a value, that value should identify a previous session between the same client and server whose security parameters the client wishes to reuse. (The reuse of session identifiers is discussed later in this chapter under "Resuming Sessions.")

- **Cipher_suites** This field contains a list of combinations for cryptographic algorithms supported by the client. This list is ordered according to the client's preference (that is, first choice first). This list is used to make the server aware of the cipher suites available to the client, but it is the server that ultimately decides which cipher will be used. If the server cannot find an acceptable choice from the list, it returns a handshake failure alert and closes the connection.

- **Compression_methods** Similar to the cipher_suites field, this field lists all supported compression methods known to the client. Again, this list is ordered according to the client's preference. Although this field is not regularly used in SSLv3, future TLS versions will require support for it.

NOTE:

After the client hello message is sent, the client waits for a server hello message. If the server returns any handshake message other than a server hello, a fatal error results and communications are halted.

The Server Hello Message

After the server processes the client hello message, it can respond with either a handshake failure alert or a server hello message. The content of the *server hello* message is similar to that of the client hello. The difference is that whereas the client hello is used to list its capabilities, the server hello is used to make decisions that are then passed back to the client.

The server hello message contains the following fields:

- **Server_version** This field contains the version that was decided on by the server; this version will be used for further communications with the client. The server bases its decision on the highest version supported by both parties. For example, if the client states that it can support SSLv3 but the server supports up to TLS (or SSLv3.1), the server will decide on SSLv3.

- **Random** This field, similar in structure to that of the client's, is used for future cryptographic operations within SSL. It must, however, be independent of and different from that generated by the client.

- **Session_id** This field provides the identity of the session corresponding to the current connection. If the session identifier that was received by the client is nonempty, the server will look in the session cache for a match. If a match is found, the server can establish a new connection, resuming the specified session state. In that case, the server returns the same value that was provided by the client, indicating a resumed session. Otherwise, this field contains a different value, identifying a new session.

- **Cipher_suite**   This field indicates the single cipher suite selected by the server from the list provided by the client.

- **Compression_method**   Similar to the cipher_suite message, this field indicates the single compression method selected by the server from the list provided by the client.

The Server Certificate Message

Immediately after the server hello message, the server can send its certificate or chain of certificates to be authenticated. Authentication is required in all cases of agreed-on key exchange (with the exception of anonymous Diffie-Hellman). The appropriate certificate type (generally an X.509v3 server certificate) must be used for the key exchange algorithm of the selected cipher suite.

This message also makes the public key available to the client. This public key is what the client uses to encrypt the actual session key.

NOTE:

A similar message type can be used for client-side authentication support.

The Server Key Exchange Message

The server sends a *server key exchange* message only when no certificate is present, when the certificate is used only for signing (as with *Digital Signature Standard* [DSS] certificates and signing-only RSA certificates), or when Fortezza key exchange is used. The message complements the cipher suite that was previously stated in the server hello message, providing the algorithm variables that the client needs in order to continue. These values depend on which algorithm has been selected. For example, with RSA key exchange (where RSA is used only for signatures), the message would contain a temporary RSA public key exponent and modulus, and a signature of those values.

The Certificate Request Message

The optional *certificate request* message requests a certificate from the client for authentication purposes. It is made up of two parameters. The first parameter indicates the acceptable certificate types (RSA—signature-only, DSS—signature-only, and so on). The second parameter indicates the acceptable distinguished names of acceptable certificate authorities.

NOTE:

This message is to be used only by non-anonymous servers (servers not using anonymous Diffie-Hellman).

The Server Hello Done Message

As the name implies, the *server hello done* message is sent by the server to the client to indicate the end of the server hello and to signal that no further associated server hello messages are coming. After this message is sent, the server waits for the client to respond. On receipt of the server hello done message, the client should verify the certificate and any certificate chain sent by the server (if required) and should verify that all server hello parameters received are acceptable.

The Client Certificate Message

The *client certificate* message is the first message that a client can send after a server hello done message is received, and it is sent only if the server requests a certificate. If the client does not have a suitable certificate (for example, an X.509v3 client certificate) to send, it should send a no_certificate alert instead. Although this alert is only a warning, it is a matter of the server's discretion whether to continue or terminate communications.

The Client Key Exchange Message

Like the server key exchange message, the *client key exchange* message allows the client to send key information to the server. Unlike the server key exchange message, however, this key information pertains to a symmetric-key algorithm that both parties will use for the session.

NOTE:

Without the information contained in this message, communications cannot continue.

The content of this message depends on the type of key exchange, as follows:

- **RSA**   The client generates a 48-byte *pre-master secret*, which it encrypts by using either the public key from the server's certificate or a temporary RSA key from a server key exchange message. This result is then sent to the server to compute the master secret key. (Computation of the master secret is discussed later in this chapter under "Cryptographic Computations.")

- **Ephemeral or Anonymous Diffie-Hellman**   The client provides its own Diffie-Hellman public parameters to the server.

- **Fortezza**   The client calculates public parameters using the public key in the server's certificate along with private parameters in the client's token. These parameters are then sent to the server.

The Certificate Verify Message

The *certificate verify* message is used to provide explicit verification of a client certificate. When using client authentication, the server authenticates the client using the private key. This message contains the pre-master secret key signed with the client's private key. The server validates the key against the client's certificate. The server is not required to authenticate itself to the client. Because the pre-master secret is sent to the server using the server's public key, only the legitimate server can decrypt it with the corresponding private key.

The Finished Message

Next, the client sends a change cipher spec message, followed immediately by the *finished* message. When the server receives the finished message, it too sends out a change cipher spec message and then sends its finished message. At this point the handshake protocol is complete and the parties can begin to transfer application data securely.

Be aware that the finished message is the first to be protected with the just-negotiated algorithms, keys, and secrets. As a result, the communicating parties can verify that the key exchange and authentication processes were successful. No acknowledgment of the finished message is required; parties can begin sending encrypted data immediately after sending the finished message. Recipients of finished messages must verify that the contents are correct.

NOTE:

The change cipher spec message is actually part of the change cipher spec protocol and not the handshake protocol.

Ending a Session and Connection

Before the end of communications, the client and the server must share knowledge that the connection is ending. This arrangement protects the session from a possible truncation attack, whereby an attacker tries to compromise security by prematurely ending communications. Either party can terminate the session by sending a close_notify alert before closing its own write session. When such an alert is received, the other party must send its own close_notify alert and close down immediately, discarding any pending writes.

NOTE:

If the SSL session is closed before either party sends a close_notify message, the session cannot be resumed.

Resuming Sessions

Public-key encryption algorithms are very slow. To improve performance, the parties can cache and reuse information exchanged during the handshake protocol. This process is called session ID reuse. If it is determined during the handshake protocol that the client and the server sides of the protocol share a session ID, the public-key and authentication operations are skipped, and the previously generated shared secret is reused during key generation.

Both parties (client and server) must agree to reuse a previous session ID. If either party suspects that the session may have been compromised or that certificates may have expired or been revoked, it should force a full handshake. Because an attacker who obtains a master secret key may be able to impersonate the compromised party until the corresponding session ID expires, the SSL specification suggests that the lifetime of cached session IDs expire after 24 hours. It also suggests that applications that run in relatively insecure environments should not write session IDs to stable storage.

Cryptographic Computations

We have used the term "shared secret" to explain how traffic is encrypted in SSL. Now let's look at the generation of the *master secret*, which is derived from the pre-master secret. In the case of RSA or Fortezza cryptography, the pre-master secret is a value generated by the client and sent to the server via the client key exchange message. In Diffie-Hellman cryptography, the pre-master secret is generated by each side (server and client) using the other party's Diffie-Hellman public values.

In each of these three cases, after a pre-master secret is generated and both sides are aware of it, the master secret can be computed. The master secret, which is used as the shared secret, is made up of several hash calculations of data previously exchanged in messages. Figure 7-18 shows the format of these calculations.

Encryption and Authentication Algorithms

SSLv3.0 supports a wide range of algorithms that provide various levels of security. These algorithms (encryption, key exchange, and authentication) support a total of 31 cipher suites, although some of them provide little or

Figure 7-18

Generating a
master secret

Master_secret = MD5(pre_master_secret + SHA('A' + pre_master_secret +
ClientHello.random + ServerHello.random)) +
MD5(pre_master_secret + SHA 'BB' + pre_master_secret +
ClientHello.random + ServerHello.random)) +
MD5(pre_master_secret + SHA 'CCC' + pre_master_secret +
ClientHello.random + ServerHello.random)) +

*The characters A, BB, and CCC are actual
ASCII values

no security in today's world. One such cipher suite is based on anonymous
Diffie-Hellman, and the specification strongly discourages its use because
it is vulnerable to man-in-the-middle attacks.

Summary

Security protocols make use of the various technologies described up to
this point in the book to provide the necessary security. All cryptographic
algorithms, whether they are symmetric, asymmetric, message digests, or
message authentication, codes do very little on their own; instead, they
are the basis for the security provided through set standard protocols
such as IPSec or SSL.

Security protocols can be placed within the various layers of the TCP/IP
networking stack. IPSec, for example, is located at the IP layer, while SSL
is located between the TCP and application layers. The lower in the
TCP/IP stack a protocol is placed, the more flexible and less user-intrusive
the protocol is.

IPSec plays an important role in securing IP networks to provide private communications. It enables a wide range of security services, not only
confidentiality but also authentication, access control, and protection
against replay attacks. These services are available through the use of
either or both the authentication header (AH) and encapsulating security
payload (ESP).

SSL provides security at the transport (TCP) layer, which is below the
application layer. The security provided by SSL can be thought of as a
secure pipe placed between a client and server. Data is authenticated con-
fidentially while in the pipe. It should be noted, however, that once either
system (client or server) receives the data, the data is returned to its
unprotected clear state.

Real-World Examples

Various products are available that provide security using the IPSec and SSL protocols. There are several toolkits available for developers who wish to build IPSec and SSL into their applications. RSA Security, Inc. provides two such commercial products, BSAFE Crypto-C/J and SSL-C/J, both of which are available for C programmers as well as Java programmers.

Other companies, however, have created end-user software and embedded hardware products using IPSec and SSL. In fact, most *virtual private networks* (VPNs) are based on the popular IPSec protocol. For example, Microsoft Windows 2000 makes use of IPSec to provide a VPN, something most end users aren't aware is available. Just as IPSec can be found in a various software and hardware products, so can SSL. SSL is by far the most widely distributed security protocol when it comes to e-commerce. One reason for SSL's widespread use is that it is incorporated in every copy of Netscape and Internet Explorer available today. SSL is also found within the operating system of various platforms. Many Linux vendors have included SSL in their systems; it provides security not only for HTTP communications, but also for other protocols as well, such as NNTP, SMTP, and FTP.

CHAPTER 8

Application-Layer Security Protocols

Like Chapter 7, this chapter looks at security protocols that are used in today's networks. But unlike the protocols described in Chapter 7, the protocols discussed in this chapter provide security services for specific applications (such as Simple Mail Transfer Protocol *(SMTP),* Hypertext Transfer Protocol *(HTTP), and so on). Figure 8-1 shows each of these application protocols along with its location in the* Transportation Control Protocol/Internet Protocol *(TCP/IP) stack. This chapter provides a detailed look at two well-known security protocols—S/MIME and SET— which operate above the application layer.*

S/MIME

Secure/Multipurpose Internet Mail Extensions (S/MIME) is a specification for securing electronic mail. S/MIME, which is based on the popular MIME standard, describes a protocol for adding cryptographic security services through MIME encapsulation of digitally signed and encrypted objects. These security services are authentication, nonrepudiation, message integrity, and message confidentiality.

Figure 8-1

Application-layer
protocols within
TCP/IP

S/MIME	SET
SMTP	HTTP
TCP	
IP	

Although S/MIME is most widely known and used for securing e-mail, it can be used with any transport mechanism that transports MIME (such as HTTP). S/MIME can even be used in automated message transfer agents, which use cryptographic security services that do not require human intervention. The S/MIME specification even points out how to use its services to encrypt fax messages sent over the Internet.

The following section describes S/MIME along with the various MIME types and their uses. It explains how to create a MIME body that has been cryptographically enhanced according to *Cryptographic Message Syntax* (CMS), a formatting standard derived from PKCS #7. Finally, it defines and illustrates how cryptographic signature and encryption services are added to MIME data.

Overview

In the early 1980s, the *Internet Engineering Task Force* (IETF) developed Request for Comment (RFC) 822, which became the specification that defined the standard format of electronic mail messages. Along with RFC 821 (which defined the mail transfer protocol), RFC 822 was the foundation of the SMTP, which was designed to carry textual messages over the Internet.

MIME, also developed by the IETF, was designed to support nontextual data (such as graphics or video data) used in Internet messages. The MIME specification adds structured information to the message body that allows it to contain nontextual information. However, MIME does not provide any security services.

In 1995, RSA Data Security, Inc., led a consortium of industry vendors in the development of S/MIME. After work on the specification was under way, RSA passed it to the IETF for further development. S/MIMEv3 is the current version. Through continued development by the IETF S/MIME working group, the protocol has incorporated a number of enhancements.

S/MIME Functionality

S/MIMEv3 currently provides the following security enhancements to MIME content:

- **Enveloped data** This function supports confidentiality services by allowing any content type in a MIME message to be symmetrically encrypted. The symmetric key is then encrypted with one or more recipients' public keys. The encrypted data and corresponding encrypted symmetric key are then attached to the data structure, along with any necessary recipient identifiers and algorithm identifiers.

- **Signed data** This function provides data integrity services. A message digest is computed over the selected content (including any algorithm identifiers and optional public-key certificates), which is then encrypted using the signer's private key. The original content and its corresponding signature are then base-64 encoded (base-64 and other encoding methods are described later in "Transfer Encoding").

- **Clear-signed data** This function allows S/MIME to provide the same data integrity services as provided by the signed data function, while at the same time allowing readers that are not S/MIME-compliant to view the original data. Following the processes just described, a digital signature is computed over the selected content, but only this digital signature (and not the original data) is base-64 encoded.

- **Signed and enveloped data** This function supports both confidentiality and integrity services by allowing either the signing of encrypted data or the encrypting of signed data.

Cryptographic Algorithms

S/MIMEv3 implements support for several symmetric content-encryption algorithms. However, some S/MIME implementations still incorporate RC2 with a key size of 40 bits, and by today's standards, a 40-bit key is too weak. However, in most current S/MIMEv3 implementations, the user can choose from various content-encryption algorithms, such as DES, Triple DES, or RC2 with a key size greater than 40; see Chapter 2.

The specification does, however, spell out all algorithms to be used for security services within S/MIMEv3. Some of them are optional, and others are required. They are as follows:

- **Digest and hashing algorithms** These must support MD5 and SHA-1; however, SHA-1 should be used.

- **Digital signature algorithms** Both sending and receiving agents must support DSA and should also support RSA.

- **Key encryption algorithms** Sending and receiving agents must support Diffie-Hellman and should also support RSA encryption.

- **Data encryption (session key) algorithms** Sending agents should support RC2/40-bit key, RC2/128-bit key, and Triple DES. Receiving agents should support RC2/128 and Triple DES but must support RC2/40.

Which algorithm is best? It's a simple matter of looking at key length; the bigger the key, the greater the security. However, sending and receiving agents are not always at the same level. For instance, the sending agent may be attempting to encrypt something with RC2/128 for added security; however, the receiving agent may only have the ability to decrypt messages with RC2/40. For this reason, the S/MIME specification defines a process for deciding which algorithm is best when you're sending S/MIME messages.

The following are the specified rules that a sending agent should use in making its decision:

1. *Known capabilities.* If the sending agent has previously received a list of cryptographic capabilities of the recipient, the sender should choose the first (most preferred) capability listed to encrypt the outgoing message.

2. *Unknown capabilities but known use of encryption.* This rule applies when the sending agent has no idea of the encryption capabilities of the recipient but has received at least one previously encrypted message from that recipient. In this case, the sending agent should encrypt the outgoing message using that algorithm.

3. *Unknown capabilities and unknown version of S/MIME.* This rule applies when a sending agent has had no previous contact with the recipient and does not know its capabilities. The sending agent should use Triple DES because of its strength and because it is required by S/MIMEv3. However, if Triple DES is not used, the sending agent should use RC2/40.

S/MIME Messages

S/MIME messages are made up of the MIME bodies and CMS objects. The latter are derived from PKCS #7 data structures.

Before any cryptographic processing takes place, a MIME entity must be prepared. A MIME entity may be a subpart of a message or the whole message, including all its subparts. The latter type of MIME entity is made up only of the MIME headers and MIME body and does not include the RFC822 headers (To:, From:, and so on). This MIME entity is then converted to canonical form, and the appropriate transfer encoding is applied (both processes are discussed in the following sections).

After the MIME entity has been created and all proper encoding has taken place, the MIME entity is sent to security services, where the chosen security function is provided (enveloping, signing, or both). This process yields a CMS (or PKCS #7) object, which in turn is wrapped up in MIME and placed with the original message, according to the selected S/MIME content type.

Canonicalization

As stated in the preceding section, each MIME entity must be converted to a canonical form. This conversion allows the MIME entity to be uniquely and unambiguously represented in the environments where the signature is created and where the signature will be verified. This same process is performed for MIME entities that will be digitally enveloped as well as signed. Canonicalization provides a standard means by which data from various platforms can be exchanged.

Transfer Encoding

Whenever data is processed by digital equipment, it can be encoded and represented in a variety of ways, such as 7-bit, 8-bit, or binary. *Transfer encoding* ensures that data is represented properly for transfer across the Internet and ensures reliable delivery. One common method is base-64 encoding, which enables arbitrary binary data to be encoded so that it may pass through a variety of systems unchanged. For example, if 8-bit data is transferred and a 7-bit device (such as a mail gateway) receives it, there is a good chance that before it is forwarded to its final destination, it may be stripped of characters.

NOTE:

As you might expect, if a digitally signed message is altered or stripped of characters, it will be selected as invalid.

Enveloped-Only Data

The process of generating an encrypted MIME entity is called *digital enveloping* and is provided for by the *enveloped-data* content type. This content type consists of encrypted content of any type and encrypted content-encryption keys for one or more recipients. For each recipient, a digital envelope (made up of the encrypted content and associated encrypted content-encryption key) is created, ensuring confidentiality for the message while it is in transit. Figure 8-2 illustrates the S/MIME enveloped-data process.

Figure 8-2

S/MIME enveloped-data process

To construct an enveloped-data content type, follow these steps:

1. For a chosen symmetric algorithm (that is, RC2, DES, and so on), generate a pseudo-random content-encryption key.

2. For each recipient, encrypt the content-encryption key. Which encryption to use depends on which key management system is used. The associated key management systems are as follows:

> **RSA key transport** The content-encryption key is encrypted in the recipient's public key.

Diffie-Hellman key agreement The recipient's public key and the sender's private key are used to generate a shared symmetric key, which is then used to encrypt the content-encryption key. **Known symmetric key** The content-encryption key is encrypted using a previously distributed symmetric key.

3. For each recipient, create a block of data containing the recipient information. This information includes the encrypted content-encryption key and other recipient-specific information (such as version and algorithm identifiers).

4. Encrypt the message using the content-encryption key.

5. Prepend the recipient information to the encrypted content, and base 64-encode the result to produce the enveloped-data value.

When the digital envelope is received, the process is reversed to retrieve the original data. First, the enveloped data is stripped of its base-64 encoding. Then the appropriate content-encryption key is decrypted. Finally, the content-encryption key is used to decrypt the original content.

Signed-Only Data

The S/MIME specification defines two methods for signing messages:

■ Application/pkcs7-mime with signed-data (usable only by S/MIME-compliant mailers)

■ Multipart/signed, also known as clear signing (usable by all mailers)

S/MIMEv3 doesn't mandate which method to use, but the specification mentions that the multipart/signed form is preferred for sent messages because of its readability by any mailer. The specification states that receiving agents should be able to handle both kinds.

Signed Data An S/MIME application/pkcs7-mime message with signed data may consist of any MIME content type, in which any number of signers in parallel can sign any type of content. Figure 8-3 illustrates S/MIME data signing.

The following steps apply to constructing a signed-data content type:

1. For each signer, select a message digest or hashing algorithm (MD5 or SHA-1).

2. Compute a message digest or hash value over all content to be signed.

Figure 8-3

S/MIME data
signing

3. For each signer, digitally sign the message digest (that is, encrypt the digest using the signer's private key).

4. For each signer, create a signer information block containing the signature value and other signer-specific information (such as version and algorithm identifier).

5. Prepend the signed content with signer information (for all signers), and then base-64-encode it to produce the signed data value.

After it is received, the signed data content type is stripped of its base-64 encoding. Next, the signer's public key is used to decrypt and reveal the original message digest. Finally, the recipient independently computes the message digest and compares the result with that of the one that was just decrypted.

Clear-Signed Data   It is possible that data you have digitally signed might be received by a recipient that is not S/MIME-compliant, rendering the original content unusable. To counter this problem, S/MIME uses an alternative structure, the multipart/signed MIME type.

The body of the multipart/signed MIME type is made up of two parts. The first part, which can be of any MIME content type, is left in the clear and placed in the final message. The contents of the second part are a special case of signed data, known as a *detached signature,* which omits the copy of the plaintext that may be contained within the signed data. Figure 8-4 illustrates the S/MIME clear-signed data process.

Figure 8-4

S/MIME clear-signed data process

Signing and Encrypting

S/MIME also supports both encryption and signing. To provide this service, you can nest enveloped-only and signed-only data. In other words, you either sign a message first or envelope the message first. The decision of which process to perform first is up to the implementer and the user.

NOTE:

The S/MIMEv3 specification (RFC2633) describes security risks involved with each technique (envelope first or signing first).

Registration Request

In addition to security functions, S/MIME defines a format for conveying a request to have a public-key certificate issued. A MIME content type, *application/x-pkcs10*, is used to request a certificate from a certification authority.

NOTE:

The specification does not mandate the use of any specific technique for requesting a certificate, whether it is through a certificate authority, a hardware token, or manual distribution. The specification does, however, mandate that every sending agent have a certificate.

Certificates-Only Messages

A *certificates-only* message is an application/pkcs7-mime and is prepared in much the same way as a signed-data message. This message, which is used to transport certificates to an S/MIME-compliant end entity, may be needed from time to time after a certification authority receives a certificate request. The certificates-only message can also be used for the transport of *certificate revocation lists* (CRLs).

Enhanced Security Services

Currently there are three optional enhanced security services that can be used to extend the current S/MIMEv3 security and certificate processing services.

- **Signed receipts**   A signed receipt is an optional service that allows for proof of message delivery. The receipt provides the originator a means of demonstrating to a third party that the recipient not only received but also verified the signature of the original message (hopefully, this means that the recipient also read the message). Ultimately, the recipient signs the entire message and its corresponding signature for proof of receipt. Note that this service is used only for signed data.

- **Security labels**   Security labels can be used in a couple of ways. The first and probably most easily recognizable approach is to describe the sensitivity of data. A ranked list of labels is used (confidential, secret, restricted, and so on). Another technique is to use the labels to control authorization and access, describing which kind of recipient should have access to the data (such as a patient's doctor, medical billing agents, and so on).

- **Secure mailing lists**   When S/MIME provides its services, sending agents must create recipient-specific data structures for each recipient. As the number of recipients grows for a given message, this processing can impair performance for messages sent out. Thus, *mail list agents* (MLAs) can take a single message and perform the recipient-specific encryption for every recipient.

Interoperability

Since the S/MIME standard first entered the public eye, a number of vendors have made efforts to incorporate it. However, a lack of interoperability is one pitfall that end users should take into account. For example, many vendors are still S/MIMEv2-compliant, whereas others have moved to S/MIMEv3 without supporting backward compatibility. Other problems include limits on the certificate processing available in various products.

To help promote product interoperability, the RSA Interoperability Test Center was established. This S/MIME test center allows vendors to perform interoperability testing on their products and to have the results published. The following Web address provides interoperability information as well as products that have been found to be S/MIME-compliant: http://www.rsasecurity.com/standards/smime/interop_center.html.

Secure Electronic Transaction (SET)

The Internet has made it easier than ever for consumers to shop, money to be transferred, and bills to be paid over the Internet at the press of a button. The price we pay for this ease of use, however, is increased opportunity for fraud. For example, Figure 8-5 illustrates how easy it is for those with very little character to fraudulently generate credit cards used for online payment, known in the industry as *payment cards*.

The *Secure Electronic Transaction* (SET) specification provides a framework for protecting payment cards used in Internet e-commerce transactions against fraud. SET protects payment cards by ensuring the confidentiality and integrity of the cardholder's data while at the same time providing a means of authentication of the card. The current version of the specification (SETv1) was initiated by MasterCard and Visa in February 1996 and was completed in May 1997.

SET is defined in three books. The first book, *Business Description,* describes the specification in business terms (that is, goals, participants,

and overall architecture). The second book, *Programmer's Guide,* is a
developer's guide, detailing the architecture, cryptography, and various
messages used in SET. The third book, *Formal Protocol Definition,* provides a formal definition of the entire SET process. (All three books were
published by Visa International and MasterCard on May 31, 1997.)

What follows is a high-level overview of the SET specification, outlining
the business requirements, functions, and participants defined in the first
book. We also cover SET certificates used and their management, describing the addition of SET-specific extensions. Finally, we look at the SET
messages and transactions.

Business Requirements

The specification defines the business requirements of SET as follows:

- To provide confidentiality of payment information and enable
  confidentiality of the associated order information
- To ensure the integrity of all transmitted data
- To provide authentication that a cardholder is a legitimate user of a
  branded payment card account

- To provide authentication that a merchant can accept branded payment card transactions through its relationship with an acquiring financial institution

- To ensure the use of the best security practices and system design techniques to protect all legitimate parties in an electronic commerce transactions

- To create a protocol that neither depends on transport security mechanisms nor prevents their use

- To facilitate and encourage interoperability among software and network providers

SET Features

To meet its stated business requirements, SET defines the following necessary features:

- **Confidentiality of information** Confidentiality provides a secure channel for all payment and account information, preventing unauthorized disclosure. SET provides for confidentiality through the use of the DES algorithm.

- **Integrity of data** Data integrity ensures that the message content is not altered during transmission. This feature is provided through the use of digital signatures using the RSA algorithm.

- **Cardholder account authentication** Cardholder authentication provides merchants a means of verifying the cardholder as legitimate. Digital signatures and X.509v3 certificates are used to implement this function.

- **Merchant authentication** Merchant authentication gives cardholders a means of verifying that the merchant not only is legitimate but also has a relationship with a financial institution. Again, digital signatures and X.509v3 certificates are used to implement this service.

- **Interoperability** Interoperability allows the use of this specification in hardware and software from various manufacturers, allowing their use by cardholders or other participants.

SET Participants

Various participants use and interact with the SET specification. Figure 8-6 illustrates a simplified overview of the participants' interactions.

Figure 8-6

Interactions among SET participants

Following are these participants and their roles in the transactions governed by SET:

- **Issuer**   The issuer is the bank or other financial institution that provides a branded payment card (such as a MasterCard or Visa credit card) to an individual. The card is provided after the individual establishes an account with the issuer. It is the issuer that is responsible for the repayment of debt, for all authorized transactions placed on the card.

- **Cardholder**   The cardholder is the individual authorized to use the payment card. The SET protocol provides confidentiality services for the cardholder's transactions with merchants over the Internet.
- **Merchant**   The merchant is any entity that provides goods and/or services to a cardholder for payment. Any merchant that accepts payment cards must have a relationship with an acquirer.
- **Acquirer**   The acquirer is a financial institution that supports merchants by providing the service of processing payment cards. In other words, the acquirer pays the merchant, and the issuer repays the acquirer.
- **Payment gateway**   The payment gateway is the entity that processes merchant payment messages (for example, payment instructions from cardholders). The acquirer or a designated third party can act as a payment gateway; however, the third party must interface with the acquirer at some point.

Dual Signatures

The SET protocol introduced dual signatures, a new concept in digital signatures. *Dual signatures* allow two pieces of data to be linked and sent to two different entities for processing. For example, within SET a cardholder is required to send an *order information* (OI) message to the merchant for processing; at the same time, a *payment instructions* (PI) message is required by the payment gateway. Figure 8-7 illustrates the dual signature generation process.

The dual signature process follows these steps:

1. A message digest is generated for both the OI and the PI.
2. The two message digests are concatenated (hashed) to produce a new block of data.
3. The new block of data is hashed again to provide a final message digest.
4. The final message digest is encrypted using the signer's private key, producing a digital signature.

A recipient of either message can check its authenticity by generating the message digest on its copy of the message, concatenating it with the message digest of the other message (as provided by the sender) and computing the message digest of the result. If the newly generated digest

Figure 8-7

Generating dual signatures

PI	= Payment information	
OI	= Order information	
PIMD	= PI message digest	
OIMD	= OI message digest	
||	= Concatenation	
POMD	= Payment/Order message digest	

matches the decrypted dual signature, the recipient can trust the authenticity of the message.

SET Certificates

The SET protocol provides authentication services for participants through the use of X.509v3, and has revocation provisions through the use of CRLv2 (both X.509v3 and CRLv2 are described in Chapter 6.). These certificates are application-specific; that is, SET has defined its own specific private extensions that are meaningful only to SET-compliant systems. SET contains the following predefined profiles for each type of certificate:

- **Cardholder certificates** function as electronic representations of payment cards. Because a financial institution digitally signs these certificates, they cannot be altered by a third party and can be generated only by the financial institution. A cardholder certificate does not contain the account number and expiration date. Instead, the account information and a secret value known only to the cardholder's software are encoded using a one-way hashing algorithm.

- **Merchant certificates** function as electronic substitutes for the payment card brand decal that appears in a store window; the decal itself is a representation that the merchant has a relationship with a financial institution allowing it to accept the payment card brand. Because the merchant's financial institution digitally signs them, merchant certificates cannot be altered by a third party and can be generated only by a financial institution.

- **Payment gateway certificates** are obtained by acquirers or their processors for the systems that process authorization and capture messages. The gateway's encryption key, which the cardholder gets from this certificate, is used to protect the cardholder's account information. Payment gateway certificates are issued to the acquirer by the payment card brand organization.

- **Acquirer certificates** are required only in order to operate a certification authority that can accept and process certificate requests directly from merchants over public and private networks. Those acquirers that choose to have the payment card brand organization process certificate requests on their behalf do not require certificates because they are not processing SET messages. Acquirers receive their certificates from the payment card brand organization.

- **Issuer certificates** are required only in order to operate a certification authority that can accept and process certificate requests directly from cardholders over public and private networks. Those issuers that choose to have the payment card brand organization process certificate requests on their behalf do not require certificates because they are not processing SET messages. Issuers receive their certificates from the payment card brand organization.

Certificate Management

The SET specification states that certificates must be managed through a strict certificate hierarchy, as shown in Figure 8-8 (certificate hierarchies are explained in Chapter 6).

In the case of SET, each certificate is linked to the signature certificate of the entity that digitally signed it. By following the trust tree to a known trusted party, a person can be assured that the certificate is valid. For example, a cardholder certificate is linked to the certificate of the issuer (or the brand organization on behalf of the issuer). The issuer's certificate is linked back to a root key through the brand organization's certificate. The public signature key of the root is known to all SET software and can be used to verify each of the certificates in turn.

Figure 8-8

SET certificate
hierarchy

Payment Processing

To provide for secure payment processing over the Internet, the SET specification defines multiple transaction types, as shown in Table 8-1.

To illustrate how SET provides security of payment processing within e-commerce transactions, we next discuss each of the following transaction types in depth:

- Purchase request
- Payment authorization
- Payment capture

Purchase Request

The purchase request transaction is made up of four messages that are exchanged between the cardholder and the merchant:

1. *Initiate request.* When the cardholder has selected a purchase and decided which payment card to use, the cardholder is ready to initiate the request. To send SET messages to a merchant, the cardholder must have a copy of the merchant's and payment

Table 8-1	Transaction	Description
SET Transaction Types	Cardholder registration	Allows the cardholder to register with a CA.
	Merchant registration	Allows a merchant to register with a CA.
	Purchase request	Message from the cardholder containing order information (OI) and payment information (PI) and sent to the merchant and bank.
	Payment authorization	Message between the merchant and payment gateway requesting payment authorization for a transaction.
	Payment capture	Message from the merchant to the payment gateway requesting payment.
	Certificate inquiry and status	A CA may send this message to either cardholders or merchants to state that more processing time is needed. *or* A cardholder or merchant may send this message to a CA to check the current status of a certificate request, or to receive the certificate if the request has been approved.
	Purchase inquiry	Allows the cardholder to check the status of authorization, capture, or credit processing of an order after the purchase response has been received.
	Authorization reversal	Allows a merchant to reverse an authorization entirely or in part.
	Capture reversal	Allows a merchant to correct errors in previous capture requests, such as those caused by human error.
	Credit	Allows a merchant to issue credit to a cardholder's account for various reasons (such as for returned or damaged goods).
	Credit reversal	Allows a merchant to correct errors in a previous credit request.
	Payment gateway certificate request	Allows a merchant to request a current copy of the payment gateway's certificates.
	Batch administration	Message between merchant and payment gateway regarding merchant batches.
	Error message	Indicates that a responder rejects a message because it fails tests of format or content verification.

gateway's key-exchange keys. The SET order process begins when the cardholder software (software that runs with your browser) requests a copy of the gateway's certificate. The message from the cardholder indicates which payment card brand will be used for the transaction.

2. *Initiate response.* When the merchant receives an initiate request message, a unique transaction identifier is assigned to the message. The merchant then generates an initiate response message containing its certificates and that of the payment gateway. This information is then digitally signed with the merchant's private key and transmitted to the cardholder.

3. *Purchase request.* Upon receipt of the initiate response message, the cardholder software verifies the certificates of both the merchant and gateway. Next, the cardholder software creates a dual signature using the OI and PI. Finally, the cardholder software generates a purchase request message containing a dual-signed OI and a dual-signed PI that is digitally enveloped to the payment gateway. The entire purchase request is then sent to the merchant.

4. *Purchase response.* When the merchant software receives the purchase request message, it verifies the cardholder's certificate contained within the message, as well as the dual-signed OI. The merchant software then begins processing the OI and attempts to gain authorization from the payment gateway by forwarding the PI. Finally, the merchant generates a purchase response message, which states that the merchant received the cardholder's request.

Upon receipt of the purchase response from the merchant, the cardholder software verifies the merchant certificate as well as the digital signature of the message contents. At this point, the cardholder software takes some action based on the message, such as displaying a message to the cardholder or updating a database with the status of the order.

Payment Authorization

During the processing of an order from a cardholder, the merchant attempts to authorize the transaction by initiating a two-way message exchange between the merchant and the payment gateway. First, an authorization request is sent from the merchant to the payment gateway; then an authorization response is received from the merchant by the payment gateway. The request and response are described as follows:

1. *Authorization request.* The merchant software generates and digitally signs an authorization request, which includes the amount to be authorized, the transaction identifier from the OI, and other information about the transaction. This information is then digitally enveloped using the payment gateway's public key. The authorization request and the cardholder PI (which is still digitally enveloped to the payment gateway) are transmitted to the payment gateway.

2. *Authorization response.* When the authorization request is received, the payment gateway decrypts and verifies the contents of the message (that is, certificates and PI). If everything is valid, the payment gateway generates an authorization response message, which is then digitally enveloped with the merchant's public key and transmitted back to the merchant.

Upon receipt of the authorization response message from the payment gateway, the merchant decrypts the digital envelope and verifies the data within. If the purchase is authorized, the merchant then completes processing of the cardholder's order by shipping the goods or performing the services indicated in the order.

Payment Capture

When the order-processing portion is completed with the cardholder, the merchant then requests payment from the payment gateway. Payment capture is accomplished by the exchange of two messages: the capture request and the capture response. This process is described as follows:

1. *Capture request.* The merchant software generates the capture request, which includes the final amount of the transaction, the transaction identifier, and other information about the transaction. This message is then digitally enveloped using the payment gateway's public key and transmitted to the payment gateway.

2. *Capture response.* The capture response is generated after the capture request is received and its contents verified. The capture response includes information pertaining to the payment for the transaction requested. This response is then digitally enveloped using the merchant's public key and is transmitted back to the merchant.

Upon receipt of the capture response from the payment gateway, the merchant software decrypts the digital envelope, verifying the signature and message data.

NOTE:

The merchant software stores the capture response and uses it for reconciliation with payment received from the acquirer.

Summary

Security protocols located at the application layer work slightly differently from those that operate on the IP (network) and TCP (transport) layers. Whereas IPSec (see Chapter 7) is used to provide security for all data being transferred across an IP network, S/MIME and SET are used solely to provide security for certain applications.

In 1995, a consortium of application and security vendors, led by RSA Data Security, Inc., designed the S/MIME protocol. Since then, the IETF S/MIME working group has taken control of S/MIME to continue its growth. S/MIME provides security not only for e-mail but also for any data that is transferred via the MIME protocol. Since its creation, S/MIME has continued to grow and improve its security services, adding support for mailing lists, signing receipts, and security labels.

SET is an open specification that provides a framework for protecting payment cards that are used in e-commerce transactions. Initiated by Visa and MasterCard in 1996, SET was completed in 1997, with the help of various other application developers and security vendors. The specification is described in three books totaling more than 900 pages.

Note that this chapter and Chapter 7 discuss only four selected protocols. Numerous others are available today, each of them supporting a specific security task.

Real-World Examples

Both S/MIME and SET have been incorporated in various applications. For secure e-mail, many companies and individuals have chosen to use S/MIME instead of a proprietary system such as PGP. In fact, many users have S/MIME-enabled mailers that they have not taken advantage of. S/MIME is incorporated in Microsoft's Outlook and Outlook Express e-mail applications as well as Netscape's Messenger software.

SET has also gained widespread use. Many of the vendors that visitors shop with daily across the Internet are SET-enabled. Currently, the merchants worldwide who use SET number in the hundreds. SET products are available not only for consumers but also for merchants, payment gateways, and SET certificate authorities. For a list of current SET-enabled products as well as the merchants that use them, visit http://www.setco.org/.

For both of these protocols, many security vendors also provide cryptographic APIs (application programming interfaces, or toolkits), which developers can use to produce secured applications. RSA Security, Inc., is one such company.

CHAPTER 9

Hardware Solutions: Overcoming Software Limitations

The performance of cryptosystems varies, and some of them come with a significant computational expense to computer systems. One way to address this problem is to apply cryptographic hardware. Cryptographic accelerators, for example, offer performance enhancements (as well as possible pitfalls). Cryptographic hardware, including various kinds of tokens, also plays a role in authentication, as does the old technology of biometrics, now being applied in new ways.

Cryptographic Accelerators

Cryptographic accelerators provide a means of performing the computationally expensive workload that usually accompanies various algorithms and protocols. Cryptographic accelerators work like math coprocessors: They implement in hardware a set of functions usually handled by software. Encoding these functions in silicon allows hardware to perform these tasks much faster.

Cryptographic accelerators provide usefulness on two fronts. First and most noticeable is increased speed, which is particularly important to e-commerce companies that interact with a considerable number of customers daily. The second benefit is a spin-off of the first one: By reducing the workload on the system's CPU, accelerators allow the system to be used more efficiently for other tasks. Figure 9-1 shows a typical *Secure Socket Layer* (SSL) accelerator card.

Figure 9-1

A typical SSL accelerator card

Another reason for the popularity of cryptographic accelerators is the certifications associated with them. NIST, for example, has certified many of them. The certification of each device depends on the safeguards that were implemented in it during manufacture.

NOTE:

Cryptographic accelerators often serve to slow down cryptographic operations because accelerators are I/O-bound. For example, a Web server that has farmed out private-key operations to a cryptographic accelerator often performs slower in SSL handshakes when the load is high. The reason for this is simple. I/O-bound operations are an order of magnitude slower than CPU-bound operations because getting the data to the hardware bus consumes an enormous amount of operating system and context-switching resources. An operating system with poor multitasking capabilities will likely be brought to its knees if it has to deal with a high number of SSL handshakes farmed out to an accelerator. Each thread must block and wait, and the CPU must manage all the blocked threads. This leads to a great deal of thread thrashing and, simply put, kills performance. For this reason, installing a cryptographic accelerator does not necessarily give you an across-the-board increase in speed. Where *and* how *the accelerator is applied are of prime importance.*

Authentication Tokens

In the realm of computer security, another important set of hardware devices is authentication tokens. Authentication tokens provide a means of authenticating and identifying an end user. Instead of memorizing passwords, end users protect their identity using a physical object that is unique to each user. An everyday analogy is the use of a driver's license to prove a person's identity.

Many tokens are designed for use with automated authentication systems. To verify the identity of the token's owner, the host system performs its authentication protocol using information encoded on the token. Because the uniqueness of the information is responsible for proving the identity of its bearer, the information must be protected against duplication or theft. Advanced tokens usually contain a microprocessor and semiconductor memory, and they support sophisticated authentication protocols that provide a high level of security.

In theory, authentication tokens enable the use of *single sign-on* (SSO) systems. As the name implies, SSO systems allow users to use an authentication token to sign on once to all applications they require access to. At the moment, true SSO is more or less a theoretical concept. In reality, even systems that use authentication tokens may have reduced sign-on capabilities.

Token Form Factors

Authentication tokens come in a variety of physical forms. The size, shape, and materials from which a token is manufactured are referred to collectively as the token's *form factor*. These parameters affect the durability, portability, security, and convenience of a given type of token. For example, some tokens have electrical contacts mounted on the outer surface of the token's casing. The electrical contacts are connected to an integrated circuit embedded in the token. When an electrostatic discharge of sufficient potential is applied to the contacts, the integrated circuit may be damaged. Because the human body can accumulate a significant static charge in dry weather, care must be taken in the design of such tokens to minimize the risk of damage from static discharges. To compensate for this, some types of tokens have contacts that are recessed in a conductive plastic casing. This type of token is less susceptible to damage from stray static discharges because the casing absorbs the charge before it reaches the contacts.

A token's form factor involves trade-offs that must be evaluated for a specific application. Tokens that have recessed contacts usually require a thicker casing than those that have surface-mounted contacts, and that can make it harder to carry the token in a pocket. Customers can sometimes select from a number of different form factors with the same functionality, making it possible to choose the form factor that is best suited to a particular application. Figure 9-2 shows three form factors.

Noncontact Tokens

Noncontact tokens, as their name implies, require no electrical or physical contact with a token reader device. Instead, noncontact tokens usually operate by transmitting data to and receiving data from a terminal, or they require that the user enter data that is then generated by the token.

Figure 9-2

Cryptographic tokens from (a) Rainbow Technologies, (b) Datakey, and (c) RSA Security

(a)

(b)

(c)

Noncontact tokens include proximity cards, one-time password generators, and handheld challenge/response calculators.

Proximity Cards

Proximity cards are noncontact tokens that use radio frequency signals to authenticate users. Proximity cards contain micro-miniature electronic tuned circuits, a switching mechanism, and a power source. These cards transmit a coded signal either when they come within a certain range of a proximity reader or when someone activates them manually. Some proximity devices are also designed to transmit continually. A user merely holds a uniquely coded proximity token or card within a given distance of a proximity reader, and the system reads the data within it. Figure 9-3 shows the XyLoc proximity card and reader from Ensure Technologies.

Figure 9-3

XyLoc proximity card and reader

NOTE:

Theoretically, authentication data (a coded signal in this case) is susceptible to replay attacks. That is, an outsider could conceivably record the signal being transmitted and replay it at a later time to gain access.

One-Time Password Generators

One-time password generators have proven to be one of the most successful types of authentication tokens to date. RSA Security, Inc., has proven this fact through its sales of the ACE/Server and SecurID products. The system has proven to be portable and to provide a very high level of security. Figure 9-4 shows a SecurID token in one of its (a) original form factors and (b) running on the Palm OS.

RSA's solution is made up of two components, which work in concert with each other. The ACE/Server is a back-end server application that houses a user's seed record. In turn, this seed is used by the ACE/Server application to produce a random six-digit numeric code on a configurable

Figure 9-4

(a) SecurID token;
(b) SecurID on Palm OS

time scale (for example, every 60 seconds a new six-digit numeric code is produced). The second component, the SecurID token, is also aware of the user's seed record. Like the ACE/Server, the SecurID produces a random numeric code. Figure 9-5 illustrates the user interaction with one-time passwords for authentication.

When users log in, they enter a four-digit PIN (known only to them) as well as the six-digit random code displayed by their token at that

Figure 9-5

Authentication via a one-time password generator

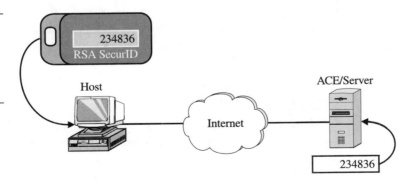

moment. In this way, the system can authenticate the user's entry against the entry in the back-end server.

Challenge/Response Calculators

Challenge/response calculators work on a premise similar to that of one-time password generators. Through the use of a back-end server component and a handheld device, an initial seed record is synchronized. In the case of challenge/response calculators, however, there is slightly more user intervention.

As users log in, they are prompted with a random challenge from the host system. The users must then enter the displayed challenge into their calculator, which performs a cryptographic operation on the challenge password and displays the result. In turn, users enter this result (the response) into the host system to gain access. Figure 9-6 illustrates the common component setup and user intervention involved with challenge/response calculators.

Figure 9-6

User intervention in challenge/ response calculators

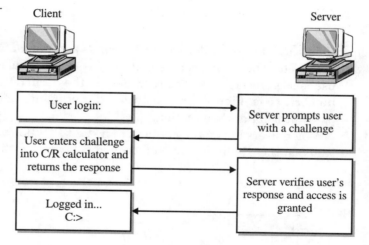

NOTE:

Challenge/response calculators tend to be protected by a PIN that the user must enter before the challenge/response sequence.

Contact Tokens

To transfer data, most tokens must make physical contact with the reader device. For example, magnetic stripe tokens (the kind used in automated teller machines) are inserted into a reader so that the magnetic stripe makes contact with an electromagnetic sensing device. Most integrated circuit tokens require an interface in which electrical contacts located on the token physically touch matching contacts on the reader to supply such functions as power, ground, and data signals. The physical arrangement and functional definition of these contacts have an impact on the interoperability of tokens and reader devices because these devices cannot communicate unless the contacts are defined in the same way.

Smart Cards

A *smart card,* an intelligent token, is a credit card-sized plastic card that contains an embedded integrated circuit chip. It provides not only memory capacity but also computational capability. The self-containment of smart cards makes them resistant to attack because they do not depend on potentially vulnerable external resources. Because of this characteristic, smart cards are often used in applications that require strong security protection and authentication.

For example, a smart card can act as an identification card to prove the identity of the cardholder. It also can be used as a medical card that stores the cardholder's medical history. Furthermore, a smart card can be used as a credit or debit bankcard and used for offline transactions. In all these applications, the card stores sensitive data, such as biometrics information of the card owner, personal medical history, and cryptographic keys for authentication. Figure 9-7 shows a Datakey smart card and RSA smart card.

Figure 9-7

(a) Datakey
smart card; (b)
RSA smart card

(a)   (b)

Smart Card Standards

Smart card standards govern the physical properties and communication characteristics of the embedded chip. ISO 7816 is the international standard for smart cards. The standard itself is made up of six parts, each describing everything from electrical properties to card dimensions. The following is a description of each part of the ISO 7816 standard:

- **ISO 7816-1** Defines the physical dimensions of contact smart cards and the placement of chips, magnetic stripes, and any embossing on the cards. It also describes the required resistance to static electricity.

- **ISO 7816-2** Defines the location, purpose, and electrical characteristics of the smart card's contacts.

- **ISO 7816-3** Describes electronic signals and transmission protocols, defining the voltage and current requirements for the electrical contacts defined in ISO 7816-2.

- **ISO 7816-4** Across all industries, defines a set of commands to provide access, security, and transmission of card data (that is, the card reads and writes to its memory).

- **ISO 7816-5** Defines *Application Identifiers* (AIDs), which are used to identify a specific application.

- **ISO 7816-6** Describes encoding rules for data needed in many applications.

Currently *Europay International, MasterCard International*, and *Visa International* (EMV) are cooperatively developing specifications to facilitate the use of smart cards for payments worldwide. These specifications build upon the ISO 7816 standards that have been developed for smart cards that use electrical contacts.

Yet another standard, which has helped to ensure interoperability, is public-key cryptography standard PKCS #11. PKCS #11 provides functional specification for personal cryptographic tokens.

Types of Smart Cards

A variety of smart cards are available, each defined according to the type of chip it uses. These chips range in their processing power, flexibility, memory, and cost. The two primary categories of smart cards—memory cards and microprocessor cards—are described in the following sections.

Memory Cards

Memory cards have no sophisticated processing power and cannot manage files dynamically. All memory cards communicate with readers through synchronous protocols. There are three primary types of memory cards:

- **Standard memory cards** These cards are used solely to store data and have no data processing capabilities. These cards are the least expensive per bit of user memory. They should be regarded as floppy disks of varying sizes without the lock mechanism. Memory cards cannot identify themselves to the reader, so the host system must recognize the type of card that is being inserted into a reader.

- **Protected/segmented memory cards** These cards have built-in logic to control access to memory. Sometimes referred to as *intelligent memory* cards, these devices can be set to write-protect some or all of the memory array. Some of these cards can be configured to restrict access to both reading and writing, usually through a password or system key. Segmented memory cards can be divided into logical sections for planned multifunctionality.

- **Stored value memory cards** These cards are designed to store values or tokens and are either disposable or rechargeable. Most cards of this type incorporate permanent security measures at the point of manufacture. These measures can include password keys and logic that are hard-coded into the chip. The memory arrays on these devices are set up as decrements, or counters, and little or no memory is left for any other function. When all the memory units are used, the card becomes useless and is thrown away or recharged.

CPU/MPU Microprocessor Multifunction Cards

These cards have on-card dynamic data processing capabilities. Multifunction smart cards allocate card memory into independent sections assigned to specific functions or applications. Embedded in the card is a microprocessor or microcontroller chip that manages this memory allocation and file access. This type of chip is similar to those found inside personal computers; when implanted in a smart card, the chip manages data in organized file structures via a *card operating system* (COS). Unlike other operating systems, this software controls access to the on-card user memory. As a result, various functions and applications can reside on the card. This means that businesses can use these cards to distribute and maintain a range of products.

These cards have sufficient space to house digital credentials (that is, public and private key-pairs). Further, through the use of the use of the on-card microprocessor chip, many of the needed cryptographic functions can be provided. Some cards can even house multiple digital credential pairs.

Readers and Terminals

Smart cards can be plugged in to a wide variety of hardware devices. The industry defines the term *reader* as a unit that interfaces with a PC for the majority of its processing requirements. In contrast, a *terminal* is a self-contained processing device.

Terminals as well as readers can read and write to smart cards. Readers come in many form factors and offer a wide variety of capabilities. The easiest way to describe a reader is according to the method of its interface to a PC. Smart card readers are available that interface to RS232 serial ports, *Universal Serial Bus* (USB) ports, PCMCIA slots, floppy disk slots, parallel ports, IRDA (*infrared data*) ports and keyboards, and keyboard wedge readers. Another way to distinguish reader types is according to onboard intelligence and capabilities. Extensive price and performance differences exist between an industrial-strength intelligent reader that supports a wide variety of card protocols and a home-style Windows based-card reader that works only with microprocessor cards and performs all the data processing in the PC.

The options available in terminals are equally numerous. Most units have their own operating systems and development tools. They typically support other functions such as magnetic stripe reading, modem functions, and transaction printing.

The Pros and Cons of Smart Cards

There is sufficient evidence in the computer industry that smart cards greatly improve the convenience and security of any transaction. They provide tamperproof storage of user and account identity. They protect against a full range of security threats, from careless storage of user passwords to sophisticated system hacks. But smart cards, like other authentication systems, are vulnerable to various attacks.

Moreover, a major drawback of smart card technology is price. The cost is considerably higher than that of software-based access control (such as passwords), creating a barrier to widespread distribution of smart card technology. As more units are sold, however, we should begin to see prices fall, making smart cards and their associated hardware more affordable.

JavaCards

A JavaCard is a typical smart card: It conforms to all smart card standards and thus requires no change to existing smart card-aware applications. However, a JavaCard has a twist that makes it unique: A *Java Virtual Machine* (JVM) is implemented in its *read-only memory* (ROM) mask. The JVM controls access to all the smart card resources, such as memory and I/O, and thus essentially serves as the smart card's operating system. The JVM executes a Java bytecode subset on the smart card, ultimately allowing the functions normally performed off-card to be performed on-card in the form of trusted *loyalty applications*. For example, instead of using the card to simply store a private key, you can now use that private key to perform a digital signature.

The advantages of this approach are obvious. Instead of programming the card's code in hardware-specific assembly language code, you can develop new applications in portable Java. Moreover, applications can be securely loaded to the card post-issuance—after it's been issued to the customer. In this way, vendors can enhance JavaCards with new functions over time. For example, bankcards that initially give customers secure Internet access to their bank accounts might be upgraded to include e-cash, frequent flier miles, and e-mail certificates.

History and Standards

Schlumberger, a leading smart card manufacturer, provided one of the first working prototypes of a Java-based card in 1996. The original implementation was made up of a smart card that housed a lightweight Java bytecode interpreter. As work continued in this field, SUN Microsystems issued the first JavaCard specification in October 1996. This specification was based on Schlumberger's experience.

It was not until February 1997 that the concept of a JavaCard finally took off, at which time Schlumberger and other smart card manufacturers formed the JavaCard Forum. By the end of 1997, the JavaCard Forum had released a new specification, JavaCard 2.0. This specification answered many of the shortcomings of the original specification and included many new concepts.

Another standard, which is of importance to JavaCards as well as to smart cards, is the *OpenCard Framework* (OCF). OCF, which was created by the OpenCard Consortium, is made up of many of the leading smart card and JavaCard manufacturers, as well as many application developers, such as Dallas Semiconductors, Gemplus, IBM Corp., Visa International, SUN Microsystems, and others.

OCF, similar to the JavaCard Forum, has been the driving force for the development Java-based systems. Unlike the JavaCard Forum, which provides development specifications for applications to be run on-card, OCF provides the development specifications for applications to be run in computers and terminals.

NOTE:

The application specifications provided by OCF are for use by systems that will communicate not only with JavaCards, but also with any smart card that follows the PKCS #11 standard.

JavaCard Operations

A JavaCard operates like a typical smart card. When the smart card reader sends a command, the JavaCard processes it and returns an answer. To maintain compatibility with existing applications for smart cards, a single JavaCard can process only one command at a time. Figure 9-8 illustrates the JavaCard components.

Figure 9-8

JavaCard
components

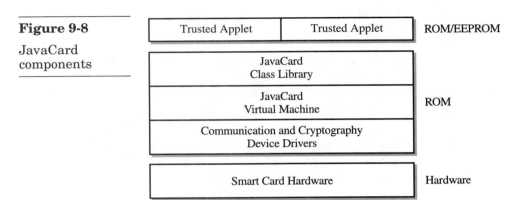

Trusted Applet	Trusted Applet	ROM/EEPROM
JavaCard Class Library		
JavaCard Virtual Machine		ROM
Communication and Cryptography Device Drivers		
Smart Card Hardware		Hardware

Other Java Tokens

Another great advancement that has taken off because of JavaCard technology is the advent of other kinds of Java tokens, including Java rings. Java rings offer the most personal of tokens: jewelry. The ring is a steel casing that houses an 8-bit microprocessor called Crypto iButton. This microprocessor is similar to one you might find on smart card. It has its own real-time clock and a high-speed math accelerator to perform 1,024-bit public-key operations. Conceivably, it can hold additional information (such as a passport, driver's license, or medical data). The Crypto iButton microprocessor is not specific to Java rings and can be found in a number of other form factors, as shown in Figure 9-9.

Figure 9-9

Crypto iButton
form factors:
(a) wristwatch;
(b) dogtag-type
token; (c) Java
ring

(a)

(b)

(c)

Biometrics

Biometrics is the science of measuring a characteristic of the human body; in its commercial application, such measurements are used to verify the claimed identity of an individual. Physical characteristics such as fingerprints, retinas and irises, palm prints, facial structure, and voice are some of the many methods being researched. Because these characteristics are relatively unique to each individual, biometrics provides an excellent means of authentication. As explained in the following sections, this technology is particularly useful for authentication when applied to commerce over the Internet.

Biometric systems are believed to provide a higher level of security than other forms of authentication, such as the use of passwords or PINs. One reason is that a biometric trait cannot be lost, stolen, or duplicated, at least not as easily as a password or PIN. Second, the use of biometrics provides nontransferable authentication. Simply stated, all other types of authentication, such as a key, are transferable. You can give someone your private key, but not your eyeball or finger (we hope).

Biometric Systems Overview

The various biometric recognition mechanisms typically operate in two modes: enrollment and verification. In the enrollment process, the user's biological feature (physical characteristic or personal trait) is acquired and stored for later use. This stored characteristic, commonly known as a *template,* is usually placed in a back-end database for later retrieval. The verification process is as you might expect. The user's characteristic is measured and compared against the stored template. The following sections describe these processes in greater detail.

Enrollment

For initial use of the biometric, each user must be enrolled by a system administrator, who verifies that each individual being enrolled is an authorized user. The biological feature is acquired by a hardware device, known as a *sensor,* which typically resides at the front end of the biometric authentication mechanism. When a physical feature is presented to the sensor, the sensor produces a signal that is modulated in response to variations in the physical quantity being measured. If, for example, the sensor is a microphone used to capture a voice pattern, the microphone produces a signal whose amplitude (voltage or current) varies with time in response to the varying frequencies in a spoken phrase.

Because the signals produced by most biometric sensors are analog, they must be converted into digital form so that they can be processed by computer. An analog-to-digital converter is therefore the next stage in most systems. Analog-to-digital converters take an analog input signal and produce a digital output stream, a numeric representation of the original analog signal. Rather than use raw data from the sensor, biometric systems often process the data to extract only the information relevant to authentication. Further processing may be used to enhance differences and compress data. When the digital representation has been processed to the desired point, it is stored. Most biometric devices take multiple samples during enrollment to account for degrees of variance in the measurement. Figure 9-10 illustrates a typical enrollment process.

Figure 9-10

Enrollment process

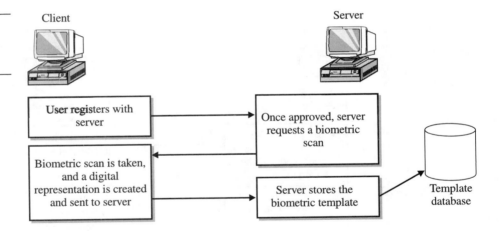

Verification

After users are enrolled, their biometrics are used to verify their identity. To authenticate someone, his or her biological feature is acquired from the sensor and converted to a digital representation, called a *live scan*. Then the live scan is compared to the stored biometric template. Typically, the live scan does not exactly match the user's stored template. Because biometric measurements almost always contain variations, these systems cannot require an exact match between the enrollment template and a current pattern. Instead, the current pattern is considered valid if it falls within a certain statistical range of values. A comparison algorithm is used to determine whether the user being verified is the same user that was enrolled.

The comparison algorithm yields a result that indicates how close the live scan is to the stored template. If the result falls into an "acceptable" range, an affirmative response is given; if the result falls into an "unacceptable" range, a negative response is given. The definition of "acceptable" differs for each biometric. For some biometrics, the system administrator may set the level of the acceptable range. If this level is set too low, however, the biometric fails to be a valid authentication mechanism. Similarly, if it is set too high, the authorized users may have trouble being authenticated. Pattern matching is fundamental to the operation of any biometric system and therefore should be considered a primary factor when you're evaluating a biometric product. Figure 9-11 illustrates a typical verification process.

Figure 9-11

Verification process

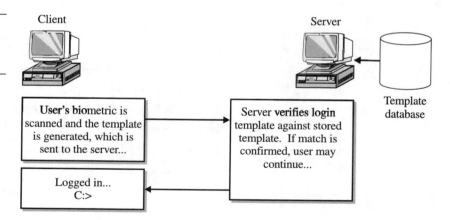

Templates

In general, most available biometric authentication mechanisms function as explained in the preceding sections. One key feature of biometrics is the template. The accumulated templates of all users are referred to as the *template database*. These databases require the same protections as password databases. The size of the templates vary from system to system. When you're testing these systems for accuracy, you should examine the templates to determine whether unique biometric features are adequately represented.

Another aspect of templates that affects biometric authentication is the approach taken by the comparison algorithm in using the template. Most devices use the template for verification, but some use it for identification. In the latter, the device takes a live scan and then compares it against the entire template database to determine whether any of the stored representations falls within the acceptable comparison algorithm range. In contrast, a biometric verification compares the live scan only against the single template of the person whom the user claims to be. For example, a user types a user name and then submits to a live scan for verification. The comparison algorithm compares the scan only to the template associated with that user name. Typically, verification biometrics are faster because they do not have to compare the live scan against the entire template database.

Recognition Methods

Just as every human body has countless unique characteristics, countless recognition methods can be used in biometrics. Let's look at some of the common biometric recognition methods in use.

Fingerprint Recognition

Fingerprint recognition is probably the most common form of biometrics available. This form of data encryption has evolved from the use of fingerprints for identification over the past several decades. By having an individual scan a fingerprint electronically to decode information, the transmitter of the data can be certain that the intended recipient is the receiver of the data. When scanned electronically, fingerprints provide a higher level of detail and accuracy than can be achieved with manual systems.

Another strength of fingerprint biometrics is that giving fingerprints is more widely accepted, convenient, and reliable than other forms of physical identification, especially when technology is used. In fact, studies have shown that fingerprint identification is currently thought to be the least intrusive of all biometric techniques. One concern of fingerprint biometrics is that latent prints left on a scanning medium will register a prior user; however, units exist that do not operate unless a "live" finger is on the medium, and they register only the later imprint. The error rate experienced with this form of encryption is approximately 1 in 100,000 scans.

One of the most important features of fingerprint biometrics is its low cost. Scanners are fairly inexpensive, and as the technology becomes more common the cost should only decrease. In fact, in anticipation of widespread use of this technology in the future, some mouse manufacturers are developing products with built-in fingerprint scanner technology.

Optical Recognition

There are two common types of optical biometrics: retinal and iris. These devices are more accurate than fingerprint and hand devices because both the retina and the iris have more characteristics to identify and match than those found on the hand. Retinal and iris scanning devices have come a long way in recent years and now allow individuals to be scanned even through eyeglasses or contact lenses. The error rate for a typical retina or iris scanner is about 1 in 2,000,000 attempts, something that further demonstrates the reliability of this technology. Two drawbacks to these devices, however, are that they have difficulty reading images of those people who are blind or have cataracts and that they currently are cumbersome to use.

The cost of these systems averages $6,500, making them somewhat unattractive for network users. But as this technology becomes more standardized and accepted, the cost should fall and become less of a factor in decision making.

Facial Recognition

In this form of biometrics, an image is examined for overall facial structure. This approach is often less reliable than more common forms such as fingerprints and iris scans. Moreover, the interpretative functions performed by the computer are much more subjective using this technology. Although one benefit of facial biometrics is that it can be applied at either at close range or over greater distances, it loses accuracy progressively as the distance increases between the individual and the scanner. Changes in lighting can also increase the error rate.

An attractive feature of facial recognition products is their low cost. Units can typically be purchased for as little as $150. At this price, this technology might lend itself to electronic commerce, but the units can be cumbersome to use and still are not as reliable as other forms of biometrics for encryption purposes.

Voice Recognition

Voice recognition offers several advantages for use in encryption. Not only is voice biometrics perfect for telecommunications applications, but also most modern personal computers already have the necessary hardware to use the applications. Even if they don't, sound cards can be purchased for as little as $50, and condenser microphones start at about $10. This means that for less than $100, individuals can possess the technology needed to have fairly reliable biometric encryption technology for use over the Internet.

This type of biometric is not as accurate, however, as some other forms. The error rate for voice recognition ranges between two percent and five percent. However, it lends itself well to use in the public telephone system and is more secure than PINs.

Some drawbacks to this technology are that voiceprints can vary over the course of the day, and if a user has a health condition such as a cold or laryngitis, it can affect verification.

Signature Recognition

Most adults are familiar with the signing of documents. In our personal lives we sign everything from personal checks to birthday cards. In the business world we sign things such as expense accounts and other official documents. This widespread practice lends itself well to the use of signature recognition as a means of biometric verification in electronic commerce. This type of signature identification, however, is different from the normal two-dimensional signature that you find on a form or document. Biometric signature recognition operates in a three-dimensional environment that uses measurements not only of the height and width but also the amount of pressure applied in a pen stroke; the latter measurement gauges the depth of the stroke as if it were made in the air. This extra dimension helps to reduce the risk of forgery that can occur in two-dimensional signatures.

One drawback to signature recognition is that people do not always sign documents in exactly the same manner. The angle at which they sign may be different because of their seating position or their hand placement on the writing surface. Therefore, even though the three-dimensional approach adds to its ability to discern impostors, this method is not as accurate as other forms of biometric verification.

Signature recognition systems are not as expensive as some of the higher-end systems such as iris scanners; they are priced more in the range of voice and fingerprint scanners, and that makes them affordable for network use.

Keystroke Recognition

This technology is not as mundane as it sounds. The concept is based on a password or PIN system but adds the extra dimension of keystroke dynamics. With this technology, not only must intruders know the correct password, but they must also be able to replicate the user's rate of typing and intervals between letters. Even if an unauthorized person is able to guess the correct password, it's unlikely that he will be able to type it with the proper rhythm unless he has the ability to hear and memorize the correct user's keystrokes.

Keystroke recognition is most likely one of the least secure of the new biometric technologies that have evolved in recent years, but it is also probably one of the least expensive and easiest to implement. It probably won't gain much attention for use in electronic commerce because similarly priced systems offer far more reliability.

Biometric Accuracy

When you're choosing a biometric authentication system, an important consideration is its accuracy. The accuracy of biometric authentication systems can be categorized by two measures: the *false acceptance rate* (FAR) and the *false rejection rate* (FRR). A system's FAR reflects the situation in which a biometric system wrongly verifies an identity by matching biometric features from individuals who are not identical. In the most common context, false acceptance represents a security hazard. Similarly, a system's FRR reflects the situation in which a biometric system is not able to verify the legitimate claimed identity of an enrolled person. In the most common context, the user of a biometric system will experience false rejection as inconvenience.

Suppliers of biometric systems often use FAR together with FRR to describe the capabilities of the system. Obviously, FRR and FAR are dependent on the threshold level. Increasing the threshold will reduce the probability of false acceptance and therefore enhance security. However, system availability will be reduced due to an increased FRR.

How these rates are determined is fundamental to the operation of any biometric system and therefore should be considered a primary factor when a biometric system is evaluated. You should be aware that manufacturers' FAR and FRR numbers are extrapolated from small user sets, and the assumptions for the extrapolations are sometimes erroneous.

You should assess these performance factors with an eye toward the type of users who will use the system. For a proper live scan to be taken, users must become familiar with the device. You can expect it to take two weeks before the false rejection rate drops off. Another user consideration is that not all users may be able to use the biometric—for example, because of an impairment that prevents them from taking an acceptable scan. In that case, you may need to provide an alternative method to grant those users access, or you may have to select a biometric based on the needs of each set of users. When selecting a biometric, also consider user acceptance. Some biometrics have met with resistance from users because the technology is too invasive.

Combining Authentication Methods

Passwords, authentication tokens, and biometrics are subject to a variety of attacks. Passwords can be guessed, tokens can be stolen, and even biometrics have certain vulnerabilities; these threats can be reduced by applying sound design principles and system management techniques during the development and operation of your authentication system. One method that can substantially increase the system's security is to use a combination of authentication techniques.

For example, an authentication system might require users to present an authentication token and also enter a password. By stealing a user's token, an attacker would still not be able to gain access to the host system because the system would require the user's password in addition to the token. Although it might be possible to guess the user's password, the host system can make this extremely difficult by locking the user out after a specified number of invalid passwords have been presented in succession. After a user's account has been locked in this manner, only the appropriate system administrator or security officer should be able to unlock the account.

Tokens can also be used to store biometric templates for user authentication. After enrollment, the user's unique template could be stored on a token rather than in a file on the host system. When the user requests access to the system, a current template is generated and compared to the enrollment template stored on the user's token. It would be preferable for this comparison to be carried out internally by the token because in that way the enrollment template would never need to leave the token. However, often this method is not possible because of the complexity of the algorithms used for the comparison. The microprocessors typically used in smart tokens cannot execute these algorithms in a reasonable time. If the template comparison is done by the host system, the host must provide adequate assurance that users' templates cannot be compromised. In addition, the token and host system should implement an authentication protocol that ensures two things: that the host system is obtaining the template from a valid token and that the token is submitting the template to a valid host. The ideal situation is to have both the biometric sensors and the comparison algorithm implemented on the token. In that case, the token can perform the entire biometric authentication process. Figure 9-12 shows one of the newer products available on the market, which combines authentication methods.

Figure 9-12

BioMouse Plus from American Biometric Company

Summary

A wide variety of cryptographic hardware is available on the market. Various tokens can be used for authentication, as can various microprocessor cards, biometrics, and accelerators. Each of these approaches has its place, for the right price.

Vendors

A great many vendors manufacture and sell cryptographic accelerators, tokens, smart cards, and biometric devices. Table 9-1 lists some of the manufacturers and the products they sell.

Table 9-1
Cryptographic
Manufacturers

Companies/ Device	Accelerators	Tokens/ Smart cards	Biometrics
nCipher http://www.ncipher.com/	Nfast		
Compaq http://www.compaq.com/	AXL300		
Rainbow Technologies http://www.rainbow.com/	CryptoSwift, NetSwift	iKey, Sentinel	
RSA Security, Inc. http://www.rsasecurity.com/		SecurID	
DataKey http://www.datakey.com/		Datakey	
Ensure Technologies http://ensuretech.com/ cgi-bin/dp/framesethome.dt/		XyLoc Security Server	
Dallas Semiconductor http://www.dalsemi.com/index.html		iButton	
GemPlus http://www.gemplus.com/		GemClub-Micro, GemStart, GemWG10	
American Biometric Company http://www.abio.com/			BioMouse Plus
AuthenTec, Inc. http://www.authentec.com/			FingerLoc, EntrePad

CHAPTER 10

Digital Signatures: Beyond Security

Thanks to the Internet, e-commerce has dramatically changed our ways of conducting business. As each day passes, paper-based transactions— including agreements that have legal force—are becoming obsolete as the use of electronic agreements transmitted over the Internet increases in popularity. The main motivation for this change is convenience. Distance, for example, is no longer a barrier to getting an agreement signed. Within seconds, an electronic agreement can travel across the world, receive an electronic (or digital) signature, and be returned completed. But this new world of e-commerce requires close attention to legal and technical issues.

Users' experiences with digital signatures (see Chapter 5) have shown that this technology can save e-commerce parties time and money. Compared with paper signatures, digital signatures offer a number of benefits:

- **Message integrity**   A digital signature is superior to a handwritten signature in that it attests to the contents of a message as well as to the identity of the signer. As long as a secure hash function is used, there is no way to take someone's signature from one document and attach it to another, or to alter the signed message in any way. The slightest change in a signed document will cause the digital signature verification process to fail. Thus, authentication allows people to check the integrity of signed documents. Of course, if signature verification fails, it may be unclear whether there was an attempted forgery or simply a transmission error.

- **Savings** The use of open systems (such as the Internet) as transport media can provide considerable savings of time and money. Furthermore, adding automation means that data can be digitally signed and sent in a timely manner.

- **Storage** Business data (contracts and similar documents) can be stored much more easily in electronic form than in paper form. Furthermore, in theory an electronic document that has been digitally signed can be validated indefinitely. If all parties to the contract keep a copy of the time-stamped document, each of them can prove that the contract was signed with valid keys. In fact, the time stamp can prove the validity of a contract even if one signer's key becomes compromised at some point after the contract was signed.

- **Risk mitigation** If properly implemented, digital signatures reduce the risk of fraud and attempts by a party to repudiate (disavow) the contract.

Before companies and individuals adopt these new techniques, however, they must first address a few legal and technical concerns. In U.S. federal law, under the Statutes of Frauds, a party that claims that a contract was made must provide proof. The traditional method of proof is the document with a handwritten signature. The question is whether an electronic document containing a digital signature is secure and therefore reliable as proof. The Federal Rules of Evidence allow computer data to be admitted as business records if a foundation is established for their reliability. As this book is being written, new federal legislation has taken effect. This legislation provides that an electronic signature has the same legal status as a handwritten signature. It should be noted, however, that these new laws are still untested.

This chapter provides insight into the many aspects of digital and electronic signatures as they apply to e-commerce. We discuss concepts and requirements, legal and technical, that users must completely understand if they hope to apply these signatures. We also look at the various relevant laws, including the newly enacted federal *Electronic Signatures in Global and National Commerce* (E-SIGN) Act. Finally, we discuss the differences between electronic and digital signatures and how each falls short if the proper concepts and requirements aren't used.

Legislative Approaches

As we've discussed, digital signatures offer a range of benefits for businesses and consumers alike. For digital signatures to make their way into mainstream, however, two barriers must be overcome:

- How to give documents that exist only in electronic form the same legal status as paper documents
- How to provide a secure, reliable, and legally sanctioned method for "signing" electronic documents that will eliminate the need to generate and sign paper documents, thereby encouraging and facilitating electronic commerce

Both problems require legislative solutions.

Legal Guidelines from the American Bar Association

The *American Bar Association* (ABA), the organization that represents the legal profession in the United States, has done considerable work on the legal aspects of digital signatures. In 1996, the ABA's Information Security Committee, Section of Science and Technology, published a document titled "Digital Signature Guidelines." These guidelines were originally drafted to provide "general, abstract statements of principle, intended to serve as long-term, unifying foundations for digital signature law across varying legal settings." Many states have chosen to model their own digital signature legislation after these guidelines.

Many legal professionals, with the exception of the ABA special interest legal groups, are playing catch-up in the fast evolving and sometimes complicated digital world. As the number of e-commerce sites using digital signatures increases, so will the need for lawyers who can render sound legal advice. Clients will begin to look to attorneys and others for guidance about the appropriate level of security for a given line of electronic business and other transactions.

It will be of the utmost importance for attorneys to cooperate closely with business and technical specialists in the procurement and deployment of computer security systems generally, and specifically those systems that require electronic signatures. The legal consequences that flow from the presence or absence of particular elements of data security will constitute risks, liabilities, and other potential costs that should be taken into account from the beginning.

Legal Concepts Related to Digital Signatures

Because electronic documents can be easily copied and modified without detection, they cannot automatically be assumed to be authentic. Moreover, unlike hand-written characters, digitally encoded characters are not unique. The signature on an electronic document is not physically connected to the document's content.

To withstand both legal and technical tests, the recipient of an electronic document containing a digital signature must be able to prove to an impartial third party (a court, a judge, or a referee before whom the parties have agreed to submit for resolution any issue or dispute) that the contents of the document are genuine and that it originated with the sender. In addition, the signature must be such that the sender cannot later disavow the contents of the document.

Before we go any further, let's review the concepts of nonrepudiation and authentication, which have been described earlier (see Chapters 5 and 6). These concepts play a key role in the legalities of digital signatures, and it is important to understand how they differ in the digital world compared with the paper world.

Nonrepudiation

Nonrepudiation, at its most basic, is the ability to prove to an impartial third party—after the fact—that a specific communication originated with and was submitted by a certain person or was delivered by a certain person. Nonrepudiation, then, defines the means that are used to prevent illegitimate breaches of contract on the same grounds. This means that evidence exists thst ties the identity of a party to the substance of a message or transaction at a certain point in time and that the evidence is sufficiently strong to prevent or rebut that party's subsequent denial of it.

The 1988 ISO Open Systems Interconnection Security Architecture standard provides a limited definition of nonrepudiation as a security service that counters repudiation, where *repudiation* is defined as "denial by one of the entities involved in a communication of having participated in all or part of the communication." Signatures, seals, recording offices, certified mail, letters of credit, notaries, auditors, and collateralized bills of lading are examples of nonrepudiable business practices traditionally employed to support legally binding business transactions.

These elements of nonrepudiation must now be incorporated into the electronic environment—in real time, with full assurance, and without a paper trail.

In the absence of this kind of rigor, how can businesses operating at Internet speed avoid or resolve disputes? It is only with a full set of digital nonrepudiation elements that irrefutable evidence can be shown in a court of law. Otherwise, businesses aren't protected against breach of contract, fraud, currency fluctuations, insolvency, credit risks, incomplete funds delivery, and operational failure.

Nonrepudiation services provide trusted evidence that a specific action occurred. The concept of nonrepudiation, as it pertains to information security and digital signatures, can be broken into three types: nonrepudiation of origin, nonrepudiation of submission, and nonrepudiation of delivery.

- **Nonrepudiation of origin**   This concept protects the recipient of a communication by guaranteeing the identity of the originator of a communication. It further confirms the time the message was sent and ensures that the message was not tampered with during transmission.

- **Nonrepudiation of delivery**   This concept protects the sender of a communication by guaranteeing essentially the same elements as does nonrepudiation of origin. As with nonrepudiation of origin, it can be used to provide the time a message was sent and to indicate whether the data was tampered with during transmission.

- **Nonrepudiation of submission**   This concept is similar to nonrepudiation of origin and delivery except that it is used to protect the sender against any claim by the recipient that the data wasn't sent or wasn't sent at a specific time.

Authentication

For the purposes of this chapter, and in relation to digital signatures, two types of authentication must be understood: signer authentication and data authentication.

For a document to have any legal force, the signer of the document must be authenticated; this concept is called *signer authentication*. If someone signs a loan certificate, for example, the bank can store the borrower's signature for use later in legal ways because the signature is believed to authenticate the borrower with a high probability. A signature should indicate who signed a document, message, or record, and it should be difficult for another person to produce the signature without authorization. If a public/private key pair is associated with an identified signer, the digital signature attributes the message to the signer. The digital signature cannot be forged unless the signer loses control of the private key (a "compromise" of the private key), such as by divulging it or losing the medium or device in which it is contained.

Data authentication is comparable to stamping a document in a way that disallows all future modifications to it. Data authentication is usually accompanied by *data origin authentication,* which binds a concrete person to a specific document (for example, by limiting the number of persons who use the stamp). A signature should identify what is signed, making it impracticable to falsify or alter either the signed matter or the signature without detection. The digital signature also identifies the signed message, typically with far greater certainty and precision than paper signatures. Verification reveals any tampering because the comparison of the hash results (one made at signing and the other made at verifying) shows whether the message is the same as when signed.

Signer authentication and data authentication are used to exclude impersonators and forgers, and they are essential ingredients in what is often called a *nonrepudiation service*. A nonrepudiation service provides assurance of the origin or delivery of data in order to protect the sender against false denial by the recipient that the data has been received, or to protect the recipient against false denial by the sender that the data has been sent. Thus, a nonrepudiation service provides evidence to prevent a person from unilaterally modifying or terminating legal obligations arising from a transaction effected by computer-based means.

Written Versus Digital Signatures

Although digital and written signatures can serve the same purposes, there are obvious physical differences. Let's look at the differences between the signatures applied to written and digital documents.

Written Documents

Traditionally, someone's signature on a literal document authenticates the origin of the data contained in it. Because people sign various documents during their lifetimes, their signatures become a part of their identity over time. By using a unique combination of pencil strokes that is very difficult for anyone else to forge, they can sign anything, almost without thinking. Additionally, loan certificates (and other documents that may have legal force) have been designed to guard against forging of a signed document. Examples include documents that use watermarks, embossing, and special ink treatment, all of which provide protection against photocopies and other forgeries.

Digital Documents

Electronic documents can easily be copied and modified without detection. To generalize this consideration, *digital information* is usually defined (loosely) as the kind of information not bounded to any concrete carrier, such as the ink on a piece of paper. Additionally, the digital information lacks *personality* (a file saved by someone can be easily updated by someone else having the appropriate permissions).

Clearly, the traditional methods of signing by appending the signature to an existing document do not work for electronic documents. Anyone can simply modify the document and append the same signature to it.

Requirements for the Use of Digital Signatures

For current digital signature legislation to withstand the test of litigation, a number of important issues must be resolved. The American Bar Association's "Guidelines for Digital Signatures" is an excellent foundation, but corporations and individuals might wish to focus on concerns not addressed in the guidelines. The following sections describe those requirements, which are essential if digital signatures are to stand up.

Public Key Infrastructures

To effectively incorporate digital signatures within an e-commerce framework, an organization should create and maintain a *public-key infrastructure* (PKI), as described in Chapter 6. To a point, having a PKI ensures that only valid keys are used in signing and verifying electronic documents.

The PKI must enforce policies whereby properly administered *certification authorities* (CAs) and *registration authorities* (RAs) are used, requiring end users to show reliable proof that authenticates them. Furthermore, public-key certificates can be housed in a central location that can be accessed by any relying party. Finally, a PKI serves to revoke or suspend certificates as needed.

Control of Key Revocation

Another important issue related to the use of digital signatures is the management of private signature keys. If an unauthorized person gains access to a private key, the thief will be able to forge the owner's signature on electronic documents. To prevent this, a user should be able to revoke a compromised signature key in the public directory. Here are some guidelines:

- All users should be able to revoke their public keys from the directory at any time. For this policy to work, CAs should save (in the public directory) information about all revoked keys.

- An authority should be able to revoke the signatures issued for its employees. A separate CA could certify digital signatures for employees of a given company.

- *Online Certificate Status Protocol* (OCSP), which was explained in Chapter 6, should be used to ensure that verifiers receive the most current revocation status.

Time-Stamping

Another issue is *time-stamping*. Digital signatures provided through the use of public-key technology can be called into question for a simple reason: If the signer of a particularly important document (for example, a loan agreement) later wishes to repudiate her signature, she can dishonestly report the compromise of her private key and ask it to be revoked. A later verifier will not be able to certify whether the signing happened before or after the revocation.

Time-stamping is a set of techniques that enable you to ascertain whether an electronic document was created or signed at (or before) a certain time. In practice, most time-stamping systems use a trusted third party called a *time-stamping authority* (TSA). A *time stamp* is the TSA's digital attestation that an identified electronic document was presented to the TSA at a certain time.

A *time-stamping service* (TSS) is a collection of methods and techniques providing long-term authentication of digital documents. The object of a TSS is to authenticate not only the document but also the moment in time at which the document is submitted for authentication. Figure 10-1 illustrates the interaction between end-users and a trusted time-stamping server available from Datum.

Figure 10-1

Time-stamping components

The importance of time-stamping becomes clear when there is a need for a legal use of electronic documents with a long lifetime. Without time-stamping, you cannot trust signed documents after the cryptographic primitives used for signing have become unreliable, nor can you resolve cases in which the signer repudiates the signing, claiming to have accidentally lost the signature key.

During recent years, especially in the context of legal regulation of the use of digital signatures, the organizational and legal aspects of time-stamping have become the subject of worldwide attention. Time-stamping helps to significantly lower the level of trust currently required of a PKI by making it possible to prove that a document was signed before the corresponding signature key was revoked. For that reason, organizations often depend on time-stamping to resolve the status of documents.

Current and Pending Legislation

Digital signature legislation has been an ongoing issue for some time. Worldwide, especially in Europe, digital signature laws have been in effect for about a decade. The *United Nations Commission on International Trade Law* (UNCITRAL), a model law on electronic commerce, took effect in 1996 and has had a major influence on signature laws worldwide. The UNCITRAL model law takes a high-level, enabling approach to electronic signatures and records, with no mention of digital signatures or cryptography.

Only during the past five years has the United States gained momentum in this legal arena. The first state law, enacted in Utah in 1995 and amended in March 1996, is widely recognized as an important and positive first step toward legal recognition of digital signature technology. The Utah act provides for the licensure of certification authorities by the Utah Department of Commerce. Utah's law also details the rights and liabilities of parties to a transaction using public-key cryptography and a licensed certification authority. In 1996, Washington state adopted legislation closely resembling the Utah law. Other states, most notably Georgia, began considering bills modeled after the Utah law, and, for a time, it seemed that a consensus was developing among the states.

Now, however, various policy issues have increasingly moved states toward approaches that are less regulatory, less technology-specific, and more incremental. For example, California and Arizona enacted legislation permitting the use of digital signatures for transactions involving state entities. This legislation authorized the two states' secretaries of state to promulgate regulations to achieve the purpose of the act. Still other states have passed laws permitting the use of electronic signatures for particular purposes, such as for medical records (Connecticut) or for budget and accounting purposes, such as electronic check signing by the treasurer (Delaware). Georgia, along with a number of states that had legislation resembling the Utah act, have allowed the bills to die and opted for further study.

The effort in Massachusetts exemplifies an attempt to craft laws that directly address the legal issues raised by electronic commerce but do not exclusively codify public-key cryptography in statute. This approach seeks generally to remove legal obstacles to electronic communications and transactions by giving legal effect to electronic signatures and electronic records. The law would also specifically provide for the admissibility of electronic signatures and records.

The problem with the state laws, however, is that no two sets of laws are the same. Building on the work in Massachusetts, the federal government is trying to provide a solution by working on new federal legislation. The U.S. House and Senate, after long negotiations, compromised on a new electronic signature bill, the Electronic Signatures in Global and National Commerce (E-SIGN) Act, on June 9, 2000. The E-SIGN Act makes electronic, or online, signatures as legally binding as ink-and-paper signatures and states that they can be used as evidence in legal proceedings.

The E-SIGN Act

President Bill Clinton signed the E-SIGN Act on June 30, 2000. E-SIGN gives legal recognition and effect to electronic signatures, contracts, and records, and it empowers the use of online contracts and provision of notices. The law became effective October 1, 2000, except for certain provisions affecting the use of electronic records to satisfy records retention requirements, which became effective March 1, 2001. E-SIGN requires a consumer to agree to electronically signed contracts and consent to receiving records over the Internet. Companies must verify that customers have an operating e-mail address and other technical means of receiving information. Some notices, such as evictions, health insurance lapses, or electricity lapses, must still come in paper form.

Under E-SIGN, federal agencies are given authority allowing them to unconditionally exempt specified types of records from the consumer consent provisions. Most notably, the legislation directs the *Securities and Exchange Commission* (SEC) to use this authority to issue a regulation that effectively allows mutual funds to provide prospective investors with an electronic fund prospectus at or before the time they access electronic sales literature, without first obtaining investor consent to the electronic format of the prospectus. In this way, funds can continue the practice, permitted under the SEC's interpretive releases, of using hyperlinks on their Web sites to give prospective investors simultaneous access to both sales literature and the fund's prospectus.

E-SIGN was originally designed to boost Internet e-commerce transactions, for both *business-to-business* (B2B) and *business-to-consumer* (B2C) markets, by eliminating paperwork arising from contracts. The effect of the E-SIGN Act is uniform nationwide legislation enabling the use of electronic records and signatures for interstate and international commerce.

Electronic Versus Digital Signatures: What's the Difference?

Simply put, an *electronic* signature is any symbol or method, accomplished by electronic means, that is executed or adopted by a party with present intention to be bound by or to authenticate a record. An electronic signature can be created by any electronic means. For example, the output of a sophisticated biometric device, such as a fingerprint computer recognition system, could qualify as an electronic signature, and so would the simple entry of a typed name at the end of an e-mail message. The principle is that the symbol or method was executed or adopted by the signer with a present intent to sign the record. This definition focuses on the traditional legal purposes of a signature and not on the particular medium or manner chosen to effect the signature.

In contrast, a *digital* signature refers to a particular implementation of public-key cryptography (such as the implementation described in Chapter 5). More formally, a digital signature can be defined as the transformation of a record using an asymmetric cryptosystem and a hash function such that a person having the initial record and the signer's public key can accurately determine (a) whether the transformation was created using the private key that corresponds to the signer's public key and (b) whether the initial record has been altered since the transformation was made.

In other words, a digital signature is created by use of a public-key system, whereas an electronic signature is produced by any computer method, including public-key systems. Digital signatures are technology-specific. Electronic signatures are technology-neutral.

The use of low-security electronic signatures, such as simply typing one's name on an e-mail, raises serious questions of proof regarding the authenticity of such a signature. However, there are times when little or no security is warranted. A given transaction or message may be informal, of little or no value, or otherwise not reasonably likely to form the basis of subsequent dispute. For example, it's common practice to conclude purely social e-mail messages with the typing of the sender's name. In this case, the name is a symbol intended to authenticate the document but not necessarily manifesting intent to be bound by the content—assuming there exists any particular content at all. In this context, the word "authenticate" means merely the intention to represent that the signer was the sender. In common practice, e-mail among friends and close colleagues is often concluded with the initials of the sender alone.

For more formal, but low-risk, electronic transactions, a more robust signature system may be desirable. This does not necessarily mean that a full-fledged public-key solution is required. For example, some business and professional online services require entry of a user name and password to access their systems. After users are on the system, they may be entitled to additional information or services, such as online dialog with an expert or authorization to view value-added proprietary documents. Here, the electronic signature is created by use of a user name and password, probably relying on access control technology far less expensive and simpler to use than public-key cryptosystems. Depending on the understanding of the parties as evidenced by contracts, disclaimers, or other conditions of use, the use of this system may authenticate the user and also by implication, or perhaps expressly, express intent to be bound by billing rates or other terms.

Following is a description of various E-SIGN provisions:

- **Technology**   E-SIGN requires that parties to a contract decide on the form of electronic signature technology. From a scanned handwritten signature to biometric-protected smart cards, E-SIGN allows the use of various forms of technology as long as both parties agree.

- **Notification**   The E-SIGN Act provides the following with regard to notification:
  1. The consumer decides whether to use an e-signature or handwritten signature; the consumer must give consent before receiving bills and other documents only in electronic form.
  2. Cancellation and foreclosure notices must be sent on paper.
  3. The vendor must conduct test e-mailings before sending subsequent e-mail notifications.
  4. The law does not allow e-signatures on adoptions, wills, and product safety recalls.

- **Rights** Consumers must be made aware of any right or option to receive a disclosure in paper form and what they must do to obtain paper copies. Furthermore, consumers must be made aware of the right to withdraw consent to have records provided electronically, including any conditions, consequences, or fees associated with doing so. The organization must describe the procedures for withdrawing consent and for updating information needed to contact the consumer electronically.

- **Consent** Consumers must be presented with and must confirm the hardware and software requirements for access and retention of electronic records and must confirm consent to the contract. Both confirmations must be visibly and conspicuously separate from all other terms and agreements.

- **Consumer obligations** The consumer is obligated to inform electronic records providers of any change in e-mail address or other location to which the electronic records may be provided. Furthermore, the consumer is obligated to notify the electronic records provider before withdrawal of consent.

- **Enforcement** The E-SIGN Act provides for its enforcement by giving authority to government agencies as needed to protect the public interest.

Dealing with Legal Uncertainties

Because the E-SIGN Act does not prescribe the technology that must be used to sign and verify an electronic document, an electronic signature could simply be a person's typed name on e-mail. All that is required is for both parties to agree to the technology. To the best of our knowledge, such a signature in no way fosters nonrepudiation and authentication, which have always been the foundation for commerce as we know it.

Ultimately, we believe that a more solid foundation will be needed. The concepts of authentication and nonrepudiation are crucial to the operation of business transactions. To separate authorized users of information from unauthorized users, there must be a reliable way to ascertain the identity of the user. The Internet was not designed with adequate technical means to achieve this identification. In fact, without the existence of the requirements listed in "Requirements for the Use of Digital Signatures," it is easy impersonate someone else.

Finally, because the validity of documents with these new electronic signatures has never been challenged in court, their legal status is truly not yet defined. It's likely that through such challenges, we will see the courts issue rulings that will better define which methods, key sizes, and security precautions are acceptable for electronic signatures to be legally binding.

Summary

Digital signatures have the potential to possess greater legal authority than handwritten signatures. Why? Digital signatures may provide a higher degree of nonrepudiation and authenticity than their handwritten counterparts. For example, if a ten-page document is signed by hand on the tenth page, one cannot be sure that the first nine pages have not been altered. However, if an electronic document is signed with a digital signature, a third party can verify that not one byte of the contract has been altered. For this and other reasons, digital signatures also save the parties time and money.

However, if digital signatures are to replace handwritten signatures, serious issues—some of which revolve around current legislation—must be answered. For example, is the current E-SIGN Act enough? Do electronic signatures provide the same level of nonrepudiation and authenticity provided by handwritten signatures?

E-SIGN is a great leap forward for both interstate and international Internet commerce. However, E-SIGN should be seen more as a foundation on which to build with current and emerging technologies, such as the use of public-key technology, PKIs, and digital notaries.

Real-World Examples

A number of relevant products can be purchased or downloaded free from the Internet. They range from enabling software to hardware that allows users to authenticate themselves to their private signing key. Following are only a couple of the available solutions.

- RSA Security, Inc., as well as a number of other security software vendors, offers developer *software development kits* (SDKs) and products. BSAFE Cert-C and Cert-J, for example, allow developers to use public-key certificates for a number of security services such as digital signatures.

- Datum carries an excellent time-stamp device to be used in conjunction with digital notaries or time-stamp authorities or to provide in-house time-stamp services.

In addition to security vendors that sell products designed for users and developers, we will likely see the advent of more businesses that will offer services to support digital signatures. Such services include certification authorities and time-stamp and digital notary services. Here are some examples:

- Digisign is one company that has already begun selling time-stamp and digital notary services.

- VeriSign is a certification authority that issues public-key certificates to end users.

Finally, we should not forget legal professionals. A great many legal professionals have taken the time to become technically savvy, and we expect to see this number increase as more related legal cases are seen in the future.

CHAPTER 11

Doing It Wrong: The Break-Ins

Over the past two decades, the computer industry has really taken off, and the number of security incidents has increased significantly. Corporations as well as individuals have learned the hard way that data can easily be accessed, disclosed, modified, or even deleted if proper security is not provided.

Over the years, companies have fallen short in their efforts to implement cryptographic solutions both in their own products and services and in attempts to protect their internal enterprise from intruders. This chapter summarizes the various types of losses that occur when a system is not properly secured. We also outline the kinds of threats and intruders that have come to be widely reported. Finally, we look at a number of case studies in which security was either overlooked or failed because of improper implementation. (We describe successful case studies in Chapter 12.)

Measuring Losses

The kinds of losses that organizations can experience because of lapses in computer security can be counted in a number of ways. Many people think first of the direct forms of loss, such as the loss of data. However, when you look closely at what is at stake, loss of data is only the beginning. Following is a short list of the types of losses that occur:

- **Loss of data or secrets**   When people hear the word "hacker," this is perhaps one of the first types of loss that they think of. This category includes the loss of user credit card numbers, compromise of financial reports, and unauthorized access to medical information.

NOTE:

The data itself need not have been stolen for a serious loss to result. Instead, an attacker may manipulate the data in such a way that it is rendered inaccurate or unusable.

- **Loss of reputation**   After a successful breach of security, end users may abandon a service or product because they're afraid to use it. Yet another aspect of this type of loss is the effect it has on assessments of a corporation by financial analysts. Sometimes an analyst's negative evaluation can have as great an impact as the break-in itself. This may be one of the main reasons that corporations seldom report break-ins and theft of data.

- **Financial losses**   In addition to direct financial thefts, loss of data and loss of reputation will result in financial losses. Financial losses can be one of the most difficult to quantify. One reason is that no one knows exactly how many current customers will not return following a break-in or, worse yet, how many potential new customers will never make the attempt.

Types of Security Threats

To implement security effectively, corporations as well as individuals need to be aware of a variety of potential threats. Let's take a look at each these threats.

> **NOTE:**
> *Each of the following threats does not necessarily require direct human interaction. Through the use of computer viruses or Trojan Horse applications, data can easily be destroyed, manipulated, or sent to an intruder for viewing.*

Unauthorized Disclosure of Data

Unauthorized disclosure of data results from an individual accessing or reading information and revealing it either accidentally or intentionally. Corporations and individuals are making greater use of networks, including private networks such as *local area networks* (LANs) and *wide area networks* (WANs) and public networks such as the Internet. As a result, some of the data stored or processed on the network may require some level of protection to ensure confidentiality. Network data or software may be compromised when it is accessed, read, and possibly released to an unauthorized individual.

A common cause of unauthorized access is the failure to encrypt sensitive information. Data can be compromised by exploiting the following types of vulnerabilities:

- Storing data in the clear (i.e., unencrypted) when it is considered sensitive enough to warrant encryption
- Failing to implement, monitor, and enforce appropriate authorization and access-control mechanisms where sensitive data is stored

Unauthorized Modification of Data

Information in digital form is often shared between many users and stored on numerous shared devices. The unauthorized modification of data includes the modification, deletion, or destruction of data or software in an unauthorized or accidental manner.

A particularly insidious event is data modification that goes undetected. When such modifications are present for long periods of time, the modified data may be spread throughout the network, possibly corrupting databases, spreadsheet calculations, and other forms of application data.

This kind of damage can compromise the integrity of application information. When undetected software changes are made, all system software can become suspect, warranting a thorough review (and perhaps reinstallation) of all related software and applications.

These kinds of unauthorized changes can be made in simple command programs (for example, in PC batch files), in utility programs used on multiuser systems, in major application programs, or in any other type of software. They can be made by unauthorized outsiders as well as those who are authorized to make software changes (although not, of course, the damaging changes we are speaking of here). These changes can divert information (or copies of the information) to other destinations, corrupt the data as it is processed, and impair the availability of system or network services.

The unauthorized modification of data and software can easily take place when data integrity services are not provided.

Unauthorized Access

Unauthorized access occurs when someone who is not authorized to use a system or network gains access, usually by posing as a legitimate user of the network. Three common methods are used to gain unauthorized access: password sharing, general password guessing, and password capture.

Password sharing allows an unauthorized user to assume the network access and privileges of a legitimate user with the latter's knowledge and acceptance. General password guessing is not a new means of unauthorized access. In password capture, a legitimate user is tricked into unknowingly revealing his or her login ID and password. Methods of password capture include the use of a Trojan Horse program. To a user, this program looks like a legitimate login program; however, it's designed solely to capture passwords.

Another method used to ultimately gain network access is to capture a login ID and password as they are transmitted across the network unencrypted. A number of methods for capturing cleartext network traffic, including passwords, are readily available.

Intruders can gain unauthorized network access by exploiting the following types of vulnerabilities:

- Lack of, or insufficient, identification and authentication schemes
- Password sharing
- The use of poor password management or easy-to-guess passwords
- Failure to patch known system holes and vulnerabilities
- The storage of network access passwords in batch files on PCs
- Lack of a time-out for login and log-off attempts

Disclosure of Network Traffic

Many users realize the importance of protecting confidential information when it is stored on their workstations or servers; however, it's also important to maintain confidentiality as the information travels across the network. The disclosure of network traffic occurs when someone who is unauthorized reads, or otherwise obtains, information as it traverses the network. Intruders can easily compromise network traffic by listening to and capturing traffic transmitted over the network transport media. Examples of attack methods include tapping into a network cable with the use of a hardware device that analyzes network traffic as it is transmitted.

Traffic analyzing software, or *sniffers*, allow intruders to access the network the traffic is traversing. One such application is Sun Microsystems' "snoop" utility, which was originally created to allow administrators to verify traffic flow across the network. But it also allows intruders running the Solaris operating system to watch the flow of network traffic.

Information that can be compromised in this way includes system and user names, passwords, electronic mail messages, application data, health records, and so on. For example, even if patient records are stored on a system in an encrypted form, they can be captured in plaintext as they are sent from a workstation or PC to a file server. Electronic mail message files, which usually have strict access rights when stored on a system, are often sent in plaintext across a wire, making them an easy target for capturing.

Disclosure of network traffic is usually the result of data sent in the clear, across both public and private networks.

Spoofing of Network Traffic

It's a basic principle of network security that data that is transmitted over a network should not be altered in an unauthorized manner—either by the network itself or by an intruder—as a result of that transmission. Network users should have a reasonable expectation that any messages they send will be received unmodified. A modification occurs when an intentional or unintentional change is made to any part of the message, including the contents and addressing information.

Spoofing of network traffic involves (1) the ability to receive a message by masquerading as the legitimate receiving destination or (2) masquerading as the sending machine and sending an unauthorized message to a destination. For an attacker to masquerade as a receiving machine, the network must be persuaded that the destination address is the legitimate address of the machine. (Network traffic can also be intercepted by listening to messages as they are broadcast to all nodes.) To masquerade as the sending machine and deceive a receiver into believing the message was legitimately sent, attackers can masquerade the address or mount a playback attack. A *playback* involves capturing a session between a sender and a receiver and then retransmitting the message (with either a new header, new message contents, or both).

Intruders can spoof or modify network traffic by exploiting the following types of vulnerabilities:

- Transmitting network traffic in plaintext
- Lack of a date/time stamp (showing sending time and receiving time)
- Failure to use message authentication codes or digital signatures
- Lack of a real-time verification mechanism (to use against playback)

Identifying Intruders

Every day, undesirable intruders make unauthorized entry into computer systems and networks. Who exactly are the intruders? These individuals range from recreational hackers to foreign intelligence agencies. Each of these groups has its own agenda and motivations. The following sections paraphrase the descriptions of various intruders that were noted in a recent Federal Bureau of Investigation Congressional statement titled "Cybercrime."

Insiders

Most corporations want to believe that their employees are the cream of the crop and would never violate corporate security. In reality, however, some employees are not what they seem. People who commit security crimes against their employers are motivated by a number of reasons; the disgruntled insider (a current or former employee) is a principal source of computer crimes for many companies. Insiders' knowledge of the target company's network often allows them to gain unrestricted access and damage the system or steal proprietary data. The 2000 survey by the Computer Security Institute and FBI reports that 71 percent of respondents detected unauthorized access to systems by insiders.

Hackers

Virtually every day we see news reports about recreational hackers, or "crackers," who crack into networks for the thrill of the challenge or to gain bragging rights in the hacker community. Remote cracking once required a fair amount of skill and computer knowledge, but recreational hackers can now download attack scripts and protocols from the World Wide Web and launch them against victim sites. Thus, even though attack tools have become more sophisticated, they have also become easier to use.

Terrorists

Increasingly, terrorist groups are using new information technology and the Internet to formulate plans, raise funds, spread propaganda, and communicate securely. Moreover, some terrorist groups, such as the Internet Black Tigers (who reportedly are affiliated with the Tamil Tigers), have been known to engage in attacks on foreign government Web sites and e-mail servers. "Cyber terrorism"—by which we mean the use of cyber tools to shut down critical national infrastructures (such as energy, transportation, or government operations) for the purpose of coercing or intimidating a government or civilian population—is thus a very real, although still largely potential, threat.

Foreign Intelligence Services

Not surprisingly, foreign intelligence services have adapted to using cyber tools as part of their espionage tradecraft. As far back as 1986, before the worldwide surge in Internet use, the KGB employed West German hackers to access U.S. Department of Defense systems in the well-known "Cuckoo's Egg" case. Foreign intelligence services increasingly view computer intrusions as a useful tool for acquiring sensitive U.S. government and private sector information.

Hactivists

Recently there has been a rise in what has been dubbed "hactivism"—politically motivated attacks on publicly accessible Web pages or e-mail servers. These groups and individuals overload e-mail servers and hack into Web sites to send a political message. Although these attacks generally have not altered operating systems or networks, they damage services and deny the public access to Web sites containing valuable information; and they infringe on others' right to communicate.

One such group, the Electronic Disturbance Theater, promotes civil disobedience online in support of its political agenda regarding the Zapatista movement in Mexico and other issues. In the spring of 2000, the group called for worldwide electronic civil disobedience, and it has taken what it terms "protest actions" against White House and Department of Defense servers. Supporters of Kevin Mitnick, recently convicted of numerous computer security offenses, hacked into the Senate Web page and defaced it in May and June 2000.

The Internet has enabled new forms of political gathering and information sharing for those who want to advance social causes; that is good for the promotion of democracy worldwide. But illegal activities that disrupt e-mail servers, deface Web sites, and prevent the public from accessing information on U.S. government and private sector Web sites should be regarded as criminal acts that deny others their human rights to communicate rather than as an acceptable form of protest.

Intruder Knowledge

How have intruders gained the knowledge that allows them to commit such serious break-ins? For the most part, few of the intruder types we've discussed have extensive knowledge of the inner workings of today's computer systems. Many of these intruders do nothing more than use the information and tools built by other intruders in the past. Many Web sites provide them with all the information and tools needed to break in or damage computer systems and networks.

This doesn't mean that the information and tools downloaded by intruders were created for the purpose of aiding such attacks. On the contrary, much of this knowledge is designed to help administrators and security officers recognize potential security holes within their systems and networks—such was the case with Sun Microsystems' snoop utility, described earlier in this chapter. It's through the use of these tools, however, that intruders are able to exploit the weaknesses inherent in many systems.

Case Studies

The following case studies illustrate various ways in which security can be improperly implemented. Each example is based on an actual account of a real corporation, although the names have not been used. In general, these real-word examples demonstrate that security breaches often focus on four areas: data at rest, data in transit, authentication, and improper implementation. It is staggering how often these four elements are involved in security lapses. By examining these cases in depth, we hope to prevent these types of incidents from reoccurring.

Data in Transit

Many Web sites are still providing communications in the clear (i.e., not encrypted). As a result, they make themselves vulnerable to attackers using sniffers, who monitor and intercept clear traffic for their own purposes. Worst yet, officials in many corporate enterprises feel that their data is safe as long as it remains within their firewalls. The problem is that with many employees within the same local area network, it is easy for an employee with sinister intentions to view, destroy, or simply manip-ulate all the data traveling up and down the lines.

For example, one software vendor that recently joined the ranks of the "dot-com" world allowed for the unsecured transfer of data between its internal servers. This meant that account numbers and cardholder infor-mation flowed across their internal network completely visible to any employee. This corporation, like many other corporations, felt that as long as security was provided for information flowing across the Internet, there was no need to enable internal security (behind their corporate firewall).

This particular corporation found out the hard way that there was need for internal security. It turned out an employee had been saving customer credit card numbers as they zoomed across their internal network.

When asked why, the employee simply stated that he could. What if the employee had posted the credit card numbers on the Internet (for the world to see)? If the press had gotten hold of that story, the corporation would have most likely lost many customers. What if the employee had used the credit card numbers to make purchases for himself? The credit card corporations involved might have lost faith in the merchant and can-celled their contracts. Fortunately, the corporation discovered the employee's file of saved credit card numbers before any real harm had been done.

The corporation could have avoided this predicament by enabling SSL (described in Chapter 7) and making use of secure e-mail through a pro-tocol such as S/MIME (described in Chapter 8).

The need for security in such situations is so obvious that we honestly don't know why it is sometimes difficult for others to grasp. No corpora-tion would have unlocked doors. We'd be willing to bet that the CEO keeps his or her possessions under lock and key, as do the company's employees. The reason is obvious: People snoop, steal, or inadvertently look at things they shouldn't.

Data at Rest

A number of corporations that provide goods and services to Internet cus-tomers actually do a great job protecting customer data in transit by mak-ing use of the SSL protocol. However, they fail to realize (or maybe they choose to forget) that data requires further protection once it's at rest. SSL does not protect data after it leaves the security of the protocol. After data is received by either the client or the server, that data is decrypted.

Nevertheless, some companies fail to adequately protect such data. One corporation, an online music vendor, recently had the misfortune of having an unauthorized "guest" break in to its systems. The attack placed more than three million credit card numbers from the company's back-end databases at risk of disclosure on the Internet. Fortunately, in this incident, it has been reported that the credit card numbers were never obtained. Still, the potential for widespread credit card fraud was there.

In news reports, the corporation's upper management stated that they didn't quite understand how the attack occurred. The company had provided for security through the use of SSL to secure connections. However, this corporation could have and should have done more in the way of security. For example, it could have encrypted the credit card numbers before placing them in the database.

Authentication

Authentication is by far one of the easiest of the security services to implement, but many corporations limit their system and network security to user ID/password schemes. Many applications, whether they reside within an enterprise or at consumer sites, incorporate nothing more than a simple password or, worse yet, a four-digit PIN.

It's easy to experience firsthand the best example of the risk incurred by companies that use inadequate authentication safeguards. All you have to do is to sit down at someone's computer who uses a certain travel-services Web site. One of the authors of this book did just that. It was a simple matter to go to the site and select the button Lost/Forgotten Password. Within one minute, the password was e-mailed directly to the user's account (which the author could easily open as well). Within all of five minutes, he could have purchased two round-trip tickets to the Caribbean. Even if an individual had to guess a password or a PIN to access the site as another person, it would take a day at most.

In the digital age, with all the information provided in this book and others like it, no new technology is needed to greatly improve authentication security. The cost of an authentication token is nothing in comparison with the money that would be lost by a fraudulent purchase at such a site.

Another example occurred recently at a medical center, where the system was hacked by an intruder who entered by using a common tool used by network administrators known as VNC (*virtual network computing*). Through the use of VNC, the intruder was able to enter the file system and gain access to various medical records. In all, the hacker accessed more than 4,000 cardiology patient records, 700 physical rehabilitation records, and every admission, discharge, and transfer record of the medical center within a five-month period.

Without regard to internal security and the sensitivity of medical records, all this data was stored in the clear. But let's focus on the more important issue: how the network was accessed in the first place. VNC in its current incarnation has very limited authentication mechanisms (i.e., user ID and password). This means that intruders need only try a number of passwords before they gain access.

In a case concerning medical records, you can easily see the losses add up. What if this sensitive data was released publicly across the Internet? There is the obvious loss of patient confidence, as well as the very real possibility of lawsuits. Furthermore, what if the medical records were modified? While it sounds like something from a movie, this could easily happen.

With that said, proper authentication could have been observed in this case. True user ID/password schemes do provide authentication to a point, but as the sensitivity of the data increases so should the degree of authentication required. At the medical center, authentication would have been best provided for by requiring the use of client-side certificates or a one-time password token.

Implementation

Improper implementation can be seen in many examples of security breaches. The fact is that it isn't easy to implement security services using cryptography. Considerable time and effort must be taken to ensure that the newly implemented system is secure.

One well-known bug, which was recently discovered, belongs to one widely used security application, which provides encryption and digital signatures to its users. In attempting to create a new key-escrow scheme (explained further in Chapter 6) that would be less intrusive to users, the application developers made a simple error.

This simple error allowed for the possible disclosure of all data that had been encrypted using its new functionality. Furthermore, the integrity of any information, which was digitally signed by the software, could be destroyed. In this case, the actual dollar losses may never be calculated, simply because we do not know exactly when this bug was first discovered (we would like to believe that it was announced as soon as it was found). The corporation who originally developed the software must now spend even more money fixing the problem that they created.

The entire incident could have been prevented by following existing security protocols (in this case, sticking with none key-escrow schemes). While we can appreciate the fact that the company went to the trouble of implementing a new less-intrusive concept, we feel developers should first have their work verified by an objective third party. There are a number of security consultants and agencies that test and even certify the security of products.

Information Security: Law Enforcement

Just as legal professionals are beginning to look at the legal ramifications of information security (see Chapter 10), various law enforcement agencies are studying related enforcement issues. Within the past year alone, the FBI has begun increasing the number of field agents in its *National Infrastructure Protection Center* (NIPC). Over the next two years, the number of field offices nationwide is to be increased to 56.

Within the past year, the U.S. Department of Justice has also initiated a new section devoted to investigating computer crime. The *Computer Crime and Intellectual Property Section* (CCIPS) has a staff of attorneys who advise federal prosecutors and law enforcement agents about various issues raised by computer and intellectual property crime. Furthermore, the staff provides ongoing work in the areas of e-commerce security, electronic privacy laws, and hacker investigation.

Various other agencies provide a broad range of security services. One such agency is the *Computer Emergency Response Team / Coordination Center* (CERT/CC). CERT/CC was originally created in 1988 by DARPA (the *Defense Advanced Research Projects Agency*, part of the U.S. Department of Defense) after the Morris Worm incident, which crippled 10 percent of all computers on the Internet. CERT/CC works on a number of initiatives, such as research into security vulnerabilities, improvement of system security, and coordination of teams to respond to large-scale incidents.

Summary

Efforts made to improve the security of computer networks provide benefits beyond the reduction of risks for corporations. They also play an integral role in keeping fear at bay for the benefit of everyone who uses such systems. To really see the B2B and B2C e-commerce markets take off, we are going to have to see improvements in information security.

Various risks and vulnerabilities plague all the players in the new digital world. The number of intruders, ranging from internal employees to teenage hackers who threaten computer systems, continues to grow. These intruders are becoming more knowledgeable and finding better tools that enable them to attack unsuspecting systems. Still, as the case studies from this chapter have shown, corporations and developers alike often refuse to do everything in their power to provide for proper security. Although law enforcement agencies are quickly coming up to speed with today's technology, they are simply "fighting fires" when it comes to dealing with digital attacks at this point. However, by incorporating proper security from the onset, corporations, developers, and users can prevent cybercrime before it happens.

CHAPTER 12

Doing It Right: Following Standards

A growing number of techniques are available to help organizations ensure that they've incorporated adequate security in their products and services as well as provided security for their own enterprises. Every security professional should know certain important concepts. Various standards, guidelines, and regulations have been developed, and various external agencies and organizations can be called on, to help ensure that security is implemented properly. The experiences of successful organizations can be helpful in understanding how security can be properly incorporated into everything from back-end enterprises to end-user products and services.

As you learned in Chapter 11, it seems as if there is no way around it: Sooner or later your network will be broken into. It's an excellent idea to operate under this assumption. To a casual outsider or to those who are new to the field of information security, this practice may seem a bit overboard or even a little paranoid. But security experts think this way so that they can stay ahead of the bad guys. In this chapter, you'll learn the various ways that companies are properly implementing security in the digital age.

Security Services and Mechanisms

A security service is a collection of mechanisms, procedures, and other controls that are implemented to help reduce the risk associated with the threat of data loss or compromise. Some services provide protection from threats, and other services provide for detection of the occurrences of any breach. For example, an identification and authentication service helps reduce the risk posed by access to the system by an unauthorized user. An example of a service that detects a security breach is a logging or monitoring service.

The following security services are discussed in this section:

- **Authentication** is the security service that can be used to ensure that individuals accessing the network are authorized.

- **Confidentiality** is the security service that can be used to ensure that data, software, and messages are not disclosed to unauthorized parties.

- **Integrity** is the security service that can be used to ensure that unauthorized parties do not modify data, software, and messages.

- **Nonrepudiation** is the security service that can be used to ensure that the entities involved in a communication cannot deny having participated in it. Specifically, the sending entity cannot deny having sent a message (nonrepudiation with proof of origin), and the receiving entity cannot deny having received a message (nonrepudiation with proof of delivery).

NOTE:

Though not discussed in this chapter, access control is the security service that helps ensure that network resources are being used in an authorized manner.

Authentication

The first step in securing system resources is to implement a service to verify the identities of users, a process referred to as *authentication*. Authentication provides the foundation that determines the effectiveness of other controls used on the network. For example, a logging mechanism provides usage information based on user ID, and an access-control mechanism permits access to network resources based on the user ID. Both controls are effective only under the assumption that the requester of a network service is the valid user assigned to that specific user ID.

Identification requires that the user be known by the system or network in some manner, usually based on an assigned user ID. However, unless the user is authenticated, the system or network cannot trust the validity of the user's claim of identity. The use is authenticated by supplying something possessed only by the user (such as a token), something only the user knows (such as a password), or something that makes the user unique (such as a fingerprint). The more of these kinds of authentication that the user must supply, the less risk there is that someone can masquerade as the legitimate user.

On most systems and networks, the identification and authentication mechanism is a scheme that combines a user ID with a password. Password systems can be effective if managed properly, but they seldom are managed properly. Authentication that relies solely on passwords often fails to provide adequate protection for systems for a number of reasons. First, users tend to create passwords that are easy to remember and hence easy to guess. On the other hand, passwords generated from random characters are difficult to guess but also difficult for users to remember. As a result, users may write down such passwords, and they are often found in areas that are easy accessible. It's not unusual, for example, to find passwords written on sticky notes mounted on computer monitors, where anyone can find them and use them to gain access to the network. The guessing of passwords is a science, and a great deal of research has been published that details the ease with which passwords can be guessed.

Proper password selection—striking a balance between the password being easy to remember for the user but difficult to guess for everyone else—has always been an issue. Password generators have been developed that produce passwords consisting of pronounceable syllables. Such passwords have greater potential of being remembered than those made of purely random characters. Some systems and network administrators require the use of an algorithm that produces random pronounceable passwords. Programs called *password checkers* enable a user to determine whether a new password is considered easy to guess and thus unacceptable.

Because of the vulnerabilities that still exist with the use of password-only mechanisms, more robust mechanisms can be used, such as token-based authentication or biometrics. A smart card–based or token-based mechanism requires that a user be in possession of the token and additionally may require the user to know a PIN or password. These devices then perform a challenge/response authentication scheme using real-time parameters. The latter practice helps prevent an intruder from gaining unauthorized access through a login session playback. These devices may also encrypt the authentication session, preventing compromise of the authentication information through monitoring and capturing.

Locking mechanisms can be used for network devices, workstations, or PCs, requiring user authentication to unlock. These tools can be useful when users must leave their work areas frequently. These locks allow users to remain logged in to the network and leave their work areas (for an acceptably short period of time) without exposing an entry point into the network.

Confidentiality

Because access control through the use of proper authentication is not always possible (because of shared drives and open networks), data confidentiality services can be used when it's necessary to protect the secrecy of information. The use of encryption through symmetric or asymmetric ciphers (or both) can reduce the risk of unauthorized disclosure, both in the case of data at rest and data in transit, by making it unreadable to those who may capture it. Only the authorized user who has the correct key can decrypt the data.

Integrity

Data integrity services provide protection against intentional and accidental unauthorized modification of data. This service can be used for data while it is at rest on a back-end database or while it is in transit across a network. This service can be provided by the use of cryptographic checksums and highly granular access-control and privilege mechanisms. The more granular the access-control or privilege mechanism, the less likely it is that an unauthorized or accidental modification can occur.

Furthermore, data integrity services help to ensure that a message is not altered, deleted, or added to in any manner during transmission across a network. Most available security techniques cannot prevent the modification of a message, but they can detect that a message has been modified (unless the message is deleted altogether).

Nonrepudiation

Nonrepudiation helps to ensure that the entities in a communication cannot deny having participated in all or part of the communication. When a major function of the network is electronic mail, this service becomes crucial. Nonrepudiation services can be provided through the use of public-key cryptographic techniques using digital signatures.

Standards, Guidelines, and Regulations

Throughout this book, we've described a number of standards, guidelines, and regulations. For example, Chapter 6 explains how the X.509 standard can be used to provide for secure public-key operations, and Chapter 7 describes the SSL and IPSec protocols, which are used to provide various security services. The following sections outline the various organizations that have made the effort to ensure that each standard, guideline, and regulation provides for a proper security implementation.

The Internet Engineering Task Force

The *Internet Engineering Task Force* (IETF) is an international community of network designers, operators, vendors, and researchers. This group is concerned with the smooth operation of the Internet and the evolution of the Internet architecture.

The technical work of the IETF is done in its *working groups,* which are organized by topic into several areas (routing, transport, security, and so on). The working groups are managed by area directors (ADs), who are members of the *Internet Engineering Steering Group* (IESG). Providing architectural oversight is the *Internet Architecture Board* (IAB). The IAB also adjudicates appeals when someone complains about the policies adopted by the IESG. The IAB and IESG are chartered by the *Internet Society* (ISOC) for these purposes. The general area director also serves as the chair of the IESG and of the IETF and is an ex officio member of the IAB.

ANSI X9

X9 is a division of the *American National Standards Institute* (ANSI) that develops and publishes voluntary, consensus technical standards for the financial services industry. X9's voting membership includes more than 300 organizations representing investment managers, banks, software and equipment manufacturers, printers, credit unions, depositories, government regulators, associations, consultants, and others.

X9 develops standards for check processing, electronic check exchange, PIN management and security, the use of data encryption, and wholesale funds transfer, among others. Standards under development include electronic payments via the Internet, financial image interchange, home banking security requirements, institutional trade messages, and electronic benefits transfer.

X9's procedures ensure that interested parties have an opportunity to participate and comment on a developing standard before it is implemented. X9 standards are also reviewed by ANSI before publication to ensure that all requirements are met. ANSI conducts an audit of X9 operations every five years.

X9 is organized into seven subcommittees. At any given time the committee has 20 to 30 active working groups and more than 80 domestic and international standards projects. Organizations that vote on more than one subcommittee constitute a parent committee that sets policy and procedures.

National Institute of Standards and Technology

The *National Institute of Standards and Technology* (NIST) has published many guidelines and standards on the topic of information security. One of its key contributions to cryptography is the federal information-processing standard (FIPS 140-1), which describes a standard for secure cryptographic modules. FIPS 140-1 is discussed more fully in the following section.

NIST also administers a certification process for software and hardware cryptographic modules.

FIPS 140-1

FIPS 140-1 specifies the security requirements that are to be satisfied by a cryptographic module that is used in a security system protecting unclassified information in computer and telecommunication systems. Cryptographic modules conforming to this standard must meet the applicable security requirements described in the standard.

The FIPS 140-1 standard was developed by a working group composed of users and vendors and including government and industry participants. To provide for a wide spectrum of data sensitivity (such as low-value administrative data, large funds transfers, and data related to human life and safety) and a diversity of application environments (such as a guarded facility, an office, and a completely unprotected location), the working group identified requirements for four security levels for cryptographic modules. Each security level offers an increase in security over the preceding level. These four increasing levels of security are designed to support cost-effective solutions that are appropriate for different degrees of data sensitivity and different application environments.

Although the security requirements specified in this standard are intended to maintain the security of a cryptographic module, conformance to this standard does not guarantee that a particular module is secure. It is the responsibility of the manufacturer of a cryptographic module to build the module in a secure manner.

Similarly, the use of a cryptographic module that conforms to this standard in an overall system does not guarantee the security of the overall system. The security level of a cryptographic module should be chosen to provide a level of security that's appropriate to the security requirements of the application, the environment in which the module is to be used, and the security services that the module is to provide. The responsible authority in each agency or department must ensure that the agency or department's relevant computer or telecommunication systems provide an acceptable level of security for the given application and environment.

NIST emphasizes the importance of computer security awareness and of making information security a management priority that is communicated to all employees. Because computer security requirements vary among applications, organizations should identify their information resources and determine the sensitivity to and potential impact of losses. Controls should be based on the potential risks. Available controls include administrative policies and procedures, physical and environmental controls, information and data controls, software development and acquisition controls, and backup and contingency planning.

NIST has developed many of the needed basic controls to protect computer information and has issued standards and guidelines covering both management and technical approaches to computer security. These include standards for cryptographic functions that are implemented in cryptographic modules as specified in the FIPS 140-1 standard. This standard is expected to be the foundation for NIST's current and future cryptographic standards.

Common Criteria

A standard known as *Common Criteria* (CC) was developed as the result of a series of international efforts to develop criteria for evaluation of information security. It began in the early 1980s, when the *Trusted Computer System Evaluation Criteria* (TCSEC) was developed in the United States. Ten years later, a European standard, the *Information Technology Security Evaluation Criteria* (ITSEC), was built on the concepts of the TCSEC. Then in 1990, the *International Organization for Standardization* (ISO) sought to develop a set of international evaluation criteria for general use. The CC project was started in 1993 in order to bring these (and other) efforts together into a single international standard for information security evaluation.

The CC aims to build consumer confidence by testing and certifying products and services. Typically, certifiers are commercial organizations operating testing laboratories accredited by ISO. Accreditors are sometimes closely involved in the determination of functional and assurance requirements for a system.

The Health Insurance Portability Act

Various regulations have been enacted at the local, state, and federal levels, each of them specifying unique requirements for the various market sectors. The *Health Insurance Portability Act* (HIPAA) is one such regulation. Handed down by the federal government and signed into law in 1996, HIPAA addresses both health insurance reform and administrative simplification. The latter section aims to standardize access to patient records and the transmission of electronic health information between organizations. Important among these administrative issues is the proposed standard for security and electronic signatures, which mandates requirements for the following:

- **Confidentiality** This requirement is designed to keep all transfers of information private. Steps must be taken to ensure that information is not made available or disclosed to unauthorized individuals.
- **Integrity** This requirement ensures that data has not been changed or altered en route or in storage.
- **Authentication** This mandate means that organizations must make sure that the person sending the message is the person he or she claims to be.
- **Nonrepudiation** This principle ensures that after a transaction occurs, neither the originator nor the recipient can deny that it took place.
- **Authorization** This requirement limits access to network information and resources to users who have been authenticated based on defined privileges.

When it comes to people's most personal information—their medical history—people have always been concerned about confidentiality. As individuals, we are secretive about every aspect of our health, from weight to illness to prescriptions to payments. When it comes to medical information, it is essential that healthcare providers implement PKI security infrastructures so that they can use digital certificates to securely store, transmit, and access health records electronically. The thought of personal information on a public network can be intimidating, and patients need to be assured that their private medical histories continue to maintain unparalleled confidentiality.

Developer Assistance

Many software developers, whether they're implementing security for a retail product or for the newest e-commerce site or they're building applications for an enterprise, have chosen to outsource the security task. A good number of security consultants, architects, and managed security services are available for hire. These individuals and companies provide a wide range of assistance in implementing security, allowing developers to spend more time working on the unique aspects of their products (where their talents are best used).

RSA Security, Inc., is one professional services organization that can assist developers in the design and implementation of security. In addition, many organizations, including RSA, can also provide certification when the system is completed.

Insurance

Many financial institutions and insurance companies have now begun insuring e-commerce Web sites. Many of these new insurers look for certification and require security audits. One way to implement insurance requirements is through the use of secure cryptographic modules (such as BSAFE, a software product family line available from RSA Security, Inc.).

American International Group, Inc. (AIG), one such insurance provider, has e-business divisions that offer insurance to companies with e-business initiatives. RSA Security, Inc., and AIG partnered in January 2000 to provide e-security to corporations. The partnership means that customers can take advantage of discounts offered by AIG for the use of RSA products.

Security Research

Sun Tzu stated it perfectly in *The Art of War*: "Know your enemy as you know yourself, and in a thousand battles you shall never perish." For organizations that are designing and implementing security systems, the most successful approach is to learn what intruders know so that you can come up with a way to stop them. The following list of Web sites is an excellent place to start to learn what the enemy knows.

http://www.cert.org/	CERT/CC is a center of Internet security expertise.
http://www.securityfocus.com/	Security Focus provides up-to-date information on current bugs. It also keeps an excellent collection of hacker-related articles.

| http://www.slashdot.org/ | This site provides information about current break-ins and describes the various known system vulnerabilities. |
| http://www.2600.org/ | This site dubs itself the "Hacker Quarterly," providing its readers with current information on system hacks and cracks. |

NOTE:

This list is by no means complete; it is merely a starting place where you can gain knowledge about security issues.

Case Studies

In contrast to the case studies presented in Chapter 11, the following case studies illustrate the ways in which corporations and developers took steps to properly implement security, focusing specifically on their techniques within the four commonly ignored areas described in Chapter 11: data at rest, data in transit, authentication, and implementation. Each case study shows how time and money can be saved by properly implementing security *before* an incident arises.

Implementation

One major hardware manufacturer recently looked into implementing a public-key infrastructure. After close analysis, company officials realized that not all the applications that the company needed secured were "PKI-ready;" that is, some of the applications did not support the use of public-key certificates. After working with various security architects and consultants, company officials learned that for this set of applications they need to provide a front-end server application that handled certificates. The employees already had one of the easiest-to-use PKI clients: a Web browser.

In this case, there is still a chance that sensitive data might be exposed at points where the new server application communicates with the legacy applications. However, the level of security at this company is now significantly higher than it was before the PKI was established.

Even if their systems and networks are never breached, this company has saved a significant amount of both time and money. Each of their legacy applications required a password to access, which meant they needed a fully staffed help desk to assist users with logging in and resetting forgotten passwords. Another cost advantage came through the use of digital signatures on electronic ordering forms, which are now legally binding (see Chapter 10).

Authentication

A California city government recently discovered that a typical city employee had to establish and memorize six to nine passwords to access various applications. With this number of passwords, city officials realized that time and money were being wasted on administering the effort to deal with lost and forgotten passwords. For those users who weren't having such problems, it was probably because they had written down the passwords next to their computer terminals, creating a serious security hazard.

The city quickly realized that they needed to reduce the average number of passwords required, while at the same time increasing security. After seeking assistance from various security groups and reviewing a variety of products, city officials decided on using biometrics. Through the use of biometric technologies, this city provided fingerprint scanners at each of its computer terminals, thereby eliminating the need for multiple passwords. As a result, trouble calls are down substantially, amounting in considerable savings. At the same time, concerns that sensitive data might be disclosed have decreased significantly.

Another example of a company making authentication more secure occurred in the banking industry. Think of how often you walk up to your ATM machine, insert your card, enter your PIN, and perform a transaction. And consider how many other PINs you may have, for example, for your brokerage account or for accounts with other banks. The more PINs you have the easier they are to forget, and having just one PIN for all your accounts puts you at risk. One major bank realized that they were spending a considerable amount of time and money on customers who were forgetting their PIN number. Still more time and money were lost because of fraud (it is not uncommon for bank users to write their PIN code down in their wallet, or worse yet, give the code to a friend who performs a transaction for them.)

Realizing the need for an authentication alternative, the bank searched out security professionals and reviewed various software and hardware packages. After a thorough look at the costs and return on investment, the bank has decided implement a biometric system. Currently they are testing both finger and iris scanners.

The actual dollar amount saved in decreased fraud was not disclosed; however, you can only imagine how much the bank lost each year. Furthermore, the costs of keeping a customer help desk to reset PINs as needed has decreased significantly.

Data at Rest

Prior to last year, one federal law enforcement agency, which works closely with the relocation of witnesses, had not provided any true security for their field agent's laptops. Imagine for a moment what exactly might happen if one of these laptops were lost or stolen?

After realizing the possibility of confidential data possibly being exposed if one of these laptops were compromised, the agency added security software that encrypts and decrypts files as needed. Furthermore, the software requires strong, two-factor authentication through the use of a one-time password token.

By simply taking the time to add strong security to each of these laptops, this agency has more than likely saved not only time and money, but possibly even lives.

Another example, although not as dramatic as the first one, involves a major U.S. airline using encryption to provide confidentiality services to its back-end databases. What is unique about this case is that the encryption is applied not only to user information required for reservations, but also to all information pertaining to users' frequent flyer mileage accounts.

After the company began to recognize just how much these miles were worth once they started adding up, they decided it was time to provide security. Through the use of a symmetric-key algorithm, their customers' information as well as the miles they had earned were safely secured.

You might think that customer information or frequent flyer miles are not the most sensitive data in the world. However, this company realized that if their customer accounts, especially corporate accounts, were ever disclosed publicly on the Internet it could mean financial disaster—not to mention the cost of paperwork if a customer's reservation was changed or removed from the database.

Data in Transit

One Canadian-based software corporation was providing a product to pharmacists and doctors that allowed for quicker prescription fulfillment. Their product simply transmitted the necessary patient data and prescription from the physician to the pharmacy. However, until recently, the data was not encrypted during transmission. The company felt that because the data was traveling across a dial-up phone line it was unnecessary to provide security.

The software corporation quickly realized that even with a dial-up phone connection, security was a necessity. However, the company was afraid that if they were to add security, that doctors and pharmacists might have difficulty using it (after all, doctors know medicine, not security). After speaking with outside security professionals, the corporation decided on the integration of the SSL protocol (discussed in Chapter 7) to provide security. The SSL protocol is virtually transparent to the end-users eliminating the difficulty factor.

The software company now knows they are selling a product that not only can protect the data as it is communicated, but also, through the use of SSL, can guarantee the data was not changed in transit. Furthermore, their market has now expanded to cover not only physicians and pharmacies using dial-up lines, but also those that use open networks (such as the Internet).

Summary

At first glance, it may appear that protecting the security of data in a network is a losing battle, but many developers, enterprises, and users have been successful in achieving this goal. This chapter tells only a few of many success stories in this arena.

As these case studies illustrate, security is a battle that you should not face alone. Instead, you should take advantage of the expertise of other professionals. Here you've seen a number of ways in which security can be ensured through the use of existing standards, protocols, algorithms, and assistance from consultants who have been shown to be of great help. Through the certification process, many users can ensure that their security methods (especially cryptography) are as well designed and well implemented as possible. It is sometimes useful to consult with a trusted third party or external agency to gain a different point of view.

Security is an important issue for businesses and other organizations that are entrusted with personal data. In the long run, everyone benefits when consumers can have faith in the technology that enables not only the efficient storage of data, but also the potential for unprecedented communication and human growth.

APPENDIX A

Bits, Bytes, Hex, and ASCII

Throughout this book, we show data as hexadecimal (often shortened to "hex") numbers. Even if the data is a series of letters, it can be represented in hexadecimal numbers. This appendix describes bits, bytes, and hexadecimal numbers and explains how ASCII characters are formed.

Using Decimal, Binary, and Hexadecimal Numbers

A computer is a *binary* machine; everything is either "on" or "off," reflecting the fact that electric power is either flowing or not flowing through a given circuit. The machine can be programmed to interpret the state of being on or off as a 0 or a 1. If you string these 0s and 1s together, you can represent anything. For example, you can represent the decimal number 105 as the binary number 1101001.

To see how binary numbers work, it might be helpful to recall how decimal numbers work. A decimal number is composed of some number of "ones," "tens," "hundreds," and so on. As Figure A-1 shows, if you start

Figure A-1

The number 8,614 is decimal, comprising four "ones," one "ten," six "hundreds," and eight "thousands." The number 10000110100110 is the binary equivalent. The numerals in the positions indicate the number of powers of 1, 2, 4, 8, and so on

counting at zero and move from right to left, each place in a decimal number represents a number of 10^ns (10 to the nth power). A computer does the same thing except that it uses "two" as its base instead of "ten." For each place in a binary number, there can be only two possible values: a 0 or a 1. In Figure A-1, the binary number is computed if you start counting at zero and move from right to left to see how many "ones," how many "twos," how many "fours," and so on, each of which represents a power of 2.

Any value that can be represented as a decimal number can also be represented as a binary number. The binary number will take up more space, but any value can be expressed. Suppose you wanted to use the decimal number 2,535,294,694. A computer would "think" of it as binary, which would look like this:

```
1001 0111 0001 1101 1000 0110 1110 0110
```

Writing such numbers can be tedious, so programmers use hexadecimal as a convenience. The word "decimal" has to do with "ten" ("dec" means "ten," as in "decade" or "decathlon"), whereas "binary" refers to "two" ("bi" means "two," as in "bicycle" or "bifocals"), and the word "hexadecimal" refers to "sixteen." So binary numbers are "base two," decimal numbers are "base ten," and hexadecimal numbers are "base sixteen." The digits used in binary numbers are

0 1

The digits used in decimal numbers are

0 1 2 3 4 5 6 7 8 9

And the digits used in hexadecimal numbers are

0 1 2 3 4 5 6 7 8 9 A B C D E F

Notice that each system has the same number of digits as what we've referred to as the "base." Base two uses two digits, base ten uses ten digits, and base sixteen uses sixteen digits. Table A-1 is a conversion table for numbers in the three bases.

	Base Two	Base Ten	Base Sixteen
Table A-1	0	0	0
	1	1	1
Binary, Decimal,	10	2	2
and Hexadecimal	11	3	3
Equivalents	100	4	4
	101	5	5
	110	6	6
	111	7	7
	1000	8	8
	1001	9	9
	1010	10	A
	1011	11	B
	1100	12	C
	1101	13	D
	1110	14	E
	1111	15	F

Hexadecimal is convenient because any group of four binary digits (a binary digit is also known as a bit) can be represented in one hexadecimal digit. This means that you can take a big binary number, break it into groups of four digits, and rewrite it in hexadecimal. For example,

```
1001 0111 0001 1101 1000 0110 1110 0110
```

can be rewritten in hex as

```
0x97 1D 86 E6
```

The 1001 has been converted to 9 (see Table A-1), the 0111 has become 7, and so on. The 0x at the front is a notational convention indicating that the number is in hexadecimal.

It's possible to think of that number as "six 1s," "fourteen 16s," "six 256s," and so on. You start counting at zero and move from right to left, and each place represents the number of 16^ns.

Using Bits and Bytes

If you put eight bits together, you have one byte. The word "byte" is simply the technical jargon for a group of eight bits. For example, 1001 0111 is a byte. It can also be represented as 0x97, so two hex digits make up one byte. The number 0x97 1D 86 E6 is 32 bits, or four bytes. A byte is also a measure of space. If your computer has 1MB of memory, that means it has space enough to load one million bytes of data into memory. A byte can have 256 possible values, from 0 to 255 (0x00 to 0xFF).

NOTE:

Actually, a megabyte is 1,048,576 bytes, which is 2^{20}. Most quantities of things in the computer industry come in powers of 2, either for technical reasons or simply because. Computers are binary machines, so hardware constraints may dictate that you use a power of 2, and in software, working with numbers that are powers of 2 can often be more convenient than using other numbers. But sometimes the only reason to use a power of 2 is that a task is being computerized. For example, in cryptography, 104-bit symmetric keys are secure enough, but that number is not a power of 2. So people use 128-bit keys. There's no technical cryptographic reason to use 128 bits instead of 104, but 128 is a power of 2. People working in computer science sometimes choose numbers simply because they are powers of 2.

Using ASCII Characters

A computer chip can interpret only 1s and 0s and therefore does not have a native way to represent letters of the alphabet. So in the 1960s, at the beginning of the computer age, the American Standards Association, calling on the contributions of computer manufacturers, programmers, and others, came up with a standard way to represent letters as numbers. Because *A* is the first letter of the English alphabet, it could have been assigned the number 0x01; *B* could have been 0x02, and so on. It could have been, but that's not what the committee chose. The people involved were interested in representing more than just letters of the alphabet. They knew that computers would also need to interpret numerals, math symbols, and punctuation marks. In addition, they would need uppercase as well as lowercase letters.

Eventually, a standard was developed specifying that the bytes 0x20 through 0x7F would be used to represent the English alphabet, numerals, certain symbols, and certain punctuation marks. That's 96 standard characters. Table A-2 shows the values and their characters. The standard is called ASCII (pronounced ASK-ee), an acronym for *American Standard Code for Information Interchange*.

As it turned out, the original 96 ASCII characters were not sufficient because some languages had special marks on their letters (called *diacritical* marks), such as the umlaut (two dots) in *ü* or the cedilla (the squiggle on the bottom) in *ç*. Other languages had larger alphabets. In addition, values for more punctuation marks and control characters were needed. Over the years, standards committees have generated additional character sets. A byte can have only 256 possible values, and that is not enough space to hold all the possible characters. As a result, some of the new standards define characters in two bytes, allowing definition of as many as 65,536 characters. Other standards specify four bytes per character, giving space for more than four million characters. Most character sets include the original ASCII values along with the added values.

All this means that if a computer is operating on the expression 0x52 53 41 53, it could be the hex representation of the decimal number 1,381,187,923, or it could be the letters *RSAS*.

Table A-2

The Core 96-Member ASCII Character Set

20	21	22	23	24	25	26	27	28	29	2A	2B	2C	2D	2E	2F
	!	"	#	$	%	&	'	(	)	*	+	,	-	.	/

30	31	32	33	34	35	36	37	38	39	3A	3B	3C	3D	3E	3F
0	1	2	3	4	5	6	7	8	9	:	;	<	=	>	?

40	41	42	43	44	45	46	47	48	49	4A	4B	4C	4D	4E	4F
@	A	B	C	D	E	F	G	H	I	J	K	L	M	N	O

50	51	52	53	54	55	56	57	58	59	5A	5B	5C	5D	5E	5F
P	Q	R	S	T	U	V	W	X	Y	Z	[	\	]	^	_

60	61	62	63	64	65	66	67	68	69	6A	6B	6C	6D	6E	6F
`	a	b	c	d	e	f	g	h	i	j	k	l	m	n	o

70	71	72	73	74	75	76	77	78	79	7A	7B	7C	7D	7E	7F
p	q	r	s	t	u	v	w	x	y	z	{			}	~	DEL

The character 0x20 is space, as in the space between two words. The character 0x7F is the DELETE key.

Using Computers in Cryptography

Keep in mind that to a computer, numbers can represent many kinds of meanings. For example, if a computer is looking at 0x42 A0 10 07, it might be looking at the decimal number 1,117,786,119, or those bits might mean something else. It could be an instruction, for example. A computer program is a series of instructions, and because a computer stores everything as binary numbers, instructions, too, can look like numbers. Moreover, each chip has its own instruction set, so a number on one computer may mean one instruction but on another computer may mean something else. For example, on one machine the bits 0x42 A0 10 07 might be the computer's way of saying, "Add the contents of register 16 to the contents of register 7 and store the result in register 7." Other values could represent memory addresses, other control characters, or some sort of data in another format.

In cryptography, though, these kinds of values are simply bytes and numbers. So when we talk about plaintext, we really mean bytes of data, no matter what meaning the owner of the data attributes to the bytes. A crypto algorithm looks at the data as bits to manipulate or numbers to crunch. Cryptography makes no distinction between bytes that represent letters of the alphabet and bytes that indicate instructions in a program. They are simply bytes.

APPENDIX B

A Layman's Guide to a Subset of ASN.1, BER, and DER

An RSA Laboratories Technical Note
Burton S. Kaliski Jr.
Revised November 1, 1993

NOTE:

*This document supersedes June 3, 1991 version, which was also published as NIST / OSI Implementors' Workshop document SEC-SIG-91-17. PKCS documents are available by electronic mail to <**pkcs@rsa.com**>.*

Abstract

This note gives a layman's introduction to a subset of OSI's Abstract Syntax Notation 1 (ASN.1), Basic Encoding Rules (BER), and Distinguished Encoding Rules (DER). The particular purpose of this note is to provide background material sufficient for understanding and implementing the PKCS family of standards.

Copyright © 1991–1993 RSA Laboratories, a division of RSA Data Security, Inc. License to copy this document is granted provided that it is identified as "RSA Data Security, Inc. Public-Key Cryptography Standards (PKCS)" in all material mentioning or referencing this document. 003-903015-110-000-000

Section 1: Introduction

It is a generally accepted design principle that abstraction is a key to managing software development. With abstraction, a designer can specify a part of a system without concern for how the part is actually implemented or represented. Such a practice leaves the implementation open; it simplifies the specification; and it makes it possible to state "axioms" about the part that can be proved when the part is implemented, and assumed when the part is employed in another, higher-level part. Abstraction is the hallmark of most modern software specifications.

One of the most complex systems today, and one that also involves a great deal of abstraction, is Open Systems Interconnection (OSI, described in X.200). OSI is an internationally standardized architecture that governs the interconnection of computers from the physical layer up to the user application layer. Objects at higher layers are defined abstractly and intended to be implemented with objects at lower layers. For instance, a service at one layer may require transfer of certain abstract objects between computers; a lower layer may provide transfer services for strings of 1's and 0's, using encoding rules to transform the abstract objects into such strings. OSI is called an open system because it supports many different implementations of the services at each layer.

OSI's method of specifying abstract objects is called ASN.1 (Abstract Syntax Notation 1, defined in X.208), and one set of rules for representing such objects as strings of 1's and 0's is called the BER (Basic Encoding Rules, defined in X.209). ASN.1 is a flexible notation that allows one to define a variety data types, from simple types such as integers and bit strings to structured types such as sets and sequences, as well as complex types defined in terms of others. BER describes how to represent or encode values of each ASN.1 type as a string of eight-bit octets. There is generally more than one way to BER-encode a given value. Another set of rules, called the Distinguished Encoding Rules (DER), which is a subset of BER, gives a unique encoding to each ASN.1 value.

The purpose of this note is to describe a subset of ASN.1, BER, and DER sufficient to understand and implement one OSI-based application, RSA Data Security, Inc.'s Public-Key Cryptography Standards. The features described include an overview of ASN.1, BER, and DER and an abridged list of ASN.1 types and their BER and DER encodings. Sections 2-4 give an overview of ASN.1, BER, and DER, in that order. Section 5 lists some ASN.1 types, giving their notation, specific encoding rules, examples, and comments about their application to PKCS. Section 6 concludes with an example, X.500 distinguished names.

Advanced features of ASN.1, such as macros, are not described in this note, as they are not needed to implement PKCS. For information on the other features, and for more detail generally, the reader is referred to CCITT Recommendations X.208 and X.209, which define ASN.1 and BER.

Section 1.1: Terminology and Notation

In this note, an octet is an eight-bit unsigned integer. Bit 8 of the octet is the most significant, and bit 1 is the least significant.

The following meta-syntax is used in describing ASN.1 notation:

BIT	Monospace denotes literal characters in the type and value notation; in examples, it generally denotes an octet value in hexadecimal
n_1	Bold italics denotes a variable
[]	Bold square brackets indicate that a term is optional
{}	Bold braces group related terms
|	Bold vertical bar delimits alternatives within a group
...	Bold ellipsis indicates repeated occurrences
=	Bold equals sign expresses terms as subterms

Section 2: Abstract Syntax Notation 1

Abstract Syntax Notation 1, abbreviated ASN.1, is a notation for describing abstract types and values.

In ASN.1, a type is a set of values. For some types, there are a finite number of values, and for other types there are an infinite number. A value of a given ASN.1 type is an element of the type's set. ASN.1 has four kinds of types: simple types, which are "atomic" and have no components; structured types, which have components; tagged types, which are derived from other types; and other types, which include the CHOICE type and the ANY type. Types and values can be given names with the ASN.1 assignment operator (::=), and those names can be used in defining other types and values.

Every ASN.1 type other than CHOICE and ANY has a tag, which consists of a class and a nonnegative tag number. ASN.1 types are abstractly the same if and only if their tag numbers are the same. In other words, the name of an ASN.1 type does not affect its abstract meaning; only the tag does. There are four classes of tags:

1. *Universal,* for types whose meaning is the same in all applications; these types are only defined in X.208.

2. *Application,* for types whose meaning is specific to an application, such as X.500 directory services; types in two different applications may have the same application-specific tag and different meanings.

3. *Private,* for types whose meaning is specific to a given enterprise.

4. *Context-specific*, for types whose meaning is specific to a given structured type; context-specific tags are used to distinguish between component types with the same underlying tag within the context of a given structured type, and component types in two different structured types may have the same tag and different meanings.

The types with universal tags are defined in X.208, which also gives the types' universal tag numbers. Types with other tags are defined in many places, and are always obtained by implicit or explicit tagging (see Section 2.3). Table B-1 lists some ASN.1 types and their universal-class tags.

ASN.1 types and values are expressed in a flexible, programming-language-like notation, with the following special rules:

- Layout is not significant; multiple spaces and line breaks can be considered as a single space.

- Comments are delimited by pairs of hyphens (--), or a pair of hyphens and a line break.

- Identifiers (names of values and fields) and type references (names of types) consist of upper- and lowercase letters, digits, hyphens, and spaces; identifiers begin with lowercase letters; type references begin with uppercase letters.

The following four subsections give an overview of simple types, structured types, implicitly and explicitly tagged types, and other types. Section 5 describes specific types in more detail.

Table B-1

Some Types and
Their Universal-
Class Tags

Type	Tag Number (Decimal)	Tag Number (Hexadecimal)
INTEGER	2	02
BIT STRING	3	03
OCTET STRING	4	04
NULL	5	05
OBJECT IDENTIFIER	6	06
SEQUENCE and SEQUENCE OF	16	10
SET and SET OF	17	11
PrintableString	19	13
T61String	20	14
IA5String	22	16
UTCTime	23	17

Section 2.1: Simple Types

Simple types are those not consisting of components; they are the "atomic" types. ASN.1 defines several; the types that are relevant to the PKCS standards are the following:

- BIT STRING, an arbitrary string of bits (1's and 0's)
- IA5String, an arbitrary string of IA5 (ASCII) characters
- INTEGER, an arbitrary integer
- NULL, a null value
- OBJECT IDENTIFIER, an object identifier, which is a sequence of integer components that identify an object such as an algorithm or attribute type
- OCTET STRING, an arbitrary string of octets (eight-bit values)
- PrintableString, an arbitrary string of printable characters

- T61String, an arbitrary string of T.61 (eight-bit) characters
- UTCTime, a "coordinated universal time" or Greenwich Mean Time (GMT) value

Simple types fall into two categories: string types and nonstring types. BIT STRING, IA5String, OCTET STRING, PrintableString, T61String, and UTCTime are string types.

String types can be viewed, for the purposes of encoding, as consisting of components, where the components are substrings. This view allows one to encode a value whose length is not known in advance (e.g., an octet string value input from a file stream) with a constructed, indefinite-length encoding (see Section 3).

The string types can be given size constraints limiting the length of values.

Section 2.2: Structured Types

Structured types are those consisting of components. ASN.1 defines four, all of which are relevant to the PKCS standards:

1. SEQUENCE, an ordered collection of one or more types
2. SEQUENCE OF, an ordered collection of zero or more occurrences of a given type
3. SET, an unordered collection of one or more types
4. SET OF, an unordered collection of zero or more occurrences of a given type

The structured types can have optional components, possibly with default values.

Section 2.3: Implicitly and Explicitly Tagged Types

Tagging is useful to distinguish types within an application; it is also commonly used to distinguish component types within a structured type. For instance, optional components of a SET or SEQUENCE type are typically given distinct context-specific tags to avoid ambiguity.

There are two ways to tag a type: implicitly and explicitly.

- Implicitly tagged types are derived from other types by changing the tag of the underlying type. Implicit tagging is denoted by the ASN.1 keywords [*class number*] IMPLICIT (see Section 5.1).

- Explicitly tagged types are derived from other types by adding an outer tag to the underlying type. In effect, explicitly tagged types are structured types consisting of one component, the underlying type. Explicit tagging is denoted by the ASN.1 keywords [*class number*] EXPLICIT (see Section 5.2).

The keyword [*class number*] alone is the same as explicit tagging, except when the "module" in which the ASN.1 type is defined has implicit tagging by default. ("Modules" are among the advanced features not described in this note.)

For purposes of encoding, an implicitly tagged type is considered the same as the underlying type, except that the tag is different. An explicitly tagged type is considered like a structured type with one component, the underlying type. Implicit tags result in shorter encodings, but explicit tags may be necessary to avoid ambiguity if the tag of the underlying type is indeterminate (e.g., the underlying type is CHOICE or ANY).

Section 2.4: Other Types

Other types in ASN.1 include the CHOICE and ANY types. The CHOICE type denotes a union of one or more alternatives; the ANY type denotes an arbitrary value of an arbitrary type, where the arbitrary type is possibly defined in the registration of an object identifier or integer value.

Section 3: Basic Encoding Rules

The Basic Encoding Rules (BER) for ASN.1 give one or more ways to represent any ASN.1 value as an octet string. (There are certainly other ways to represent ASN.1 values, but BER is the standard for interchanging such values in OSI.)

There are three methods to encode an ASN.1 value under BER, the choice of which depends on the type of value and whether the length of the value is known. The three methods are primitive, definite-length encoding; constructed, definite-length encoding; and constructed, indefinite-length encoding. Simple nonstring types employ the primitive, definite-length method; structured types employ either of the constructed methods; and simple string types employ any of the methods, depending on whether the length of the value is known. Types derived by implicit tagging employ the method of the underlying type, and types derived by explicit tagging employ the constructed methods.

In each method, the BER encoding has three or four parts:

1. **Identifier octets**   These identify the class and tag number of the ASN.1 value, and indicate whether the method is primitive or constructed.

2. **Length octets**   For the definite-length methods, these give the number of contents octets. For the constructed, indefinite-length method, these indicate that the length is indefinite.

3. **Contents octets**   For the primitive, definite-length method, these give a concrete representation of the value. For the constructed methods, these give the concatenation of the BER encodings of the components of the value.

4. **End-of-contents octets**   For the constructed, indefinite-length method, these denote the end of the contents. For the other methods, these are absent.

The three methods of encoding are described in the following sections.

Section: 3.1: Primitive, Definite-Length Method

This method applies to simple types and types derived from simple types by implicit tagging. It requires that the length of the value be known in advance. The parts of the BER encoding are as follows:

Identifier Octets

There are two forms: low tag number (for tag numbers between 0 and 30) and high tag number (for tag numbers 31 and greater).

Low-Tag-Number Form   One octet. Bits 8 and 7 specify the class (see Table B-2), bit 6 has value "0," indicating that the encoding is primitive, and bits 5–1 give the tag number.

Table B-2	Class	Bit 8	Bit 7
Class Encoding in Identifier Octets	universal	0	0
	application	0	1
	context-specific	1	0
	private	1	1

High-Tag-Number Form Two or more octets. First octet is as in low-tag-number form, except that bits 5–1 all have value "1." Second and following octets give the tag number, base 128, most significant digit first, with as few digits as possible, and with the bit 8 of each octet except the last set to "1."

Length Octets

There are two forms: short (for lengths between 0 and 127), and long definite (for lengths between 0 and $2^{1008} - 1$).

Short Form One octet. Bit 8 has value "0" and bits 7–1 give the length.

Long Form Two to 127 octets. Bit 8 of first octet has value "1" and bits 7–1 give the number of additional length octets. Second and following octets give the length, base 256, most significant digit first.

Contents Octets

These give a concrete representation of the value (or the value of the underlying type, if the type is derived by implicit tagging). Details for particular types are given in Section 5.

Section 3.2: Constructed, Definite-Length Method

This method applies to simple string types, structured types, types derived from simple string types and structured types by implicit tagging, and types derived from anything by explicit tagging. It requires that the length of the value be known in advance. The parts of the BER encoding are as follows.

Identifier Octets

As described in Section 3.1, except that bit 6 has value "1," indicating that the encoding is constructed.

Length Octets

As described in Section 3.1.

Contents Octets

The concatenation of the BER encodings of the components of the value:

- For simple string types and types derived from them by implicit tagging, the concatenation of the BER encodings of consecutive substrings of the value (underlying value for implicit tagging)
- For structured types and types derived from them by implicit tagging, the concatenation of the BER encodings of components of the value (underlying value for implicit tagging)
- For types derived from anything by explicit tagging, the BER encoding of the underlying value

Details for particular types are given in Section 5.

Section 3.3: Constructed, Indefinite-Length Method

This method applies to simple string types, structured types, types derived from simple string types and structured types by implicit tagging, and types derived from anything by explicit tagging. It does not require that the length of the value be known in advance. The parts of the BER encoding are as follows:

Identifier Octets

As described in Section 3.2.

Length Octets

One octet, 80.

Contents Octets

As described in Section 3.2.

End-of-Contents Octets

Two octets, 00 00.

Since the end-of-contents octets appear where an ordinary BER encoding might be expected (e.g., in the contents octets of a sequence value), the 00 and 00 appear as identifier and length octets, respectively. Thus the end-of-contents octets are really the primitive, definite-length encoding of a value with universal class, tag number 0, and length 0.

Section 4: Distinguished Encoding Rules

The Distinguished Encoding Rules (DER) for ASN.1 are a subset of BER, and give exactly one way to represent any ASN.1 value as an octet string. DER is intended for applications in which a unique octet string encoding is needed, as is the case when a digital signature is computed on an ASN.1 value. DER is defined in Section 8.7 of X.509.

DER adds the following restrictions to the rules given in Section 3:

1. When the length is between 0 and 127, the short form of length must be used.
2. When the length is 128 or greater, the long form of length must be used, and the length must be encoded in the minimum number of octets.
3. For simple string types and implicitly tagged types derived from simple string types, the primitive, definite-length method must be employed.
4. For structured types, implicitly tagged types derived from structured types, and explicitly tagged types derived from anything, the constructed, definite-length method must be employed.

Other restrictions are defined for particular types (such as BIT STRING, SEQUENCE, SET, and SET OF), and can be found in Section 5.

Section 5: Notation and Encodings for Some Types

This section gives the notation for some ASN.1 types and describes how to encode values of those types under both BER and DER.

The types described are those presented in Section 2. They are listed alphabetically here.

Each description includes ASN.1 notation, BER encoding, and DER encoding. The focus of the encodings is primarily on the contents octets; the tag and length octets follow Sections 3 and 4. The descriptions also explain where each type is used in PKCS and related standards. ASN.1 notation is generally given only for types, although for the type OBJECT IDENTIFIER, value notation is given as well.

Section 5.1: Implicitly Tagged Types

An implicitly tagged type is a type derived from another type by changing the tag of the underlying type.

Implicit tagging is used for optional SEQUENCE components with underlying type other than ANY throughout PKCS, and for the extendedCertificate alternative of PKCS #7's Extended-CertificateOrCertificate type.

```
ASN.1 notation:
[[class] number] IMPLICIT Type
class = UNIVERSAL  |  APPLICATION  |  PRIVATE
```

where **Type** is a type, **class** is an optional class name, and **number** is the tag number within the class, a nonnegative integer.

In ASN.1 "modules" whose default tagging method is implicit tagging, the notation [[*class*] *number*] **Type** is also acceptable, and the keyword IMPLICIT is implied. (See Section 2.3.) For definitions stated outside a module, the explicit inclusion of the keyword IMPLICIT is preferable to prevent ambiguity.

If the class name is absent, then the tag is context-specific. Context-specific tags can only appear in a component of a structured or CHOICE type.

Example   PKCS #8's `PrivateKeyInfo` type has an optional `attributes` component with an implicit, context-specific tag:

```
PrivateKeyInfo ::= SEQUENCE {
  version Version,
  privateKeyAlgorithm PrivateKeyAlgorithmIdentifier,
  privateKey PrivateKey,
  attributes [0] IMPLICIT Attributes OPTIONAL }
```

Here the underlying type is `Attributes`, the class is absent (i.e., context-specific), and the tag number within the class is 0.

BER Encoding

Primitive or constructed, depending on the underlying type. Contents octets are as for the BER encoding of the underlying value.

Example   The BER encoding of the `attributes` component of a `PrivateKeyInfo` value is as follows:

- The identifier octets are 80 if the underlying `Attributes` value has a primitive BER encoding, and a0 if the underlying `Attributes` value has a constructed BER encoding.
- The length and contents octets are the same as the length and contents octets of the BER encoding of the underlying `Attributes` value.

DER Encoding

Primitive or constructed, depending on the underlying type. Contents octets are as for the DER encoding of the underlying value.

Section 5.2: Explicitly Tagged Types

Explicit tagging denotes a type derived from another type by adding an outer tag to the underlying type.

Explicit tagging is used for optional SEQUENCE components with underlying type ANY throughout PKCS, and for the `version` component of X.509's `Certificate` type.

```
ASN.1 notation:
[[class] number] EXPLICIT Type
class = UNIVERSAL | APPLICATION | PRIVATE
```

where ***Type*** is a type, ***class*** is an optional class name, and ***number*** is the tag number within the class, a nonnegative integer.

If the class name is absent, then the tag is context-specific. Context-specific tags can only appear in a component of a SEQUENCE, SET, or CHOICE type.

In ASN.1 "modules" whose default tagging method is explicit tagging, the notation [[***class***] ***number***] ***Type*** is also acceptable, and the keyword EXPLICIT is implied. (See Section 2.3.) For definitions stated outside a module, the explicit inclusion of the keyword EXPLICIT is preferable to prevent ambiguity.

Example 1   PKCS #7's ContentInfo type has an optional content component with an explicit, context-specific tag:

```
ContentInfo ::= SEQUENCE {
  contentType ContentType,
  content
    [0] EXPLICIT ANY DEFINED BY contentType OPTIONAL }
```

Here the underlying type is ANY DEFINED BY contentType, the class is absent (i.e., context-specific), and the tag number within the class is 0.

Example 2   X.509's Certificate type has a version component with an explicit, context-specific tag, where the EXPLICIT keyword is omitted:

```
Certificate ::= ...
  version [0] Version DEFAULT v1988,
...
```

The tag is explicit because the default tagging method for the ASN.1 "module" in X.509 that defines the Certificate type is explicit tagging.

BER Encoding

Constructed. Contents octets are the BER encoding of the underlying value.

Example   The BER encoding of the content component of a Content-Info value is as follows:

- Identifier octets are a0.
- Length octets represent the length of the BER encoding of the underlying ANY DEFINED BY contentType value.

- Contents octets are the BER encoding of the underlying ANY DEFINED BY contentType value.

DER Encoding

Constructed. Contents octets are the DER encoding of the underlying value.

Section 5.3: ANY

The ANY type denotes an arbitrary value of an arbitrary type, where the arbitrary type is possibly defined in the registration of an object identifier or associated with an integer index.

The ANY type is used for content of a particular content type in PKCS #7's ContentInfo type, for parameters of a particular algorithm in X.509's AlgorithmIdentifier type, and for attribute values in X.501's Attribute and AttributeValueAssertion types. The Attribute type is used by PKCS #6, #7, #8, #9, and #10, and the AttributeValue-Assertion type is used in X.501 distinguished names.

ASN.1 Notation

ANY [DEFINED BY *identifier*]where *identifier* is an optional identifier.

In the ANY form, the actual type is indeterminate.

The ANY DEFINED BY *identifier* form can appear only in a component of a SEQUENCE or SET type for which *identifier* identifies some other component and only if that other component has type INTEGER or OBJECT IDENTIFIER (or a type derived from either of those by tagging). In that form, the actual type is determined by the value of the other component, either in the registration of the object identifier value, or in a table of integer values.

Example X.509's AlgorithmIdentifier type has a component of type ANY:

```
AlgorithmIdentifier ::= SEQUENCE {
  algorithm OBJECT IDENTIFIER,
  parameters ANY DEFINED BY algorithm OPTIONAL }
```

Here the actual type of the `parameter` component depends on the value of the `algorithm` component. The actual type would be defined in the registration of object identifier values for the `algorithm` component.

BER Encoding

Same as the BER encoding of the actual value.

Example   The BER encoding of the value of the `parameter` component is the BER encoding of the value of the actual type as defined in the registration of object identifier values for the `algorithm` component.

DER Encoding

Same as the DER encoding of the actual value.

Section 5.4: BIT STRING

The `BIT STRING` type denotes an arbitrary string of bits (1's and 0's). A `BIT STRING` value can have any length, including zero. This type is a string type.

The `BIT STRING` type is used for digital signatures on extended certificates in PKCS #6's `ExtendedCertificate` type, for digital signatures on certificates in X.509's `Certificate` type, and for public keys in certificates in X.509's `SubjectPublicKeyInfo` type.

ASN.1 Notation

```
BIT STRING
```

Example   X.509's `SubjectPublicKeyInfo` type has a component of type `BIT STRING`:

```
SubjectPublicKeyInfo ::= SEQUENCE {
  algorithm AlgorithmIdentifier,
  publicKey BIT STRING }
```

BER Encoding

Primitive or constructed. In a primitive encoding, the first contents octet gives the number of bits by which the length of the bit string is less than the next multiple of 8 (this is called the "number of unused bits"). The second and following contents octets give the value of the bit string, converted to an octet string. The conversion process is as follows:

1. The bit string is padded after the last bit with zero to seven bits of any value to make the length of the bit string a multiple of 8. If the length of the bit string is a multiple of 8 already, no padding is done.

2. The padded bit string is divided into octets. The first eight bits of the padded bit string become the first octet, bit 8 to bit 1, and so on through the last eight bits of the padded bit string.

In a constructed encoding, the contents octets give the concatenation of the BER encodings of consecutive substrings of the bit string, where each substring except the last has a length that is a multiple of eight bits.

Example The BER encoding of the BIT STRING value "01101110010111 0111" can be any of the following, among others, depending on the choice of padding bits, the form of the length octets, and whether the encoding is primitive or constructed:

03 04 06 6e 5d c0	**DER encoding**
03 04 06 6e 5d e0	**Padded with "100000"**
03 81 04 06 6e 5d c0	**Long form of length octets**
23 09	**Constructed encoding:**
03 03 00 6e 5d	**"0110111001011101" + "11"**
03 02 06 c0	

DER encoding

Primitive. The contents octets are as for a primitive BER encoding, except that the bit string is padded with zero-valued bits.

Example The DER encoding of the BIT STRING value "01101110010111 0111" is

```
03 04 06 6e 5d c0
```

Section 5.5: CHOICE

The CHOICE type denotes a union of one or more alternatives.

The CHOICE type is used to represent the union of an extended certificate and an X.509 certificate in PKCS #7's ExtendedCertificate-OrCertificate type.

ASN.1 notation

```
CHOICE {
  [identifier₁] Type₁,
  ...,
  [identifierₙ] Typeₙ }
```

where ***identifier***$_1$, . . ., ***identifier***$_n$ are optional, distinct identifiers for the alternatives, and ***Type***$_1$, . . ., ***Type***$_n$ are the types of the alternatives. The identifiers are primarily for documentation; they do not affect values of the type or their encodings in any way.

The types must have distinct tags. This requirement is typically satisfied with explicit or implicit tagging on some of the alternatives.

Example PKCS #7's `ExtendedCertificateOrCertificate` type is a `CHOICE` type:

```
ExtendedCertificateOrCertificate ::= CHOICE {
  certificate Certificate, -- X.509
  extendedCertificate [0] IMPLICIT ExtendedCertificate
}
```

Here the identifiers for the alternatives are `certificate` and `extendedCertificate`, and the types of the alternatives are `Certificate` and `[0] IMPLICIT ExtendedCertificate`.

BER encoding

Same as the BER encoding of the chosen alternative. The fact that the alternatives have distinct tags makes it possible to distinguish between their BER encodings.

Example The identifier octets for the BER encoding are `30` if the chosen alternative is `certificate`, and `a0` if the chosen alternative is `extendedCertificate`.

DER encoding

Same as the DER encoding of the chosen alternative.

Section 5.6: IA5String

The `IA5String` type denotes an arbitrary string of IA5 characters. IA5 stands for International Alphabet 5, which is the same as ASCII. The character set includes non-printing control characters. An `IA5String` value can have any length, including zero. This type is a string type.

The `IA5String` type is used in PKCS #9's electronic-mail address, unstructured-name, and unstructured-address attributes.

ASN.1 notation

`IA5String`

BER encoding

Primitive or constructed. In a primitive encoding, the contents octets give the characters in the IA5 string, encoded in ASCII. In a constructed encoding, the contents octets give the concatenation of the BER encodings of consecutive substrings of the IA5 string.

Example   The BER encoding of the `IA5String` value "test1@rsa.com" can be any of the following, among others, depending on the form of length octets and whether the encoding is primitive or constructed:

```
16 0d 74 65 73                            DER encoding
   74 31 40 72 73 61 2e 63 6f 6d
16 81 0d                                  Long form of length octets
   74 65 73 74 31 40 72 73 61 2e 63 6f 6d
36 13                                     Constructed encoding:
   16 05 74 65 73 74 31                   "test1" + "@" + "rsa.com"
   16 01 40
   16 07 72 73 61 2e 63 6f 6d
```

DER Encoding

Primitive. Contents octets are as for a primitive BER encoding.

Example   The DER encoding of the `IA5String` value "test1@rsa.com" is

```
16 0d 74 65 73 74 31 40 72 73 61 2e 63 6f 6d
```

Section 5.7: INTEGER

The `INTEGER` type denotes an arbitrary integer. `INTEGER` values can be positive, negative, or zero, and can have any magnitude.

The `INTEGER` type is used for version numbers throughout PKCS, for cryptographic values such as modulus, exponent, and primes in PKCS #1's RSAPublicKey and RSAPrivateKey types and PKCS #3's DHParameter type, for a message-digest iteration count in PKCS #5's PBEParameter type, and for version numbers and serial numbers in X.509's Certificate type.

ASN.1 Notation

```
INTEGER [{ identifier₁(value₁) ... identifierₙ(valueₙ) }]
```

where *identifier*$_1$, . . ., *identifier*$_n$ are optional distinct identifiers and *value*$_1$, . . ., *value*$_n$ are optional integer values. The identifiers, when present, are associated with values of the type.

Example X.509's Version type is an INTEGER type with identified values:

```
Version ::= INTEGER { v1988(0) }
```

The identifier v1988 is associated with the value 0. X.509's Certificate type uses the identifier v1988 to give a default value of 0 for the version component:

```
Certificate ::= ...
  version Version DEFAULT v1988,
...
```

BER Encoding

Primitive. Contents octets give the value of the integer, base 256, in two's complement form, most significant digit first, with the minimum number of octets. The value 0 is encoded as a single 00 octet.

Some example BER encodings (which also happen to be DER encodings) are given in Table B-3.

DER Encoding

Primitive. Contents octets are as for a primitive BER encoding.

Integer Value	BER Encoding
0	02 01 00
127	02 01 7F
128	02 02 00 80
256	02 02 01 00
-128	02 01 80
-129	02 02 FF 7F

Table B-3

Example BER Encodings of INTEGER Values

Section 5.8: NULL

The NULL type denotes a null value.

The NULL type is used for algorithm parameters in several places in PKCS.

ASN.1 Notation

NULL

BER Encoding

Primitive. Contents octets are empty.

Example The BER encoding of a NULL value can be either of the following, as well as others, depending on the form of the length octets:

```
05 00
05 81 00
```

DER Encoding

Primitive. Contents octets are empty; the DER encoding of a NULL value is always 05 00.

Section 5.9: OBJECT IDENTIFIER

The OBJECT IDENTIFIER type denotes an object identifier, a sequence of integer components that identifies an object such as an algorithm, an attribute type, or perhaps a registration authority that defines other object identifiers. An OBJECT IDENTIFIER value can have any number of components, and components can generally have any nonnegative value. This type is a nonstring type.

OBJECT IDENTIFIER values are given meanings by registration authorities. Each registration authority is responsible for all sequences of components beginning with a given sequence. A registration authority typically delegates responsibility for subsets of the sequences in its domain to other registration authorities, or for particular types of objects. There are always at least two components.

The OBJECT IDENTIFIER type is used to identify content in PKCS #7's ContentInfo type, to identify algorithms in X.509's AlgorithmIdentifier type, and to identify attributes in X.501's Attribute and AttributeValueAssertion types. The Attribute type is used by PKCS #6, #7, #8, #9, and #10, and the AttributeValueAssertion type is used in X.501 distinguished names. OBJECT IDENTIFIER values are defined throughout PKCS.

ASN.1 Notation

```
OBJECT IDENTIFIER
```

The ASN.1 notation for values of the OBJECT IDENTIFIER type is

```
{ [identifier] component₁ ... componentₙ }
componentᵢ = identifierᵢ | identifierᵢ (valueᵢ) | valueᵢ
```

where *identifier*, $identifier_1$, . . ., $identifier_n$ are identifiers, and $value_1$, . . ., $value_n$ are optional integer values.

The form without *identifier* is the "complete" value with all its components; the form with *identifier* abbreviates the beginning components with another object identifier value. The identifiers $identifier_1$, . . ., $identifier_n$ are intended primarily for documentation, but they must correspond to the integer value when both are present. These identifiers can appear without integer values only if they are among a small set of identifiers defined in X.208.

Example Both of the following values refer to the object identifier assigned to RSA Data Security, Inc.:

```
{ iso(1) member-body(2) 840 113549 }
{ 1 2 840 113549 }
```

(In this example, which gives ASN.1 value notation, the object identifier values are decimal, not hexadecimal.) Table A-4 gives some other object identifier values and their meanings.

Object Identifier Value	Meaning
{ 1 2 }	ISO member bodies
{ 1 2 840 }	US (ANSI)
{ 1 2 840 113549 }	RSA Data Security, Inc.
{ 1 2 840 113549 1 }	RSA Data Security, Inc. PKCS
{ 2 5 }	Directory services (X.500)
{ 2 5 8 }	Directory services—algorithms

Table B-4

Some Object Identifier Values and Their Meanings

BER Encoding

Primitive. Contents octets are as follows, where $value_1, \ldots, value_n$ denote the integer values of the components in the complete object identifier:

1. The first octet has value $40 \times value_1 + value_2$. (This is unambiguous, since $value_1$ is limited to values 0, 1, and 2; $value_2$ is limited to the range 0 to 39 when $value_1$ is 0 or 1; and, according to X.208, n is always at least 2.)

2. The following octets, if any, encode $value_3, \ldots, value_n$. Each value is encoded base 128, most significant digit first, with as few digits as possible, and the most significant bit of each octet except the last in the value's encoding set to "1."

Example The first octet of the BER encoding of RSA Data Security, Inc.'s object identifier is $40 \times 1 + 2 = 42 = 2a_{16}$. The encoding of $840 = 6 \times 128 + 48_{16}$ is $86\ 48$, and the encoding of $113549 = 6 \times 128^2 + 77_{16} \times 128 + d_{16}$ is $86\ f7\ 0d$. This leads to the following BER encoding:

```
06 06 2a 86 48 86 f7 0d
```

DER Encoding

Primitive. Contents octets are as for a primitive BER encoding.

Section 5.10: OCTET STRING

The OCTET STRING type denotes an arbitrary string of octets (eight-bit values). An OCTET STRING value can have any length, including zero. This type is a string type.

The OCTET STRING type is used for salt values in PKCS #5's PBE Parameter type, for message digests, encrypted message digests, and encrypted content in PKCS #7, and for private keys and encrypted private keys in PKCS #8.

ASN.1 Notation

```
OCTET STRING [SIZE ({size | size₁..size₂})]
```

where *size*, *size₁*, and *size₂* are optional size constraints. In the OCTET STRING SIZE (*size*) form, the octet string must have *size* octets. In the OCTET STRING SIZE (*size₁..size₂*) form, the octet string must have between size1 and size2 octets. In the OCTET STRING form, the octet string can have any size.

Example PKCS #5's PBEParameter type has a component of type OCTET STRING:

```
PBEParameter ::= SEQUENCE {
  salt OCTET STRING SIZE(8),
  iterationCount INTEGER }
```

Here the size of the salt component is always eight octets.

BER Encoding

Primitive or constructed. In a primitive encoding, the contents octets give the value of the octet string, first octet to last octet. In a constructed encoding, the contents octets give the concatenation of the BER encodings of substrings of the OCTET STRING value.

Example The BER encoding of the OCTET STRING value 01 23 45 67 89 ab cd ef can be any of the following, among others, depending on the form of length octets and whether the encoding is primitive or constructed:

04 08 01 23 45 67 89 ab cd ef	**DER encoding**
04 81 08 01 23 45 67 89 ab cd ef	**Long form of length octets**
24 0c	**Constructed encoding:**
04 04 01 23 45 67	**01 ... 67 + 89 ... ef**
04 04 89 ab cd ef	

DER Encoding

Primitive. Contents octets are as for a primitive BER encoding.

Example The BER encoding of the OCTET STRING value 01 23 45 67 89 ab cd ef is

    04 08 01 23 45 67 89 ab cd ef

Section 5.11: PrintableString

The PrintableString type denotes an arbitrary string of printable characters from the following character set:

    A, B, ..., Z
    a, b, ..., z
    0, 1, ..., 9
    (space) ' ( ) + , - . / : = ?

This type is a string type.

The PrintableString type is used in PKCS #9's challenge-password and unstructured-address attributes, and in several X.521 distinguished names attributes.

ASN.1 Notation

`PrintableString`

BER Encoding

Primitive or constructed. In a primitive encoding, the contents octets give the characters in the printable string, encoded in ASCII. In a constructed encoding, the contents octets give the concatenation of the BER encodings of consecutive substrings of the string.

Example The BER encoding of the `PrintableString` value "Test User 1" can be any of the following, among others, depending on the form of length octets and whether the encoding is primitive or constructed:

`13 0b 54 65 73 74 20 55 73 65 72 20 31`	**DER encoding**
`13 81 0b 54 65 73 74 20 55 73 65 72 20 31`	**Long form of length octets**
`33 0f`	**Constructed**
`13 05 54 65 73 74 20`	**encoding:**
`13 06 55 73 65 72 20 31`	**"Test " + "User 1"**

DER Encoding

Primitive. Contents octets are as for a primitive BER encoding.

Example The DER encoding of the `PrintableString` value "Test User 1" is

`13 0b 54 65 73 74 20 55 73 65 72 20 31`

Section 5.12: SEQUENCE

The SEQUENCE type denotes an ordered collection of one or more types.
The SEQUENCE type is used throughout PKCS and related standards.

ASN.1 Notation

```
SEQUENCE {
    [identifier₁] Type₁ [{OPTIONAL | DEFAULT value₁}],
    ...,
    [identifierₙ] Typeₙ [{OPTIONAL | DEFAULT valueₙ}]}
```

where $identifier_1$, . . ., $identifier_n$ are optional, distinct identifiers for the components, $Type_1$, . . ., $Type_n$ are the types of the components, and $value_1$, . . ., $value_n$ are optional default values for the components. The identifiers are primarily for documentation; they do not affect values of the type or their encodings in any way.

The OPTIONAL qualifier indicates that the value of a component is optional and need not be present in the sequence. The DEFAULT qualifier also indicates that the value of a component is optional, and assigns a default value to the component when the component is absent.

The types of any consecutive series of components with the OPTIONAL or DEFAULT qualifier, as well as of any component immediately following that series, must have distinct tags. This requirement is typically satisfied with explicit or implicit tagging on some of the components.

Example X.509's Validity type is a SEQUENCE type with two components:

```
Validity ::= SEQUENCE {
    start UTCTime,
    end UTCTime }
```

Here the identifiers for the components are start and end, and the type of both components is UTCTime.

BER Encoding

Constructed. Contents octets are the concatenation of the BER encodings of the values of the components of the sequence, in order of definition, with the following rules for components with the OPTIONAL and DEFAULT qualifiers:

- If the value of a component with the OPTIONAL or DEFAULT qualifier is absent from the sequence, then the encoding of that component is not included in the contents octets.
- If the value of a component with the DEFAULT qualifier is the default value, then the encoding of that component may or may not be included in the contents octets.

DER Encoding

Constructed. Contents octets are the same as the BER encoding, except that if the value of a component with the DEFAULT qualifier is the default value, the encoding of that component is not included in the contents octets.

Sectopm 5.13: SEQUENCE OF

The SEQUENCE OF type denotes an ordered collection of zero or more occurrences of a given type.

The SEQUENCE OF type is used in X.501 distinguished names.

ASN.1 Notation

```
SEQUENCE OF Type
```

where *Type* is a type.

Example X.501's RDNSequence type consists of zero or more occurrences of the RelativeDistinguishedName type, most significant occurrence first:

```
RDNSequence ::= SEQUENCE OF RelativeDistinguishedName
```

BER Encoding

Constructed. Contents octets are the concatenation of the BER encodings of the values of the occurrences in the collection, in order of occurrence.

DER Encoding

Constructed. Contents octets are the concatenation of the DER encodings of the values of the occurrences in the collection, in order of occurrence.

Section 5.14: SET

The SET type denotes an unordered collection of one or more types.

The SET type is not used in PKCS.

ASN.1 Notation

```
SET {
   [identifier₁] Type₁ [{OPTIONAL | DEFAULT value₁}],
   ...,
   [identifierₙ] Typeₙ [{OPTIONAL | DEFAULT valueₙ}]}
```

where $identifier_1, \ldots, identifier_n$ are optional, distinct identifiers for the components, $Type_1, \ldots, Type_n$ are the types of the components, and $value_1, \ldots, value_n$ are optional default values for the components. The identifiers are primarily for documentation; they do not affect values of the type or their encodings in any way.

The OPTIONAL qualifier indicates that the value of a component is optional and need not be present in the set. The DEFAULT qualifier also indicates that the value of a component is optional, and assigns a default value to the component when the component is absent.

The types must have distinct tags. This requirement is typically satisfied with explicit or implicit tagging on some of the components.

BER Encoding

Constructed. Contents octets are the concatenation of the BER encodings of the values of the components of the set, in any order, with the following rules for components with the OPTIONAL and DEFAULT qualifiers:

- If the value of a component with the OPTIONAL or DEFAULT qualifier is absent from the set, then the encoding of that component is not included in the contents octets.
- If the value of a component with the DEFAULT qualifier is the default value, then the encoding of that component may or may not be included in the contents octets.

DER Encoding

Constructed. Contents octets are the same as for the BER encoding, except that:

- If the value of a component with the DEFAULT qualifier is the default value, the encoding of that component is not included.
- There is an order to the components, namely ascending order by tag.

Section 5.15: SET OF

The SET OF type denotes an unordered collection of zero or more occurrences of a given type.

The SET OF type is used for sets of attributes in PKCS #6, #7, #8, #9, and #10, for sets of message-digest algorithm identifiers, signer information, and recipient information in PKCS #7, and in X.501 distinguished names.

ASN.1 Notation

```
SET OF Type
```

where **Type** is a type.

Example X.501's RelativeDistinguishedName type consists of zero or more occurrences of the AttributeValueAssertion type, where the order is unimportant:

```
RelativeDistinguishedName ::=
   SET OF AttributeValueAssertion
```

BER Encoding

Constructed. Contents octets are the concatenation of the BER encodings of the values of the occurrences in the collection, in any order.

DER Encoding

Constructed. Contents octets are the same as for the BER encoding, except that there is an order, namely ascending lexicographic order of BER encoding. Lexicographic comparison of two different BER encodings is done as follows: Logically pad the shorter BER encoding after the last octet with dummy octets that are smaller in value than any normal octet. Scan the BER encodings from left to right until a difference is found. The smaller-valued BER encoding is the one with the smaller-valued octet at the point of difference.

Section 5.16: T61String

The `T61String` type denotes an arbitrary string of T.61 characters. T.61 is an eight-bit extension to the ASCII character set. Special "escape" sequences specify the interpretation of subsequent character values as, for example, Japanese; the initial interpretation is Latin. The character set includes nonprinting control characters. The `T61String` type allows only the Latin and Japanese character interpretations, and implementors' agreements for directory names exclude control characters [NIST92]. A `T61String` value can have any length, including zero. This type is a string type.

The `T61String` type is used in PKCS #9's unstructured-address and challenge-password attributes, and in several X.521 attributes.

ASN.1 Notation

```
T61String
```

BER Encoding

Primitive or constructed. In a primitive encoding, the contents octets give the characters in the T.61 string, encoded in ASCII. In a constructed encoding, the contents octets give the concatenation of the BER encodings of consecutive substrings of the T.61 string.

Example The BER encoding of the `T61String` value "clés publiques" (French for "public keys") can be any of the following, among others, depending on the form of length octets and whether the encoding is primitive or constructed:

```
14 0f                                            DER encoding
   63 6c c2 65 73 20 70 75 62 6c 69 71 75 65 73
14 81 0f                                          Long form of length octets
   63 6c c2 65 73 20 70 75 62 6c 69 71 75 65 73
34 15                                            Constructed encoding:
   14 05 63 6c c2 65 73                          "clés" + " " + "publiques"
   14 01 20
   14 09 70 75 62 6c 69 71 75 65 73
```

The eight-bit character c2 is a T.61 prefix that adds an acute accent (´) to the next character.

DER Encoding

Primitive. Contents octets are as for a primitive BER encoding.

Example The DER encoding of the `T61String` value "clés publiques" is

```
14 0f 63 6c c2 65 73 20 70 75 62 6c 69 71 75 65 73
```

Section 5.17: UTCTime

The `UTCTime` type denotes a "coordinated universal time" or Greenwich Mean Time (GMT) value. A `UTCTime` value includes the local time precise to either minutes or seconds, and an offset from GMT in hours and minutes. It takes any of the following forms:

```
YYMMDDhhmmZ
YYMMDDhhmm+hh'mm'
YYMMDDhhmm-hh'mm'
YYMMDDhhmmssZ
YYMMDDhhmmss+hh'mm'
YYMMDDhhmmss-hh'mm'
```

where:

> *YY* is the least significant two digits of the year
>
> *MM* is the month (01 to 12)
>
> *DD* is the day (01 to 31)
>
> *hh* is the hour (00 to 23)
>
> *mm* are the minutes (00 to 59)
>
> *ss* are the seconds (00 to 59)
>
> Z indicates that local time is GMT, + indicates that local time is later than GMT, and – indicates that local time is earlier than GMT
>
> *hh'* is the absolute value of the offset from GMT in hours
>
> *mm'* is the absolute value of the offset from GMT in minutes

This type is a string type.

The `UTCTime` type is used for signing times in PKCS #9's signing-time attribute and for certificate validity periods in X.509's `Validity` type.

ASN.1 Notation

`UTCTime`

BER Encoding

Primitive or constructed. In a primitive encoding, the contents octets give the characters in the string, encoded in ASCII. In a constructed encoding, the contents octets give the concatenation of the BER encodings of consecutive substrings of the string. (The constructed encoding is not particularly interesting, since `UTCTime` values are so short, but the constructed encoding is permitted.)

Example   The time this sentence was originally written was 4:45:40 P.M. Pacific Daylight Time on May 6, 1991, which can be represented with either of the following `UTCTime` values, among others:

```
"910506164540-0700"
"910506234540Z"
```

These values have the following BER encodings, among others:

```
17 0d 39 31 30 35 30 36 32 33 34 35 34 30 5a

17 11 39 31 30 35 30 36 31 36 34 35 34 30 2D 30 37 30
      30
```

DER Encoding

Primitive. Contents octets are as for a primitive BER encoding.

Section 6: An Example

This section gives an example of ASN.1 notation and DER encoding: the X.501 type `Name`.

Section 6.1: Abstract Notation

This section gives the ASN.1 notation for the X.501 type `Name`.

```
Name ::= CHOICE {
  RDNSequence }

RDNSequence ::= SEQUENCE OF RelativeDistinguishedName

RelativeDistinguishedName ::=
  SET OF AttributeValueAssertion

AttributeValueAssertion ::= SEQUENCE {
    AttributeType,
    AttributeValue }

AttributeType ::= OBJECT IDENTIFIER

AttributeValue ::= ANY
```

The `Name` type identifies an object in an X.500 directory. `Name` is a CHOICE type consisting of one alternative: `RDNSequence`. (Future revisions of X.500 may have other alternatives.)

The `RDNSequence` type gives a path through an X.500 directory tree starting at the root. `RDNSequence` is a SEQUENCE OF type consisting of zero or more occurrences of `RelativeDistinguishedName`.

The `RelativeDistinguishedName` type gives a unique name to an object relative to the object superior to it in the directory tree. `RelativeDistinguishedName` is a SET OF type consisting of zero or more occurrences of `AttributeValueAssertion`.

The `AttributeValueAssertion` type assigns a value to some attribute of a relative distinguished name, such as country name or common name. `AttributeValueAssertion` is a SEQUENCE type consisting of two components, an `AttributeType` type and an `AttributeValue` type.

The `AttributeType` type identifies an attribute by object identifier. The `AttributeValue` type gives an arbitrary attribute value. The actual type of the attribute value is determined by the attribute type.

Section 6.2: DER Encoding

This section gives an example of a DER encoding of a value of type `Name`, working from the bottom up.

The name is that of the Test User 1 from the PKCS examples [Kal93]. The name is represented by the following path:

```
              (root)
                 |
         countryName = "US"
                 |
organizationName = "Example Organization"
                 |
     commonName = "Test User 1"
```

Each level corresponds to one RelativeDistinguishedName value, each of which happens for this name to consist of one AttributeValue-Assertion value. The AttributeType value is before the equals sign, and the AttributeValue value (a printable string for the given attribute types) is after the equals sign.

The countryName, organizationName, and commonUnitName are attribute types defined in X.520 as:

```
attributeType OBJECT IDENTIFIER ::=
  { joint-iso-ccitt(2) ds(5) 4 }

countryName OBJECT IDENTIFIER ::= { attributeType 6 }
organizationName OBJECT IDENTIFIER ::=
  { attributeType 10 }
commonUnitName OBJECT IDENTIFIER ::=
  { attributeType 3 }
```

AttributeType

The three AttributeType values are OCTET STRING values, so their DER encoding follows the primitive, definite-length method:

```
06 03 55 04 06     countryName
06 03 55 04 0a     organizationName
06 03 55 04 03     commonName
```

The identifier octets follow the low-tag form, since the tag is 6 for OBJECT IDENTIFIER. Bits 8 and 7 have value "0," indicating universal class, and bit 6 has value "0," indicating that the encoding is primitive. The length octets follow the short form. The contents octets are the concatenation of three octet strings derived from subidentifiers (in decimal): $40 \times 2 + 5 = 85 = 55_{16}$; 4; and 6, 10, or 3.

AttributeValue

The three `AttributeValue` values are `PrintableString` values, so their encodings follow the primitive, definite-length method:

```
13 02 55 53                                              "US"
13 14                                                    "Example
   45 78 61 6d 70 6c 65 20 4f 72 67 61 6e 69 7a 61       Organization"
   74 69 6f 6e
13 0b                                                    "Test User 1"
   54 65 73 74 20 55 73 65 72 20 31
```

The identifier octets follow the low-tag-number form, since the tag for `PrintableString`, 19 (decimal), is between 0 and 30. Bits 8 and 7 have value "0" since `PrintableString` is in the universal class. Bit 6 has value "0" since the encoding is primitive. The length octets follow the short form, and the contents octets are the ASCII representation of the attribute value.

AttributeValueAssertion

The three `AttributeValueAssertion` values are `SEQUENCE` values, so their DER encodings follow the constructed, definite-length method:

```
30 09                       countryName = "US"
 06 03 55 04 06
 13 02 55 53
30 1b                       organizationName = "Example Organization"
 06 03 55 04 0a
 1 3 14  . . .  6f 6e
30 12                       commonName = "Test User 1"
 06 03 55 04 0b
 13 0b ... 20 31
```

The identifier octets follow the low-tag-number form, since the tag for `SEQUENCE`, 16 (decimal), is between 0 and 30. Bits 8 and 7 have value "0" since `SEQUENCE` is in the universal class. Bit 6 has value "1" since the encoding is constructed. The length octets follow the short form, and the contents octets are the concatenation of the DER encodings of the `attributeType` and `attributeValue` components.

RelativeDistinguishedName

The three RelativeDistinguishedName values are SET OF values, so their DER encodings follow the constructed, definite-length method:

```
31 0b
   30 09 ... 55 53

31 1d
   30 1b ... 6f 6e

31 14
   30 12 ... 20 31
```

The identifier octets follow the low-tag-number form, since the tag for SET OF, 17 (decimal), is between 0 and 30. Bits 8 and 7 have value "0" since SET OF is in the universal class. Bit 6 has value "1" since the encoding is constructed. The length octets follow the short form, and the contents octets are the DER encodings of the respective Attribute-ValueAssertion values, since there is only one value in each set.

RDNSequence

The RDNSequence value is a SEQUENCE OF value, so its DER encoding follows the constructed, definite-length method:

```
30 42
   31 0b ... 55 53
   31 1d ... 6f 6e
   31 14 ... 20 31
```

The identifier octets follow the low-tag-number form, since the tag for SEQUENCE OF, 16 (decimal), is between 0 and 30. Bits 8 and 7 have value "0" since SEQUENCE OF is in the universal class. Bit 6 has value "1" since the encoding is constructed. The length octets follow the short form, and the contents octets are the concatenation of the DER encodings of the three RelativeDistinguishedName values, in order of occurrence.

Name

The Name value is a CHOICE value, so its DER encoding is the same as that of the RDNSequence value:

```
30 42
   31 0b
      30 09
         06 03 55 04 06    attributeType = countryName
         13 02 55 53       attributeValue = "US"
   31 1d
      30 1b
         06 03 55 04 0a    attributeType = organizationName
         13 14                attributeValue = "Example Organization"
            45 78 61 6d 70 6c 65 20 4f 72 67 61 6e 69 7a 61
            74 69 6f 6e
   31 14
      30 12
         06 03 55 04 03    attributeType = commonName
         13 0b                attributeValue = "Test User 1"
            54 65 73 74 20 55 73 65 72 20 31
```

References

PKCS #1   RSA Laboratories. *PKCS #1: RSA Encryption Standard.* Version 1.5, November 1993.

PKCS #3   RSA Laboratories. *PKCS #3: Diffie-Hellman Key-Agreement Standard.* Version 1.4, November 1993.

PKCS #5   RSA Laboratories. *PKCS #5: Password-Based Encryption Standard.* Version 1.5, November 1993.

PKCS #6   RSA Laboratories. *PKCS #6: Extended-Certificate Syntax Standard.* Version 1.5, November 1993.

PKCS #7   RSA Laboratories. *PKCS #7: Cryptographic Message Syntax Standard.* Version 1.5, November 1993.

PKCS #8   RSA Laboratories. *PKCS #8: Private-Key Information Syntax Standard.* Version 1.2, November 1993.

PKCS #9   RSA Laboratories. *PKCS #9: Selected Attribute Types.* Version 1.1, November 1993.

PKCS #10   RSA Laboratories. *PKCS #10: Certification Request Syntax Standard.* Version 1.0, November 1993.

X.200   CCITT. *Recommendation X.200: Reference Model of Open Systems Interconnection for CCITT Applications.* 1984.

X.208	CCITT. *Recommendation X.208: Specification of Abstract Syntax Notation One (ASN.1).* 1988.
X.209	CCITT. *Recommendation X.209: Specification of Basic Encoding Rules for Abstract Syntax Notation One (ASN.1).* 1988.
X.500	CCITT. *Recommendation X.500: The Directory—Overview of Concepts, Models and Services.* 1988.
X.501	CCITT. *Recommendation X.501: The Directory—Models.* 1988.
X.509	CCITT. *Recommendation X.509: The Directory—Authentication Framework.* 1988.
X.520	CCITT. Recommendation X.520: The Directory—Selected Attribute Types. 1988.
[Kal93]	Burton S. Kaliski Jr. *Some Examples of the PKCS Standards.* RSA Laboratories, November 1993.
[NIST92]	NIST. Special *Publication 500-202: Stable Implementation Agreements for Open Systems Interconnection Protocols.* Part 11 (Directory Services Protocols). December 1992.

Revision History

June 3, 1991, Version

The June 3, 1991, version is part of the initial public release of PKCS. It was published as NIST/OSI Implementors' Workshop document SEC-SIG-91-17.

November 1, 1993, Version

The November 1, 1993, version incorporates several editorial changes, including the addition of a revision history. It is updated to be consistent with the following versions of the PKCS documents:

PKCS #1	*RSA Encryption Standard.* Version 1.5, November 1993.
PKCS #3	*Diffie-Hellman Key-Agreement Standard.* Version 1.4, November 1993.

PKCS #5	*Password-Based Encryption Standard*. Version 1.5, November 1993.
PKCS #6	*Extended-Certificate Syntax Standard*. Version 1.5, November 1993.
PKCS #7	*Cryptographic Message Syntax Standard*. Version 1.5, November 1993.
PKCS #8	*Private-Key Information Syntax Standard*. Version 1.2, November 1993.
PKCS #9	*Selected Attribute Types*. Version 1.1, November 1993.
PKCS #10	*Certification Request Syntax Standard*. Version 1.0, November 1993.

The following substantive changes were made:

Section 5	Description of T61String type is added.
Section 6	Names are changed, consistent with other PKCS examples.

Further Technical Details

In this appendix, you will find extra information not covered in the main body of the book. It is a deeper look at some of the topics described. This information is not necessary for a proper understanding of the main concepts, but should be interesting reading for those who want to explore cryptography a little further.

How Digest-Based PRNGs Work

As mentioned in Chapter 2, most PRNGs (*pseudo-random number generators*) are based on digest algorithms. The algorithm takes a seed and—just as sowing a botanical seed produces a plant—produces a virtually unlimited number of pseudo-random numbers. Here is a typical implementation using SHA-1 as the underlying digest algorithm.

Suppose the user wants two 128-bit session keys. The first step is give the seed to the PRNG, which digests it using SHA-1. The seed is the "message" of the message digest. This produces a 20-byte internal value, commonly called the *state*, which must be kept secret. Next, the user asks the PRNG for 16 bytes (the data of the first 128-bit session key). The PRNG uses SHA-1 to digest the state. Now the state, rather than the seed, is the message of the message digest. The digest produces 20 bytes. The user needs only 16, so the PRNG outputs the first 16 bytes.

The user then requests 16 more bytes (the data of the second 128-bit session key). The PRNG has four left over from the last call; it could return them, but it also needs 12 more to fill the second request. To get the next 12 bytes, the PRNG changes the state somehow and digests the resulting new state. Because the PRNG has changed the state, this next block of 20 bytes will be different from the first block. The PRNG now has 20 new bytes. It returns the four left over from the first digest and the first 12 from the current digest.

Each time the PRNG produces output, it either returns leftovers or changes the state, digests the state, and returns as many bytes from that result as needed.

How does a PRNG change the state? It may simply add one to the current state. Recall that if you change a message, even if only by one bit, the resulting output will be significantly different. No matter what the input message is, the output will always pass tests of randomness. So if the PRNG takes a current state and adds one to it, digesting the new state will produce completely different, pseudo-random output. If the current state is

    0xFF FF FF FF . . . FF

then adding one to it will change the state to

    0x00 00 00 00 . . . 00

It's certainly possible to change the state by adding a different constant. Instead of adding 1, the PRNG could add a 20-byte number. In that way, all bytes of the state are manipulated in each operation.

A simpler PRNG would not bother with an internal state. Instead, it would digest the seed to create the first block of output and then would digest the first block of output to create the second block. Such a PRNG would be horrible.

Here's why. Suppose Ray (the attacker from Chapter 3) wants to read Pao-Chi's e-mail. The first thing Ray does is to get Pao-Chi to send him some encrypted e-mail—that is, to send him a few digital envelopes. With this e-mail, what Ray has is several 128-bit session keys (and possibly some initialization vectors if the encryption algorithm is a block cipher with a feedback mode). These keys are a series of pseudo-random bytes, each block produced by digesting the preceding block. With a little work, Ray can figure out a block boundary. Now Ray eavesdrops on Pao-Chi's future e-mails. What is the 128-bit session key used for the next e-mail?

It's simply the digest of the last block that Ray has. That's why good digest-based PRNGs use an internal state.

If the underlying digest algorithm is truly one-way (meaning that no one can determine the message from the digest), no one will be able to figure out what the state was that produced any particular pseudo-random output. If no one can figure out what the state is at any point in time, no one can compute what the next bytes will be.

Feedback Modes

In Chapter 2 you learned about block ciphers. A block cipher encrypts each block independently, so if the same block of plaintext appears more than once in a message, the resulting ciphertext block also will be repeated. This repetition could help an attacker. For example, suppose a company encrypts employee information in a database using the same key for each entry. If two entries contain the same block of ciphertext for "salary," anyone seeing that matching block would know that those two people earn the same salary.

Feedback modes make certain that each block of ciphertext is unique. (Except for that, they offer no additional security.) The most common feedback mode (described in Chapter 2) is *cipher block chaining* (CBC). When you encrypt data in CBC mode, each block of plaintext is XOR'd with the preceding block of ciphertext before the block is encrypted. There is no previous ciphertext for the first block, so it is XOR'd with an *initialization vector* (IV).

The term for no feedback is *electronic codebook* (ECB). Following are some other feedback modes.

Cipher Feedback Mode*

In *cipher feedback* (CFB) mode, you encrypt a block of data and XOR the plaintext with this encrypted block to produce the ciphertext. The block of data you encrypt is the preceding ciphertext. The first block has no preceding ciphertext, so it uses an IV. To create the first block of ciphertext, you encrypt the IV and XOR it with the plaintext. Now you save the

*(Source: RSA Labs)

resulting ciphertext for the next block. For the second block, you encrypt the preceding ciphertext (the result of the preceding XOR) and XOR the result of that with the plaintext. For example, suppose that the first plaintext block begins with the word "Goal." Here's the process.

1. Encrypt the IV. IV = 0xA722B551 . . . becomes 0x38F01321 . . . .

2. XOR the plaintext with the encrypted IV. Goal = 0x476F616C becomes 0x7F9F724D, which is the ciphertext.

3. Encrypt the preceding ciphertext. 0x7F9F724D . . . becomes 0xE1250B77 . . . .

4. XOR the plaintext with the encrypted preceding ciphertext, and repeat until the entire message is encrypted.

It's possible to define CFB mode so that it uses feedback that is less than one full data block. In fact, with CFB, it's possible to define a block size as one byte, effectively converting a block cipher into a stream cipher. Suppose you're using AES, a block cipher with a block size of 16 bytes. Here's what to do. First, use a 16-byte IV and encrypt it. You now have a block of 16 bytes that is the encrypted IV. Grab one byte of plaintext and XOR it with the most significant byte of the encrypted IV. Now that you've used that byte, throw it away by shifting the block of encrypted IV to the left. That leaves the least significant byte open. Fill it with the ciphertext (the result of the XOR). Now go on to the next byte of plaintext.

CFB mode is as secure as the underlying cipher, and using the XOR operation conceals plaintext patterns in the ciphertext. Plaintext cannot be manipulated directly except by the removal of blocks from the beginning or the end of the ciphertext.

Output Feedback Mode*

Output feedback (OFB) mode is similar to CFB mode except that the quantity XOR'd with each plaintext block is generated independently of both the plaintext and the ciphertext. Here's how to use this mode. For the first block of ciphertext, encrypt the IV and call this quantity the cipher block. Now XOR the cipher block with the plaintext. For the second block, encrypt the cipher block to create a new cipher block. Now XOR this new cipher block with the next block of plaintext.

---

*(Source: RSA Labs)

Assuming again that the first block of plaintext is "Goal," here's how OFB works.

1. Encrypt the IV to produce the cipher block. IV = 0xA722B551 . . . becomes 0x38F01321 . . . .

2. XOR the plaintext with the encrypted IV. Goal = 0x476F616C becomes 0x7F9F724D, which is the ciphertext.

3. Encrypt the preceding cipher block. 0x38F01321 . . . becomes 0x9D44BA16 . . . .

4. XOR the plaintext with the encrypted preceding cipher block, and continue in the same manner.

Feedback widths less than a full block are possible, but for security reasons they're not recommended. OFB mode has an advantage over CFB mode in that any bit errors that might occur during transmission are not propagated to affect the decryption of subsequent blocks. Furthermore, this mode can be programmed to take advantage of precomputations to speed the process. In CBC and CFB, you can't do the next step until completing the preceding step. Here, you can compute cipher blocks before computing the XOR or loading the next block of plaintext.

A problem with OFB mode is that the plaintext is easily manipulated. An attacker who knows a plaintext block m_i can replace it with a false plaintext block x by computing m_i XOR x to the corresponding ciphertext block c_i. Similar attacks can be used against CBC and CFB modes, but in those attacks some plaintext blocks will be modified in a manner that the attacker can't predict. Yet the very first ciphertext block (the initialization vector) in CBC mode and the very last ciphertext block in CFB mode are just as vulnerable to the attack as the blocks in OFB mode. Attacks of this kind can be prevented using, for example, a digital signature scheme or a MAC scheme.

Counter Mode*

Because of shortcomings in OFB mode, Whitfield Diffie has proposed an additional mode of operation termed *counter* mode. It differs from OFB mode in the way the successive data blocks are generated for subsequent

---

*(Source: RSA Labs)

encryptions. Instead of deriving one data block as the encryption of the preceding data block, Diffie proposes encrypting the quantity i + IV mod block bits for the ith data block.

Here's how it works. First, encrypt the IV and XOR it with the first block of plaintext. Now add 1 to the IV (if the IV were 0xFF FF ... FF, the addition would produce 0x00 00 ... 00; that's what the mod block bits means). Encrypt this new block, and XOR it with the next block of plaintext. If the cipher uses 8-byte blocks and the first block of data is "Goal #14," then counter mode would look like this:

1. Encrypt the IV to produce the cipher block. IV = 0xA722B551 041A3C96 becomes 0x38F01321 7922E09B.

2. XOR the plaintext with the encrypted IV. Goal #14 = 0x476F616C 20233134 becomes 0x7F9F724D 5901D1AF, which is the ciphertext.

3. Encrypt IV + 1. 0xA722B551 041A3C97 becomes 0x674B9B01 CFA38027.

4. XOR the plaintext with the encrypted IV + 1, and repeat the process.

Cryptanalysis of this method continues, but most cryptographers express confidence that counter mode will be a good alternative to CBC because this feedback mode can take advantage of precomputations and hence speed the process.

How to Plug Information Leaks from IV and Salts

One concern of cryptographers is the concept of leaking information. For example, the IV for a block cipher and the salt in PBE are not secret. Anyone eavesdropping on a digital conversation protected by a block cipher with a feedback mode will know what the IV is. Someone who finds a password-protected session key will know the salt. That's no problem because knowing the IV or salt does not help an attacker. But where did that IV and salt come from? A PRNG? The same PRNG that produced the session key? If it did, it means that the program has leaked information about the session key. The session key is related to the IV or salt (or both), and the attacker knows what those values are.

Certainly if the PRNG uses a good digest with an internal state, knowledge of the IV or salt will not lead the attacker to the session key. Even though a relationship exists between the values, an attacker will not be able to exploit that relationship.

Nonetheless, information is leaking, and it's extremely simple to plug the hole. When you generate a session key, you use a PRNG with a good seed. For the IV or salt, you use a different PRNG seeded with the time of day.

You want every IV and salt you use to be unique. To do that, you use a different PRNG with a different salt each time. The time will be different for each instance, so there is a simple seed that will guarantee a different salt and IV each time. In Chapter 2, you saw that the time alone is a poor seed. That's because you don't want the attacker to do a brute force attack on the seed to reconstruct the PRNG and then reproduce the secrets generated by the PRNG. But if the thing generated by the PRNG is public, it doesn't matter whether the attacker can reproduce the seed. Knowledge of the seed in this case allows the attacker only to reconstruct a PRNG and reproduce values that have already been made public.

So to avoid leaking information, you use two PRNGs: one for generating secrets, and another one for generating salts and IVs. For performance reasons, you shouldn't waste time collecting a good seed for the PRNG that generates the salt and IV; simply use the time. It's fast, and it guarantees different output each time you use the PRNG.

Tamper-resistant Hardware*

In Chapter 3, you learned that some hardware devices are built to be tamper-resistant. Usually this means that they detect when someone is trying to access data through some means other than normal channels. How can these devices be made tamper-resistant?

Many techniques are used to make hardware tamper-resistant. Some of these techniques are intended to thwart direct attempts at opening a device and reading information from its memory; others offer protection against subtler attacks, such as timing attacks and induced hardware-fault attacks.

---

*(Source: RSA Labs)

At a very high level, here are a few general techniques used to make devices tamper-resistant:

- Employing sensors of various types (for example, light, temperature, and resistivity sensors) to detect malicious probing
- Packing device circuitry as densely as possible (dense circuitry makes it difficult for attackers to use a logic probe effectively)
- Using error-correcting memory
- Using nonvolatile memory so that the device can tell whether it has been reset (or how many times it has been reset)
- Using redundant processors to perform calculations and ensuring that all the calculated answers agree before outputting a result

RSA Padding

Chapter 4 describes the RSA digital envelope, in which a session key is encrypted with an RSA public key. The RSA public exponent is often 3, which means that to encrypt data, you treat the session key as a number and raise it to the 3rd power modulo the modulus. That's the same as finding $s \times s \times s \bmod n$, where s is the session key as a number, and n is the modulus. Most RSA keys are 1,024 bits, so the modulus is 1,024 bits long.

Modular multiplication means that the answer will always be less than the modulus. You compute the product, and if it is less than the modulus, there's no more work; if it's greater than the modulus, you reduce the result. To reduce a number means that you divide the intermediate result by the modulus and take the remainder as the answer. For example,

$$10 \times 10 \bmod 35 = 100 \bmod 35 = \text{rem}\,(100 \times 35) = 30$$

Because 10×35 is 2 with a remainder of 30 ($100 - 2 \times 35 = 100 - 70$), the answer is 30. The number 100 has been reduced to 30 modulo 35.

This reduction is essentially the reason RSA (and Diffie-Hellman and DSA) is secure. You compute an intermediate value and then reduce it. The attacker may know what the reduction is, but what was the intermediate value? If the attacker knows the intermediate value, it would not be hard to find the original number, but for each final number there are simply far too many possible intermediate values. That is, with big enough keys, any one of trillions upon trillions of intermediate values produces the same final answer, and each intermediate value comes from a different starting point. A 1,024-bit modulus means that there are about 2^{1024} possible starting points, so there are about 2^{1024} possible intermediate values an attacker would have to examine to find the correct one. You saw in Chapter 2 how long it would take to examine 2^{128} keys, so you can imagine that using brute force to find the correct intermediate value among 2^{1024} possible numbers is not a viable option. That's why attackers would use other mathematical techniques, such as factoring or solving the discrete log problem, to break the algorithm, but those other techniques also take millions of years.

When you multiply two numbers, the size of the result is the sum of the sizes of the operands (or possibly one bit less). Assuming the session key you're encrypting is 128 bits long (the most common session key size), the size of $s \times s$ is 256. Because the RSA modulus is 1,024 bits long, the product $s \times s$ is smaller than the modulus, so no reduction is necessary. Finally, $s \times (s \times s)$ will be a 384-bit number (a 128-bit number times a 256-bit number). That, too, is less than the modulus, so no reduction is necessary.

So if you found $s \times s \times s \bmod n$, you would not do any reductions, and an attacker would know the intermediate value (it's the final result) and would be able to compute the original number s. The solution to this problem is to pad the data (see also Chapter 2). Here's how. Start with s, but make it a bigger number so that when finding $s \times s \times s$, you create intermediate answers larger than n and you have to reduce. Of course, you must pad in such a way that when decrypting, the recipient knows what the pad bytes are and can throw them away.

PKCS #1 Block 02 Padding

The most common padding scheme for RSA is defined in the Public Key Cryptography Standard #1 (PKCS #1; see the accompanying CD). It works like this. Start with a block that is the same size as the modulus. If the modulus is 1,024 bits, the block is 128 bytes long. The session key will fill 16 of those bytes (assuming that the session key is 128 bits), and this means that you'll need 112 bytes of padding. The padding comes first, followed by the key. So the first 112 bytes of the block are padding, and the last 16 bytes are the session key.

The first byte of padding is 00, the next byte is 02, and then the next 109 bytes are random or pseudo-random values, none of which can be 00. Finally, the 112th byte of padding is 00. If the session key were

```
FF FF FF FF    FF FF FF FF    FF FF FF FF    FF FF FF FF
```

then a padded block might look like this:

```
00 02 D0 CE 21 83 41 73 F6 84 32 06 A8 A6 AD 13
2B 65 27 86 28 EF 0E 8C CA 4F 20 C0 19 95 fE 6C
3E 69 1A 49 9C B7 CE 80 8A 9D C7 3D EC 6F 64 3A
A5 65 A0 A4 35 9A CA D4 CB CD 1D C8 60 6B E2 7F
2B BD 27 E1 47 F2 18 F0 65 41 9E 0D 1A CD B4 3D
24 14 C4 78 A6 A6 F3 1E 07 61 B6 C4 49 A0 77 18
BB 0E C7 72 E3 F1 79 1C 02 90 23 04 82 69 63 00
FF FF FF FF FF FF FF FF FF FF FF FF FF FF FF FF
```

This block, then, becomes the value to encrypt. Cubing this number (cubing means to multiply a number by itself three times) will produce a number larger than the modulus, so reduction is necessary. The answer (ciphertext) might look something like this.

```
A0 2E 7D bE 8F 7A 3B DD 04 01 26 03 CC AF F5 7F
34 3F 49 22 C4 DC 48 09 E8 33 3B B0 59 DA D2 E7
B3 38 23 A7 D6 EB F1 B7 ED 3C 7B 45 81 4E 4F 3C
F4 BC 93 42 A8 8E 02 A9 05 1A fB 81 3E 8F 06 05
22 F3 90 9F 9B 35 13 A6 89 EC C3 5F 3F 6F 1D 9F
54 DE CB C0 0F F3 2F FF 1B 45 CA 80 B6 69 63 DF
54 C1 A7 B4 A2 D6 F5 53 E5 5D F1 D5 B9 F4 9E 5F
74 4C CD 72 C1 29 B7 FF D5 29 05 13 AD 04 BA 15
```

The recipient would decrypt this and recover the original padded value. That individual (more precisely, the recipient's software) would then need to *unpad,* or throw away the pad bytes, keeping only the session key. The first byte is 00, and the second byte is 02; those are simple—throw them away. Now throw away all the ensuing bytes that are not 00: the 109 random or pseudo-random numbers. The padding routine must never use 00 as one of those bytes, so during unpadding, the end of the padding is easy to spot; it's the first instance of 00. When the unpad routine reaches 00, it knows there's no more padding. It throws away the 00, and the rest of the bytes are the session key.

The Bleichenbacher Attack

In 1998, Daniel Bleichenbacher, a cryptographer at Bell Labs, came up with an attack against PKCS #1 Block 02 padding. This attack takes advantage of the fact that the decryptor looks for specific bytes in specific locations. After decryption, the recipient will see whether the first byte is 00 and the second byte is 02 and whether there is a 00 after some random values.

Suppose that Ray, our attacker from Chapter 3, has an encrypted message from Pao-Chi to Gwen. If Ray can decrypt the RSA digital envelope portion of the communication, he will have the session key and can decrypt the message. Here's how the attack works. First, Ray computes a bogus RSA digital envelope that looks like Pao-Chi's envelope. To do that, Ray uses a special mathematical formula and uses as input Pao-Chi's correct envelope and a random or pseudo-random number (for details, see the RSA Labs Bulletin number 7, June 26, 1998, written by Daniel Bleichenbacher, Burt Kaliski, and Jessica Staddon). Ray then sends the substitute envelope to Gwen. If Gwen responds by saying that something went wrong, that the envelope didn't unwrap properly, Ray uses the same formula to create a new, different envelope using Pao-Chi's envelope and a different number (probably just the previous number plus 1) and sends the new envelope to Gwen. When an envelope unwraps improperly, it means that the first byte is not 00, or the second byte is not 02, or maybe there's no 00 to indicate the end of padding. Ray continues to send fake envelopes to Gwen until she responds by saying the envelope unwrapped properly.

When Ray has a fake envelope that works, he can figure out what Pao-Chi's original envelope is. The fake envelope and Pao-Chi's are related; Ray created the fake one based on the correct one and a number he chose. He uses this relationship to break the encryption. This technique does not break the private key; rather, it recovers only one envelope. Ray's fake envelope, when decrypted, does not produce the same thing Pao-Chi encrypted; rather, the result is something that simply looks like a digital envelope. It has the leading 00 02, and somewhere along the line there's another 00 to indicate the end of the padding. Gwen (or rather the software she uses to open the envelope) simply assumes that the numbers following this second 00, whatever those numbers happen to be, make up a session key. They don't—this is a bogus envelope—but to Gwen it looks like a legitimate envelope because all the marker bytes are there in the correct location.

Bleichenbacher's research indicates that Ray will probably need to send about 1,000,000 (one million) fake envelopes to recover one message. In some situations, he might even need to send 20,000,000 fake envelopes.

This attack is not likely to work using e-mail because Ray would have to wait for Gwen to open the one million e-mails and send a response to each one, and eventually Gwen would stop trying to open any e-mail from Ray. But it might work if the recipient is using an automated responder. An example is an SSL server that simply responds to "hits," sending an error message when something goes wrong and opening a session when all goes right.

There are simple ways to thwart this attack (see the bulletin previously cited), and in fact, the SSL specification has a built-in countermeasure. It is probably safe, in the real world, to continue using PKCS #1 Block 02 padding when you're creating digital envelopes. However, if you want to avoid this attack, you can use a different padding scheme. The next section describes a padding scheme that's immune to the Bleichenbacher attack.

Optimal Asymmetric Encryption Padding

In 1995, two cryptographers-Mihir Bellare of the University of California at San Diego and Phillip Rogaway of the University of California at Davis-proposed a new way to pad RSA digital envelopes. They named this technique *Optimal Asymmetric Encryption Padding* (OAEP).

Suppose the RSA key is 1,024 bits and the session key is 128 bits. You create a buffer of 128 bytes (the same size as the RSA modulus) and place the session key at the end, just as in PKCS #1 Block 02. You now need 112 bytes of padding to precede the session key. The first byte is 00. The next 20 bytes, known as the seed, are random or pseudo-random. The next 20 bytes are the SHA-1 digest of some known data. (This known data is part of the algorithm identifier, the information you pass to the recipient indicating what you did to create the envelope.) The next 70 bytes are all 00, and then the last pad byte is 01. For example, assuming the session key is 16 bytes of 0xFF, at this point, you would have something that looks like this.

```
00 14 86 6A 90 11 B4 DE 48 66 25 03 9B E2 57 F5
2B BD 27 E1 47 F2 18 F0 65 41 9E 0D 1A CD B4 3D
24 C4 78 A6 A6 F3 1E 07 61 00 00 00 00 00 00 00
00 00 00 00 00 00 00 00 00 00 00 00 00 00 00 00
00 00 00 00 00 00 00 00 00 00 00 00 00 00 00 00
00 00 00 00 00 00 00 00 00 00 00 00 00 00 00 00
00 00 00 00 00 00 00 00 00 00 00 00 00 00 00 01
FF FF FF FF FF FF FF FF FF FF FF FF FF FF FF FF
```

You're not finished yet. From the seed, you create a mask 107 bytes long. The mask-generating function is based on SHA-1. Then, you XOR the mask with next 107 bytes, which are the digest, all the 00 bytes, the 01, and the session key. In the following, the underlined values have been masked.

```
00 14 86 6A 90 11 B4 DE 48 66 25 03 9B E2 57 F5
2B BD 27 E1 47 36 C2 B2 3A 61 C8 B8 86 20 30 1C
B9 C5 fD 13 E3 bE 37 9C F5 EF 79 1C 02 90 23 04
82 69 63 AA AF 37 30 64 66 D6 CD AF 35 58 99 BC
6F 3C 7E 14 AE 9D D1 FB F7 D1 F6 97 93 D9 B0 A6
8A D8 C4 44 87 F2 EC 77 EE 2D 9B F8 41 02 D8 50
23 00 57 49 EF D1 61 98 41 51 4D C8 A6 4D 74 A7
19 E4 4D 80 86 A9 6F AB 1E 57 98 B2 41 59 2F EA
```

Finally, you use this resulting value (the 107 bytes after the XOR operation) as a second seed to create a mask for the original seed. Then you XOR the original seed with this new mask.

```
00 8B 60 80 FE DE CA AF 72 77 4E 46 32 4D 6A F1
E3 82 37 5C DA 36 C2 B2 3A 61 C8 B8 86 20 30 1C
B9 C5 fD 13 E3 bE 37 9C F5 EF 79 1C 02 90 23 04
82 69 63 AA AF 37 30 64 66 D6 CD AF 35 58 99 BC
6F 3C 7E 14 AE 9D D1 FB F7 D1 F6 97 93 D9 B0 A6
8A D8 C4 44 87 F2 EC 77 EE 2D 9B F8 41 02 D8 50
23 00 57 49 EF D1 61 98 41 51 4D C8 A6 4D 74 A7
19 E4 4D 80 86 A9 6F AB 1E 57 98 B2 41 59 2F EA
```

The result looks random. To unpad, you skip the first 21 bytes (the decryptor knows the first byte is 00 and the next 20 bytes are the seed). You use the rest of the data as a seed (this is the second seed) to create a mask. You XOR this mask with the 20 bytes after the first byte (remember, the first byte is 00). Now you've reconstructed the original seed. You use the original seed to create a mask to XOR with the remaining 107 bytes. Then, you digest the known data and compare it to the 20 bytes after the seed. Also, you check to make sure that the next 70 bytes are all 00 and that the last byte before the session key is 01. If all these checks pass, the recipient has the session key.

OAEP has some variants. Different digest algorithms with different seed sizes are possible. The first byte might be a random byte instead of 00 (although there are mathematical limitations on what that byte can be).

Using this padding scheme means that a Bleichenbacher attack will almost certainly fail. The chances that someone could create a fake envelope that produces a valid OAEP block are so astronomically small that it will virtually never happen. The reason is the digesting. Remember that digest algorithms produce dramatically different output when the input is changed, even slightly. A fake envelope would have to decrypt to something that by sheer chance created some digests that, after the XOR operation, created the 70 bytes of 00 followed by the one byte of 01 in the appropriate place.

Timing Attacks

How long does it take for your computer to perform a private-key operation (creating a digital signature or opening a digital envelope)? It turns out that there are slight variations in the amount of time needed to perform asymmetric algorithm operations. The actual time is dependent on the key itself and the input data.

Here's what we mean. Take two private keys, both of them the same algorithm (RSA, DH, DSA, or ECC) and the same size. Now perform the same operation (sign, encrypt, key agree) with the same data. How long *exactly* did each operation take? With one key it might take 0.2007415517 milliseconds, and with the second 0.2007415548 milliseconds. The difference is tiny, but there is a difference.

Or suppose that the time can be computed in cycles. One key makes the computation in 90,288,451 cycles, and another key uses 90,289,207 cycles. If you're not familiar with computer cycles, one cycle is one "tick" of the computer's internal clock. A hertz is one cycle per second, so a 450 megahertz (450MHz) computer can operate at 450 million cycles per second. Most processors can perform one integer addition in one cycle and one integer multiplication in two to six cycles (some processors might need 27 cycles to do one integer multiplication). So a 450MHz processor could do 450 million additions or 75 million to 225 million multiplications in one second. Actually, it gets complicated with pipelining and multiprocessing and integer units and floating-point units, but the point is that time can be measured in cycles as well as seconds.

However time is measured, the variations in time can aid an attacker. Knowing the input data (for example, what you're signing) and exactly how long it took you to perform the private-key operation (such as signing), an attacker can gain information about your private key. This is known as a *timing attack*. The attacker almost certainly needs timings from many private-key operations (each operation working on different input data) to figure out the entire key. The more exact the time, the fewer data points the attacker needs.

Highly controlled experiments on simple machines running simple software implementations have had some success in measuring the times of various operations. More success has been found timing tokens and other slow processors. But often the experiments have required hundreds if not thousands of timings to collect enough information on a particular key. Furthermore, using the *Chinese Remainder Theorem* (CRT; see Chapter 4) for RSA operations and Montgomery multiplication helps thwart the attack. (Peter Montgomery is a researcher who came up with a clever way to perform the internal operations of RSA, DH, DSA, and some ECC much faster.) Data and instruction caching may skew the measurements. Another way to defeat this attack is to prevent the attacker from knowing the input, an approach known as *blinding*. The attacker knows what the input is, but if you alter it before signing and then alter the resulting signature to compensate for the original alteration, the exact data operated on by the private key is unknown. Unfortunately, blinding is a drain on performance, adding another 40 percent to the total signature time.

In real-world applications, a timing attack may not be practical because virtually all current implementations of RSA employ CRT and the implementations of all public-key algorithms employ Montgomery math. Furthermore, attackers often have no way of knowing how long it took to perform the operation, or the measurements were not accurate enough. Possibly the target did not make enough private-key computations before changing keys.

In some situations, a timing attack may be more practical. One example is an SSL server performing private-key operations automatically. An attacker could request an SSL connection and time the response and then repeat the request, time the response again, and so on hundreds or thousands of times. For each SSL connection, the server creates a digital signature, each time signing something different. This is exactly what the attacker needs: knowledge of the data being signed, different data being signed each time, and many iterations.

No one has demonstrated a successful timing attack in real-world situations, including an attack on an SSL server. CRT and Montgomery math may be all that's needed to prevent a successful attack, or other operations may mask the signature time. But you may need to be aware of the possibility of a timing attack, especially if, in the future, you use a smart card in someone else's reader. In that case, blinding may become a prudent countermeasure.

Kerberos*

In Chapter 5, you learned about authentication using digital signatures. You may have heard about Kerberos, an alternative authenticating technique.

Kerberos is an authentication service developed by the Project Athena team at MIT, based on a 1978 paper by Roger Needham and Michael Schroeder. The first general-use version was version 4. Version 5, which addressed certain shortfalls in version 4, was released in 1994. Kerberos uses secret-key ciphers for encryption and authentication. Version 4 used only DES. Unlike a public-key authentication system, Kerberos does not produce digital signatures. Instead, Kerberos was designed to authenticate requests for network resources rather than to authenticate authorship of documents. Thus, Kerberos does not provide for future third-party verification of documents.

In a Kerberos system, a designated site on each network, called the Kerberos server, performs centralized key management and administration. The server maintains a database containing the secret keys of all users, authenticates the identities of users, and distributes session keys to users and servers that wish to authenticate one another. Kerberos requires trust in a third party (the Kerberos server). If the server is compromised, the integrity of the whole system is lost. Public-key cryptography was designed precisely to avoid the necessity to trust third parties with secrets.

Kerberos is generally considered adequate within an administrative domain; however, across domains, the more robust functions and properties of public-key systems are often preferred. Some developmental work has been done to incorporate public-key cryptography into Kerberos.

For detailed information on Kerberos, read "The Kerberos Network Authentication Service (V5)" (J. Kohl and C. Neuman, RFC 1510) at ftp://ftp.isi.edu/in-notes/rfc1510.txt.

---

*(Source: RSA Labs)

DH, ECDH, DSA, and ECDSA Certificates

In Chapter 6, you learned about certificates. The minimum contents of a certificate are the owner's name, public key, and the CAs signature. For RSA, the public key is the modulus and public exponent. For DH, ECDH, DSA, and ECDSA, the public key consists of the system parameters and a public value.

Often, messages contain certificates. For example, if Pao-Chi sends a signed message to Daniel, Daniel needs Pao-Chi's certificate to verify the signature. Pao-Chi can include his certificate as part of the message, saving Daniel the trouble of searching for it in public directories. If Satomi wants to pose as Pao-Chi, she could send a message with a certificate containing Pao-Chi's name but not his true public key. But she will have to get that certificate signed by a CA whose certificate was signed by the root that Daniel will use. Satomi will have to break the root's key to become the root (and hence create her own CA) or break a CA's key to create a valid certificate. That's not likely, so including the certificate in a message is no security problem.

Because messages contain certificates and because larger messages are sometimes expensive, it's often desirable to create smaller certificates. A protocol or company might demand that names be short (for example, that they carry no title, mailing address, fax number, or other such information) or that there be no extensions or attributes.

In the past, people have proposed shrinking public keys. DH, ECDH, DSA, or ECDSA keys can be compressed by excluding the system parameters. Everyone would have to get the system parameters in some other way.

But this is not a good idea. The purpose of a certificate is to guarantee that an attacker could not replace a true public key with a fake one. But if the parameters are not part of the certificate, an attacker could replace the parameters. Someone using a public key extracted from a certificate (creating a digital envelope or verifying a signature) would be certain of using the correct public value but not the correct parameters. If Satomi, for example, replaces the parameters on Pao-Chi's machine and if Pao-Chi tries to send a message to Daniel, he will create something that Daniel cannot read. Satomi almost certainly won't be able to read it either (she would still need to know Daniel's private value), so all she would be doing by changing the parameters would be creating a nuisance. This is a denial-of-service attack because her actions would deny Pao-Chi and Daniel the service of secure communication.

To prevent this problem, the company could enforce a policy in which everyone uses the same system parameters. It could create some system parameters and distribute them to all employees, each of whom would create individual public and private key pairs. This is generally not a security problem; sharing system parameters does not weaken the math. Some cryptographers warn that if "too many" people share system parameters (good luck getting one of those cryptographers to quantify "too many"), it might be possible to introduce weaknesses, but for the most part, sharing parameters does not aid an attacker. In such a situation, Satomi could not replace the system parameters on Pao-Chi's machine because he would know what the true parameters were; they're his. Presumably, Pao-Chi will have those parameters protected in such a way that Satomi could not alter them without his knowledge.

This parameters policy could work for communications among all the employees at Pao-Chi's company, but how could people outside the company guarantee a public key's authenticity? Everyone else would also need the system parameters. Suppose the company created a second certificate, this one for the parameters. That would mean two certificates would be required to verify one public key, defeating the purpose of saving space.

The best way to distribute DH, ECDH, DSA, and ECDSA keys is to include the system parameters in the certificate.

Problems with Using SSL to Protect Credit Cards

Chapter 7 describes the *Secure Socket Layer* (SSL), the latest version of which is known as *Transport Layer Security* (TLS). Many companies use SSL exclusively to protect credit card transactions. Unfortunately, that may not be a wise policy.

SSL encrypts data while in transit, so if someone runs a sniffer program on the Internet—checking traffic to see whether any credit card numbers are sent in the clear—SSL will protect the transaction. However, credit card numbers sent over the Internet usually are not stolen in transit; instead, they are stolen while in storage. Rather than eavesdropping on Internet messages, thieves break into servers storing sensitive material.

When you operate a Web site, you're essentially making your local files available for the world to see. Recall the discussion of permissions in Chapter 1. You can set the permissions on your files so that only certain users have read or write access to them. A Web server has, in effect, set the read permission on many of its files to the entire world.

One mistake made by companies is to store the credit card numbers on the Web server. In fact, an MSNBC reporter discovered that on January 13, 2000, when he "was able to view nearly 2,500 credit card numbers stored by seven small e-commerce Web sites within a few minutes, using elementary instructions provided by a source. In all cases, a list of customers and all their personal information was connected to the Internet and either was not password-protected or the password was viewable directly from the Web site." (source: www.msnbc.com) The companies may set the permissions of the files containing the numbers to exclude the world, or they may not. It doesn't matter. As you saw in Chapter 1, simple OS permissions are no real deterrent to the majority of hackers and crackers.

The best policy is to store credit card numbers encrypted. Another possibility is to use a protocol, such as SET, in which credit cards numbers are transmitted using a digital envelope, the public key creating the envelope belonging to the issuing bank. Hence, a merchant never sees the credit card in the clear and can never store it unsecurely. Because SET has not been widely adopted, the credit card companies and banks may devise a new protocol.

One way consumers can protect themselves is to read the security policies of the e-commerce companies from which they might wish to make purchases. The following quotations indicate policies that are less than secure:

> " . . . uses SSL, an advanced encryption technology that protects
> your credit card information."

> "We use Secure Sockets Layer (SSL) technology to protect the
> security of your online order information."

The point is not that SSL has no value but rather that SSL does not address the storage issue. It is not a silver bullet that solves all security problems.

Here is a policy that is starting to get the right idea:

> "To ensure that your information is even more secure, once we
> receive your credit card information, we store it on a server that
> isn't accessible from the Internet."

Finally, here are quotes from a couple of security policies of Web sites that are truly interested in security.

"Every time you send us your credit card number and your billing and shipping information, we use the industry-standard Secure Sockets Layer (SSL) technology to prevent the information from being intercepted. We also encrypt your credit card number when we store your order and whenever we transfer that information to participating merchants."

"Within those systems, sensitive information is encrypted to protect your personal data, like credit card numbers."

Chapter Review

Chapter 1 Review

Chapter Summary

After reading this chapter, the students should understand the following.

Security Provided by Computer Operating Systems

■ Users access data on a computer or network through an operating system (OS).

■ Operating systems have built-in permissions, which provide certain people conditional access to the computer.

■ Login procedures involve a username and password.

■ A system administrator, also known as a superuser, is in charge of creating and closing user accounts, and maintaining the systems and the network.

■ The username of the superuser is generally "root", or "su", or "administrator".

■ A cracker is most likely to succeed by logging on to a network as a superuser.

■ A password-cracking software automates exhaustive password searches.

■ The application 10phtCrack allows system administrators to test the passwords in use by their users.

Attacks that Bypass Operating Systems

- The OS organizes data under a directory file structure, and uses file extensions to direct users to the data they want on the hard disk.
- The process of reconstructing the lost or damaged files on a disk, in the event of a computer failure or natural disaster, is called data recovery.
- In the event of serious disk-drive failures, data recovery may be possible only through specialized hardware devices.
- A memory reconstruction attack involves an examination by an attacker of previously allocated computer memory that is freed when a program ends. The memory managers in many operating systems use the hard drive as virtual memory. It temporarily copies to the hard drive any data from the memory that has been allocated but is not being used.
- In UNIX, the OS "dumps core" in response to certain system errors.

Added Protection Through Cryptography

- Password protection, though widely used, is not adequate.
- Cryptography encrypts data and adds security to the process of authenticating people's identity.
- Cryptographic techniques for providing data secrecy can be adapted to create strong digital identities.

The Role of Cryptography in Data Security

- Privacy involves ensuring that no one can break into files to read sensitive data.
- Data integrity is a mechanism that alarms users if something has been altered.
- The practice of authentication is used to verify identities.
- Nonrepudiation is the legal driving force that impels people to honor their word.
- Cryptography is not foolproof; all crypto can be broken, and if implemented incorrectly, it adds no real security.

Key Terms

Hacker   A person who breaks into computer networks to steal information, commit vandalism, or disrupt service. They are also known as crackers.

Cracker   A person who breaks into computer networks to steal information, commit vandalism, or disrupt service. They are also known as hackers.

Permissions   Permissions allow only certain people to access a computer. Certain built-in permissions exist in all operating systems.

Login procedure   The login procedure involves checking for the appropriate credentials, usually a username and a password, of a user.

System administrator   The person charged with creating and closing user accounts, and maintaining the systems and network.

Password cracking software   Applications that automate exhaustive password searches.

Read-protected file   A file that cannot be opened and read.

Directory file structure   The OS organizes data under a directory file structure.

File extensions   File extensions direct users to the data they want on the hard disk.

Data recovery   The process of reconstructing the lost or damaged files on a disk, in the event of a computer failure or natural disaster.

Core dump   A term used for a program exiting ungracefully in response to certain errors.

Memory reconstruction attack   An examination by an attacker of previously allocated computer memory that is freed when a program ends.

Virtual memory   The hard disk is used as virtual memory in many operating systems. The memory manager temporarily copies to the hard disk any data from memory that has been allocated but is momentarily not being used.

Cryptography   The process of encrypting data to protect it.

Data integrity   This mechanism alarms users when some data has been altered.

Privacy   This process ensures that no one can break into files to read sensitive data.

Nonrepudiation   The legal driving force that impels people to honor their word.

Key Terms Quiz

Use the Key Terms list to complete the sentences that follow. (Not all terms will be used.)

1. _____ is the process of encrypting data to protect it.

2. User access to a computer is permitted via a _____.

3. A _____ is a person in charge of creating and closing user accounts.

4. Applications that automate exhaustive password searches are called

_____.

5. The structure that the OS uses to organize data is called a _____.

6. The _____ process helps prevent total loss of data on a disk, in the event of a natural disaster or computer failure.

7. The memory managers in many operating systems use the hard drive as _____ memory.

8. In UNIX systems, the term _____ has become synonymous with a program exiting ungracefully in response to certain errors.

9. _____ allow only certain users access to the computer.

10. The mechanism that alarms users when some data has been altered is called _____.

Multiple-Choice Quiz

1. Which of the following options is not an operating system?
   a. DOS
   b. Linux
   c. Windows 95
   d. Word 95

2. A system administrator is also known as a _____.
   a. base user
   b. encryptor
   c. security analyst
   d. superuser

3. _____ software automates exhaustive password searches.
   a. Automation
   b. Authentication
   c. Password-cracking
   d. Password-searching

4. The application 10phtCrack is used for _____.
   a. automating exhaustive password searches
   b. gaining illegal entry into university networks
   c. assigning a student with a username and password
   d. testing the passwords in use by the network users

5. An operating system uses _____ to direct users to the data they want on the hard disk.
   a. directories
   b. encryption
   c. file extensions
   d. passwords

6. A(n) _____ attack involves an examination of previously allocated computer memory that is freed when a program ends.
   a. file lock
   b. infringement
   c. memory reconstruction
   d. password test

7. Cryptographic techniques for providing data secrecy can be adapted to create strong _____ identities.

    a.   binary

    b.   digital

    c.   public key

    d.   private key

8. The term _____ is the legal driving force that impels people to honor their word.

    a.   authentication

    b.   data encryption

    c.   nonrepudiation

    d.   privacy

9. The practice of _____ is used to verify identities.

    a.   authentication

    b.   data encryption

    c.   encryption

    d.   nonrepudiation

10. Which of the following is not applicable to the product Inspector Copier?

    a.   It is manufactured by Reynolds Data Recovery.

    b.   It performs data recovery.

    c.   It swaps the current virtual memory for the real memory.

    d.   It does not reference the OS installed on the devices.

11. The user name of a(n) _____ is usually "root".

    a.   base user

    b.   encryptor

    c.   security analyst

    d.   system administrator

12. Which of the following statements is not applicable to a system administrator?

    a.   They are also known as superusers.

    b.   They have permission to circumvent the OS permissions.

    c.   The username of the system administrator is usually "root".

    d.   They encrypt system data.

13. The _____ technique can be used by attackers to circumvent OS protections.

    a.   data encryption

    b.   data mirroring

    c.   data recovery

    d.   data analysis

14. The username and password of a guest account is _____, respectively.

    a.   admin and admin

    b.   admin and guest

    c. guest and admin
    d. guest and guest

15. People who break into computer networks to steal information are known as
_____.

    a. crackers
    b. encryptors
    c. users
    d. sys admins

Essay Quiz

1. How do operating systems function?
2. What are the ways in which a cracker logs on to a system?
3. Explain the limitations of cryptography in data security.

Lab Projects

Lab Project 1.1

Michael, the system administrator at Zenstro Micro Systems, needs to test the strength of the passwords applied by the network users. List the ways he can do this.

Lab Project 1.2

Zenstro Micro Systems provides credit card verification and validation for customers of a major bank. The employees of Zenstro Micro Systems are required to compare and validate information received over the net with the data residing on their database. The company is setting up its intranet. Which security mechanisms should the network administrator employ to ensure authorized access and confidentiality of the data being transmitted over the network?

Chapter 2 Review

Chapter Summary

After reading this chapter, the students should understand the following.

Understanding the Basics of Symmetric-Key Cryptography

■ Symmetric-key cryptography, also known as secret-key cryptography, is a method of cryptography that uses the same key for both encryption and decryption.

■ Encryption is the process of converting sensitive data to gibberish, while decryption is the process of converting gibberish to the original data.

- An algorithm, which is a list of instructions to be performed in a particular order, is used for encryption and decryption.
- The data to be kept secret is called plaintext or cleartext.
- The encrypted data is called ciphertext.
- A key is a number or a set of numbers that the algorithm uses to convert plaintext into ciphertext.
- The study of breaking cryptographic systems is called cryptanalysis.
- The cryptographer develops crypto systems, while the cryptanalyst looks for weaknesses in algorithms.
- A key is a number or a set of numbers that the algorithm uses to convert plaintext into ciphertext. In symmetric-key cryptography, the key is made up of only numbers, and the same key is used to encrypt and decrypt data.
- Different keys can be used for different data files.
- A random number generator (RNG) is a device that generates random numbers based on unpredictable inputs, such that the numbers are unrepeatable.
- A pseudo-random number generator (PRNG) is an algorithm that generates repeatable numbers based on inputs, called seeds. To pass the test of randomness, the seed must change each time a new number is to be generated.
- The reasons for using a PRNG, instead of just using a seed, include its speed, and entropy, which is chaos. The greater the entropy, the more random the output.
- Most PRNGs use message digests to perform their functions.

Attacks on Encrypted Data

- To decrypt data, an attacker must either identify the key or break the algorithm.
- In a brute-force attack, the attacker tries every possible key until the right key is identified.
- Cryptographic keys are measured in bits, and the range of possible keys is called the key size.
- The most commonly used symmetric-key size is 128 bits.
- Longer keys are more secure.
- A known-plaintext attack is a type of attack in which the attacker computes the key from a chunk of ciphertext and deciphers its corresponding plaintext.
- The best strategy to prevent attacks on encrypted data is to select a strong algorithm, and further deter an attacker by using a longer key.

Symmetric Algorithms: The Key Table

- All symmetric ciphers use the key to build a key table in a process known as key setup or initialization.

- A key table is a pseudo-random array of a particular size in a particular format. The key table does the encryption.

- The algorithm produces a good scramble with a good key table, and the resultant ciphertext is very different from the original plaintext, thus preventing exploitation of the algorithm's weakness by an attacker.

Symmetric Algorithms: Block Versus Stream Ciphers

- There are two types of symmetric-key algorithms: block ciphers and stream ciphers.

- A block cipher operates on blocks of data that are 8 to 16 bytes long. Block ciphers break the plaintext into blocks and operate on each block independently.

- Adding extra bytes to an incomplete block of data to make it complete is known as padding.

- The most common feedback mode is cipher block chaining (CBC).

- Stream ciphers are very similar to one-time pads.

- A stream cipher uses an algorithm that generates a pad based on the key. This is generated on-the-fly, only when needed.

- Stream ciphers use the XOR operation for encryption and decryption.

- Stream ciphers are much faster and use far less code as compared to block ciphers.

- If key reusability is desired, use a block cipher.

- If interoperability is desired, use the Advanced Encryption Standard (AES) algorithm, which is a block cipher.

- If speed is desired, use a stream cipher.

Digital Encryption Standard

- Digital Encryption Standard (DES) is a block cipher that uses a 56-bit key to build a key table.

- DES uses the key table to perform bit manipulations on plaintext.

- Triple DES, a widely used replacement for DES, uses three keys of 56 bits each. Triple DES performs the algorithm three times; however, it is very slow, and thus reduces application performance.

- In response to the cryptanalytic weakness and performance problems of Triple DES, commercial companies developed new block ciphers. These include RC2 and RC5, IDEA, Cast, Safer, and Blowfish.

- The commercial DES replacements use algorithms that can operate on variable-sized and bigger keys, and are much faster than Triple DES.

- The AES algorithm is expected to become the worldwide algorithm standard.

Key Terms

Cryptography   The process of converting readable data into gibberish, with the ability to recover the original data from the gibberish.

Symmetric-key cryptography   An algorithm uses a key to convert information into gibberish, which looks like random bits. Then the same algorithm uses the same key to recover the original data. It is also called secret-key cryptography.

Secret-key cryptography   An algorithm uses a key to convert information into gibberish, which looks like random bits. Then the same algorithm uses the same key to recover the original data. It is also called symmetric-key cryptography.

Encryption   The process of converting sensitive data into gibberish, which looks like random bits.

Decryption   The process of converting gibberish, which looks like random bits into the original data.

Secret number   The number that must be inputted into a program to encrypt and decrypt a file, without which the program will not run.

Plaintext   The data that the user wants to keep secret. Also called cleartext.

Cleartext   The data that the user wants to keep secret. Also called plaintext.

Ciphertext   The data that is encrypted is called ciphertext.

Algorithm   A list of instructions to be performed in a particular order. It uses a key to convert information into random bits and recover the original data.

Key   A number or a set of numbers that the algorithm uses to convert plaintext into ciphertext. Cryptographic keys are measured in terms of bits.

Cryptanalysis   The study of breaking cryptographic systems.

Cryptanalyst   A person who looks for weaknesses in cryptography algorithms.

Cryptographer   A person who develops crypto systems.

Rubber-hose attack   The cryptanalytic technique to determine the origin of an algorithm, whether it originates in a mathematical operation or in a machine.

Binary   Numbers that are in a sequence of 1's and 0's.

Random number generator (RNG)   A device that generates random numbers based on unpredictable inputs, such that the numbers are unrepeatable.

Pseudo-random number generator (PRNG)   An algorithm that generates repeatable numbers based on inputs, called seeds. To pass the test of randomness, the seed must change each time a new number is to be generated.

Message digests   A device that takes recognizable bits and bytes and mixes them up into a random, unrecognizable blob. Most PRNGs use message digests.

Brute-force attack A type of attack in which the attacker tries every possible key until the right key is identified.

Key size The range of possible keys.

Padding data Adding extra bytes to an incomplete block to make it complete.

Known plaintext attack A type of attack in which the attacker computes the key from a chunk of ciphertext and deciphers its corresponding plaintext.

Key table A pseudo-random array of a particular size in a particular format.

Key value Keys of varying lengths are sometimes used. In such cases, the algorithm needs a key value that is the same size from one use to the next.

Key setup The process of building a key table. It is also called initialization.

Initialization The process of building a key table. It is also called key setup.

Block cipher A type of symmetric-key algorithm that operates on blocks of data.

Stream cipher A type of symmetric-key algorithm, very similar to a one-time pad.

Key stream In cryptography, the "pad" is known as a key stream.

Key Terms Quiz

Use the Key Terms list to complete the sentences that follow. (Not all terms will be used.)

1. Symmetric-key cryptography is also known as _____.

2. Converting sensitive data into junk value requires the use of a(n)

_____.

3. Plaintext is also known as _____.

4. An algorithm encrypts plaintext into ciphertext using a _____.

5. The study of breaking cryptographic systems is known as _____.

6. _____ takes recognizable bits and bytes and mixes them up into a random, unrecognizable blob.

7. In a(n) _____ attack, the attacker tries every possible key until the right key is identified.

8. The type of symmetric-key algorithm that operates on blocks of data is called _____ and the type of symmetric-key algorithm, very similar to a one-time pad, is called _____.

9. The process of building a key table is called _____.

10. In cryptography, the "pad" is known as a _____.

Multiple-Choice Quiz

1. _____ involves converting sensitive data into random bits.

   a. Ciphering
   b. Decryption
   c. Encryption
   d. Replacement

2. The data that the user wants to keep secret is called a(n) _____.

   a. algorithm
   b. ciphertext
   c. key
   d. plaintext

3. After the data is encrypted it is called a(n) _____.

   a. algorithm
   b. ciphertext
   c. key
   d. plaintext

4. A(n) _____ looks for weaknesses in cryptography algorithms.

   a. cryptanalyst
   b. cryptographer
   c. encryptor
   d. decryptor

5. A person who develops crypto systems is called a(n) _____.

   a. cryptanalyst
   b. cryptographer
   c. encryptor
   d. decryptor

6. The main difference between a random number generator and a pseudo-random number generator is that _____.

   a. pseudo-random number generation is very speedy.
   b. pseudo-random numbers are now obsolete.
   c. pseudo-random numbers are repeatable.
   d. random numbers generation works on the concept of entropy.

7. Cryptographic keys are measured in _____.

   a. bits
   b. locks
   c. megahertz
   d. watts

8. In a _____ attack, the attacker computes the key from a chunk of ciphertext and deciphers its corresponding plaintext.

    a. brute-force
    b. known-plaintext
    c. Trojan horse
    d. vulnerability

9. Key setup is also known as _____.

    a. authentication
    b. encryption
    c. initialization
    d. verification

10. Adding extra bytes to an incomplete block of data to complete it is known as

_____.

    a. ciphering
    b. filling
    c. inserting
    d. padding

11. The algorithm _____ came be to be the new standard, known as Advanced Encryption Standard (AES) invented by Belgian researchers.

    a. IDEA
    b. Rijndael
    c. RC4
    d. DEC

12. The most commonly used stream cipher is _____.

    a. Blowfish
    b. DEC
    c. IDEA
    d. RC4

13. If the user needs to reuse keys, _____ ciphers are preferred.

    a. asymmetric
    b. block
    c. streamw
    d. None of the above

14. If interoperability is an issue, _____ algorithms should be used.

    a. AES
    b. DES
    c. RC4
    d. RSA

15. DES is a block cipher that uses a _____-bit key.

   a.   40

   b.   56

   c.   126

   d.   156

16. The most commonly used symmetric-key size is _____ bits.

   a.   40

   b.   56

   c.   128

   d.   156

Essay Quiz

1. How does symmetric cryptography work?

2. What is an RNG?

3. What are the differences between block ciphers and stream ciphers?

Lab Projects

Lab Project 2.1

Blake, the system administrator, wants to implement a higher level of security in his organization. Based on his research, he wants to encrypt sensitive information on the network. List the steps he should follow to encrypt data.

Lab Project 2.2

Ricardo, the system administrator of Helix Systems, is experimenting with the use of ciphers. Identify the right type of ciphers for the following:

1. A Database

2. E-mail

3. SSL

4. File encryption

Give reasons for your choice of cipher.

Chapter 3 Review

Chapter Summary

After reading this chapter, the students should understand the following.

Password-Based Encryption

■ The process of keeping all the keys safe and available for use is known as key management.

■ The key used to encrypt megabytes of information, or bulk data, is generally known as the session key.

■ A session is an instance of encryption.

■ One of the ways to secure the session key is to encrypt it using a symmetric-key algorithm.

■ The process of encrypting the session key itself requires a key. This key is called the key encryption key (KEK).

■ Password-based encryption (PBE) is used to build the KEK.

■ In PBE, a password and a salt is used to build the KEK. The KEK is then used to encrypt the session key.

■ Passwords do not have much entropy. Hence using a mixing algorithm on the password (and salt) ensures that the KEK looks random.

■ The purpose of salt is to prevent precomputations. The salt does not add security; it only prevents a dictionary attack.

■ When the user wants to share the data with other people and keep it stored encrypted, they would have to use both a session key and a KEK.

■ It is also preferable to use both the session key and the KEK since it is much easier to break a password than to break a key.

■ A PBE program will function even with the wrong password. Some of the ways of checking if the password is correct at the time of entering it are salt, eight-byte number, and algorithm identifier.

■ There are two ways to break the PBE: The attacker could use brute-force on the KEK, or the attacker could guess the password.

■ Choose a strong password that does not appear in a dictionary and hence would foil a brute-force attack.

■ Password generators are programs that work like PRNGs but produce keystrokes instead of numbers.

Hardware-Based Key Storage

■ A cryptographic key can be stored on a hardware device, such as a token or crypto accelerator.

■ A token is a tiny computer that stores cryptographic keys.

- Smart card and USB port attachments are the most common types of tokens.
- A token contains a small chip with a processor, an operating system of sorts, and limited input/output, memory, and hard drive storage space.
- The advantage of using tokens is that an attacker does not have access to them, thus greatly reducing the risk of a remote attack.
- Smart cards are simple plastic cards that contain a microprocessor.
- Smart card readers transfer a symmetric key between the smart card and the computer.
- The Universal Serial Bus (USB) port is the industry standard for attaching plug-and-play devices.
- A token can also generate big random passwords and store them.
- Crypto accelerators are larger hardware crypto devices, as compared to tokens. They have specialized chips that perform faster cryptographic operations and store data more securely than general-purpose microprocessors.
- The storage space of a crypto accelerator is not visible. Access using normal channels is very limited. If attackers attempt to open the cover to physically access the hard drive, the device erases itself.
- The limitation of a crypto accelerator is that it is constantly attached to the computer, thereby increasing its vulnerability. On the other hand, tokens are connected only for a few seconds at a time, limiting their vulnerability.
- Tokens and crypto accelerators usually come with a RNG.

Biometrics

- Biometrics is a technique that uses a person's unique physical characteristics to verify their identity.
- The most well-known biometric is the fingerprint.
- Other biometrics include retina scans, voiceprints, and DNA.
- Biometric devices are not widely used due to their high costs and unreliability.

Key Terms

Key management   The process of keeping all the keys safe and available for use.

Dictionary attack   An attacker using precomputed keys from a dictionary, created from common passwords and their associated keys.

Salt   A tiny bit of near-random data inserted where too much regularity would be undesirable. A cryptographic salt is used to prevent dictionary attacks.

Key encryption key (KEK)   The key used to encrypt the session key.

Password-based encryption (PBE)   Builds the KEK.

Brute-force on the password (BFP) The BFP process involves five steps. They include getting a candidate password, performing the mixing to build a candidate key, doing the key setup, decrypting the ciphertext, and performing the check.

Brute-force on the key (BFK) The BFK process involves five steps. They include getting a candidate key, doing the key setup, decrypting ciphertext and yielding plaintext, and checking the plaintext.

Tokens Tiny computers that can store cryptographic keys. Each token contains a small chip with a processor, an operating system and limited input/output, memory, and hard drive storage space.

Crypto accelerators Large hardware crypto devices that store cryptographic keys. Special chips perform faster cryptographic operations and store data more securely than general-purpose microprocessors.

Smart card A plastic card that contains a microprocessor and which can be used to store keys.

Smart card readers These transfer a symmetric key between the smart card and the computer.

Universal Serial Bus (USB) port This port is the industry standard for attaching plug-and-play devices.

Biometrics A technique that uses a person's unique physical characteristics to verify their identities.

Keystrokes The characters associated with the keys on a keyboard.

Password generators Programs that generate passwords. They work like PRNGs but produce keystrokes.

Session key The key used to encrypt megabytes of information, or bulk data.

Key Terms Quiz

Use the Key Terms list to complete the sentences that follow. (Not all terms will be used.)

1. The process of keeping all the keys safe and available for use is known as
_____.

2. A _____ attack involves the use of precomputed keys, created from common passwords and their associated keys.

3. The PBE program uses the _____ to encrypt the session key.

4. The key used to encrypt megabytes of information, or bulk data is called
_____.

5. Tiny computers that can store cryptographic keys are called _____.

6. A _____ transfers a symmetric key between the smart card and the computer.

7. The most popular port for attaching plug-and-play devices is the _____ port.

8. The large hardware crypto devices having specialized chips that perform faster cryptographic operations and offer higher data security are called _____.

9. _____ is a technique that uses a person's unique physical characteristics to verify their identity.

10. Password generators that are programs generating passwords, work like PRNGs but produce _____.

Multiple-Choice Quiz

1. What does KEK stand for?

   a.   Kernel encryption key
   b.   Key encryption key
   c.   Knowledge encryption key
   d.   Known encryption key

2. The key used to encrypt the session key is known as a(n) _____.

   a.   asymmetric key
   b.   key encryption key
   c.   public key
   d.   private key

3. A salt is used to prevent a _____ attack.

   a.   brute-force
   b.   password-based
   c.   dictionary
   d.   known-plaintext

4. What is the first step in encrypting bulk data?

   a.   Collect the salt and password.
   b.   Generate a random or pseudo-random session key.
   c.   Generate a salt.
   d.   Store the encrypted session key.

5. Which of the following statements is not applicable to a dictionary attack?

   a.   A dictionary attack is faster than a brute-force attack.
   b.   A dictionary attack tries more passwords than a brute force attack.
   c.   A dictionary attack cannot be prevented by a salt.
   d.   A dictionary attack involves creating a dictionary of common passwords and their associated keys.

6. The brute-force on the password (BFP) process involves _____ stages.

    a.   four
    b.   five
    c.   six
    d.   seven

7. Smart cards and USB port attachments are the most common types of _____.

    a.   biometric techniques
    b.   crypto accelerators
    c.   PDAs
    d.   tokens

8. The _____ port is the industry standard for attaching plug-and-play devices.

    a.   PCMCIA
    b.   i-Button
    c.   1-Wire
    d.   USB

9. The larger hardware crypto devices are called _____.

    a.   crypto accelerators
    b.   microprocessors
    c.   PDAs
    d.   tokens

10. Which of the following statements is not applicable to a crypto accelerator?

    a.   It performs cryptographic operations faster than general-purpose microprocessors.
    b.   Its storage space is visible.
    c.   It has a specialized chip.
    d.   It stores data more securely.

11. The most well-known biometric is the _____.

    a.   fingerprint
    b.   gait recognition
    c.   retina scan
    d.   voiceprint

12. Which of the following is not a biometric application?

    a.   fingerprint
    b.   DNA
    c.   retina scan
    d.   tokens

13. Password generators are programs that, unlike PRNGs, produce _____.

    a.   characters
    b.   keys
    c.   keystrokes
    d.   numbers

14. The first step of the brute-force on the key (BFK) process is _____.

    a. checking the plaintext
    b. doing key setup
    c. decrypting some ciphertext
    d. getting the candidate key

15. Using a(n) _____ algorithm on the password ensures the randomness of the KEK.

    a. asymmetric
    b. iterative
    c. mixing
    d. recursive

Essay Quiz

1. Why is it necessary to use both the session key and the KEK?

2. List the steps involved in decrypting bulk data.

3. List some biometrics. Why are biometric devices not widely used?

Lab Projects

Lab Project 3.1

Fullmen and Kueller Ltd. needs to protect their client data. This data is stored in the company's database. Rachel, the system administrator, has decided that the login procedure, using usernames and passwords, is flawed. They need to bolster company security by implementing additional mechanisms. Preventing remote attacks is of high priority. What mechanisms would suit their needs?

Lab Project 3.2

Rachel, the system administrator, wants to simulate a brute-force attack on a key. List the steps involved in the process.

Chapter 4 Review

Chapter Summary

After reading this chapter, the students should understand the following.

Key Distribution and Sharing

■ The key distribution problem refers to the problem of how two or more people can securely send keys over unsecured lines.

■ The key distribution solution involves one party generating a key in advance, encrypting it using PBE, and sending the encrypted key to each other.

- If the key is exchanged in person, the number of meetings to share the key exponentially increases as the number of parties increases.
- This can be solved by having all the involved parties share the same key, in which a "key master" gives the key to all employees.
- Limitations are that employees leaving the company will continue to have the key and in the event of an attacker cracking one message, they will crack them all.

Using a Trusted Third Party

- If sharing keys in advance is not viable, a trusted third party (TTP) can be used.
- The TTP and the party involved share a KEK.
- The TTP has to exchange keys with all the parties in person. To make things easier, a hierarchy of TTPs can be created.
- If two correspondents are in the same office, they can use the services of a shared TTP.
- If two correspondents are in separate offices, each one communicates with their own TTP, then the two TTPs communicate with each other to bridge the gap.
- The TTP approach defeats the purpose of encryption, since the TTP can read all the encrypted messages.
- To solve the key distribution problem, public-key cryptography is used.

Public-Key Cryptography and the Digital Envelope

- Asymmetric-key cryptography, also known as public-key cryptography, is a method of cryptography that uses two different keys: one key is used exclusively for encryption, the other for decryption.
- The relationship between these keys is mathematical.
- The key that is made public without jeopardizing security is called a public key. The public key is used to encrypt data in asymmetric-key cryptography.
- The private key is used to decrypt data in asymmetric-key cryptography.
- Only the owner of the private key can recover the session key and decrypt the bulk data.
- Public key algorithms are slow, as compared to symmetric-key crypto.
- The process of encrypting bulk data using symmetric-key crypto, and encrypting the symmetric key with a public-key algorithm is called a digital envelope.
- Public-key algorithms can be broken by determining what the private key is, based on the public key.
- An attacker can break the public-key algorithm or perform a brute force attack to find the private key.

How Public-Key Cryptography Works

- Public-key crypto operates on the data as numbers.
- The foundation of any good public-key crypto is a one-way function—that is, the class of math problems on which public-key crypto is built.

- The three most widely used algorithms for solving the key distribution problem are RSA, Diffie-Hellman (DH), and Elliptic Curve Diffie-Hellman (ECDH).
- The RSA algorithm encrypts data. If the user feeds plaintext to the algorithm along with the public key, they get ciphertext as a result.
- With the digital envelope, the plaintext is the session key.
- It is possible to use RSA to encrypt data, but it is not as fast as symmetric algorithms.
- The best way to use RSA is to create a digital envelope.
- The most commonly used RSA key size is 1024 bits.
- An RSA public key consists of two numbers: a modulus and a public exponent.
- An RSA private key consists of two numbers: a modulus and a private exponent.
- The modulus is the product of two very large prime numbers.
- To generate an RSA key pair, the user has to decide on the public exponent (e), find two large primes (p and q) that work with the (e) chosen, multiply (p) and (q) to get the modulus (n), and finally compute the private exponent (d) based on (e), (p), and (q).
- $\varphi(n)$ is known as Euler's phi-function.
- In RSA, the only one-way function is multiplication.
- The process of determining the original two numbers, when the product of those two numbers is available, is called factoring.
- The DH algorithm does not encrypt data, instead it generates a secret.
- The DH algorithm uses public-key technology to generate a symmetric session key.
- Two parties can generate the same secret and use it to build a session key for use in a symmetric algorithm. This procedure is called key agreement or key exchange.
- Secret value is the number generated when the private key of one party is used along with the public key of the second party.
- A DH public key consists of a generator, a modulus, and a public value.
- To generate a DH key pair, the user has to find the prime (p) first, then a generator (g) that works well with the (p), and then a random or pseudo-random (x). The public value $(y) = g^x \bmod p$.
- The user can use a single prime as a modulus.
- The elliptic curves used in cryptography fall into two main categories called "odd" and "even."
- Elliptic curves can also be categorized as F_p, F2 Polynomial, and F2 Optimal Normal.
- Not all of the flavors of elliptic curves are used in crypto.
- A cryptographic EC is discrete (only integers, no fractions or decimals).
- A discrete log refers to a logarithm that works with the math of integers only—no fractions or decimals.
- The bigger the range, the more secure the curve, and the slower the computations.
- An elliptic curve has points, with x and y coordinates.

- The graphical form of elliptic curves can be described with scalar multiplication.
- The technical term for the specific range over which an elliptic curve is defined is Field.
- It is possible to use Elliptic Curve Cryptography (ECC) for encryption, although it is not widely used due to security and performance issues.

Comparing the Algorithms

- An algorithm's security, key size, performance, transmission size, and interoperability form the criteria while evaluating it for a situation.
- ECC is based on the EC discrete log problem. DH is based on the discrete log problem. RSA is based on factoring.
- ECC is newer and less understood.
- With regard to security, some people prefer RSA because DH and ECDH are susceptible to man-in-the-middle attacks.
- In RSA, only the initiator of the contact can generate the session key. While, with DH and ECDH, both parties contribute to generating the session key.
- The bigger the key, the greater the level of security, and the slower the speed of the public-key algorithm.
- A 1024-bit DH key is equivalent to a 160-bit ECC key, according to the general perception.
- Based on the performance of the public-key operations, RSA is comparatively faster than the DH and the ECDH algorithms.
- Based on the performance of the private-key operations, ECC is somewhat faster than DH and RSA.
- With RSA and DH, the transmission size is the same as the key size. With ECDH, the transmission size is twice the key size.
- If interoperability is required, RSA is the de facto standard.

Protecting Private Keys

- A token or a smart card can be used to store the private key.
- For servers, crypto accelerators can be used.

Key Recovery

- The most common form of key recovery is the RSA digital envelope.
- The three basic entities that can act as a key recovery agent are a trusted third party; a group of trustees, each holding a portion of the key; and a group of trustees using a threshold scheme.
- The method implemented to restore keys that get lost is called key recovery.
- The most common form of key recovery is the RSA digital envelope.

■ The practice of giving keys to a third party so that the third party can read sensitive material on demand is called key escrow.

■ The advantage of recovering the key via a trusted third party is that key recovery is easy.

■ The disadvantage of recovering the key via a trusted third party is that the TTP has access to all the keys.

■ The advantage of recovering the key via a group of trustees is that no one individual can recover the keys secretly. This is because the secret is split into multiple digital envelopes.

■ The commonest key recovery method involves threshold schemes.

■ Threshold schemes are also known as secret sharing, or secret splitting.

■ A secret must be split into several shares, some number of which must be combined to recover the secret.

■ The threshold method has many advantages. It prevents one single individual from obtaining keys surreptitiously. It is possible to reconstruct the keys even if trustees are absent. Further, if one of the trustees leaves the company, there is no need to restart the key recovery process, as the key can be recovered only if many people act together.

Key Terms

Asymmetric-key cryptography   A method of cryptography that uses two separate keys for encryption and decryption.

Key distribution problem   Refers to the problem of how two or more people can securely send keys over unsecured lines.

Asymmetric-key cryptography   Also known as public-key cryptography, it is a method of cryptography that uses two different keys—one key for encryption and the other for decryption.

Public key   The key that is made public without jeopardizing security. The key used to encrypt data in asymmetric-key cryptography.

Private key   The key used to decrypt data in asymmetric-key cryptography.

Digital envelope   The process of encrypting bulk data using symmetric-key crypto, and encrypting the symmetric key with a public-key algorithm.

One-way function   The class of math problems on which public-key crypto is built. It is the foundation of any good public-key crypto.

Modulus   The product of two very large prime numbers.

Factoring   The process of determining the original two numbers, when the product of those two numbers is available.

Key agreement   The procedure in which two parties generate the same secret and use it to build a session key for use in a symmetric algorithm. It is also known as key exchange.

Secret value   The number generated when the private key of one party is used along with the public key of the second party.

Point   A point is an x, y coordinate.

Scalar   The mathematical term for a single number.

Field   The technical term for the specific range over which an elliptic curve is defined.

RSA   The most commonly used public-key algorithm for solving the key distribution problem which is based on factoring.

Key recovery   The method implemented to restore keys that get lost.

Key escrow   The practice of giving keys to a third party so that the third party can read sensitive material on demand.

Threshold schemes   Threshold schemes offer an attractive means of implementing key recovery with checks and balances. A secret must be split into several shares, some number of which must be combined to recover the secret. It is also known as secret sharing or secret splitting.

Key recovery agent   A trusted third party, or a group of trustees, each holding a portion of the key, entrusted with the job of key recovery.

Euler's phi-function $\varphi(n)$ is known as Euler's phi-function.

Key Terms Quiz

Use the Key Terms list to complete the sentences that follow. (Not all terms will be used.)

1. A method of cryptography that uses two different keys for encryption and decryption is called _____.

2. The key used to encrypt data in asymmetric-key cryptography is called

_____.

3. The _____ algorithm is based on factoring.

4. The foundation of any good public-key crypto is a(n) _____.

5. The process of determining the original two numbers, when the product of those two numbers is available, is called _____.

6. The procedure in which two parties generate the same secret and use it to build a session key for use in a symmetric algorithm is called _____.

7. The specific range over which an elliptic curve is defined is called

_____.

8. An elliptic curve has _____, with x and y coordinates.

9. The practice of giving keys to a third party so that they can read sensitive material on demand is called _____.

10. _____ is known as Euler's phi-function.

Multiple-Choice Quiz

1. The most commonly used public-key algorithm for solving the key distribution problem is _____.

    a.   DH

    b.   ECDH

    c.   Rijndael

    d.   RSA

2. Public-key crypto operates on the data as _____.

    a.   ASCII text

    b.   bits

    c.   characters

    d.   numbers

3. What does ECDH stand for?

    a.   Encryption Curve Diffie-Hellman

    b.   Electronic Curve Diffie-Hellman

    c.   Elliptic Curve Diffie-Hellman

    d.   Extended Curve Diffie-Hellman

4. Which of the following is not applicable to the RSA algorithm?

    a.   It was developed by Ron Rivest, among others.

    b.   It is the most commonly used public-key algorithm.

    c.   It is faster than a symmetric algorithm.

    d.   The best way to use RSA is to create a digital envelope.

5. The most commonly used RSA key size is _____ bits.

    a.   256

    b.   512

    c.   612

    d.   1024

6. In RSA, the one-way multiplication function is _____.

    a.   addition

    b.   division

    c.   multiplication

    d.   subtraction

7. The product of two primes is called a _____.

    a.   factor

    b.   modulus

    c.   private exponent

    d.   public exponent

8. The _____ is used for finding large primes.

    a.   Chinese Remainder Theorem

    b.   DH algorithm

    c.   phi-function by Euler

    d.   Fermat test

9. What does a DH public-key consist of?

    a.   A modulus and a private value

    b.   A generator and a public value

    c.   A generator, a modulus, and a public value

    d.   A generator, a modulus, and a private value

10. Which of the following is not a kind of elliptic curve?

    a. F_p

    b.   F2 Polynomial

    c.   F2 Normal

    d.   F2 Optimal Normal

11. DH and ECDH are more susceptible to a _____ attack.

    a.   brute-force

    b.   dictionary

    c.   man-in-the-middle

    d.   known-plaintext

12. A 1024-bit DH key is equivalent to a _____-bit ECC key.

    a.   160

    b.   1024

    c.   1528

    d.   2024

13. Based on the performance of the public key operations, which one of the following algorithms is the fastest?

    a.   DH

    b.   ECC

    c.   IDEA

    d.   RSA

14. Secret splitting is another term for _____.

    a.   digital envelopes

    b.   key escrow

    c.   key recovery

    d.   threshold schemes

15. Which of the following algorithms is comparatively faster for receiving the contact or opening a digital envelope?

    a.   DH

    b.   ECC

    c.   IDEA

    d.   RSA

Essay Quiz

1. What is a digital envelope?

2. What are the limitations of ECC with regard to interoperability?

3. What are the RSA, DH, and ECC standards based on?

Lab Projects

Lab Project 4.1

Craig and McHill Ltd. have decided to use a public-key algorithm to protect their sensitive data. Most of the clients of Craig and McHill Ltd. reside in Europe. Performance and speed are of utmost importance, although a standard level of security is required. Which algorithm would suit their needs?

Lab Project 4.2

Craig and McHill Ltd. use the Diffie-Hellman algorithm for their data security needs. Thomas, the system administrator, needs to generate a DH key pair. What are the steps involved in the process?

Chapter 5 Review

Chapter Summary

After reading this chapter, the students should understand the following.

Uniqueness of a Digital Signature

■ Digital signature is a technique of encrypting data with a private key and decrypting it with a public key.

■ Digital signatures depend on two fundamental assumptions: first, the private key is safe, with only the owner having access to it; and second, the private key is the only way to produce a digital signature.

■ Anything that is encrypted with a private key is a digital signature.

■ Signature uniqueness for any signature scheme is yet to be proven.

Message Digests

■ Public-key crypto is slow. Hence it's not good to encrypt the entire plaintext. Instead of encrypting the entire plaintext with the private key, encrypting a representative of the data is a better option.

■ Message digest is a representative of data in cryptography. It is an algorithm that takes any input and produces a fixed length, pseudo-random output.

- The word "digest" means to reduce or condense. The Secure Hash Algorithm (SHA-1) digest condenses messages to 20 bytes, irrespective of their size.

- Digests appear random, but they are not truly random. They are pseudo-random.

- Two similar messages produce two completely different digests.

- A message cannot be reconstructed from the digest. It is a one-way function and has no trap door.

- No message can produce a particular digest.

- No two messages produce the same digest.

- A collision occurs when two messages—any two messages—produce the same digest.

- The pigeonhole principle says that sooner or later some messages will collide in the same digest.

- Collisions exist, but no one can find a collision on demand (for some algorithms, no one has found a collision, even by accident.)

- An attacker changing a message slightly and producing the same digest indicates that the algorithm is broken.

- Message digest also checks for data integrity, which describes data the user can count on, at least in terms of authenticity.

- The three important digest algorithms are MD2, MD5, and SHA-1.

- Ron Rivest created the MD2 digest algorithm. It produces a 128-bit (16-byte) digest; therefore, it has 2^{128} possible digest values. Nobody was able to find collisions on demand with any arbitrary message, but certain classes of messages produced collisions.

- MD5 was much stronger and faster than MD2. It is a 16-byte digest. MD5 has not been broken and no one has found collisions, but some internals of the algorithm are vulnerable.

- SHA-1 contains stronger internals than MD5 and it produces a longer digest (160 bits). It has survived cryptanalysis and is recommended by the crypto community.

- Someone trying to surreptitiously change the original message will result in a new fake message producing a different digest. When the digest produced by the algorithm does not represent the data, it is an indication of a problem.

- The digital signature and the keyed digest are two methods to prevent the alteration of a digest.

- The most common keyed digest is called hash-based message authentication checksum (HMAC).

- HMAC is a hash-based message authentication algorithm, which checks data by summing it.

- A MAC detects changes in the data and sum, using a digest, block cipher, or stream cipher and key, respectively.

Back to Digital Signatures

■ Each chunk of data has its own signature. No single digital signature is associated with an individual or key pair, but it is unique to the data signed and the keys used.

■ Different signatures are produced whether an individual signs two messages with the same key or two individuals sign the same data with different keys. This prevents anyone from taking a valid signature and appending it to a different message.

■ A way to check if messages have been altered in transit is to digest and compare the messages sent and received. They must match.

■ Another method is to check the algorithm identifier, pad bytes, and digest. This will make it harder to spoof.

■ Tying a signature to a digest and the algorithm prevents an attacker from substituting an alternative digest algorithm.

Implementing Authentication, Data Integrity, and Nonrepudiation

■ A message digest ensures data integrity such that what the sender sends is what the receiver receives.

■ A digital signature authenticates that the other entity in the data exchange is shown to be the entity it claims to be and that the data is verified to have come from that entity.

■ A digital signature provides nonrepudiation such that a signer cannot later disavow any knowledge of the message.

Understanding the Algorithms

■ The RSA algorithm is used to sign, but the DH algorithm only performs key exchanges.

■ The Digital Signature Algorithm (DSA) is based on the discrete log problem, like the DH. It can be adapted to create signatures.

■ The most common way to create signatures is to use ECC and is called ECDSA. It uses elliptic curves.

■ RSA is used to encrypt a digest with a private key to produce a digital signature. To forge an RSA signature, one must have the private key.

■ DSA does not encrypt data, though it can be used to create a digital signature.

■ The security of DSA lies in the discrete log problem, the same problem that gives DH its security. The size of the DSA keys will be the same as that of DH keys.

■ In ECDSA, the signer has the digest, k (a pseudo-random number), and the private key. The output is r and s. The verifier has the digest, s (one part of the signature), and the public key. Output is v. If v and r are the same, the signature is verified; if they are not the same, something went wrong.

Comparing the Algorithms

■ Security: DSA and ECDSA produce and compare surrogate numbers. If the two numbers at the signer's and verifier's end match, the signature is verified. RSA does not follow this method. No surrogate is involved; the verifier compares the signer's value. Since DSA and ECDSA compare surrogates, it opens an avenue of attack not possible with RSA. So, though the probability of an attack on DSA and ECDSA is low, it is lower still with RSA.

■ Performance: RSA performance does not change while DSA and ECDSA are slightly more time-consuming than their DH counterparts. ECC is a faster signature scheme.

■ Transmission Size: DSA and ECDSA signatures are about 340 bits, regardless of key size. An RSA signature is the same size as the key.

■ Interoperability: RSA has become the de facto standard. DSA has become a part of most cryptographic packages. ECC is less prevalent.

Protecting Private Keys

■ Many protocols require users to have two keys: a digital envelope (or a KEK) and a separate signing key. So two private keys have to be protected.

■ If the user loses a private key, there are ways to revoke, or cancel, the public key affiliated with it.

■ Losing a signing key poses a bigger risk than any other key, because it permits the attacker to pose as you. The damage is significantly less if a digital envelope, or KEK, is stolen since it exposes the user's secrets to them, but does not allow them to act on the user's behalf.

Introduction to Certificates

■ Digital certificate, which is actually a name, public key, and signature, is a way to know whether or not a public key belongs to the purported individual. If someone takes an existing certificate and replaces the public key or name with an imposter's, it can be detected.

■ The certificate is signed by the certificate authority (CA.)

■ CA's certificate is signed by the root and the root key is distributed outside the certificate hierarchy.

Key Recovery

■ Applying a key recovery plan for signing keys is not a good idea, as it would nullify nonrepudiation.

■ Anyone losing a signing key does not invalidate existing signatures, as only the public key is needed to be verified.

■ New signatures require a new key pair to be generated and a new public key to be distributed.

Key Terms

Digital signature   When data is encrypted with a private key and decrypted with a public key, the technique is called a digital signature in the crypto community.

Message digest   The representative of data in cryptography is a message digest. It is an algorithm that takes any length of input and mixes it to produce a fixed-length, pseudo-random output.

MD2   An algorithm that produces a 128-bit (16-byte) digest; therefore, it has 2128 possible digest values.

MD5   An algorithm that is much stronger and much faster than MD2, and like MD2, is a 16-byte digest.

SHA-1   An algorithm that contains stronger internals than MD5 and produces a 160-bit digest.

HMAC   A hash-based message authentication algorithm, which checks data by summing it. It detects changes in the data or sum, using a digest, block cipher, or stream cipher and key, respectively.

Data integrity   The process of sending data along with a check to ensure that the information is not altered.

Authentication   Checking the identity of the user who has sent the data.

Nonrepudiation   Refers to checking and recording the identity of the signer such that they cannot later disavow any knowledge of the message.

RSA   An algorithm used to encrypt a digest with a private key to produce a digital signature.

DSA   An algorithm that does not encrypt data, although it can be used to create a digital signature.

Digital certificate   A method to determine if a public key belongs to the purported entity. It contains a name, public key, and signature.

Collisions   A collision occurs when two messages—any two messages—produce the same digest.

Interoperability   The capability of software and hardware on different machines from different vendors to share data.

Key Terms Quiz

Use the Key Terms list to complete the sentences that follow. (Not all terms will be used.)

1. When data is encrypted with a private key and decrypted with a public key, the technique is called a(n) _____.

2. _____ refers to checking and recording the identity of the signer such that they cannot later disavow any knowledge of the message.

3. _____ is a way to ensure that a public key belongs to the purported individual.

4. _____ is an algorithm that contains stronger internals than MD5 and it produces a longer digest (160 bits).

5. _____ is an algorithm that takes any input and produces a fixed length, pseudo-random output.

6. _____ occur when two messages produce the same digest.

7. The ability of software and hardware on different machines from different vendors to share data is called _____.

8. _____ is an algorithm that does not encrypt data but creates a digital signature.

9. _____ is an algorithm used to encrypt a digest with a private key to produce a digital signature.

10. _____ is a hash-based message authentication algorithm, which checks data by summing it.

Multiple-Choice Quiz

1. MD2 produces a _____ byte digest.
   a.   18
   b.   17
   c.   16
   d.   21

2. SHA-1 produces a(n) _____-byte digest.
   a.   18
   b.   20
   c.   24
   d.   16

3. Message digest is an algorithm that takes any input and produces a _____ output.
   a.   fixed length
   b.   smaller
   c.   random length
   d.   random

4. HMAC is an algorithm that _____.
   a.   is not recommended by cryptographers
   b.   checks for changes in the data by summing it
   c.   produces a 128-bit digest, with 2128 possible digest values
   d.   was created by Ron Rivest

5. _____ is the strongest of the digest algorithms and has survived cryptanalysis and is recommended by the crypto community.

   a.   MD2

   b.   MD5

   c.   SHA-1

   d.   RSA

6. _____ is a way to ensure that the public key belongs to the purported entity.

   a.   Algorithm identifier

   b.   Collision

   c.   Digital certificate

   d.   Digital envelope

7. Digital signatures depend on two fundamental assumptions: _____.

   a.   The safety of the private key, and the private key being the only way to produce a digital signature

   b.   The safety of the public key, and the private key being the only way to produce a digital signature

   c.   Only the owner having access to the signing key, and the recovery plan for it.

   d.   The protection of the root key and the ability to generate a new symmetric key.

8. The pigeonhole principle says _____.

   a.   some messages will collide in the same digest

   b.   no message can collide in the same digest

   c.   messages will collide, but in another digest

   d.   the number of possible digests is finite

9. _____ helps in confirming the data and identity of the signer.

   a.   Authentication

   b.   Identification

   c.   Nonrepudiation

   d.   Recognition

10. A digital certificate binds a name to a _____ key.

   a.   public

   b.   private

   c.   root

   d.   signing

11. Checking and recording the identity of the signer is called _____.

   a.   recognition

   b.   nonrepudiation

   c.   authentication

   d.   identification

12. Anything that is encrypted with a _____ is a digital signature.

   a.   private key

   b.   public key

   c.   root key

   d.   signing key

13. The number of possible digests with SHA-1 is _____.

   a. 2^{128}
   b. 2^{160}
   c. 2^{281}
   d. 2^{1024}

14. The most common keyed digest is called _____.

   a. HMAC
   b. MD2
   c. MD5
   d. SHA-1

15. _____ can be based on a digest, block cipher, or stream cipher.

   a. HMAC
   b. MD2
   c. MD5
   d. SHA-1

Essay Quiz

1. Explain digital signatures and list the various signature algorithms.

2. What is a message digest? List the properties of a message digest.

3. Why is it important to protect signing keys?

Lab Project

Lab Project 5.1

Steve, a new worker in Deor-i Shipping Company, has been put in charge of loading ships with cargo bound for different places. Deor-i Shipping is a fully automated company with all the transfer of information taking place through the local network. Due to apparent security reasons, the company uses digital signature process to send information. Steve, being new to computers, has to be taught about the working of a digital certificate. Explain the process of producing the digital certificate, such that no one can take an existing certificate and replace the public key with an imposter's.

Chapter 6 Review

Chapter Summary

After reading this chapter, the students should understand the following.

Public-Key Certificates

■ Public-key certificates (PKC) are tamperproof data packets that attest to the binding of a public-key to an end user. These certificates are issued and digitally signed by trusted third-party certification authorities (CA) and contain the user's name, public key, and other identifying information.

■ Of the various certificates in use, the most widely accepted certificate format is the International Telecommunication Union's X.509 Version 3. This format is profiled in the RFC2459.

■ The X.509 certificate Versions 2 and 3 are structured with the issuer unique identifier and the subject unique identifier.

■ Standard Version 3 certificate extension fields have three parts marked extension type, extension criticality, and extension value.

■ In a public-key certificate, the entity names for both the issuer and the subject must be unique.

■ X.509 Version 3 grants greater flexibility with names. Entities can be identified by one or more names.

■ Of the various certificates in use, the most widely accepted certificate format is the International Telecommunication Union's X.509 Version 3. This format is profiled in the RFC2459.

■ The syntax for all certificates that conform to the X.509 standards is expressed using the Abstract Syntax Notation 1 (ASN.1).

Components of a PKI

■ A public-key infrastructure involves a collaborative process between these entities: the Certification Authority (CA), the Registration Authority (RA), a certificate repository, a key recovery server, and an end user.

■ In a PKI, the CA issues, manages, and revokes certificates for a community of end users by authenticating its end users and then digitally signing the certificate information before disseminating it.

■ A CA provides its own public key to all its certified end users and all relying parties who may use the certification information.

■ A registration authority (RA) commonly accepts and verifies information about new registers, generates keys on behalf of end users, accepts and authorizes requests for key backup and recovery, accepts and authorizes requests for certification revocation, and distributes or recovers hardware devices, such as tokens, as needed.

■ A certificate directory is a central storage location, used by a certification authority that provides a single point for certificate administration and distribution.

■ A key recovery server gives the CA a simple way of backing up private keys at the time of creation and recovering them later.

■ Management protocols assist in online communication between end users and management within a PKI.

■ Management protocols should support the following functions: registration, initialization, certification, key recovery, key update, revocation, and cross-certification.

■ Operational protocols are those protocols that enable the transfer of certificates and revocation status information among directories, end users, and relying parties.

Registering and Issuing Certificates

■ Registration is the point where end users and the CA establish trust. Cross validation of the parties involved is carried out, and upon establishment of a trust relationship, the certificate request is initiated.

Revoking a Certificate

■ Certificates are created with the belief that they will be valid and useful throughout the expected lifetime indicated in the Validity field. However, sometimes certificates require revocation before reaching the end of their lifetime due to instances of mistrust or expiration of the end user key(s).

■ The most common method used for revoking certificates is by using a Certificate Revocation List (CRL).

■ CRL distribution points or CRL partitions are several small CRLs that are accessed by CA-supplied pointers within the Issuing Distribution Point extension. Relying servers retrieve and process these smaller CRLs more easily and save time, money, and bandwidth.

■ Delta CRLs list only incremental changes that have occurred since the preceding CRL.

■ Indirect CRLs are provided to the relying parties by a third party that did not necessarily issue the certificate.

■ An Authority Revocation List (ARL) lists the revocations for a CA certificate.

■ The CA provides a server, known as an OCSP responder, which contains the current revocation information. Relying parties can query the OCPS responder to determine the status of a given certificate.

Trust Models

■ Trust models are used to describe the relationship between end users, relying parties, and the CA. The two most widely used trust models are certificate hierarchies and cross-certification.

■ The push model is the model wherein the sender pushes an entire chain of certificates when sending one certificate to the recipient. The recipient can immediately verify all certificates.

■ The pull model sends only the sender's certificate and relies on the recipient to pull in the CA's certificate. As each certificate contains the issuer's name, the recipient knows the destination where such certificates can be verified.

Managing Key Pairs

■ Management of key pairs is defined by (a) the policies based on which it was generated and (b) the intended purpose of the key.

■ Keys can be generated by the end user and a trusted third party (TTP).

■ Password protection, PCMCIA cards, tokens, biometrics, and Smart cards are used to protect private keys.

■ The ANSI X9.57 standard requires that private keys, used for nonrepudiation, be created, used, and destroyed within one secure module.

■ Key pairs, in use, can be affected by issues of compromise, both internal and external, and therefore, for the benefit of relying parties, they need to be constantly updated.

■ A key's purpose dictates the method of storage of the key pair.

■ A key pair has a limited lifetime but usually the requirement for having a key pair exceeds that lifetime. In such cases, end users acquire additional key pairs. For the benefit of the relying parties, a history of the key pairs is maintained.

The Future of PKI

■ Roaming certificates and key pairs allow users dynamic access, available in the end user's system memory for the duration of the use, to their public/private keys from a secure central server.

■ Attribute certificates (AC) do not contain a public key for an individual. Instead, they bind an entity to a set of authorization attributes.

■ A certificate policy statement (CPS) is a statement of the practices which the certification authority employs in issuing certificates.

Key Terms

Public key infrastructure (PKI)   A system of digital certificates, certificate authorities, and other registration authorities that verify and authenticate the validity of each party involved in an Internet transaction.

Certification authority (CA)   A trusted third-party (TTP) organization that issues digital certificates used to create digital signatures and public-private key pairs.

Registration authority (RA)   An approval agent for the issuance of a new certificate. They do not actually issue the certificate, but they act strictly as a vetting agent. Once they have verified the actual identity of the user, they will send the approval to the CA, who will actually issue the certificate.

X.509 Version 3   The most widely used standard for defining digital certificates.

Relative distinguished name (RDN)   An entity included as the subject in a request for a certificate. The elements in an RDN are defined by its attributes and do not need to include a name. With respect to CryptoAPI, an RDN is defined by a CERT_RDN structure, which in turn points to an array of CERT_RDN_ATTR attribute structures. Each attribute structure specifies a single attribute.

Distinguished name (DN)   Entity composed of one or more RDNs, and each RDN is composed of one or more attribute-value assertion (AVAs)

Absolute value assertion (AVA)   Consists of an attribute identifier and its corresponding value information.

Abstract Syntax Notation 1 (ASN.1)   Describes the syntax for various data structures, providing well-defined primitive objects as well as a means to define complex combinations of those primitives. It also has two sets of rules that govern encoding: Basic Encoding Rules (BER) and Distinguished Encoding Rules (DER).

Lightweight Directory Access Protocol (LDAP)   An interoperable protocol designed to provide access to the X.500 Directory while not incurring the resource requirements of the Directory Access Protocol (DAP). This protocol is specifically targeted at simple management applications and browser applications that provide a simple read/write interactive access to the X.500 Directory and is intended to be a complement to the DAP itself.

Certificate Management Protocol (CMP)   Defines the conventions for all key and certificate management functions within a PKI.

Certification Revocation List (CRL)   A signed data structure containing a time-stamped list of revoked certificates for end users.

Authority Revocation List (ARL)   A signed data structure containing a time-stamped list of revoked CA certificates.

Online Certificate Status Protocol (OCSP)   One of two common schemes for maintaining the security of a server and other network resources. The other, older method is known as Certificate Revocation List (CRL).

Attribute certificates (AC)   These do not contain a public key for an individual. Instead, they bind an entity to a set of authorization attributes.

A certificate policy (CP)   A named set of rules that indicate the applicability of a certificate to a particular community and/or a class of application with common security requirements.

Certificate policy statement (CPS)   A statement of the practices which the certification authority employs in issuing certificates.

Roaming certificates (RC)   These and key pairs allow users dynamic access to their public/private keys from a secure central server.

Delta CRL   A list of only incremental changes that have occurred since the preceding CRL.

Key Terms Quiz

Use the Key Terms list to complete the sentences that follow. (Not all terms will be used.)

1. A trusted third-party (TTP) organization that issues digital certificates for creating digital signatures and public-private key pairs is called a(n) _____.

2. A distinguished name (DN) is composed of one or more _____.

3. Each RDN is composed of one or more _____.

4. The syntax for all certificates that conform to the X.509 standard is expressed using _____.

5. A signed data structure containing a time-stamped list of revoked certificates for end users is called a(n) _____.

6. An interoperable protocol designed to provide access to the X.500 Directory, while not incurring the resource requirements of the Directory Access Protocol (DAP), is called _____.

7. The conventions for all key and certificate management functions within a PKI are defined by _____.

8. Certificates that do not contain a public key for an individual and instead bind an entity to a set of authorization attributes are called _____.

9. A named set of rules that indicate the applicability of a certificate to a particular community and/or a class of applications with common security requirements is called a(n) _____.

10. A statement of the practices which the certification authority employs in issuing certificates is called a(n) _____.

Multiple-Choice Quiz

1. A tamperproof set of data that attests to the binding of a public key to an end user is called _____.
    a. Certification authorities (CA)
    b. Public-key infrastructure (PKI)
    c. Public-key certificate (PKC)
    d. Internet Protocol Security (IPSec)

2. In a public-key certificate, entity names for both the issuer and the subject must be _____.
    a. identical
    b. less than six characters long
    c. similar
    d. unique

3. The syntax for all certificates that conform to the X.509 standard is expressed using _____.
    a. Open Systems Interconnection (OSI)
    b. Abstract Syntax Notation 1 (ASN.1)
    c. Uniform Resource Locator (URL)
    d. Attribute Value Assertions (AVAs)

4. Who can serve as an intermediate entity between the certification authority (CA) and its end users, assisting the CA in its day-to-day certificate processing functions?
    a. A registration authority
    b. A certificate directory
    c. A time-stamping authority
    d. A public certification authority

5. What provides CAs a simple way of backing up private keys at the time of creation and recovering them later?

    a. Attribute Value Assertions (AVAs)
    b. Lightweight Directory Access Protocol (LDAP)
    c. The Key Recovery Server
    d. Registration authorities

6. Protocols that enable the transfer of certificates and revocation status information between directories, end users, and relying parties are called _____.

    a. Certificate Management Protocols
    b. Management Protocols
    c. Operational Protocols
    d. Certificate Management Message Format Protocols

7. Which of the following is not a valid certificate extension of X.509 Version 3?

    a. Key usage
    b. Authority key identifier
    c. CRL distribution point
    d. ARL distribution point

8. _____ is a profile for the X.509 Version 3.

    a. RFC 2459
    b. RFC 1777
    c. RFC 1778
    d. RFC 0475

9. RDN is composed of one or more _____.

    a. DNs
    b. AVAs
    c. CRLs
    d. ARLs

10. PKI involves a collaborative process between the CA, RA, certificate repository, _____, and the end user.

    a. time-stamp server
    b. key recovery server
    c. CRL server
    d. ARL server

11. ARLs are distinguished from CRLs via the _____ field.

    a. Authority key identifier
    b. CRL number
    c. Issuing distribution point
    d. Issuer alternative name

12. _____ lists only incremental changes that have occurred since the preceding CRL.

    a.   ARL

    b.   CRL

    c.   Indirect CRL

    d.   Delta CRL

13. _____ certificate's policy governs its CRL time intervals.

    a.   An attribute

    b.   A roaming

    c.   A PKI

    d.   An X.509

14. _____ allows relying parties to check the validity of a digital certificate in real time.

    a.   Base CRL

    b.   Indirect CRL

    c.   Delta CRL

    d.   OCSP

15. Cross-certification is a _____ trust model.

    a.   hierarchical

    b.   nonhierarchical

    c.   public

    d.   private

Essay Quiz

1. A goal of the directory is to provide an infrastructure to use distinguished names for every communication entity. As a result, names in X.509 certificates are more complex than e-mail addresses. What are the benefits of using such complex names in business applications?

2. Is it necessary to provide security and access control to certificate directories?

3. How is cross-certification more secure than a pure certificate hierarchy?

Lab Projects

Lab Project 6.1

OPK Research Repository is an online research library with an array of Microsoft Word and Adobe Acrobat documents containing sensitive research information on nuclear physics. These documents are stored in public folders. As an existing system policy, user rights on these public folders cannot be modified, yet certain users should be allowed access to specific documents on the basis of authorization and access rights.

Suggest a viable solution that only allows access to authorized users to specific documents in these public folders.

Chapter 7 Review

Chapter Summary

After reading this chapter, the students should understand the following.

Network and Transport Security

■ Security protocols are used to secure the application, systems, and networks.

Internet Protocol Security

■ Internet Protocol Security (IPSec), a framework of open standards, ensures confidentiality, integrity, and authenticity of data communication across a public IP network.

■ IPSec provides security at the IP layer by selecting security protocols, determining algorithms, and implementing cryptographic keys.

■ The two protocols used are the authentication header (AH) protocol, which supports access control, data origin authentication, connectionless integrity, and rejection of replay attacks, and the encapsulating security payload (ESP) protocol, which supports confidentiality, access control, limited traffic-flow confidentiality, and the rejection of replay attacks.

Authentication Header Protocol

■ AH provides data integrity, and authentication services for IP packets using a keyed-hash function as it is faster than using digital signature technology.

■ AH does not provide confidentiality protection, so data can still be viewed as it travels across a network.

■ ICV is a truncated version of a message authentication code (MAC) and is computed using the following fields:

   ■ IP header fields that either do not change or whose values are predictable upon arrival at the endpoint for the AH security association.

   ■ The entire contents of the AH header except for the Authentication Data Field.

   ■ All upper-level protocol data, which is assumed to be immutable in transit.

■ AH services can be employed in two ways: transport mode or tunnel mode.

The Encapsulating Security Payload Protocol

■ The encapsulating security payload (ESP) protocol provides confidentiality services for IP data while in transit across untrusted networks. Optionally, it also provides authentication services.

■ ESP format varies with the type and mode of encryption being used.

■ The IPSec ESP standard currently requires compliant systems to have two cryptographic algorithms.

■ ESP services can be employed in two modes: transport mode or tunnel mode. The EPS data is called trailers and is appended to the end of each packet.

Security Associations

■ To communicate, each pair of hosts using IPSec must establish a security association (SA) between them.

■ An SA establishes a one-way relationship between the sender and the receiver; for peer communication, a second SA is required.

■ SA lets the user construct classes of security channels. If the user needs extra security, the rules of SA will reflect so—for example, the rules would specify stronger encryption.

■ A Single SA allows users to deploy either AH or ESP (not both) to implement security for IP packets. There is no restriction on the use of multiple SAs (referred to as an SA bundle).

■ The order in which the SAs are bundled is defined by the security policy.

■ There are two ways of combining SAs: transport adjacency and iterated tunneling.

■ A user can also combine transport adjacency and iterated tunneling.

Security Databases

■ IPSec contains two nominal databases: Security Policy Database (SPD) and Security Association Database (SAD).

■ SPD: This database specifies the policies that determine the disposition of all IP traffic, inbound or outbound.

■ SPD is responsible for all traffic and must be consulted during the processing of all traffic. To support this, SPD requires entries for inbound and outbound traffic. These entries are defined by a set of selectors, or IP and upper-layer protocol field values.

■ SAD: This database contains parameters that are associated with each currently active security association.

Key Management

■ IPSec provides key management, such as supplying a means of negotiating with other people the protocols, encryption algorithms, and keys to be used in data exchange. IPSec also requires users to keep track of all such agreements.

■ An IPSec-compliant system must support both manual and automated SA and cryptographic key management. These can be described as manual and automated.

■ Internet key exchange (IKE) is a hybrid of two protocols. It integrates Internet Security Association and Key Management Protocol (ISAKMP) with the Oakley key exchange protocol.

Secure Socket Layer

■ Secure Socket Layer (SSL) is the Internet protocol for session-based encryption and authentication. It provides a secure pipe between two parties to defeat eavesdropping, tampering, and message forgery.

■ SSL works at the transport layer and is independent of the application protocol used. Thus, application protocols can transparently layer on top of SSL.

Session and Connection States

■ The systems discussed in this chapter are composed of states and associated state transitions.

■ A state machine is the combination of all possible states and state transitions for a particular object. SSL has two state machines, one for the client side of the protocol and another for the server side. Each endpoint must implement the matching side of protocol.

■ The interaction between the state machines is called a handshake.

■ The SSL handshake protocol coordinates the states of client and server, enabling each one's protocol machine to operate consistently even though the state is not exactly parallel.

■ An SSL session can include multiple secure connections, and parties can have multiple simultaneous sessions.

The Record Layer Protocol

■ SSL record layer operates on the data transmitted to and received from the upper application layers. It is in this layer that the data is encrypted, decrypted, and authenticated.

■ The party receiving this information reverses the process and obtains the data.

The Change Cipher Spec Protocol

■ The change cipher spec protocol exists to signal a transistion in the ciphering strategies.

■ This protocol consists of a single message. Before finishing the handshake, both the client and the server send this message to notify each other that subsequent records will be protected under the just-negotiated cipher specifications and associated keys.

■ An unexpected change cipher spec message should generate an unexpected_message alert.

The Alert Protocol

■ The alert protocol conveys alert messages and their severity to parties in an SSL session.

■ When either party detects an error, the detecting party sends a message to the other.

■ If the alert message has a fatal result, both parties close the connection. For a nonfatal error, both parties can cache information to resume the connections.

The Handshake Protocol

■ The SSL handshake protocol is responsible for establishing the parameters of the current session state.

■ The client initiates a client hello message to begin communications. The contents of this message provide the server with data about variables that are supported by the client.

■ After the server processes the client hello message, it can respond with either a handshake failure alert or several hello messages.

■ The server hello message is sent by the server to the client and is used to make decisions that are then passed back to the client.

■ The server's certificate, or a chain of certificates to be authenticated, is sent immediately after the server hello message.

■ The server sends a server key exchange message only when no certificate is present, and the certificate is used only for signing or when Fortezza key exchange is used.

■ The optional certificate request message requests a certificate from the client for authentication purposes and is made up of two parameters. The first parameter indicates the acceptable certificate type. The second parameter indicates the acceptable distinguished names of acceptable certificate authorities.

■ The server hello done message is sent by the server to the client to indicate the end of the server hello. It also signals that no further associated server hello messages are coming. On receipt of the server hello done message, the client should verify the certificate and the certificate chain. The client should also verify that all server hello parameters received are acceptable.

■ The client certificate message is the first message that a client can send after a server hello done message is received and is sent only if the server requests a certificate.

■ The client key exchange message allows the client to send key information to the server. The key information pertains to a symmetric-key algorithm that both parties will use for the session.

■ The certificate verify message is used to provide explicit verification of a client certificate. The server authenticates the client using a private key. The server is not required to authenticate itself to the client.

■ The client sends a change cipher spec message, followed immediately by the finished message. When the server receives the finished message, it too sends a change cipher spec message, followed by the finished message. Now the handshake protocol is complete and the parties can transmit application data securely.

■ Before ending the communications, the client and the server must share the information that the connection is ending. Either party can end communication by sending a close_notify alert before closing its own write session. The other party must send its own close_notify alert and close down immediately, discarding any pending writes.

- Public key encryption algorithms are very slow, hence to improve performance the parties can cache and reuse information exchanged during the handshake protocol. This process is called session ID reuse.

- Both parties (client and server) must agree to reuse a previous session ID. The SSL specifications suggest that the lifetime of cached session IDs expires after 24 hours.

- Master secret is derived from the pre-master secret. After the generation of pre-master secret and both the sides (client and server) are aware of it, the master secret can be computed. The master secret, which is used as the shared secret; is made up of several hash calculations of data previously exchanged in the message.

Key Terms

Security The term refers to techniques for ensuring that data stored in a computer cannot be read or compromised. Most security measures involve data encryption and passwords.

Protocol An agreed-upon format for transmitting data between two devices.

Encryption The translation of data into a secret code is called encryption. Encryption is the most effective way to achieve data security.

Packet It is a piece of a message transmitted over a packet-switching network. One of the key features of a packet is that it contains the destination address in addition to the data.

Nodes In networks, a node is a processing location. It can be a computer or some other device, such as a printer. Every node has a unique network address.

IP Address It is an identifier for a computer or device on an IP network. Networks using the IP protocol, route messages based on the IP address of the destination.

Header A header is a unit of information that precedes a data object. In a network transmission, a header is part of the data packet and contains transparent information about the file or the transmission.

Firewall A system designed to prevent unauthorized access to or from a private network. Firewalls can be implemented in both hardware and software, or a combination of both.

Network A group of two or more computer systems linked together.

Blowfish It is a symmetric encryption algorithm designed by Bruce Schneier in 1993 as an alternative to existing encryption algorithms. Blowfish is available for free use by any, and the technology is unpatented and free of license.

Routers A device that forwards data packets along networks. A router is connected to at least two networks. Routers are located at gateways, the places where two or more networks connect.

IP (Internet Protocol) IP specifies the format of packets, and the addressing scheme. IP is something like the postal system. It allows you to address a package and drop it in the system, but there's no direct link between you and the recipient.

Decryption The process of decoding data that has been encrypted into a secret format. Decryption requires a secret key or password.

Session It is the period of time a user interfaces with an application. The user session begins when the user accesses the application and ends when the user quits the application.

Transport layer The transport layer is the fourth layer of the OSI reference model. It provides transparent transfer of data between end systems using the services of the network layer (for example, IP) below to move data between the two communicating systems.

Key Terms Quiz

Use the Key Terms list to complete the sentences that follow. (Not all terms will be used.)

1. _____ is an identifier for a computer or device on an IP network.

2. An agreed-upon format for transmitting data between two devices is called _____.

3. _____ is a device connected to at least two networks and forwards data packets along these networks.

4. _____ is the period of time a user interfaces with an application.

5. _____ is a term that refers to techniques for ensuring that data stored in a computer cannot be read or compromised.

6. A system designed to prevent unauthorized access to or from a private network, _____ can be implemented in both hardware and software, or a combination of both.

7. The translation of data into a secret code is called _____, and is the most effective way to achieve data security.

8. It is a unit of information that precedes a data object. In a network transmission, a(n) _____ is part of the data packet and contains transparent information about the file or the transmission.

9. This symmetric encryption algorithm is an alternative to existing encryption algorithms. It is _____.

10. In networks, a(n) _____ is a processing location. It can be a computer or some other device, such as a printer.

Multiple-Choice Quiz

1. AH protocol supports _____.
   a. Access control
   b. Confidentiality
   c. Compression
   d. Recognition

2. ESP protocol supports _____.

    a.   certification
    b.   identification
    c.   confidentiality
    d.   authorization

3. AH header has the following field: _____.

    a.   Next Header
    b.   Last Header
    c.   Pay Number
    d.   Integrity Check Value

4. IPSec architecture document _____ describes the combination of security associations that must be supported.

    a.   RFC5643
    b.   RFE3745
    c.   RFC2401
    d.   RFC2004

5. ESP header has the following field: _____.

    a.   Reserved
    b.   Sniffers
    c.   Padding
    d.   Cast

6. For peer communication _____ SA(s) is/are needed.

    a.   one
    b.   two
    c.   three
    d.   four

7. Security Association is not identified by _____.

    a.   a transport latency
    b.   a security parameter index
    c.   an IP destination address
    d.   a security protocol identifier

8. SPD and SAD are covered under _____.

    a.   Security associations
    b.   Security database
    c.   Security networks
    d.   National security

9. Key management is _____.

    a.   automatic
    b.   manual
    c.   semi-manual
    d.   not needed at all

10. Which of these is not an SSL specification?

    a. Session identifier
    b. Master secret
    c. Sequence numbers
    d. Padding

11. In the record layer, a header is added to _____ record(s).

    a. each
    b. alternate
    c. one in three
    d. one in ten

12. Which of the following message is fatal?

    a. Unexpected_message
    b. Parameter_failure
    c. Decompression_revoked
    d. Certificate_failure

13. The server hello message contains the following field: _____.

    a. Server_id
    b. Reserved
    c. Random
    d. Compression_suite

14. The server hello done message is sent by the _____.

    a. client to the server
    b. server to the client
    c. router to the client
    d. server to router

15. The client certificate message is the first message a client sends after receiving a _____.

    a. server key exchange message
    b. server certificate message
    c. certificate request message
    d. server hello done message

Essay Quiz

1. What is security association?

2. Explain the following:

    ▪ Main Mode

    ▪ Aggressive Mode

    ▪ Quick Mode

3. List the steps that take place in the record layer.

Lab Project

Lab Project 7.1

KOPL Systems is an E-Mail Service Provider. KOPL faces a major information security concern in carrying out their business: they have to deal with a massive amount of e-mails traversing through the internet that need protection from Internet sniffers and spoofers.

Suggest a system so that KOPL Systems can provide an integrity and confidentiality security mechanism for e-mails even while the mails traverse through the network.

Chapter 8 Review

Chapter Summary

After reading this chapter, the students should understand the following.

S/MIME

- S/MIME and SET are the two well-known security protocols that operate above the application layer.
- Secure/Multipurpose Internet Mail Extensions (S/MIME) is a specification for securing electronic mail. It is based on the MIME standard.
- S/MIME describes a protocol for adding cryptographic security services through MIME encapsulation of digitally signed and encrypted objects.
- S/MIME is most widely used for securing e-mail. It can also be used with any mechanism transporting MIME, in automated message transfers using cryptographic security services without human intervention, and to encrypt fax messages sent over the Internet.
- MIME, developed by the Internet Engineering Task Force (IETF), was designed to support non-textual data, such as graphics or video data, used in Internet messages. However, MIME did not provide any security services.
- S/MIMEv3 is the current version.
- S/MIMEv3 provides the following security enhancements to MIME content: enveloped data, signed data, clear-signed data, and signed and enveloped data.
- The enveloped data function supports confidentiality services by allowing any content type in a MIME message to be symmetrically encrypted.
- The signed data function provides data integrity services, by computing a message digest over the selected content.
- The clear-signed data function allows S/MIME to provide data integrity services, in addition to allowing non-S/MIME–compliant readers to view the original data.
- The signed and enveloped data function supports both confidentiality and integrity services by allowing either the signing of encrypted data or the encrypting of signed data.

- S/MIMEv3 implements support for several symmetric content-encryption algorithms like DES, Triple DES, or RC2 with a key size greater than 40.
- The algorithms to be used for security services within S/MIMEv3 are digest and hashing algorithms, digital signature algorithms, key encryption algorithms, and data encryption algorithms.
- Digest and hashing algorithms must support MD5 and SHA-1. However, SHA-1 should be used.
- In case of digital signature algorithms, both sending and receiving agents must support DSA and should also support RSA.
- In case of key encryption algorithms, both sending and receiving agents must support DH and also support RSA encryption.
- In case of data encryption (session key) algorithms, sending agents should support RC2/40-bit key, RC2/128-bit key, and Triple DES. Receiving agents should support RC2/40 and Triple DES, but must support RC2/40.
- The S/MIME specification defines a process to decide the best algorithm to send messages, depending on cryptographic capabilities, use of encryption, and the S/MIME version.
- If the sender has a list of cryptographic capabilities of the recipient, the most preferred capability should be chosen to encrypt the outgoing message. Or the algorithm used in a previously received encrypted message should be chosen. However, in the absence of a previous reference, Triple DES or RC2/40 should be used.
- S/MIME messages comprise MIME bodies and CMS objects, which are derived from PKCS #7 data structures.
- Before any cryptographic processing takes place, a MIME entity must be prepared and converted to canonical form, and the appropriate transfer encoding applied. Then it must be sent to security services. Finally, the CMS (or PKCS #7) object yielded must be wrapped up in MIME and placed with the original message.
- Canonicalization allows the MIME entity to be uniquely and unambiguously represented in the environments where the signatures are created and will be verified. It provides a standard means by which data from various platforms can be exchanged.
- Transfer encoding ensures that the data is represented properly for transfer across the Internet and ensures reliable delivery. One common method of transfer encoding is base-64 encoding.
- The process of generating an encrypted MIME entity is called digital enveloping and is provided for by the enveloped-data content type.
- The key management systems are RSA key transport, the Diffie-Hellman agreement, and the known symmetric key.
- The S/MIME specification defines two methods for signing messages. They are Application/pkcs7-mime and Multipart/signed.
- The multipart/signed method is preferred for sent messages because of its readability by any mailer.

- The body of a multipart/signed MIME type is made up of two parts: any MIME content type, and detached signatures.

- A detached signature is a special case of signed data, which omits the copy of the plaintext that may be contained within the signed data.

- S/MIME supports both encryption and signing.

- A MIME content type, application/x-pkcs10, is used to request a certificate from a certificate authority.

- A certificates-only message is an application/pkcs7-mime and is used to transport certificates to an S/MIME-compliant end entity. It can also be used for the transport of certificate revocation lists (CRLs).

- Three enhanced security services for the current S/MIMEv3 security and certificate processing services include signed receipts, security labels, and secure mailing lists.

- A signed receipt is an optional service that allows for proof-of-message delivery. This service is used only for signed data.

- Security labels are used to describe the sensitivity of data and to control authorization and access.

- Mail list agents take a single message and perform the recipient-specific encryption for every recipient.

- The limitations of S/MIME include a lack of interoperability and limits on the certificate processing available in various products.

SET

- The Secure Electronic Transaction (SET) specification provides a framework for protecting payment cards used in Internet e-commerce transactions against fraud.

- MasterCard and Visa initiated the current version of the SET specification (SETv1).

- SET offers features like confidentiality of information, integrity of data, cardholder account authentication, merchant authentication, and interoperability. It uses the DES and RSA algorithms and X.509v3 certificates to provide these features.

- The participants in a SET transaction are the issuer, the cardholder, the merchant, the acquirer, and the payment gateway.

- The issuer is the bank or other financial institution that provides a branded payment card to an individual.

- The cardholder is the individual authorized to use the payment card.

- The merchant is an entity that provides goods or services to a cardholder for payment.

- The acquirer is the financial institution that supports merchants by providing the service of processing payment cards.

- The payment gateway is the entity that processes merchant payment messages.

- Dual signatures allow two pieces of data to be linked and sent to two different entities for processing.

■ The SET protocol provides authentication services for participants through the use of X.509v3. It has revocation provisions through the use of CRLv2.

■ Cardholder certificates function as electronic representations of payment cards.

■ Merchant certificates function as electronic substitutes for the payment card brand decal that appears in the store window.

■ Payment gateway certificates are obtained by acquirers or their processors for the systems that process authentication and capture messages.

■ Acquirer certificates are required only in order to operate a CA that can accept and process certificate requests directly from merchants over networks.

■ Issuer certificates are required only in order to operate a CA that can accept and process certificate requests directly from cardholders over networks.

■ Certificates must be managed through a strict certificate hierarchy.

■ The purchase request transaction is made up of four messages: initiate request, initiate response, purchase request, and purchase response.

■ The payment authorization transaction is made up of two messages: authorization request and authorization response.

■ The payment capture transaction is accomplished by the exchange of two messages: the capture request and the capture response.

Key Terms

Secure/Multipurpose Internet Mail Extensions (S/MIME) A specification for securing electronic mail. It describes a protocol for adding cryptographic security services through MIME encapsulation of digitally signed and encrypted objects.

Request for Comment (RFC) 822 The specification that defined the standard format of electronic mail messages. It was designed to carry textual messages over the Internet.

CMS object One of the two components of S/MIME messages. It is derived from PKCS #7 data structures.

Canonicalization The process that allows the MIME entity to be uniquely and unambiguously represented in the environments where the signature is created and will be verified.

Transfer encoding Transfer encoding ensures that the data is represented properly for transfer across the Internet and ensures reliable delivery.

Base-64 encoding A method of transfer encoding which enables arbitrary binary data to be encoded so that it may pass through a variety of systems unchanged.

Digital enveloping The process of generating an encrypted MIME entity.

Enveloped-data content type Consists of encrypted content of any type and encrypted content-encryption keys for one or more recipients.

Detached signature A special case of signed data which omits the copy of the plaintext that may be contained within the signed data.

Application/x-pkcs10   A MIME content type that is used to request a certificate from a certificate authority.

Signed receipt   An optional service that allows for proof-of-message delivery. This service is used only for signed data.

Security labels   A security service that uses a ranked list of labels to describe the sensitivity of data and to control authorization and access.

Mail list agents (MLAs)   A security service that takes a single message and performs the recipient-specific encryption for every recipient.

Secure Electronic Transaction (SET)   A specification that provides a framework for protecting payment cards used in Internet e-commerce transactions against fraud.

Issuer   The bank or a financial institution that provides a branded payment card.

Cardholder   The individual authorized to use the payment card.

Merchant   An entity that provides goods and/or services to a cardholder for payment.

Acquirer   The financial institution that supports merchants by providing the service of processing payment cards.

Payment gateway   The entity that processes merchant payment messages.

Dual signatures   A concept that allows two pieces of data to be linked and sent to two different entities for processing.

X.509v3   An application-specific certificate through which the SET protocol provides authentication services for participants.

CRLv2   An application-specific certificate through which the SET protocol has revocation provisions.

Cardholder certificates   An electronic representation of payment cards, in which the account information and a secret value known only to the cardholder's software are encoded using a one-way hashing algorithm.

Merchant certificates   These function as electronic substitutes for the payment card brand decal that appears in the store window.

Key Terms Quiz

Use the Key Terms list to complete the sentences that follow. (Not all terms will be used.)

1. _____ is a specification for securing electronic mail.

2. _____ are used to describe the sensitivity of data and to control authorization and access.

3. The SET specification has revocation provisions through the use of
_____.

4. A MIME content type _____ is used to request a certificate from a certificate authority.

5. The SET specification provides authentication services for participants through the use of _____.

6. The components of an S/MIME object are MIME bodies and _____.

7. The _____ specification protects payment cards used in Internet e-commerce transactions against fraud.

8. The entity that processes merchant payment messages is called _____.

9. The concept that allows two pieces of data to be linked and sent to two different entities for processing is called _____.

10. _____ function as electronic representations of payment cards.

Multiple-Choice Quiz

1. The _____ S/MIME function supports confidentiality services by allowing symmetric encryption of any content type in a MIME message.

   a. clear-signed data
   b. enveloped data
   c. signed and enveloped data
   d. signed data

2. The _____ algorithms must support MD5 and SHA-1.

   a. data encryption
   b. digest and hashing
   c. digital signature
   d. key encryption

3. Which of the following transactions allows a merchant to correct errors in previous capture requests?

   a. Authorization reversal
   b. Capture reversal
   c. Credit reversal
   d. Payment gateway certificate request

4. _____ provide(s) a standard means of transferring data across various platforms.

   a. Canonicalization
   b. Digital enveloping
   c. Dual signatures
   d. Transfer Encoding

5. In the RSA transport key management system, the _____ is encrypted in the recipient's public key.

   a. content-encryption key
   b. key encryption key
   c. private key
   d. session key

6. A _____ omits the copy of the plaintext that may be contained within the signed data.

    a.   CMS object
    b.   detached signature
    c.   digital envelope
    d.   dual signature

7. A _____ is an application/pkcs7-mime used to transport certificates to an S/MIME-compliant end entity.

    a.   certificates-only message
    b.   detached signature
    c.   digital envelope
    d.   dual signature

8. A _____ is an optional service that allows for proof-of-message delivery.

    a.   payment gateway
    b.   secure mailing list
    c.   security label
    d.   signed receipt

9. The current version of the SET specification is _____.

    a.   SETv1
    b.   SETv2
    c.   SETv3
    d.   SETv4

10. SET provides for confidentiality through the use of _____.

    a.   Digital signatures
    b.   DES algorithms
    c.   RSA algorithms
    d.   X.509v3 certificates

11. Digital signatures and _____ are used to implement cardholder account authentication.

    a.   Payment getaways
    b.   DES algorithms
    c.   RSA algorithms
    d.   X.509v3 certificates

12. The use of digital signatures using the RSA algorithm provides _____.

    a.   cardholder account authentication
    b.   confidentiality of information
    c.   integrity of data
    d.   merchant authentication

13. The financial institution that supports merchants by providing the service of processing payment cards is called a(n) _____.

    a.   acquirer

    b.   cardholder

    c.   issuer

    d.   merchant

14. What is the final step in the dual signature generation process?

    a.   Encrypting a final message digest using the signer's private key.

    b.   Generating a message digest for both the OI and the PI.

    c.   Hashing the new block of data.

    d.   Hashing the two message digests.

15. _____ function as electronic substitutes for the payment card brand decal that appears in the store window.

    a.   Acquirer certificates

    b.   Cardholder certificates

    c.   Issuer certificates

    d.   Merchant certificates

Essay Quiz

1. Explain payment gateway certificates.

2. How is payment capture accomplished?

3. What are the four messages that make up the purchase request transaction?

Lab Project

Lab Project 8.1

Peter McClure, the system administrator of Symonds International, wants to construct an enveloped data content type. List the steps to do this.

Chapter 9 Review

Chapter Summary

After reading this chapter, the students should understand the following.

- Cryptographic hardware play two types of roles, cryptographic accelerators (for better processing speed and better performance of cryptographic systems) and authentication tokens (identification and authentication services).

Cryptographic Accelerators

- Cryptographic accelerators, like math coprocessors, implement in hardware a set of functions usually handled by software.

- Encoding the functions in silicon takes a heavy computational workload required for authentication, such as algorithms and protocols, off the system hardware and software, thus increasing system speed and allowing optimization of system resources.

■ Most cryptographic accelerators are certified by certifying authorities, such as the National Institute of Standards and Technology (NIST), making them dependable and safe.

Authentication Tokens

■ Authentication tokens are hardware devices that help authenticate and identify an end user.

■ The token has unique information encoded on it, which the host system uses to perform authentication protocol and identify the owner.

■ Duplication or theft of the unique authentication information can provide unauthorized access to system resources.

■ Advanced authentication tokens contain a microprocessor and semiconductor memory, and they support sophisticated authentication protocols that provide a higher level of security than ordinary authentication tokens.

■ The shape, size, and manufacturing material of an authentication token are called its form factors. These factors affect the durability, probability, security, and convenience of a token.

■ There are two types of authentication tokens, noncontact and contact.

■ Noncontact tokens require no electrical or physical contact of the token with an authentication information reader. They operate by transmitting data to, and receiving data from, a terminal or reader, or they require a user to enter data that is then generated by the token—for example, passwords or secure IDs.

■ There are mainly three types of noncontact tokens: proximity cards, one-time password (OTP) generators, and handheld challenge/response calculators.

■ Contact tokens must make physical contact with the reader to transfer data—for example, in automated teller machines (ATMs). The electrical contacts located on the token physically touch the matching contacts on the reader to supply power, ground, and data signals. The contacts on the token and reader are defined in the same way to enable readability of data and interoperability of devices.

■ A Smart card is a credit card–sized plastic card that contains an embedded integrated circuit chip. This chip contains both memory and computational capacity.

■ Self-containment of authentication information and mechanisms on these cards makes them resistant to attacks, and therefore, they are preferred in applications that require strong security protection and authentication. An example of Smart cards is banking debit cards. The physical properties and communication characteristics of the embedded chip are governed by Smart card standards, so that they are universally accepted and interoperable. ISO 7816 is the international standard for Smart cards.

■ Depending upon the type of chip used, a variety of Smart cards is available. The chips vary in processing power, flexibility, memory, and cost. The two primary categories of Smart card are memory cards and microprocessor cards.

■ Memory cards have no sophisticated processing power and cannot manage files dynamically. There are three primary types of memory cards: standard, protected/segmented, and stored value memory cards.

■ Microprocessor multifunction cards have on-card dynamic data processing capabilities. These cards, with the help of a microprocessor embedded in them, allocate card memory to specific functions or applications. This data is managed in organized file structures using a card operating system (COS), which controls access to the on-card user memory.

■ All Smart cards interact with a processing device, a reader or a terminal, that can read data from the card and authenticate it. Although both reader and terminal primarily authenticate content, they differ in the functionality they provide. Readers are units that interface with a PC for the majority of their processing requirements, whereas terminals are self-contained processing devices. Terminals as well as readers can read and write to the Smart cards.

■ JavaCard is a Smart card with a Java Virtual Machine (JVM) in its read-only memory (ROM) mask. JVM serves as the Smart card's operating system (OS), allows embedding of information in portable Java instead of using hardware-specific assembly code. Also, the use of Java enables the adding of functionality to cards post-issuance.

■ A JavaCard operates like a Smart card. Upon receiving a command from a Smart card reader, a JavaCard processes it and returns an answer confirming whether or not the details are valid.

■ A JavaCard can process one command at a time.

Biometrics

■ Biometrics is the science of measuring human body characteristics, which can then be used to verify the identity of an individual.

■ The biometric recognition mechanism operates in two modes: enrollment and verification.

■ In enrollment, the biological features of users are acquired by a handheld device called a sensor, which are then converted into a digital signal. Most sensors take multiple samples to account for degrees of variance in the measurement.

■ In verification, the biological feature of users are acquired from the sensor and converted to a digital representation. This is called a live scan and is then compared to the stored biometric template. The live scan is considered valid if it falls within a certain statistical range of values.

■ The accumulated templates of all users are referred to as the template database. These databases require the same protection as a password database.

■ The user can use any of the following recognition methods: fingerprint recognition, optical biometrics, facial recognition, voice recognition, signature recognition, and keystroke recognition.

■ The accuracy of biometrics authentication can be recognized in terms of its false acceptance rate (FAR) and the false rejection rate (FRR).

■ Suppliers often use FAR together with FRR to describe the capabilities of the system.

Combining Authentication Methods

■ Passwords, authentication tokens, and biometrics are subject to a variety of attacks. Combining authentication techniques can help counter the vulnerabilities of individual systems and increase the security.

Key Terms

Noncontact tokens   Tokens that do not require any electrical or physical contact with a reader. They either operate by exchanging data with a terminal or require the user to enter data that is then generated by the token.

Contact tokens   Tokens that must make physical contact with the reader to transfer the data. Most integrated circuit tokens require an interface in which electrical contacts located on the token physically touch the matching concepts on the reader.

Proximity cards   Noncontact cards that use radio frequency signals to authenticate users. The coded signal is either transmitted manually or when cards come within a certain range of a proximity reader.

Smart cards   A credit card–sized plastic card that contains an embedded integrated circuit chip. The self-containment of these cards makes them resistant to attacks and suitable for applications that require strong security protection and authentication.

PCMCIA   Acronym for Personal Computer Memory Card International Association, an international standards body and trade association with over 200 member companies that was founded in 1989 to establish standards for Integrated Circuit cards and to promote interchangeability among mobile computers where ruggedness, low power, and small size were critical.

Readers   A unit that reads and writes data from, and to, a Smart card and interfaces with a PC for most of its processing requirements.

Terminals   A self-contained processing device that reads and writes data to and from the Smart card.

Biometrics   The science of measuring human body characteristics, which can then be used to verify the identity of an individual.

Enrollment   A phase in biometric verification. The biological features of users are acquired by a handheld device called a sensor, which are then converted into a digital signal. Most sensors take multiple samples to account for degrees of variance in the measurement.

Biometric verification   A verification method in which the biological feature of a user is acquired from the sensor and converted to a digital representation and then stored as a template to verify user identity against.

Optical recognition   Method of capturing measurements of the retina and iris to identify and authenticate users later.

Fingerprint recognition   A recognition method in which fingerprints are scanned and used as templates for authentication later.

FAR   A situation in which a biometric system wrongly verifies an identity by matching the features from individuals who are not identical, and which would create a security hazard.

FRR   A situation in which a biometric system is not able to verify the legitimate claimed identity of an enrolled user, and which would result in inconvenience for the user.

Live scan   A method in which the biological feature of users are acquired from the sensor and converted to a digital representation.

Key Terms Quiz

Use the Key Terms list to complete the sentences that follow. (Not all terms will be used.)

1. _____ is the most reliable biometric technology for user authentication.

2. A _____ is a self-contained processing device.

3. A _____ is the digital representation of a biological feature.

4. _____ is a method in which the biological feature of users are acquired from the sensor and converted to a digital representation.

5. When a biometric system wrongly verifies an identity by matching the features from individuals who are not identical, the situation is called _____.

6. Biometrics is the science of measuring _____, which can then be used to verify the identity of an individual.

7. The devices that use radio frequency signals to authenticate users are called _____.

8. _____ contain an embedded integrated circuit chip having memory and computational capacity.

9. _____ make physical contact with the reader to transfer the data.

10. A situation in which a biometric system is unable to verify the legitimate claimed identity of an enrolled user is called its _____.

Multiple-Choice Quiz

1. Cryptographic accelerators provide _____.
   a.   increased speed
   b.   increased security
   c.   increased computational expense
   d.   All of the above

2. Authentication tokens _____.

    a.   authenticate the user performing the transaction
    b.   identify the user performing the transaction
    c.   authenticate the device used for the transaction
    d.   validate the transaction

3. Tokens that have recessed contacts usually require a _____ casing than those that have surface-mounted contacts.

    a.   thinner
    b.   thicker
    c.   wider
    d.   narrower

4. Noncontact tokens include _____.

    a.   proximity cards
    b.   one-time password generators
    c.   challenge/response calculators
    d.   All of the above

5. Java rings are steel casings that contain _____ called Crypto iButtons.

    a.   magnetic chips
    b.   microprocessors
    c.   math accelerators
    d.   None of the above

6. A _____ can be regarded as a floppy disk of varying sizes without the lock.

    a.   JavaCard
    b.   reader
    c.   standard memory card
    d.   proximity card

7. A _____ improves the security and provides tamperproof storage of user and account identity.

    a.   Smart card
    b.   proximity card
    c.   terminal
    d.   reader

8. A _____ is so designed that it stores values or tokens and is either disposable or rechargeable.

    a.   stored value memory card
    b.   microprocessor multifunction card
    c.   JavaCard
    d.   HTMLCard

9. Tokens based on JavaCard technology are _____.

    a.   Java rings and Crypto iButtons
    b.   Crypto iButtons and Dogtag-type tokens

    c.   Dogtag-type tokens and Java rings

    d.   None of the above

10. _____ are used to acquire biological features in biometrics.

    a.   Face identifiers

    b.   Sensors

    c.   Gamma-ray face scanners

    d.   Latent scanners

11. JVM executes a Java _____ subset on the Smart card.

    a.   bytecode

    b.   bitcode

    c.   10-bit code

    d.   10-byte code

12. A _____ manages data as organized file structures on a Smart card.

    a.   microprocessor

    b.   card operating system

    c.   malfunction card

    d.   microcontroller chip

13. Biometric signature recognition operates in a _____ environment.

    a.   one-dimensional

    b.   three-dimensional

    c.   four-dimensional

    d.   two-dimensional

14. _____ defines Application Identifiers (AIDs), which are used to identify a specific application.

    a.   ISO 7816-1

    b.   ISO 7816-3

    c.   ISO 7816-5

    d.   ISO 7816-6

15. _____ defines the physical dimensions of contact Smart cards and the placement of chips, magnetic stripes, and any embossing on the cards.

    a.   ISO 7816-1

    b.   ISO 7816-3

    c.   ISO 7816-5

    d.   ISO 7816-6

Essay Quiz

1. What are authentication tokens and how do they work?

2. Explain the difference in the working of noncontact and contact tokens.

3. What is the meaning of enrollment and verification in the biometric recognition process?

Lab Project

Lab Project 9.1

The management of an R & D facility in San Jose desires to provide restricted access to its employees to various parts of the building. The building will be divided into five secure zones depending on the sensitivity of the tasks and research. However, the security of each of the zones may be lifted on specific occasions to allow unrestrained access.

Recommend a cost-effective solution that will yield the desired result.

Chapter 10 Review

Chapter Summary

After reading this chapter, the students should understand the following.

Introduction

- Electronically transmitted agreements and transactions offer convenience but also have legal and technical ramifications that emanate from the inherent vulnerabilities of the involved systems and components. To counter the vulnerabilities, digital signatures offer benefits in message integrity, savings, storage, and risk mitigation.

- In the US federal law, under the Statutes of Frauds, a party that claims that a contract was made must provide proof. A signed document is considered proof. The traditionally accepted signature is still the handwritten signature.

- A new, yet to be tested, legislation provides that an electronic signature has the same legal status as a handwritten signature.

Legislative Approaches

- Digital signatures, to become mainstream legal proof, must overcome the following barriers: Documents that exist only in the electronic form do not have the same legal status as paper documents; and, the method for signing electronic documents must be secure, reliable, and legally sanctioned so that the need to generate and sign paper documents would be completely eliminated.

Legal Guidelines from the American Bar Association

- The American Bar Association (ABA) Information Security Committee, Section of Science and Technology, published a document titled Digital Signature Guidelines in 1996. These guidelines were originally drafted to provide "general, abstract statements of principle, intended to serve as longterm, unifying foundations for digital signature law across varying legal settings."

Legal Concepts Related to Digital Signatures

- Nonrepudiation defines the means to prevent illegitimate breaches of contracts on the grounds that a specific communication originated with, and was submitted by, a certain person, or was delivered by a certain person.

■ Nonrepudiation services provide trusted evidence that a specific action occurred.

■ With businesses operating at the speed of the Internet, it is only with a full set of digital, nonrepudiable elements that irrefutable evidence can be presented in a court of law.

■ The three types of nonrepudiation pertaining to information security and digital signature are nonrepudiation of origin of communication by guaranteeing the identity of the sender, nonrepudiation of delivery of the communication message to guarantee that the data was not altered in transit, and nonrepudiation of submission of data by the sender to guarantee that the data was sent at a specific date and time.

■ Nonrepudiation services use signer authentications and data authentications designed to exclude impersonators or forgers.

■ Electronic documents, unlike written documents, carry information that is not bound to any concrete carrier such as paper or ink. This information can also be easily modified or updated by anyone with appropriate permissions. Therefore, the traditional method of signing by appending a signature to an existing document does not work for electronic documents.

Requirements for the Use of Digital Signatures

■ Public-key infrastructure (PKI) ensures that only valid keys are used in signing and verifying electronic documents.

■ PKI must enforce policies using properly administered certification authorities (CA) and registration authorities (RA) requiring end users to show reliable proof that authenticate them.

■ PKI also serves to revoke or suspend a certificate, if needed.

■ An unauthorized person with access to a private key can forge the owner's signature on electronic documents. To reduce the risks presented by unauthorized access, the following guidelines should be used:

  ■ All users should be able to revoke their public keys from the directory at any time. CAs should save (in the public directory) information about all revoked keys.

  ■ An authority should be able to revoke the signatures issued, using a CA, for its employees and should use a separate CA to do so.

  ■ Online Certificate Status protocol (OCSP) should be used to ensure that verifiers receive the current revocation status only.

■ Time stamping helps resolve cases where the signer repudiates signing, claiming to have lost, whether accidentally or incidentally (revocation), the signature key.

■ In addition, time stamping provides a means to trust signed documents even after the cryptographic primitives used for signing the documents have become unreliable.

Current and Pending Legislations

■ The E-SIGN act was signed on June 30, 2000. The E-SIGN law became effective, fully, on March 1, 2001.

■ E-SIGN requires a consumer to agree to electronically signed contracts and consent to receiving records over the Internet. Companies must verify that customers have an operating e-mail address and other technical means of receiving information.

■ Under E-SIGN, federal agencies have the authority to unconditionally exempt specified types of records from the consumer consent provisions.

■ E-SIGN was originally designed to boost Internet e-commerce transactions, for business-to-business (B2B) and business-to-consumer (B2C) markets, by ensuring security of these transactions and eliminating paperwork arising from contracts.

■ While an electronic signature is any symbol or method accomplished by any electronic means (including public-key systems), a digital signature refers to an implementation of public-key cryptography specific to a certain technology.

Key Terms

Digital signature   The transformation of a record using an asymmetric crypto system and a hash function such that a person having the initial record and the signer's public key can accurately determine (a) whether the transformation was created using the private key that corresponds to the signer's public key, and (b) whether the initial record has been altered since the transformation was made.

Nonrepudiation   Ensures that entities in a communication cannot deny having participated in all or part of the communication.

Repudiation   The denial by one of the entities involved in a communication of having participated in all or part of the communication.

Nonrepudiation of origin   Protects the recipient of a communication by guaranteeing the identity of the originator of the communication. It also confirms the time of sending the document and ensures the integrity of communication.

Nonrepudiation of delivery   Protects the sender of a communication by guaranteeing the identity of the receiver of the communication. It also confirms the time and the intact integrity of the communication.

Nonrepudiation of submission   Similar to nonrepudiation of origin and delivery except that it protects the sender against any claim by the recipient that the data wasn't sent or wasn't sent at a specific time.

Signer authentication   For a document to have any legal force, the signer of the document must be authenticated.

Data authentication   The process of stamping a document in a manner that disallows any future modifications.

Data origin authentication   Binds a concrete person to a specific document.

A nonrepudiation service   Provides evidence to prevent a person from unilaterally modifying or terminating legal obligations arising from a transaction effected by computer-based means.

Public-key infrastructure (PKI)   A system of digital certificates, certificate authorities, and other registration authorities that verifies and authenticates the validity of each party involved in an Internet transaction.

Certification authority (CA)   A trusted third-party (TTP) organization or company that issues digital certificates used to create digital signatures and public-private key pairs.

Registration authority (RA)   An approval agent for the issuance of a new certificate. They do not actually issue the certificate, but instead act strictly as a vetting agent. Once they have verified the actual identity of the user, they will send the approval to the CA, who will actually issue the certificate.

Time stamping   A set of techniques that enable you to ascertain whether an electronic document was created or signed at (or before) a certain time.

Time Stamping Authority (TSA)   A trusted third party that creates time-stamp tokens in order to indicate that a datum existed at a particular point in time.

Time stamp   The TSA's digital attestation that an identified electronic document was presented to the TSA at a certain time.

Time-stamping services (TSS)   A collection of methods and techniques providing longterm authentication of digital documents along with the moment in time the document is submitted for authentication.

E-SIGN   This act gives legal recognition and effect to electronic signatures, contracts, and records, and it empowers the use of online contracts and the provision of notices.

Key Terms Quiz

Use the Key Terms list to complete the sentences that follow. (Not all terms will be used.)

1. _____ provide trusted evidence that a specific action occurred.

2. _____ protects the sender of a communication by guaranteeing the identity of the receiver of the communication.

3. _____ binds a concrete person to a specific document.

4. _____ uses an asymmetric crypto along with a hash function to encrypt a record for protecting its integrity and confidentiality.

5. The process of ensuring that no future modifications can be made to a document after it leaves the sender's computer is called _____.

6. _____ protects the sender against any claim by the recipient that the data wasn't sent or wasn't sent at a specific time.

7. _____ is a trusted third-party organization or company that issues digital certificates used to create digital signatures and public-private key pairs.

8. _____ is a collection of methods and techniques providing longterm authentication of digital documents along with the moment in time the document was submitted for authentication.

9. _____ is the denial by one of the entities involved in a communication of having participated in all or part of the communication.

10. The fact that only valid keys are used in signing and verifying electronic documents is ensured by _____.

Multiple-Choice Quiz

1. The digital signature guidelines have been developed by _____.
    a.   OCSP
    b.   OSISA
    c.   ABA
    d.   ANSI

2. _____ involves protecting the sender against any claim by the recipient that either the data wasn't sent or wasn't sent at the specific time.
    a.   Nonrepudiation of admission
    b.   Nonrepudiation of origin
    c.   Nonrepudiation of delivery
    d.   Nonrepudiation of submission

3. Nonrepudiation of origin guarantees the _____ of the originator of a communication.
    a.   integrity
    b.   identity
    c.   confidentiality
    d.   authority

4. Data origin authentication binds (a) _____.
    a.   concrete person to a specific document
    b.   recipient to the sender
    c.   data to a system
    d.   sender to the recipient

5. A _____ is a way to ensure that the public key belongs to the purported individual.
    a.   digital password
    b.   digital passport
    c.   digital certificate
    d.   digital token

6. Signer authentication and data authentication are essential components of what is often called a _____.
    a.   nonrepudiation service
    b.   data authentication service
    c.   data security service
    d.   data storage service

7. To effectively incorporate digital signatures within an e-commerce framework, an organization should create and maintain a(n) _____.

    a. OCSP
    b. CA
    c. PKI
    d. RA

8. To allow users to revoke their public keys from the directory at any time, a(n) _____ should save information about all revoked keys in the public directory.

    a. CA
    b. OCSP
    c. KPI
    d. RA

9. To ensure that verifiers receive the most current revocation status, a(n) _____ should be used.

    a. RA
    b. CA
    c. OCSP
    d. PKI

10. Most time-stamping systems use a trusted third-party authority called a _____.

    a. time-stamping authority
    b. registration authority
    c. certification authority
    d. time-management authority

11. The _____ is an example of a digital signature.

    a. Smart card recognition system
    b. text entry at the end of an e-mail message
    c. fingerprint recognition system
    d. private key

12. _____ is an algorithm that does not encrypt data, yet it can be used to create a digital signature.

    a. DSA
    b. ECDSA
    c. SHA-1
    d. DSS

13. As per the E-SIGN act, which of the following still needs to be sent in the paper form?

    a. Electricity lapses
    b. An insurance premium receipts confirmation
    c. Credit card statements
    d. An electronic fund prospectus

14. The digital signatures guidelines have been drafted by ABA's _____ committee.

    a. Information security

    b.   Privacy and computer crime

    c.   E-privacy law

    d.   Technical standardization law

15. _____ are technology-neutral.

    a.   Digital signatures

    b.   Electronic signatures

    c.   Public keys

    d.   Private keys

Essay Quiz

1. List the benefits of digital signatures?

2. What is the difference between digital and written documents, although both aim to serve the same purpose?

3. Which attributes of digital signatures, or potential attributes, provide it with the potential of being a greater legal authority than handwritten signatures?

Lab Project

Lab Project 10.1

ABZ Fertilizers sends a number of CD-ROMs containing payroll information to its bank. This information is processed by the MMC bank at the end of each month. The MMC bank now wants to move to an Internet-based solution for which legislation requires them to encrypt all personal and financial data transferred electronically. The bank has an internal PKI service but can't interoperate with their customers. What should the bank do to move on to an Internet-based solution?

Chapter 11 Review

Chapter Summary

After reading this chapter, the students should understand the following.

Measuring Losses

■ Breach of security or a lapse in security can lead to the loss of data (and system resources), money, and/or the reputation of the victim.

■ Sometimes the loss is direct, and at other times, a result of a direct loss (indirect)—for example, the loss of faith in a company as a result of the compromise of system security.

■ Indirect losses can be a more serious concern than direct losses. For example, the theft of data is not as serious a possibility of ill-intended manipulation of the stolen data by the attacker. Any such manipulation will render the original data inaccurate or unusable.

■ Unauthorized disclosure of data can occur when an unauthorized user, either accidentally or intentionally, can access or read information not intended for that user. Disclosed data may be further compromised by being passed on to an unauthorized individual.

■ Unauthorized disclosure of data occurs when sensitive data is stored in unencrypted form, or when the sensitive data's storage location or environment is not protected by appropriate authorization and access-control mechanisms.

■ Unauthorized modification of data, intentionally or unintentionally, involves addition to or deletion or destruction of data or software, compromising the integrity of data.

■ If the compromised data spreads throughout the network, it may corrupt databases, spreadsheet calculations, and possibly all other forms of application information, making an organization-wide impact. Such unauthorized modifications of data can also affect system information, impairing the availability of system or network services.

■ Unauthorized modification of data and software can easily take place when data integrity services are not provided.

■ Unauthorized access to data occurs when a user who is not authorized to view or use a system or a network gains access to it.

■ Unauthorized access generally occurs through illegitimate or inadvertent disclosure of passwords and user IDs to a system.

■ Unauthorized access is the most compromising security breach as it's the primary platform for intruder access into the system. Unauthorized access gives the intruder the ability to evoke other security threats.

■ Disclosure of network traffic occurs when data in transit is intercepted (sniffed) by unauthorized users.

■ Spoofing of network traffic involves the intruders receiving a message by masquerading as the legitimate receiving destination or by masquerading as the sending computer and transmitting an unauthorized message to a destination.

■ Spoofing of network traffic can occur when data transmitted over a network is in plaintext, lacks a date/time stamp, does not use method authentication codes (or digital signature), or lacks a real-time verification mechanism (effective against playback attacks).

Identifying Intruders

■ Insiders with knowledge of the target company's network often gain unrestricted access in order to damage the system or to steal proprietary data.

■ Hackers break into a network for the thrill of it, or to gain bragging rights in the hacker community.

- Terrorist groups use new information technology and the Internet to formulate plans, raise funds, spread propaganda, communicate securely, and use coercive tactics against governments and civilian population.

- Foreign intelligence services increasingly view computer intrusion as a useful tool for acquiring sensitive (government and private sector) information and have adopted cyber tools as part of their espionage tradecraft.

- Hactivists generally do not alter operating systems or networks but damage services by disrupting e-mail servers or defacing web sites often deny the public access to web sites containing valuable information. Such criminal attacks infringe on peoples' right to communicate.

Key Terms

Sniffers   Software used by intruders to analyze network traffic.

Snoop   A utility originally created by Sun Microsystems to allow administrators to verify traffic flow across networks. Snoop also allows intruders running the Solaris OS to watch the flow of network traffic.

Spoofing   A process that involves making the transmission appear to be emanating from an authorized source.

Playback   An attack that involves capturing a session between a sender and a receiver and then retransmitting the message with a new header, new message content, or both.

Insiders   People who commit information security crimes against their employers.

Hackers   Individuals who gain unauthorized access to computer systems for the purpose of stealing and corrupting data. Originally, the term hacker was a complimentary slang term for a computer enthusiast.

Cyber terrorism   The use of cyber tools to shut down critical national infrastructure (such as energy, transportation, or government operations) for the purpose of coercing or intimidating a government or civilian population.

Hactivism   Defines politically motivated attacks on publicly accessible web pages or e-mail servers.

Hactivists   Group and individual attackers who overload e-mail servers or hack and deface web sites to send a political message.

SSL protocol   A layered security protocol that allows client/server applications to communicate securely over the Internet.

National Infrastructure Protection Center (NIPC)   A division of the FBI that looks at the legal ramifications of information security and related enforcement issues.

Computer Crime and Intellectual Property Section (CCIPS)   Area of the US Department of Justice that is devoted to investigating computer crime.

Computer Emergency Response Team/Coordination Center (CERT/CC)   Originally created in 1988 by the Defense Advanced Research Projects Agency (DARPA) to provide a broad range of information security services. CERT/CC initiatives include research into security vulnerability, improvement of system security, and coordination of teams to respond to large-scale incidents.

Key Terms Quiz

Use the Key Terms list to complete the sentences that follow. (Not all terms will be used.)

1. Disclosure of network traffic occurs when intruders analyze network traffic using

_____.

2. The _____ utility was originally created to allow administrators to verify traffic flow across the network.

3. Alteration of data transmitted over the network by an intruder using masquerading techniques is called _____.

4. In a(n) _____ attack, an intruder captures a communication session over the network and then retransmits the modified message.

5. A disgruntled employee who commits a security crime against an employer is called a(n) _____.

6. _____ are intruders who gain unauthorized access to systems or networks.

7. Coercing the public using cyber tools is referred to as _____.

8. A politically motivated cyber attack disrupting the services of an e-mail server is called

_____.

9. Implementing the _____ protocol protects a client/server application from an eavesdropping threat.

10. _____ of the US Department of Justice is devoted to investigating computer crime.

Multiple-Choice Quiz

1. The commonest cause of unauthorized disclosure of sensitive data is _____.
   a.   failure of a real-time system procedure
   b.   storing unencrypted data
   c.   failure to patch a system bug
   d.   storing network passwords in batch files on PCs

2. Individuals revealing information to unauthorized recipients pose the threat of

_____.
   a.   unauthorized modification of data
   b.   unauthorized access
   c.   disclosure of network traffic
   d.   unauthorized disclosure of data

3. Unauthorized modification of data and software occurs when _____ services are not provided.

    a.   authentication
    b.   data integrity
    c.   data confidentiality
    d.   authorization

4. Data _____ services are used to reduce the risk of unauthorized disclosure of data.

    a.   integrity
    b.   confidentiality
    c.   packet
    d.   authentication

5. _____ is the method employed by attackers to trick legitimate users into revealing their passwords.

    a.   Password sharing
    b.   Password guessing
    c.   Password capture
    d.   Password batch storage

6. Disclosure of network traffic occurs when an intruder accesses or reads information by _____.

    a.   cracking the password and accessing the network
    b.   analyzing data residing in the database
    c.   breaching the integrity of the file system
    d.   analyzing data traversing over the network transport media

7. Sun Microsystems' _____ is a utility for analyzing network traffic.

    a.   Snoop
    b.   Spoof
    c.   Sniff
    d.   Scoop

8. The ability to masquerade as either a sender or a receiving destination to gain unauthorized access to either a location and information or to compromise the integrity of transmitted information is called _____.

    a.   sniffing
    b.   spoofing
    c.   snooping
    d.   strafing

9. In playback attacks, an intruder captures a session between a sender and a receiver and then retransmits the message after _____.

    a.   modifying the content of the message
    b.   modifying the header and footer of the message

    c.   modifying the header, footer and content

    d.   None of the above. Playback involves resending the message as is.

10. People who commit cyber crimes against their employers are called _____.

    a.   hackers

    b.   crackers

    c.   terrorists

    d.   insiders

11. Originally, the term _____ was a complimentary slang term for a computer enthusiast.

    a.   crackers

    b.   intruders

    c.   hackers

    d.   hactivists

12. The act of politically motivated cyber crimes is called _____.

    a.   hackvism

    b.   hactivism

    c.   cyber crimes

    d.   cyber terrorism

13. The _____ division of the FBI deals with the legal ramifications of information security.

    a.   NIPC

    b.   FedCIRC

    c.   FIRST

    d.   CSSPAB

14. CCIPS of the _____ is dedicated to investigating computer crimes.

    a.   Department of Justice

    b.   Federal Bureau of Investigation

    c.   National Security Agency

    d.   Department of Defense

15. CERT/CC was originally created in 1988 by _____.

    a.   CERIAS

    b.   FIRST

    c.   DISA

    d.   DARPA

Essay Quiz

1. State three forms of losses to an organization in case of a lapse in the security of data.

2. Why do e-mail messages with strict access rights make easy targets for capture while in transit by system intruders using sniffers?

3. List the vulnerabilities that intruders can exploit to spoof network traffic.

Lab Projects

Lab Project 11.1

A new online bookstore expects to receive a lot of customer information, including credit card details, in the near future. The store wants to set up a security system to ensure protection of the expected customer information the moment it leaves the customer's desk. Describe the steps that the store should take when setting up the security system to ensure that all sensitive user information is secure.

Chapter 12 Review

Chapter Summary

After reading this chapter, the students should understand the following.

Security Services and Mechanisms

■ Security services are mechanisms, procedures, and other controls collectively implemented to reduce risks associated with the threat of data loss and to help detect the occurrence of a security breach.

■ Authentication security services are used to validate the identity and authority of users accessing the system. They provide the foundation that helps determine the effectiveness of other controls used in the network.

■ The most common and most generally used authentication mechanism is a scheme that combines a user ID and a password.

■ The ideal password should be easy for the user to remember and difficult for others to guess.

■ An authentication system that relies solely on passwords often fails to provide adequate protection and can be replaced by more robust mechanisms, like token-based authentication or biometrics.

■ Confidentiality is the mechanism in which data is encrypted using symmetric or asymmetric ciphers or both. As a result, only an authorized user, one who has the correct key, can decrypt the data, thus reducing the risk of unauthorized disclosure of data at rest or data in transit.

■ Data integrity services help to ensure that a data packet is not altered, deleted, or added to in any manner while at rest or during transmission across a network. Data integrity services can be provided by using cryptographic checksums and highly granular access-control and privilege mechanisms.

■ Nonrepudiation is a security mechanism ensuring that a transferred message has been sent and received by the parties claiming to have done so. Nonrepudiation services are provided through the use of public-key cryptographic techniques using digital signatures.

Standards, Guidelines, and Regulations

■ The Internet Engineering Task Force (IETF) is an international community of network designers, operators, vendors, and researchers. The IETF ensures the smooth operation of the Internet and the evolution of the Internet architecture.

■ The X9 division of the American National Standards Institute (ANSI) develops standards for check processing, electronic check exchange, PIN management and security, financial industry use of data encryption, and wholesale funds transfer, among others.

■ The National Institute of Standards and Technology (NIST) has published various guidelines and standards on the topic of information security. NIST also administers a certification process for software and hardware cryptographic modules.

■ The FIPS 140-1 standard specifies the security requirements that are to be satisfied by a cryptographic module that is used in a security system protecting unclassified information in computer and telecommunication systems.

■ Various organizations like the IETF, ANSI, and NIST, among others, have made an effort to ensure that each security standard (for example, Common Criteria), guideline (for example, FIPS 140-1), and regulation (for example, the Health Insurance Portability Act) provides for a proper security implementation.

Developer Assistance

■ Most software developers outsource the security tasks to professional services organizations that assist developers in the design and implementation of security and provide certification when the system is completed.

Key Terms

Security service   A collection of mechanisms, procedures, and other controls that are implemented to reduce risks associated with the threat of data loss and to help detect the occurrence of a security breach.

Authorization   A security service that limits access to network information and resources to users who have been authenticated based on defined privileges.

Authentication   A security service that helps to identify and validate the identity and authority of the users accessing the system.

Data confidentiality   A security service used to prevent the unauthorized disclosure of data, software, and messages on an open network or in a shared environment.

Data integrity services   Services used to provide protection against unauthorized (intentional or accidental) modification of data.

Nonrepudiation   Ensures that entities in a communication cannot deny having participated in all or part of the communication.

Internet Engineering Task Force (IETF)   A large, open, international community of network designers, operators, vendors, and researchers concerned with the smooth operation of the Internet and the evolution of the Internet architecture.

Internet Engineering Steering Group (IESG)   Responsible for technical management of IETF activities and the Internet standards process. As part of the ISOC, it administers the process according to the rules and procedures that have been ratified by the ISOC Trustees. The IESG is directly responsible for the actions associated with entry into, and movement along, the Internet "standards track," including final approval of specifications as Internet Standards.

Internet Society (ISOC)   Addresses issues that confront the future of the Internet and is the organization home for the groups responsible for Internet infrastructure standards, including the Internet Engineering Task Force (IETF) and the Internet Architecture Board (IAB).

Internet Architecture Board (IAB)   Provides architectural oversight and adjudicates appeals when someone complains about the policies adopted by the IESG.

American National Standards Institute (ANSI)   A private, nonprofit organization (501(c)3) that administers and coordinates the U.S. voluntary standardization and conformity assessment system.

ANSI X9   A division of ANSI that develops and publishes voluntary, consensus technical standards for the financial services industry.

National Institute of Standards and Technologies (NIST)   Founded in 1901, NIST is a nonregulatory federal agency within the U.S. Commerce Department's Technology Administration. It publishes many guidelines and standards on the topic of information security. It also administers a certification process for software and hardware cryptographic modules.

Federal Information Processing Standard (FIPS) 140-1   Defines the standard security requirements for Cryptographic Modules (FIPS PUB 140-1).

Common Criteria (CC)   Represents the outcome of a series of international efforts to develop criteria for evaluation of information security that is broadly useful within the international community.

The Health Insurance Portability Act (HIPAA)   The HIPAA of 1996 helps healthcare providers to implement PKI security infrastructures and use digital certificates to securely store, transmit, and access health records electronically.

Public Key Infrastructure (PKI)   A system of digital certificates, Certificate Authorities, and other registration authorities that verifies and authenticates the validity of each party involved in an Internet transaction.

Key Terms Quiz

Use the Key Terms list to complete the sentences that follow. (Not all terms will be used.)

1. _____ restricts access to network information and resources on the basis of authenticated privileges.

2. _____ prevents an unauthorized user from accessing the system.

3. The risk of unauthorized disclosure of data can be reduced with the help of _____.

4. _____ refers to the validity of data.

5. An entity's participation in a communication is validated using the _____ security mechanism.

6. _____ is responsible for providing architectural oversight.

7. _____ is responsible for the evolution of the Internet architecture.

8. The standards for using data encryption in the financial industry have been set by the _____ division of the _____.

9. The _____ standard defines the criteria for evaluating information security.

10. _____ defines standards that help healthcare service providers ensure the confidentiality of health records.

Multiple-Choice Quiz

1. _____ help reduce the risk associated with the threat of data loss or compromise.

    a. Data services
    b. Security services
    c. TCP/IP
    d. IEEE

2. _____ is the security service used to help prevent unauthorized modification of data.

    a. Authorization
    b. Authentication
    c. Data integrity
    d. Confidentiality

3. The authorized use of network resources is ensured by using _____.

    a. access control
    b. nonrepudiation
    c. network control
    d. open networks

4. Data _____ is used to reduce the risk of unauthorized disclosure of data.

    a. integrity
    b. confidentiality
    c. packets
    d. authentication

5. A Smart card–based authentication mechanism is an example of _____.

    a. token-based mechanism
    b. AI-based mechanism
    c. password-based mechanism
    d. biometrics

6. Nonrepudiation is the security mechanism most suited for _____.

    a.   CRC

    b.   electronic mail

    c.   file locking

    d.   placing files in a local drive

7. The _____ standard can be used for providing secure public-key operations.

    a.   IPSec

    b.   SSL

    c.   X.509

    d.   FIPS version 2

8. Area directors, the working groups of IETF, are members of _____.

    a.   IAB

    b.   IESG

    c.   ISOC

    d.   ANSI

9. The X9 division of ANSI develops and publishes voluntary, consensus technical standards for the _____ industry.

    a.   healthcare

    b.   financial

    c.   defense

    d.   telecommunications

10. _____, published by NIST, describes the standard for secure cryptographic modules.

    a.   ITSEC

    b.   FIPS 140-1

    c.   CC

    d.   HIPPA

11. The Common Criteria (CC) standard was developed to define criteria for evaluating _____.

    a.   information security

    b.   asymmetric ciphers

    c.   symmetric ciphers

    d.   data integrity

12. Primarily, the HIPPA regulation addresses the _____ security mechanism.

    a.   authentication

    b.   integrity

    c.   confidentiality

    d.   nonrepudiation

13. Which of the following standards was signed into law in 1996?

    a.   FIPS 140-1

    b.   TCSEC

    c.   CC

    d.   HIPPA

14. _____ is a common, easy-to-use PKI client.

    a.   A web browser

    b.   File manager

    c.   An applet

    d.   Network node

15. In which of the following cases can encryption, using symmetric or asymmetric ciphers, reduce the risk of unauthorized disclosures?

    a.   Only when data is at rest

    b.   Only when data is in transit

    c.   Both when data is at rest and in transit

    d.   When data is at rest, not in transit

Essay Quiz

1. The most widely used authentication mechanism is a scheme that combines a user ID and password. Such a mechanism can be effective if managed properly, but passwords are seldom managed properly. State the reasons that make passwords difficult to manage. List any two alternate, robust authentication mechanisms.

2. FIPS 140-1 identifies the requirements for four security levels for cryptographic modules. State the objectives for this identification.

3. What are security services?

Lab Project

Lab Project 12.1

Cryocto Inc. has been hired to manage the information security services over a developing intranet of a sensitive research facility. Cryocto Inc. is required to secure data confidentiality and communication as first steps. Which security mechanisms should be used to meet this requirement?

Index

Symbols

128 bits, symmetric key size, 33
7816 standard, smart cards, 276

A

ABA (American Bar Association), digital
    signature guidelines, 295
access control, 324
ACE/Server, 272
acquirer certificates, 259
ACs (Attribute Certificates), PKI, 203
Adleman, Len, 94
AES (Advanced Encryption Standard), block
    cipher, 45, 50
Aggresive mode, IKE, establishing SAs, 225
AH (Authentication Header), 211
    fields, 212
    transport mode, 213
    tunnel mode, 214
Alert protocol, SSL, 232
algorithm identifier bytes, digital
    signatures, 156
algorithms, 159
    AES, 45, 50
    block ciphers, 38
        feedback modes, 40
        padding, 39–40
    breaking, 30
    comparisons
        interoperability, 122
        key sizes, 119
        performance, 121
        security, 117–118
        transmission sizes, 122
    DES, 45–46, 49
    DH, 94, 105, 108
    digital signature security, 163–164
    DSA, 161
    ECDH, 111–114

ECDSA, 163
elliptic curve, 94
encryption, 19
ESP, 216
Gemstar, 23
hash, 143
historical overview, 23–25
key tables, 38
keys, 22
    brute force attacks, 30, 33
    generating keys, 22
    known plaintext attacks attacks, 36
    measuring time of attacks, 37
    random number generation, 26–27
    seed attacks, 34
MD2, 148
MD5, 148
NIST standards, 50
public key, breaking, 93
RC4, 24, 98
RC5, 98
Rijndael, 50
RSA, 94, 98–99, 102–104, 160
S/MIME, 245
security, publicly known, 25
SHA-1, 143, 149
SSL authentication/encryption, 240
stream ciphers
    key streams, 44–45
    one-time pads, 41, 44
    RC4, 45
threshold, 130–131
Triple DES, 47
XOR operations, 42–43
ANSI (American National Standards Institute),
    X9 security standards, 328
application-layer security protocols, 243
application/pkcs7 content type, MIME, 252
ARLs (Authority Revocation Lists),
    PKI, 190
ASN.1 (Abstract Syntax Notation 1),
    encoding rules, 179
asymmetric key cryptography, 88

attackers, 19
  breaking algorithms, 30
  See also hackers.
attacks
  authentication, 319
  bypassing OS, 6
  data at rest, 318
  data in transit, 317
  data recovery, 7
  implementation errors, 320
  memory reconstruction, 9
  passwords, 5
    PBE, slowing down, 64
authentication, 12, 159, 324
  attacks, 319
  biometrics, 326
  digital signatures, 298
  nonrepudiation, 327
  passwords, 325
  SSL, algorithms, 240
  user IDs, 325
Authentication Data field
  AH, 212
  ESP headers, 216
authentication tokens, 269
  biometrics, 282
  challenge/response calculators, 274
  contact tokens, 275
  form factors, 270
  JavaCards, 279–281
  memory cards, 277
  multifunction smart cards, 277
  one-time password generators, 272
  proximity cards, 271
  smart cards, 275
    readers, 278
authorization requests, SET, 262
automated authentication systems,
    tokens, 269

B

base CRLs, PKI, 189
BER (Basic Encoding Rules), ASN.1, 179
BFK (brute-force on the key), 64
BFP (brute-force on the password), 64

biometrics, 75–76, 282
  accuracy of systems, 288
  authentication, 326
  comparison algorithms, 285
  enrollment process, 282
  facial recognition, 286
  fingerprint recognition, 285
  iris recognition, 286
  keystroke recognition, 288
  retina recognition, 286
  signature recognition, 287
  templates, 284
  verification process, 283
  voice recognition, 287
block ciphers, 38
  AES, 45
  Blowfish, 49
  commercial DES replacements, 49
  DES, 45–46
  feedback modes, 40
  padding, 39–40
Blowfish block cipher, 49
breaches in security, 309–310
breaking algorithms, 30, 93
brute force attacks
  breaking algorithm keys, 30, 33
  PBE passwords, 63, 68
BSAFE Crypto-C/J, 242
BSAFE SSL-C/J, 242
bulk data encryption, PBE, 60–61
business requirements, SET, 254–255
bypassing OS attacks, 6

C

calculating ICVs, IPSec, 213
canonicalization of MIME entities,
    S/MIME, 247
cardholder certificates, SET, 258
CAs (Certificate Authorities), 172, 180
  digitally signed certificates, 180
  Keon certificate server, 207
  self-signed certificates, 180
case studies
  security authentication, 334
  security implementations, 333–336
Cast block cipher, 49

CBC (Cipher Block Chaining), 40
CC security standard (Common
        Criteria), 330
CCIPS (Computer Crime and Intellectual
        Property Section), 321
CERT Web site (Computer Emergency Response
        Team), 332
CERT/CC (Computer Emergency Response
        Team/Coordination Center), 321
certificate chains
    PKI, 194–195
    X.509, 194
certificate directories, PKI, 181
certificate hierarchies, PKI, 192
certificate request messages, SSL, 237
certificates
    digitally signed, 180
    PGP, 172
    PKI
        ACs, 203
        issuance, 184
        registering, 184
        revocation, 185
        roaming, 201–202
        suspending, 190
    policies, 204
    self-signed, 180
    SET, 258–259
    smart cards, 202
    X.509, 172–174
        CPS qualifiers, 176
        CRLs, 175
        extension fields, 175–176
        OIDs, 176
        TLS, 176
        unique identifiers, 174
        URIs, 176
certificates-only messages, S/MIME, 252
CESG (British Communications Electronic
        Security Group), 95
chaining certificates. *See* certificate chains.
challenge/response authentication, 326
challenge/response calculators, 274
change cipher spec protocol, SSL, 231
checks, PBE, 61
ciphertext, 19
    salt, 58
    XOR operations, 43

clear-signed data types, S/MIME, 250
cleartext. *See* plaintext.
clients
    certificate messages, SSL, 237
    hello messages, 234
    key exchange messages, 238
CMMF (Certificate Management Message
        Format), 183
Cocks, Clifford, 95
collisions, message digests, 145–146
combining SAs, 219
commercial DES replacements, 49
comparing algorithms
    interoperability, 122
    key sizes, 119
    performance, 121
    security, 117–118
    transmission sizes, 122
comparison algorithms, biometrics, 285
confidentiality of data, 326
connections, SSL
    states, 228
    terminating, 239
contact tokens, 275
content types, MIME
    application/pkcs7, 252
    enveloped-data, 248
    multipart/signed, 250
    signed-data, 249
COS (card operating system), 277
CPS qualifiers (Certification Practice
        Statement), X.509 certificates, 176
CPSs (Certificate Practice
        Statements), 204–205
crackers, 2
    password attacks, 5
    See also hackers.
CRLs (Certificate Revocation Lists)
    PKI, 185
        CRLs, 189
        distribution points, 189
        extensions, 187–188
        fields, 186
        indirect CRL, 189
    X.509 certificates, 175
cross-certification certificates, PKI, 193
CRT (Chinese Remainder Theorem), 104
cryptanalysis, 20

crypto accelerators, 69, 73–75, 267
Crypto iButton, 281
cryptographers, 20
cryptographic accelerators, 28
cryptography, 11–12, 15–19

D

data at rest attacks, 318
data in transit attacks, 317
data
  authentication, 298
  encryption, 60–61
  integrity checking, 12, 159, 326
    message digests, 153
  origin authentication, 298
  recovery attacks, 7
  security, 12
decryption, 17–19
  PBE, 61
  session keys, 55
delta CRLs, PKI, 189
deploying PKIs, 201
Dept. of Justice, CCIPS (Computer Crime and Intellectual Property Section), 321
DER (Distinguished Encoding Rules), ANSI.1, 179
DES (Digital Encryption Standard), block cipher, 45–46
developers and security, 331
DH algorithm, 94, 105
  discrete log problem, 108
  key agreement, 108
  public keys, 108
  session keys, 106
dictionary attacks, 57, 63
Diffie, Whitfield, 93
digital envelopes, 91–92
  key recovery, 123
  S/MIME entities, 248
digital signatures, 137–139, 154, 158
  ABA guidelines, 295
  algorithms, 163–164
    identifier bytes, 156
  authentication, 298
  differences from electronic signatures, 304

differences from written document signatures, 299
  E-SIGN Act, 303, 306
  key revocation, 300
  legal issues, 296
  legislative issues, 302–303
  message integrity, 293
  nonrepudiation, 296–297
  padding bytes, 156
  PKI, 300
  private keys, 141, 154, 158
  storage advantages, 294
  time stamping, 301
digitally signed certificates, 180
discrete log problem, 108
distribution points, CRLs, 189
DNs (Distinguished Names), X.500, 178
DSA algorithm, 160–161
dual signatures, 257

E

E-SIGN Act (Electronic Signatures in Global and National Commerce), 294, 303, 306
ECDH algorithm, 111–114
ECDSA algorithm, 163
El Gamal, Taher, 160
electronic signatures, differences from digital signatures, 304
elliptic curves
  algorithms, 94
  points, 112
Ellis, James, 95
encryption, 16–18
  AES standard, 50
  algorithms, 19
    block ciphers, 38–40, 45
    commercial DES replacements, 49
    DES, 46
    ESP, 216
    key tables, 38
    keys, 22
    RC4 stream cipher, 45
    stream ciphers, 41, 44–45
    Triple DES, 47
    XOR operations, 42–43
crypto accelerators, 73–75

keys, 19–21
PBE, 55
    bulk data, 60–61
S/MIME, 251
SSL algorithms, 240
Enigma machine, 23
enrollment process, biometrics, 282
Ensure Technologies, XyLoc proximity cards, 272
entity names, X.509, 178
entropy, PRNGs, 29
entrust PKIs, 201
enveloped-data content types, S/MIME, 248
error alert messages, SSL, 232
escrow. *See* key escrow.
ESP (Encapsulating Security Payload), 211
    encryption algorithms, 216
    header fields, 216
    trailers, 217–218
    transport mode, 217
    tunnel mode, 218
Euler, Leonhard, 101
Euler's phi-function, 101
Extended Euclidean Algorithm, 101
extensions
    CRLs, 187–188
    X.509 certificates, 175–176

F

facial recognition, biometrics, 286
factoring, 102
FAR (false acceptance rate), biometrics, 288
FBI, NIPC (National Infrastructure Protection
    Center), 321
feedback modes, block ciphers, 40
Fermat test, 100
fields
    AH, 212
    CRLs, 186
    ESP headers, 216
    X.509 certificates, 173–174
files, read protection, 3
fingerprints
    authentication, 325
    biometric recognition, 285
Finished messages, SSL, 239

FIPS 140-1 (Federal Information-Processing
    Standard), 329
floppy drive certificates, 202
foreign intelligence services, security
    attacks, 316
form factors, authentication tokens, 270
formats for certificates
    PGP, 172
    X.509, 172–174
FRR (false rejection rate), biometrics, 288
functions of S/MIME, 245

G–H

Gemstar algorithm, 23
generating
    algorithm keys, 22
    key pairs, PKI, 197
Hacker Quarterly Web site, 333
hackers, 2
    password attacks, 5
    security attacks, 315
hactivists, security attacks, 316
handshakes, SSL, 228, 233
hard drives, permissions, 8
hardware-based key storage, 69
hash algorithms, 143
hash payloads, IKE quick mode, 226–227
headers
    AH, 211
        fields, 212
        transport mode, 213
        tunnel mode, 214
    ESP fields, 216
    SSL records, 231
Hellman, Martin, 93
HIPAA (Health Insurance Portability
    Act), 330
historical overview of algorithms, 23–25
histories, PKI key pairs, 200
HMAC (hash message authentication
    checksum), 151–153

I

IAB (Internet Architecture Board), 327
ICVs (Integrity Check Values), IPSec, 213
IDEA block cipher, 49
identification parameters, SAs, 219
IESG (Internet Engineering Steering Group), 327
IETF (Internet Engineering Task Force), security standards, 327
IKE (Internet Key Exchange), 210, 224
  aggresive mode, 225
  main mode, 224
  quick mode, 226–227
implementation errors and security breaches, 320
indirect CRLs, PKI, 189
insiders, security attacks, 315
insourced PKIs, 201
Inspector Copier, 7–8
insurance for e-commerce sites, 332
integrity services, 326
Intel RNG, 27
intelligent memory cards, 277
interoperability, algorithm comparisons, 122
intruders
  foreign intelligence servicess, 316
  hackers, 315
  hactivists, 316
  identifying, 314
  insiders, 315
  terrorists, 315
IP Destination Address parameter, SAs, 219
IP packets, security, 219
IPSec (Internet Protocol Security), 209–210
  AH (Authentication Header), 211
    service modes, 213
  ESP (Encapsulating Security Payload), 211
    encryption algorithms, 216
    service modes, 217
  ICVs (Integrity Check Values), 213
  key management, 223–224
  MTU (Maximum Transferable Unit), 223
  replay attack prevention, 211
  SAD (Security Association Database), 222
  SAs (Security Associations), 218–219
  SPD (Security Policy Database), 222

IRDA ports, smart card readers, 278
iris recognition, biometrics, 286
ISAKMP (Internet Security Association and Key Management Protocol), 224
ISO (International Organization for Standardization), 330
  security standards, 330
  smart card standards, 72, 276
ISOC (Internet Society), 327
issuer certificates, SET, 259
issuing certificates, PKI, 184
iterated tunneling, SAs, 219
ITSEC (Information Technology Security Evaluation Criteria), 330
IVs (Initialization Vectors), CBC, 40

J–K

Java rings, 281
JavaCard Forum, 280
JavaCards, 279–281
JavaScript Source password generator, 69
KEKs (key encryption keys), 54, 85–86
  mixing algorithms, 56
  reasons for usage, 58
Keon certificate server, 207
Keon Web PassPort, 207
key agreement, 108
key distribution problem, 82–84
  asymmetric key cryptography, 88
  DH algorithm, 105, 108
  digital envelopes, 91–92
  ECDH algorithm, 111, 113–114
  public key cryptography, 88–89
  RSA algorithm, 98–99, 102–104
  sharing keys in person, 83
key escrow, 125, 182
key exchange, 108
key management
  IPSec, 223–224
  PKI, 197
key masters, 84
key pairs, PKI, 197–200
key recovery, 125
  digital envelopes, 123
  servers, 182
  threshold schemes, 127–130
  trustees, 126

TTPs, 124
key revocation, digital signatures, 300
key size, algorithms, 32
key streams, stream ciphers, 44–45
key tables, algorithms, 38
keyed digests, HMAC, 151–153
keys
    128 bit size, 33
    algorithms, 22, 119
        attacks, 30, 33–37
        generating, 22
        random number generation, 26–27
    encryption, 19–21
    hardware-based storage, 69
    session keys, 54
keystroke recognition, biometrics, 288
known plaintext attacks, 36
Koblitz, Neal, 94
Kravitz, David, 160

L

L0phtCrack, 5
LDAP (Lightweight Directory Access
        Protocol), 181
legal issues, digital signatures, 296
legislative issues, digital
        signatures, 302–303
live scan biometrics, 283
losses due to security breaches, 309–310
loyalty applications, JavaCards, 279

M

magnetic stripe tokens, 275
main mode, IKE, 224
management protocols, PKI, 182–183
managing SET certificates, 259
manual key management, 224
manual public-key distribution, 171
master secrets, SSL, 240
MD2 algorithm, 148
MD5 algorithm, 148
measuring time of algorithm attack, 37
memory cards, 277
memory reconstruction attacks, 9

merchant certificates, SET, 259, 265
Merkle, Ralph, 95
message digests, 143–144, 148–149
    collisions, 145–146
    data integrity, 153
    PRNGs, 30
    randomness, 142
message integrity, digital signatures, 293
messages
    S/MIME
        certificates-only, 252
        MIME entities, 247
        signing, 249
    SSL
        alerts, 232
        certificate request, 237
        certificate verify, 238
        client certificate, 237
        client hello, 234
        client key exchange, 238
        finished, 239
        server certificate, 236
        server hello, 235
        server key exchange, 236
Microsoft Outlook/Express, S/MIME
        support, 265
Miller, Victor, 94
MIME (Multipurpose Internet Mail
        Extensions), 244
    application/pkcs7 content type, 252
    entities, S/MIME, 247–248
    enveloped-data content types, 248
    multipart/signed data types, 250
    signed-data content types, 249
mixing algorithms, 56
MLAs (mail list agents), 253
modular exponentiation, 108, 161
modulus, RSA public keys, 99
MTU (Maximum Transferable Unit),
        IPSec, 223
multifunction smart cards, 277
multipart/signed data types, MIME, 250
multiple key pairs, PKI, 199
multiprime RSA algorithm, 104

N

names, X.509, 178
Netscape
  Messenger, S/MIME support, 265
  SSL, 227
    seed generation, 35
  TLS, 228
networks
  security protocols, 209
  traffic
    interception, 313
    spoofing, 314
Next Header field
  AH, 212
  ESP headers, 216
NIPC (National Infrastructure Protection
    Center), 321
NIST (National Institute of Standards and
    Technology), 328
  algorithm standards, 50
  FIPS 140-1, 329
  security standards, 328
nonce exchange, IKE main mode, 224
noncontact tokens, 270–271
nonrepudiation, 159
  authentication, 327
  digital signatures, 296–297
  services, 298
NSA (National Security Agency), 95
numbers, random generation, algorithm keys,
    26–27

O

Oakley key management protocol, 224
OCF (OpenCard Framework), smart card
    standards, 280
OCSP (Online Certificate Status Protocol),
    190–191, 300
OIDs (Object Identifiers), X.509
    certificates, 176
one way functions, public key
    cryptography, 96
one-time pads, stream ciphers, 41, 44
one-time password generators, 272

operational protocols, PKI, 184
Oracle 8i, symmetric key example, 51
origins of public key cryptography, 95
OSes (operating systems), 2
  bypass attacks, 6
  memory reconstruction attacks, 9
  permissions, 3
  security, 2–3
Outlook/Outlook Express, S/MIME
    support, 265
outsourcing PKIs, 201

P

Pad Length field, ESP headers, 216
padding
  block ciphers, 39–40
  bytes, digital signatures, 156
  field, ESP headers, 216
participants, SET, 256
partitions, CRLs. *See* distribution points.
passwords
  attacks, 5
  authentication, 325
  checkers, 325
  cracking, 5
  generators, 67
  PBE
    brute-force attacks, 68
    guidelines on selection, 65
    slowing down attacks, 64
  superusers, 4
  three try limitations, 66
  token storage, 72–73
Payload Data field, ESP headers, 216
Payload Length field, AH, 212
payments, SET
  authorization requests, 262
  capture transaction, 263
  gateway certificates, 259
PBE (Password-Based Encryption), 55, 90
  brute-force attacks, 63
  bulk data encryption, 60–61
  checks, 61
  decryption, 61
  dictionary attacks, 63

KEKs, 55, 58
passwords
  brute force attacks, 68
  generators, 67
  guidelines on selection, 65
  slowing attacks, 64
salt, 55–57
session keys, 58
performance, algorithm comparisons, 121
permissions, 3, 8
permissive links, 96
PGP (Pretty Good Privacy), 172
pigeonhole principle, 145
PINs (Personal Identification Numbers)
  authentication, 326
  tokens, 71
PKCs (Public-Key Certificates), 172
PKI (Public-Key Infrastructure), 171
  ACs (Attribute Certificates), 203
  ARLs (Authority Revocation Lists), 190
  CAs (Certificate Authorities), 180
  certificates
    chains, 194
    cross-certification, 193
    directories, 181
    hierarchies, 192
    issuing, 184
    policies, 204
    registering, 184
    revoking, 185
    suspending, 190
  CPSs (Certificate Policy Statements),
    204–205
  CRLs (Certificate Revocation Lists), 185
    base CRLs, 189
    delta CRLs, 189
    distribution points, 189
    extensions, 187–188
    fields, 186
    indirect CRLs, 189
  digital signatures, 300
  insourced, 201
  Keon certificate server, 207
  Keon Web PassPort, 207
  key management, 197
  key pairs, 197
    histories, 200
    updating, 199

key recovery servers, 182
management protocols, 182–183
multiple key pairs, 199
OCSP, 190–191
operational protocols, 184
private keys, protecting, 197
RAs (RegistrationAuthorities), 180
roaming certificates, 201–202
trust models, 191
trust paths, 193
plaintext, 19, 43
platform support for S/MIME, 253
playback attacks, 314
points on elliptic curves, 112
pre-master secrets, SSL, 240
Prime Number Theorem, 100
prime numbers, public key
    cryptography, 100
privacy, 12
private CAs, 180
private keys
  digital signatures, 141, 154, 158
  PKI, 197–199
  protecting, 123
PRNGs (Pseudo-Random Number Generators)
  entropy, 29
  message digests, 30
  seeds, 28
protected smart cards, 277
protecting private keys, 123, 197
protocols
  AH, 211
  application-layer security, 243
  change cipher spec, 231
  CMMF, 183
  ESP, 211
  IPSec, 209–210
  ISAKMP, 224
  LDAP, 181
  network security, 209
  Oakley, 224
  OCSP, 190
  PKI management, 182–183
  PKI operations, 184
  S/MIME, 244
  SSL, 227, 230
  transport security, 209
proximity cards, 271

public CAs, 180
public exponents, RSA public keys, 99
public key cryptography, 88–89
  algorithms, breaking, 93
  DH algorithm, 108
  functionality, 94
  one way functions, 96
  origins, 95
pull model, certificate chains, 195
push model, certificate chains, 195

Q-R

quick mode, IKE, 226–227
random number generators, algorithm
    keys, 26–27
randomness, message digests, 142
RAs (Registration Authorities), 180
RC2 algorithm, 49
RC4 algorithm, 24, 45, 98
RC5 algorithm, 49, 98
RDNs (Relative Distinguished Names),
    X.500, 178
read protection, 3
readers
  smart cards, 278
  tokens, 71
receiving agents, S/MIME, 246
recognition methods in biometrics, 285–288
Record layer, SSL, 230–231
registering certificates, PKI, 184
registration requests, S/MIME, 251
relying parties, 171
replay attacks, 211, 272
repudiation, 297
Reserved field, AH, 212
responders, OCSP, PKI, 190–191
restarting SSL sessions, 240
retina recognition, biometrics, 76, 286
revocation
  certificates, PKI, 185
  keys, digital signatures, 300
Reynolds Data Recovery, 7
Rijndael algorithm, 50
Rivest, Ron, 94
RNGs (Random Number Generators), 27
roaming certificates, PKI, 201–202

RSA algorithm, 94, 98–99, 102–104, 160
RSA Security, Inc.
  key challenges, 33
  one-time password generators, 272
  security implementations, 332

S

S/MIME (Secure/Multipurpose Internet Mail
    Extensions), 243–244
  algorithms, 245
  certificates-only messages, 252
  clear-signed data types, 250
  encryption, 251
  enveloped-data content types, 248
  interoperability, 253
  messages
    MIME entities, 247
    signing, 249
  MIME entities, 247–248
  MLAs (Mail List Agents), 253
  receiving agents, 246
  registration requests, 251
  security, 245, 252
  sending agents, 246
  signing, 251–252
SAD (Security Association Database), IPSec, 222
safer block cipher, 49
salt, 55–58
SAs (Security Associations)
  AH transport mode, 214
  AH tunnel mode, 214
  combining, 219
  IKE, aggressive mode, 225
  IP packet security, 219
  IPSec, 218–219
  iterated tunneling, 219
  transport adjacencies, 219
scalar multiplication, ECDH
    algorithm, 113–114
Schlumberger JavaCards, 279–280
Schnorr, Claus, 160
scrambling values, algorithms, 38
secret key cryptography. *See* symmetric keys.
secret sharing/splitting, 127
secure mailing lists, S/MIME, 252
secure payment processing, SET, 260

SecurID token, 272
security
  algorithms
    comparisons, 117–118
    publicly known, 25
  authentication, 324–326, 334
  biometrics, 75–76
  cryptography, 11–12
  digital signature algorithms, 163–164
  IETF standards, 327
  implementation case studies, 333–336
  insurance for e-commerce sites, 332
  IP packets, SAs, 219
  losses due to breaches, 309–310
  nonrepudiation, 327
  OSes, 3
  program developers, 331
  protocols, 209
  useful Web sites, 332
Security Focus Web site, 332
security labels, S/MIME, 252
Security Parameters Index field
  AH, 212
  ESP headers, 216
Security Parameters Index parameter,
    SAs, 219
Security Protocol Identifier parameter,
    SAs, 219
security threats
  authentication attacks, 319
  data at rest, 318
  data in transit, 317
  foreign intelligence, 316
  hackers, 315
  hactivists, 316
  implementation errors, 320
  insiders, 315
  intruders, 314
  network traffic, 313–314
  terrorists, 315
  unauthorized access, 312
  unauthorized data disclosure, 311
  unauthorized data modification, 311–312
seeds
  breaking algorithms, 34
  Netscape SSL generation, 35
  PRNGs, 28
segmented memory smart cards, 277

selectors, SPD entries, 222
self-signed certificates, 180
sending agents, S/MIME, 246
Sequence Number field
  AH, 212
  ESP headers, 216
server messages, 235–236
service delivery modes, ESP, 217–218
service modes, AH, 213
session keys, 54, 106
  encrypting, 55
  reasons for usage, 58
sessions, SSL, 228, 239–240
SET (Secure Electronic Transaction), 253
  business requirements, 254–255
  certificates, 258–259
  dual signatures, 257
  participants, 256
  payments
    authorization requests, 262
    capture transactions, 263
    secure processing, 260
    purchase request transactions, 260
    vendors and merchants, 265
SHA-1 algorithm, 143, 149
Shamir, Adi, 94, 130
shared secrets, SSL, 227
sharing keys in person, 83
signature recognition, biometrics, 287
signed receipts, S/MIME, 252
signed-data content types, MIME, 249
signer authentication, 298
signing S/MIME messages, 249–251
Slash Dot Web site, 333
smart cards, 69–71, 275
  authentication, 326
  certificates, 202
  ISO standards, 72, 276
  JavaCards, 279–281
  memory cards, 277
  multifunction, 277
  private keys, 123
  pros and cons, 278
  readers, 278
sniffers, 313
Snoop utility, 313
SPD (Security Policy Database), IPSec, 222
spoofing network traffic, 314

SSL (Secure Sockets Layer), 35, 227–228
  accelerator cards, 268
  alert protocol, 232
  authentication algorithms, 240
  certificates
    request messages, 237
    verify messages, 238
  change cipher spec protocol, 231
  clients
    certificate messages, 237
    hello messages, 234
    key exchange messages, 238
  connection states, 228
  encryption algorithms, 240
  error alert messages, 232
  finished messages, 239
  handshakes, 228, 233
  master secrets, 240
  pre-master secrets, 240
  RC4 algorithm, 24
  record layer, 230–231
  seed generation, 35
  servers
    certificate messages, 236
    hello messages, 235
    key exchange messages, 236
  sessions
    resuming, 240
    states, 228
    terminating, 239
  shared secrets, 227
  state machine, 228
SSO systems, authentication tokens, 270
standards for smart cards, 276
state machine, SSL, 228
storage advantages, digital signatures, 294
stored value memory cards, 277
stream ciphers
  key streams, 44–45
  one-time pads, 41, 44
  RC4, 45
superusers, passwords, 3–4
suspending certificates, PKI, 190
symmetric algorithms
  block ciphers, 38
    AES, 45
    commercial DES replacements, 49

    DES, 45
    feedback modes, 40
    padding, 39–40
  RC4 stream ciphers, 45
  stream ciphers
    key streams, 44–45
    one-time pads, 41, 44
  XOR operations, 42–43
symmetric keys, 33
  cryptography, 15–19, 51
  management, 53–55
system administrators, 3

T

TCSEC (Trusted Computer System Evaluation Criteria), 330
templates, biometrics, 284
terminals, smart cards, 278
terminating SSL sessions, 239
terrorists, security attacks, 315
third-party PKIs, 201
threats to security
  authentication, 319
  data at rest, 318
  data in transit, 317
  foreign intelligence services, 316
  hackers, 315
  hactivists, 316
  implementation errors, 320
  insiders, 315
  intruders, 314
  network traffic interception, 313
  spoofing network traffic, 314
  terrorism, 315
  unauthorized access, 312
  unauthorized data disclosure, 311
  unauthorized data modification, 311–312
three try password limitations, 66
threshold algorithms, 130–131
threshold schemes, key recovery, 127–130
time stamping, digital signatures, 301
TLS (Transport Layer Security), 176, 228
tokens, 69–71
  authentication, 269–270, 325
  noncontact tokens, 270–271

number generators, 75
password storage, 72–73
private keys, 123
traffic analysis programs, 313
trailers, ESP, 217–218
transaction processing, SET, 260
transfer encoding, MIME entities, 247
transmission sizes, algorithm
    comparisons, 122
transport adjacencies, SAs, 219
Transport mode
  AH, 213
  ESP, 217
transport security protocols, 209
Triple DES (Triple Digital Encryption
    Standard), 47
trust, PKI, 191–193
trustees, key recovery, 126
TSAs (Time-Stamping Authorities), 301
TTPs (trusted third parties)
  KEKs, 85–86
  key recovery, 124
Tunnel mode
  AH, 214
  ESP, 218

U

unauthorized access, 312
unauthorized data disclosure, 311
unauthorized data modification, 311–312
UNCITRAL (United Nations Commission on
    International Trade Law), 302
unique identifiers, X.509 certificates, 174
updating key pairs, PKI, 199
URIs (Uniform Resource Identifiers), X.509
    certificates, 176
USB ports, tokens, 72
user IDs, authentication, 325
user names, 3
user-input seed collectors, 28

V

vendors, SET, 265
verification process, biometrics, 283
Verisign PKIs, 201
VNC (Virtual Network Computing), 319
voice recognition, biometrics, 76, 287

W

Web sites, security strategies, 332
Weierstrass equation, 112
Weierstrass, Karl, 112
Williamson, Malcolm, 95
written signatures, differences from
    digital signatures, 299

X

X.500, 178
X.509, 172
  certificates
    chains, 194
    CPS qualifiers, 176
    CRLs, 175
    extension fields, 175–176
    fields, 173–174
    OIDs, 176
    TLS, 176
    unique identifiers, 174
    URIs, 176
  entity names, 178
X9 security standards, 328
XOR operations, 42–43
XyLoc proximity card, 272

INTERNATIONAL CONTACT INFORMATION

AUSTRALIA
McGraw-Hill Book Company
Australia Pty. Ltd.
TEL +61-2-9900-1800
FAX +61-2-9878-8881
http://www.mcgraw-hill.com.au
books-it_sydney@mcgraw-hill.com

CANADA
McGraw-Hill Ryerson Ltd.
TEL +905-430-5000
FAX +905-430-5020
http://www.mcgraw-hill.ca

GREECE, MIDDLE EAST, & AFRICA
(Excluding South Africa)
McGraw-Hill Hellas
TEL +30-210-6560-990
TEL +30-210-6560-993
TEL +30-210-6560-994
FAX +30-210-6545-525

MEXICO (Also serving Latin America)
McGraw-Hill Interamericana Editores
S.A. de C.V.
TEL +525-1500-5108
FAX +525-117-1589
http://www.mcgraw-hill.com.mx
carlos_ruiz@mcgraw-hill.com

SINGAPORE (Serving Asia)
McGraw-Hill Book Company
TEL +65-6863-1580
FAX +65-6862-3354
http://www.mcgraw-hill.com.sg
mghasia@mcgraw-hill.com

SOUTH AFRICA
McGraw-Hill South Africa
TEL +27-11-622-7512
FAX +27-11-622-9045
robyn_swanepoel@mcgraw-hill.com

SPAIN
McGraw-Hill/
Interamericana de España, S.A.U.
TEL +34-91-180-3000
FAX +34-91-372-8513
http://www.mcgraw-hill.es
professional@mcgraw-hill.es

UNITED KINGDOM, NORTHERN,
EASTERN, & CENTRAL EUROPE
McGraw-Hill Education Europe
TEL +44-1-628-502500
FAX +44-1-628-770224
http://www.mcgraw-hill.co.uk
emea_queries@mcgraw-hill.com

ALL OTHER INQUIRIES Contact:
McGraw-Hill/Osborne
TEL +1-510-420-7700
FAX +1-510-420-7703
http://www.osborne.com
omg_international@mcgraw-hill.com

Additional Online Resources

RSA Laboratories' Frequently Asked Questions

Version 4.1, 2000, RSA Security Inc.

http://www.rsasecurity.com/rsalabs/faq/index.html

Public-Key Cryptography Standards

The Public-Key Cryptography Standards are specifications produced by RSA Laboratories in cooperation with secure systems developers worldwide for the purpose of accelerating the deployment of public-key cryptography. First published in 1991 as a result of meetings with a small group of early adopters of public-key technology, the PKCS documents have become widely referenced and implemented. Contributions from the PKCS series have become part of many formal and de facto standards, including ANSI X9 documents, PKIX, SET, S/MIME, and SSL.

Further development of PKCS occurs through mailing list discussions and occasional workshops, and suggestions for improvement are welcome. For more information, please use our contact form available online at https://www.rsasecurity.com/go/labs.html. PKCS available online at http://www.rsasecurity.com/rsalabs/pkcs/index.html.

CryptoBytes Technical Newsletter

The technical newsletter on cryptography from RSA Laboratories, the research center of RSA Security Inc.

http://www.rsasecurity.com/rsalabs/cryptobytes/index.html.

Bulletins

In addition to other publications, RSA Laboratories publishes short bulletins about topical issues of cryptographic concern. The aim is both to update the general cryptographic community on recent and important news and also to brief RSA Security customers and licensees about relevant technical issues that might be of interest.

http://www.rsasecurity.com/rsalabs/bulletins/index.html

Crypto Blunders

By Steve Burnett

http://www.datastreamconsulting.com/_notes/_notes/crypto_blunders_wp.pdf

What's on the CD-ROM

The Bonus CD-ROM included with *RSA Security's Official Guide to Cryptography Keller Graduate School of Management of DeVry University Edition* includes the Working Model Edition of Microsoft's® Visual Basic® 6.

System Requirements

- Personal Computer with 486DX/66 (Pentium 90 or higher microprocessor recommended)

- Microsoft Windows 95 or later, Windows NT 4.0, with Service Pack 3 or later (Service Pack 3 included)

- Minimum memory: 24MB for Windows 95 or later, 24MB for Windows NT 4.0 (32MB recommended for all)

- Hard disk space required:

  - Typical Installation: 52MB

  - Maximum Installation: 65MB

- Microsoft Internet Explorer 4.01 Service Pack 1 (included), additional hard disk space required for Microsoft Internet Explorer: 43MB Typical, 59MB Maximum

- CD-ROM drive

- VGA or higher-resolution monitor (super VGA recommended)

- Microsoft Mouse or compatible pointing device

Online help available at www.microsoft.com.

Licensed Software

This program is reproduced by McGraw-Hill/Osborne under a special arrangement with Microsoft Corporation. For this reason, McGraw-Hill/Osborne is responsible for the product warranty and for support. If your diskette is defective, please return it to McGraw-Hill/Osborne, which will arrange for its replacement. PLEASE DO NOT RETURN IT TO MICROSOFT CORPORATION. Any product support will be provided, if at all by McGraw-Hill/Osborne. PLEASE DO NOT CONTACT MICROSOFT CORPORATION FOR PRODUCT SUPPORT. End users of this Microsoft program shall not be eligible for upgrades, promotions or other benefits available to "registered owners" of Microsoft products.